Institutional Responses to Drug Demand in Central Europe

Public Policy and Social Welfare
A Series Edited by Bernd Marin

European Centre Vienna

Volume 27

Patrick Kenis, Flip Maas, Robert Sobiech (Eds.)

Institutional Responses to Drug Demand in Central Europe

An Analysis of Institutional Developments in the Czech Republic, Hungary, Poland and Slovenia

Ashgate
Aldershot • Brookfield USA • Singapore • Sydney

Published by

Ashgate Publishing Limited
Gower House
Croft Road
Aldershot
Hants GU11 3HR
England

Ashgate Publishing Company
Old Post Road
Brookfield
Vermont 05036
USA

This publication has been prepared by the European Centre for Social Welfare Policy and Research, on the basis of its collaboration with the United Nations International Drug Control Programme – UNDCP. The findings, conclusions and interpretations as expressed in this publication should in no way be taken to reflect the policies or opinions of the UNDCP.

Copy-editing and DTP: Willem Stamatiou
European Centre for Social Welfare Policy and Research
Berggasse 17, 1090 Vienna, Austria

British Library Cataloguing-in-Publication Data. A catalogue record for this book is available from the British Library.

ISBN 0-7546-0982-0

Printed by Facultas Verlags- und Buchhandels AG, Vienna, Austria

Contents

Preface

The countries of Central and Eastern Europe, including the four Central European countries investigated in detail in this study – the Czech Republic, Hungary, Poland and Slovenia – suffered from a rapidly deteriorating drug problem in the 1990s, resulting from both supply (push) and demand (pull) effects.

Increases in drug use have been most marked among young persons. There was a strong demand, notably with regard to synthetic drugs such as amphetamines and ecstasy. These substances, imported from Western Europe as well as produced locally, spread among young persons across Central and Eastern Europe following (negative) role models observed in Western Europe. Use of cannabis increased as well. Life-time prevalence of drug use was found in the Europe-wide ESPAD studies, conducted in 1999, to affect already 35% of the 15-16 years old students in the Czech Republic (the second highest such rate in Europe after the UK), 26% in Slovenia (the sixth highest rate in Europe), 18% in Poland (about European average) and 12% in Hungary. The rates increased in the four Central European countries by more than 80% over the 1995 to 1999 period (based on un-weighted average prevalence rates in the four countries), slightly less than in the whole of Central and Eastern Europe (almost 95%), though clearly more than in Western Europe (some 15%).

In addition, the countries of Central and Eastern Europe suffered from supply effects. Following the end of the iron curtain, the countries of Central Europe found themselves located in the midst of major international drug trafficking cross-roads. They were affected by criminal networks shipping opiates from Afghanistan to Western Europe via Turkey, the Balkan countries and the countries of Central Europe to Western Europe. Moreover, they saw themselves located on an emerging trafficking route from Afghanistan via Central Asia and the Russian Federation to Western Europe. All of this resulted in "spill-overs" to the local market due to the fact that local drug trafficking groups and other sub-contracted services providers are sometimes paid "in kind" and subsequently sell the drugs to the local market. Given transition problems, social and economic conditions were conducive to the spread of drug abuse.

Against this background, an appropriate institutional response to deal with the emerging drug problem had to be developed. The present study investigates in detail the institutional response of demand reduction activities in the four countries, their strengths and weaknesses, both on a country by country basis as well as in the form of cross-country comparisons. It thus provides a wealth of information for policy makers, both in terms of availability of services and areas for improvement. One important element of the study has been the in-depth investigation of the views of the various players in different organizations, as this is an important element to understand the further development of drug policies and changes in the institutional framework.

The study of these four countries is of particular interest as they offer almost "laboratory type" conditions for comparative social science research: all four countries emerged from similar socio-political environments, suffered more or less similar transition problems and were subject to similar demand and supply factors. While it is still difficult to measure the long-term effectiveness of the institutional response in terms of demand reduction objectives, available data suggest that the four countries have, for example, been successful – so far – in preventing the outbreak of a large-scale injecting drug use (IDU) related HIV/AIDS epidemic as suffered by several other countries in Eastern Europe. While in Central and Eastern Europe as a whole the number of newly diagnosed HIV cases related to injecting drug use exploded in recent years, rising more than six-fold between 1996 and 2000 according to data collected by EuroHIV (from 6,800 to 42,300 cases or 110 per million inhabitants in 2000), the corresponding numbers in the four central European countries remained stable at comparatively low levels (6 cases per million inhabitants taking the four countries together). Investment in the creation of appropriate demand reduction institutions seems to have contributed to these results.

An important side effect of the process in which the present study was elaborated, was the creation of a network of social science researchers in Central European countries with the ability to investigate, monitor and evaluate the structure of and changes in demand reduction institutions. The project, thus, did not only gather and analyse information on the institutional set-up of demand reduction institutions. It also helped to build up a cross-national network of dedicated social science researchers who are able to investigate the institutional side of the demand reduction field and to undertake cross-country research. Follow-up activities in some of the countries participating in the project have already shown that there is a clear demand for such kind of research, which may gain even further in importance in view of the fact that the four countries will be among the first in the forthcoming round of EU enlargement. In this context, special thanks should be given to the researchers participating in this project, to the European Centre for Social Welfare Policy and Research which – in close consultation with UNDCP – successfully monitored and guided the research activities, and to the Austrian Government, which – due to its financial contribution – enabled this research.

Thomas Pietschmann
UNDCP, Research Section

CHAPTER 1

Drug Demand Reduction in Central European Countries: Analysing the Institutional and Organizational Responses

Patrick Kenis

1 Introduction

Drug demand reduction (DDR) has become an important issue in Central European Countries. Since 1989 the supply and demand in illicit drugs has rapidly increased and new approaches to deal with the demand in illicit drugs have been developed. The study on which the present volume is based, induces to describe and assess the institutional and organizational responses to DDR in four Central European Countries – Czech Republic, Hungary, Poland and Slovenia – as it had been developed at the end of the 1990s. Before presenting the basic concepts and the methodology of this study in somewhat more detail it is important to indicate a number of starting-points on which the study is based.

First, the original objective of the study was to have in place a "sustainable network of researchers ... with the ability to investigate, monitor and evaluate the structures of and changes in institutions in the area of drug control" (UNDCP Project Document, 1997: 9). What could be a better proof that these researchers are in place than the present publication ? As the subsequent chapters will demonstrate, the project did not only result in a group of researchers who have gained the ability to investigate institutions in the area of DDR but actually resulted in some excellent and innovative country and comparative studies. These studies are not only original because they have collected and analysed data on DDR in Central European countries, which were previously not available. They also include types of approaches and analysis, which have not yet been carried out even in Western European countries. For example, the analysis of the relationship between the attitude of organizations with respect to illicit drugs and the type of activities they develop is unprecedented.

Second, in contrast to most studies in the field of drugs, the starting-point of this study is not the epidemiological situation. The starting point here, is to study the organizational and institutional responses to drug demand. Most often it is believed that if we would only know what the problem is (i.e. have accurate epidemiological figures) we would know what to do. Apart from the fact that having accurate epidemiological figures on a phenomenon such as drug demand is not only extremely difficult, these figures often do not automatically and unambiguously tell us how to respond. Even if we would know how to respond, the question still remains whether we can respond to these challenges, given the often-existing considerable barriers in implementing policies and practices. Taking the organizational and institutional responses as a starting point has a number of advantages. Rather than concentrating on what *should* be done the attention is on what *is* done. An interesting question then becomes whether activities are developed because of the problem load (i.e. the epidemiological situation) or whether other factors or rationalities explain the patterns of response. Moreover, such an approach takes also the knowledge of the organizations that are actually active in the field of drug demand reduction much more into account. Instead of having epidemiologists developing figures which then tell organizations what they have to do, it seems more effective and sensible to study together with DDR organizations why they are doing what (for a similar approach, see Kenis and Marin, 1997 and Nöstlinger and Heller, 1998).

Third, although it was clear from the outset of this study that the object of the study would be in the first place the institutional and organizational responses to DDR, the research design as such was not predefined. Rather than taking a research design or research instruments, which have been developed in other projects or other regions, one of the innovative approaches of this study was that the researchers from the Central European countries themselves developed a research design, adapted to their own needs and context. For example, compared to earlier studies mapping organizational and institutional responses, the group of researchers thought it imperative to include information of the organizations' perception on the drug problem, the national drug policy and their attitudes towards drugs.

2 Defining the organizational and institutional response

Generally speaking, the degree of institutional and organizational response is defined as the degree to which an organization or a group of organizations responds to drug demand, i.e. where they develop specific activities, which are focussed to deal directly or indirectly with reducing the number of drug users and/or reducing the negative personal and social consequences of the use of drugs. Any type of organization which offers any type of activity, which contributes to dealing with the above-mentioned problems is defined here as having an organizational response to drug demand as long as the activities are provided in a specific and specialized way.[1] Organizations can be statutory organizations, non-profit organizations, private organizations, exclusive organizations, inclusive organizations, professional organizations, local or national organizations, small or large ones, membership organizations, old or new ones, etc. Organizations are considered in the present study as having an organizational response as long as they provide at least one activity in the area of drug demand reduction. Activities in the area of drug demand reduction where grouped in nine activity clusters (see Table 1).

Table 1: Clusters of Activities Analysed

- Prevention / information
- Treatment and care
- Rehabilitation (after care)
- Research / documentation
- Funding / fund-raising
- Co-ordination
- Interest representation
- Policy development / legislation
- Training of professionals

Consequently, any organization providing activities in any of these clusters is part of the organizational fields studied.

Finally, it should be mentioned that – as will be seen in the following chapters – the degree of organizational response can be analysed on different levels. It can be analysed on the level of the single organization, i.e. it can be assessed to which extent a single organization develops specific responses as a reaction to drug demand (the organizational level). Moreover, a specific group of organizations, such as public organizations or non-profit organizations can be assessed on their organizational response (the sectoral level). Finally, also organizations in a specific territorial setting, e.g. a province or country, can be assessed on their organizational response.

3 Countries Covered and Research Methods Applied

The data presented in this volume are the results of a cross-national comparative study in four Central European countries, which first developed, and than applied a common research design.

The selection of countries was based on practical considerations. The reason why central European countries were selected is related to the general objective of the project, i.e to develop research capacities in drug demand reduction in Eastern and Central European countries. That we started the research specifically with the Czech Republic, Hungary, Poland and Slovenia was related to the fact that we could successfully identify interested researchers in these countries and that these countries can be considered to be rather similar in their institutional developments in the after 1989 period. Since all researchers involved were expected to work for a small part of their time on the project, we also had to limit the coverage of organizations included in the research. We decided to include all national organizations in the study as well as a sample of organizations from one or two local levels. We considered that comparing different countries could best be done through a comparison of their national levels. But we also considered that countries might vary much in the way the local level is involved in drug demand reduction activities. For this reason we also included for each country one or two local level studies. Table 2 gives a summary of the different organizational fields included in this study.

The research carried out consisted of two larger components, each with identifiable steps. The first step of the first component of the research project was to agree on a common and comparable research design for mapping the institutional and organizational response. As indicated before, the research design resulted from a process in which the researchers from the Central European Countries played a crucial role. The choices, which we made here, and the rationality on which these choices were based are presented in part 4 of this chapter.

Table 2: Organizational fields included in the study and some of their basic characteristics

Organization fields	Number of organizations	Legal status (public/non-profit/private)	Orientation (exclusive/ inclusive)
Czech Republic (CZ)	49	24 / 23 / 2	20 / 29
National level	15	10 / 5 / 0	4 / 11
Prague	25	9 / 14 / 2	13 / 12
Ústí nad Labem	9	5 / 4 / 0	3 / 6
Hungary (H)	46	26 / 16 / 3	14 / 32
National level	24	14 / 9 / 1	6 / 18
Budapest	17	8 / 6 / 2[1]	7 / 10
Szeged	5	4 / 1 / 0	1 / 4
Poland (PL)	49	16 / 31 / 2	17 / 32
National level	37[2]	11 / 25 / 1	10 / 27
Lodz	12	5 / 6 / 1	7 / 5
Slovenia (SLO)	37	20 / 16 / 1	9 / 28
National level	23	12 / 10 / 1	3 / 20
Ljubljana	6	4 / 2 / 0	6 / 8
Piran, Izola, Koper	8	4 / 4 / 0	

Notes: 1 One organization indicated to have no legal status.
2 Originally 38 national organizations had been identified. One organization at the national level refused to participate in the study.

In a second step, the organizations, which develop drug demand reduction activities in the different organizational fields (national and local levels) were identified. The procedure for identifying the organizations was done somewhat differently by the country teams (this is explained in the respective country chapters). Generally speaking, all teams used a combination of the following methods: inclusion of the general known organizations, requests for information from experts in the field, and applying the so-called "reputational method" (i.e. asking previously identified organizations whether they know of any other organizations within their organizational field that also provide DDR activities).

In a third research step, all identified organizations received a standardized inventory sheet from which the organizational characteristics, the

DDR activities they develop, perceptions of the drug problem and of policy and information about co-ordination with other DDR organizations was gathered. In a fourth research step the data were entered in SPSS. In addition, the research design foresaw the collection of a set of contextual data on the institutional, social and epidemiological context. During the final step of the first component, country reports were produced presenting the institutional and organizational responses to drug demand reduction at the national level and at the selected local levels. These country reports (Czech Republic, Hungary, Poland and Slovenia) are included in the present Volume (Chapters 2 to 5).

The second component consisted of the production of a series of comparative studies based on selected data. It was decided that two researchers from different countries co-operated with each other in developing such a comparative study. This resulted in four comparative chapters, which are also included in this publication (Chapters 6 to 9). In addition, a chapter has been added analysing the networks of the organizations in the national DDR fields in the different countries (Chapter 10).

4 Some Dimensions in the organizational response to drug demand

As decribed above, the study presented here is based on two principal research components. For the first component original data have been collected on the bases of a comparative research design and presented in four country studies. For the second component, the collected data have been used to develop five cross-national analyses. We will now give a short introduction to the rationality of the choices we made with regard to the data collected and the type of analysis carried out.

One of the principal starting points of the research was to describe the organizational fields (i.e. the DDR fields on the national and local level) in a comprehensive and effective way. It was the objective to arrive at an understanding of which institutions are involved in drug demand reduction, the way they are involved and their motives for it. Asking these questions has the advantage that they transcend the more commonly used drug policy research categories (e.g. the degree of prohibition versus legislation, harm reduction versus repression, policy statements, etc.). The approach in the present study describes organizational fields in terms of the institutional context, differentiation and integration.

The *institutional context* refers to the fact that strategies develop within a specific context. The importance of describing the institutional context is based on the assumption that the logic and consequences of institutional devices can only be understood when the context in which such strategies have developed is taken into account. The scope of a strategy (e.g. to develop DDR activities) is determined by the type and degree of options and restrictions organizations are institutionally constrained by. In the case of strategies on the local level, for example, options for actions are very much determined by the formal competencies municipalities have in the area of drug demand reduction. In the present study the institutional context was taken into account along the following dimensions: history of the DDR policy, legislation, government concepts and strategies, financing of DDR, co-ordination practices in the field of DDR and the epidemiological development.

Describing organizational fields in terms of *differentiation* implies questions, such as: which are the relevant organizations in the DDR field and how do these organizations differ? The way and degree in which organizations differ in the different DDR fields has been described in this study along the following dimensions: legal status of the organization, inclusive or exclusive DDR organization, size of the organization (in terms of staff and budget), goals and objectives, the activities provided and the perception of the drug problem and the DDR policy, and the attitude towards drugs. The rationale for describing organizational fields in terms of differentiation is based on the idea that the degree and type of differentiation can be indicative for such questions as the effectiveness of the DDR field (e.g. in terms of the range of activities provided), the division of labour within the DDR field (e.g. between public and non-profit organizations) or the potential differences in opinions or conflicts within a DDR field (e.g. in terms of conflicts concerning drug policies and/or attitudes with regard to drugs).

In addition, the organizational DDR fields have been described in terms of *integration*. Integration or co-ordination refers to the way in which these differentiated DDR fields are integrated. Data on integration have in the present study been collected using formal network analysis (for more details see Chapter 10) and covered the following types of integration: exchange of clients, exchange of support, exchange of expertise, exchange of resources, common activities, strategic co-operation, informal communication and the prominence attributed. The rationale behind mapping types and degrees of integration of an organizational field is related to the fact that effective DDR strategies and policies often can only be achieved by common efforts of different organizations. Consequently, it is important to understand how, why and under what circumstance organizations co-operate. Moreover, in a field like DDR, outcomes can often not readily be attributed to the activities of individual organizations, i.e. they are contingent on integrated and co-ordinated actions of many different agencies.

In particular, the combined analysis of differentiation and integration is promising. From organizational and policy studies we know that those systems or fields which are at the same time highly differentiated and highly integrated often produce the most promising outputs. This combination is however far from evident since it can be assumed that the more a field is differentiated the more difficult integration becomes. Consequently, any study exploring this problem and the solutions, which have been developed to deal with it can contribute to more effective policies and practices.

In the present volume four country studies are presented following the above logic of inquiry. For practical reasons only two of the four studies have included the integration dimension (Czech Republic and Slovenia). This dimension is, however, dealt with in a separate comparative chapter (Chapter 10), which includes data on all four countries. Every single country study presents a detailed view of the institutional context and forms and degrees of differentiation of their respective national and local DDR fields. In general, it can be said that all four countries (the Czech Republic, Hungary, Poland and Slovenia) have witnessed since 1989 a significant change in their organizational DDR fields, as the country chapters will demonstrate. It is interesting to see, however, that although epidemiological patterns since 1989 are not very different across these countries, the organizational response differs quite significantly.

On the basis of the same data presented in the country reports and on the basis of the same research philosophy presented above, five comparative studies have been included in this volume.

The first study (Chapter 6 by Csémy and Elekes) addresses the question whether there is a relationship between the problem load with regard to illicit drugs and the drug policy developed. This is indeed a question, which interests many, since it is generally assumed that the policy response should reflect the range and type of the problem load. Or seen from the reverse angle, the question might become even more interesting: does DDR policy have any effect on the prevalence and the consequences of the use of drugs? Trying to answer these questions is, of course, extremely ambitious for theoretical, methodological as well as for data quality reasons. But since the project brought together more or less comparative epidemiological data and mapped institutional and organizational responses in a comparative way, we could not resist the temptation to at least look what would happen addressing this question. As we will see, the conclusion of this chapter is consistent with the policy literature in general: an absence of a direct correspondence between the type and degree of drug problems and the degree and type of drug policies. The institutional and organizational response in the area of DDR seems to be a compromise between needs and problems on the one hand and institutional capacities, social possibilities, and resources on the other. Needs are not only determined by the factual scope and the nature of the problem, but also by the way the problem is perceived by experts, civil service, the general public and the population at risk.

Chapter 7 (by Györy and Sobiech) is a comparative analysis of factors determining the perception of the drug problem and the opinions on national policies by the organizations involved in DDR. The following determinants are included in the analysis: the type of knowledge utilized by organizations in their activities, whether activities of organizations are directed towards individuals and clients or policies, the maturity of the organizations, and the type of professionals employed. Without going into detail, the conclusions of the study are that both factors, i.e. the perception of the drug problem in the country and the opinions on national policies, vary considerable across countries but also across types of organizations. This proofs that the environment of organizations is not an objective fact and that, consequently, the strategies of organizations (e.g. with respect to the activities they provide) are a result of the way the environment is perceived by them (what Weick (1998) has called the "enacted environment").

The third comparative study (Chapter 8 by Krch and Cvelbar) is an analysis of the division of labour between non-governmental organizations (NGOs) and governmental organizations. An analysis of the role of NGOs compared with governmental organizations is particularly interesting in the case of Central European countries. DDR originally concentrated in these countries on the medical treatment of illicit drug users in public institutions. In all countries except Poland more than 80% of non-governmental organizations started drug demand reduction activities after 1992. On the basis of the comparative analysis a number of interesting conclusions are drawn. The importance of NGOs seems indeed to have increased over the years in all countries studied. Although there are differences between NGOs and governmental organizations in terms of budget, staff, etc. the difference in the type of activities they provide seems, interestingly enough, less significant. The logic seems not to be that there is a fine-tuned division of labour between governmental organizations and NGOs. On the one side, NGOs often seem to become active in areas in which also governmental organizations are involved. On the other side, they seem to develop actions in areas, which are relatively underdeveloped on the basis of the feeling that "somebody has to do it".

The next comparative chapter (Chapter 9 by Dekleva and Zamecka) takes as starting point the attitudes that organizations have with regard to drugs. The question addressed here is whether these attitudes discriminate between the countries studied and the different types of DDR organizations. This is an important question since generally it is assumed that it are exactly these differences in attitudes between actors in the DDR field which often make practice and policy such a complicated issue. But, do attitudes actually differ significantly and if yes, in which way? The data collected on attitudes in the survey have been analysed in order to arrive at a permissive/restrictive scale. Then, this composed variable has been used to compare countries, types of organizations, perception of the drug policy and the organizations' activities. This analysis produces a number of highly interesting results, some of which one would have expected while others are rather surprising. For example, the fact that the more restrictive organizations tend to be founded earlier might not come as a surprise. On the other side, the fact that restrictive organizations also tend to have more voluntary workers is rather surprising. Surprising is also that the permissive/restrictive attitudes are not related to the type of activities organizations provide. This seems to confirm the phenomena often observed in organizational research that there is a difference between what organizations say and what they do (what Brunsson (1989) has called "The Organization of Hypocrisy", but which has, however, not necessarily to be seen as something negative).

In the last comparative chapter (Chapter 10 by Kenis and Loos) the so-called network data have been analysed. In order to analyse the integration of the different DDR fields at the national level, data were collected on different types of relationships that organizations in these fields have amongst each other. Data are available on the exchange of clients, the exchange of support, the exchange of expertise, the exchange of resources, common activities, strategic co-operation, informal communication and the prominence attributed. On the basis of these data the chapter addresses two principal questions. First, what is the density of relationships within the networks or, in other words how close are the different organization co-operating with each other and in which respect. The second question is: how centralized are the networks and who are the most central actors, or in other words "who is in charge?". As will be demonstrated, the four national networks differ substantially with respect to the answers to these questions.

5 Afterword

This Volume is the outcome of a project of which the principal objective was to create a sustainable network of researchers. We hope that this book proofs that this goal has been more than reached. On top of this we have now, for the first time, a detailed institutional and organizational analysis of DDR fields in Central Europe available. The different organizational and local fields have been described in great detail on the basis of a common research design. Moreover, a number of comparative analyses have been carried out on the basis of the data. It is hoped that what is available now will at least in some way lay better groundwork for informed policy.

It is also hoped that on the basis of the data, further empirical analysis will be carried out. We hope that the presentation of the data, the questions formulated and the numerous hypothetical statements in the different chapters stimulate further research in the direction set out here. In order to stimulate this we have added the original questionnaire, which was used in the research (see Annex). It should also be noted that every table in this Volume which does not indicate a source has our primary dataset as its origin. At the end of every country chapter (Chapters 2 to 5) we have added the list of organizations, which are part of our dataset. Throughout the different chapters the general rule was, however, that the anonymity of the organizations should be respected. Apart from some cases, where with their consent the organizations are specifically mentioned, all data are presented in an anonymous and aggregated manner.

This Volume would never have come about without the help of many organizations and dedicated persons. First of all we would like to thank the 181 organizations active in the field of DDR who shared their time, insights and information with us – without whom this study simply could not have been undertaken. We would also like to thank those who have been decisive in the initial phase of this project and who helped to get the study of the ground. From the UNDCP we particularly thank Sandeep Chawla, head of the Research Section and Thomas Pietschmann, who has all the time been involved in stimulating the research, taking part in discussions during project meetings and providing feed-back to its intermediate results. The project was funded with resources from the Federal Ministry of Foreign Affairs of Austria, and we particularly would like to thank Dr. Irene Freudenschuss-Reichl, Permanent Representative of Austria to the United Nations until recently for her support. From the European Centre for Social Welfare Policy and Research we thank Bernd Marin, Director and Vanessa Proudman, Andrea Hovenier and Nicola Oberzaucher, who were involved at several stages during the development of the project. We also thank Stefan Loos for his contribution in developing Chapter 10 of this publication. We particularly thank Willem Stamatiou from the European Centre for his dedicated help in getting this Volume to the printer.

And of course goes our highest gratitude and appreciation to the involved researchers in the project: Zsuzsanna Elekes and Tünde Györy from Hungary, Ladislav Csemy and Frantisek David Krch from the Czech Republic, Renata Cvelbar and Bojan Dekleva from Slovenia, and Joanna Zamecka and Robert Sobiech from Poland. Robert Sobiech took particularly care to co-ordinate activities related to data and was responsible also for the SPSS database.

Note

1 This means that organizations, which do not explicitly deal with drug demand in a different or differentiated way, have been excluded from this study. An example of such an organization would be one providing housing facilities for people in crisis situations: such an organization might also do this for persons using drugs, perhaps without having knowledge of their particular condition or disregarding it.

References

Brunsson, N. (1989) *The Organization of Hypocrisy. Talk, Decisions, and Actions in Organizations.* Chichester etc. : Wiley.

Kenis, P./Marin, B. (1997) *Managing AIDS – Organizational Responses in Six European Countries.* Ashgate: Aldershot.

Nöstlinger, C./Heller, F. (1998) *Prioritizing the Scope of HIV/Aids Action. An Applied Action Research Project.* Final report for the Commission of the European Union. Brussels.

UNDCP Project Document (1997) *Developing Social Research Capacities in Drug Control.* Vienna: UNDCP.

Weick, K.E. (1988) 'Enacted Sensemaking in Crisis Situations', *Journal of Management Studies* 24 (4).

Part I

Country Studies

CHAPTER 2

The Drug Problem in the Czech Republic
In Search of an Institutional Structure

Ladislav Csémy and Franti‰ek David Krch

1 Policy conditions: The institutional, social and epidemiological context

1.1 *Introduction*

After 1989, the Czech Republic opened up to a process of economic transformation and social change. This brought about not only fundamental changes in the drug scene, but also in legislation, public administration, general health and the welfare system, and, consequently, in the institutional context of drug demand reduction. While the standards of prevention, treatment and harm reduction in Western European countries developed gradually in relation to the growing severity of the problem, in the Czech Republic the situation changed very quickly, and often hastily, during the 1990s. The increasing frequency of drug abuse and the problems related to the production, distribution and illegal use of drugs have turned the topic into a public issue which is resulting in pressure to find new ways to reduce demand for illegal drugs. The relatively fast development of a number of non-governmental institutions was enabled by the following factors: legislative changes, the comparatively privileged status of the drug issue, international contacts, the experience of experts and increasing demands for their services and, in the beginning, a rather non-competitive environment. These institutions focused mainly on providing services that were mediated by the state only to a limited extent or not at all.

Besides the newly created private organizations, a network of institutions established before 1989 already existed which included professional and lay associations, church and charity organizations, and foundations. Facilities for outpatient and inpatient treatment were mostly focused on psychiatric treatment and were originally intended for the treatment of alcohol dependency. In addition, there was a relatively well-developed network of regional hygiene services focused on general health prevention (mainly the prevention of infectious diseases). Some of these institutions still exist today and some have been privatized. Other institutions have disappeared or have lost their importance.

In the light of the growing popularity of the drug issue, of higher institutional demand and the relative accumulation of financial resources as well as the rising interest of international institutions (UN, Council of Europe etc.), there has also been an increase in the number of institutions that state drug demand reduction as one of their activities. It has started to pay off in a political or financial sense to engage in some kind of activity in this field. By contrast, other institutions have been forced to deal with the issue because of the increasing and changing nature of the drug problem. Drugs have become a topic of public discussion (e.g. in the media and in school curricula) and a specific problem in certain regions (large cities, industrial areas with high unemployment rates) and among certain social groups (e.g. recruits, immigrants, children under 15, and certain ethnic minorities). This has created demand for specific activities and institutions focused on drug demand reduction.

1.2 *Human resources and economic conditions*

The increasing need for services and their growing potential in the field of drug demand reduction have influenced the growth of professional and financial resources. The first experts dealing with primary prevention of drug dependency and treatment were usually recruited from the hygienic services network or from institutions working in the treatment of alcohol dependency and addiction to other substances. During the 1990s, the number of experts dealing with drug issues increased. Furthermore, a larger number of experts had an educational background rather than a medical background, and the number of volunteers grew steadily. Professional resources have multiplied and adjusted themselves to demand and to the more differentiated institutional context. While at the end of the 1980s, work with so-called chronic patients prevailed in the treatment of drug dependence and a major role was played by medical professionals, in the 1990s, the focus shifted to contact and prevention drop-in centres. The importance of social work has also grown. At institutions, the psychosocial and hygienic aspects of the initial stages of dependency have come to be seen as more important. Telephone help lines have been established, programmes for groups experimenting with drugs and extra-curricular youth school programmes have been set up. The changes in the system of education after 1990 (broader availability of university-educated experts in different fields) has contributed to the enlargement and differentiation of the available pool of human resources.

Until 1989, state support was the single major source of financing for any institution. At the beginning of the 1990s, the funding sources changed substantially and became more differentiated. A new source of financing were the contributions from international organizations. Some of these contributions covered only part of a particular programme or specifically required co-financing by the recipient state, which increased the pressure to make local financial resources available. Financial support from foundations, churches, charities as well as from the private sector also grew. The Act on Health Insurance (1990) enabled the creation of private medical facilities. Payment systems (of health insurance companies) for the performance of individual medical services led to the growth of private outpatient facilities (Hampl, 1997). A legislative amendment in 1997 introduced payment per patient (per capita) and set the limits on the number of medical procedures. This resulted in an increased attention for patients with minor psychiatric problems at some outpatient facilities. The fact that some procedures were not covered by health insurance or that health insurance companies did not conclude contracts with some individual health care providers (especially non-physicians) led to the search and creation of new financial resources on the one hand, and to a search for safeguards for the adequate use of these resources on the other. For example, the Ministry of Health of the Czech Republic (The National Drug Commission/NDC, 1999) in 1998 financed 28 projects from the DDR (drug demand reduction) budget submitted by state health institutions to reduce drug demand, 39 from civic associations, five from charities, two from foundations and two projects from non-governmental health institutions and others.

At the central level, drug policy is presently financed by the competent ministries and under the budgetary chapter "General Administration" by district offices and city authorities and by the administrations of the so-called statutory towns (NDC, 1998). The aim of the anti-drug programme of the government for the years 1998-2000 was to create a unified and co-ordinated system of financing for drug policy at the national and local levels. The government took the following measures to achieve this goal:

- Precise definition of the responsibilities of individual ministries.
- Creation of a central database of subjects financed by state or public funds in the field drug demand reduction (the database is administered by the National Drug Commission).
- Unification of the procedures used by the individual ministries for granting subsidies.
- Standardization of tender procedures.
- Introduction of a system of accreditation and licences issued by certain ministries.
- Strengthening of control mechanisms.
- Reinforcement of the budget item "Anti-Drug Policy" in the chapter "General Administration" of the state budget (NDC, 1998).

It is still difficult to identify the exact amounts and proportion of financial resources allocated to the anti-drug policy within the individual ministries. For instance, within the Ministry of the Interior, certain anti-drug activities are part of the daily routine of the police in the Czech Republic. The total amounts of financial resources allocated in the budgetary chapters of the ministries for the government's anti-drug policy were EUR 2,392,146 (CZK 86.5 million) in 1997, EUR 2,511,062 (CZK 90.8 million) in 1998 and the estimate for 1999 was EUR 2,134,956 (CZK 77.2 million) (NDC, 1999).

At the local level (NDC, 1998), the district or town authorities prepare their own draft budgets. They contribute 10-30% of the total budget of the specific anti-drug project from their own resources; the remaining portion of the budget comes from the central government. On the basis of the draft budgets, the amounts credited to the district or town authorities from the state budget are allocated to the budgetary chapter "General Administration". At the beginning of each year, the district or city authorities receive a certain minimum flat rate to ensure a "minimum level" of anti-drug activity in the area (maximum of 30%). The disbursement of the remaining financial resources has to be targeted and has to take local priorities and the quality of the projects submitted into account.

1.3 *Governmental concepts and strategies*

In 1993, the Czech Government approved the "Concept and Programme of the Anti-Drug Policy". Since then, a focused effort has been observed towards institutional integration and the establishment of an institutional infrastructure that is able to meet the needs of education, communication, co-operation and the sharing of information between the various institutions that deal with the drug problem in the Czech Republic. The above-mentioned government document, which set the framework of anti-drug activities between 1993 and 1996 was based on the United Nation's Action Programme, approved at the UN's extraordinary session in 1991. The document stipulated the responsibilities and competencies of the individual ministries. The creation of the National Drug Commission (NDC), whose role is to comprehensively co-ordinate drug issues at the national executive level, was of principal importance. The NDC is an advisory body to the government on drug issues. In order to ensure efficient co-ordination, the commission created *ad hoc* working groups in various areas of anti-drug activities. A permanent Council of Representatives of Ministries exists, which ensures the standard co-ordination of the relevant ministries. The NDC also cooperates with experts in other fields of anti-drug activities, with professional associations and NGOs (NGOs are represented in the Council of Representatives of Ministries). The Commission co-ordinates the allocation of the financial resources and is responsible for international cooperation in the area of drugs (NDC, 1998).

At the local level, the NDC co-ordinates the anti-drug policy through anti-drug co-ordinators who work under the district and city authorities and at the offices of statutory towns. The Permanent Council of Co-ordinators provides co-ordination and methodological guidance to the anti-drug co-ordinators of the district and city authorities. In Prague, the Anti-drug Commission of the Capital of Prague (ACCP) was established as an advisory body to the Council of Town Deputies. There are representatives of the institutions involved in drug demand reduction activities in the Commission, as well as representatives of the police.

On 20 November 1997, the NDC approved a document entitled "The Concept and Programme of the Anti-drug Policy for the Years 1998-2000" which was subsequently approved by the Government at its meeting of 23 February 1998 (NDC, 1998). The document contains a list of 94 tasks for the competent ministries and for the authorities of the state and public administration. The document was prepared on the basis of negotiations between the individual ministries. A number of experts representing professional associations, specialized institutions, the state and NGOs participated in drafting the individual parts of the document. The document entrusts individual ministries with concrete duties. The Ministry of Health for example, was required to create a so-called "Minimum Network of Health Care" for problem drug users and for drug addicts, to set standards for individual types of care, to introduce the accreditation system, to create a specialized educational unit for addictions, etc. The Ministry of Education, Youth and Sports was required to introduce the so-called "Minimum Programme of Prevention" to schools and educational institutions, and to establish principles for efficient primary prevention that function as quality standards for the allocation of the financial resources. The Ministry of Justice had to create a complex, long-term system of education for judges, public attorneys and higher court officials, to ensure the development of probation services and, among other things, to introduce so-called "drug-free zones" in prisons in the Czech Republic. The Ministry of Labour and Social Affairs was to prepare a concept of re-socialization and post-penitentiary care for drug-addicts, and to initiate a concept of re-socialization facilities for people who had completed treatment in the most affected regions in the Czech Republic. In 1998, the Ministry of Health and the Ministry of Justice started to cooperate in the area of coerced treatment of drug addicts who are in prison (NDC, 1998).

1.4 Legislation

Legislative measures form an important part of the government's anti-drug policy. In 1997, the existing (obligatory) punishment of a prison sentence was complemented by another alternative: "renunciation of the punishment under supervision". Aspects of probation have been introduced into the Criminal Code, in which the punishment is combined with supervision and support. Amendment No. 113/1997 of the Collection of Laws of the so-called "Customs Act" strengthened the competencies of customs' bodies in fighting organized drug crime. The Amendment of the Criminal and Offence Act No. 112/1998 of the Collection of Laws introduced a more severe punishment for drug-related crimes, i.e., the lower limits of the punishments were raised. The amendment also declared it against the law to be in the possession of amounts of illegal drugs larger than the amount defined as serving only personal consumption purposes. This offence is not heard before a court, but is penalized by an administrative authority. A fine of up to EUR 415 (CZK 15,000) may be imposed. The Act No. 167/1998 of the Collection of Laws reflects the provisions of Article 12 of the United Nations' Convention against Illicit Trafficking in Narcotic Drugs and Psychotropic Substances. Both acts entered into force on 1 January 1999. Criminal prosecution was extended to also cover the manufacturing of substances that contain narcotics as well as the unauthorized sale of such substances. In December 1998, the Ministry of the Interior defined the limits for "a small amount of drugs" for personal use. These are, for example, 20 marijuana cigarettes weighing 1 g, or 10 doses of heroin (each of 100 mg of substance) (NDC, 1999). At present, the Ministry of Labour and Social Affairs is preparing a draft Act on Probation and Mediation Services.

Law enforcement is mainly the competence of the Ministry of the Interior (Police of the Czech Republic), the Ministry of Justice (legislation, prisons, state attorneys, in part also the courts) and the Ministry of Finance (customs authorities). The Ministry of Health is responsible for approving the handling and preparation of psychotropic drugs, their import and export as well as for supervising the legal handling of such substances (Inspectorate for Narcotics and Psychotropic Substances). In 1991, the Agreement on the Establishment of the National Co-ordinating Office for Narcotics that would serve as a body co-ordinating the activities of the police and customs authorities was signed. After the separation of the Czechoslovak Federal Republic, the National Drug Information Service was established on 1 January 1993. The creation of a new border with the Slovak Republic had a negative impact from the point of view of anti-drug activities, i.e. it became necessary to establish, equip and organize new customs offices. Another negative development was the re-routing of drug trafficking as a result of the war in the countries of former Yugoslavia. In the beginning of 1995, the National Anti-Drug Office of the Czech Police was established as a result of the reorganization of the Criminal Police Department. This Department is part of the Czech Republic's Police Unit for the Detection of Organized Crime.

In 1997, 1,152 persons were charged with the illegal production and sale of drugs. In 1998, 1,530 persons were prosecuted on the same charges. Compared to 1992, in 1998 the rate of offenders sentenced on drug-related charges increased by more than 17 times. In 1998, the number of persons sentenced on drug-related charges was 1.5% of the total number of persons sentenced in the same year. A share of 81% of the offenders sentenced were younger than 30 years, 9.6% of the offenders sentenced were women. In 1998, the number of places for a differentiated prison sentence for drug addicts increased to a total of 144 places (NDC, 1998 and 1999). Despite the decreasing age of problem drug users, the Ministry of Education only had four educational reform facilities for juveniles (two of them in Prague) that also provided care for juvenile drug users (NDC, 1999).

1.5 Co-ordination

Besides the vertical co-ordination, which was initiated mainly by the government of the Czech Republic and which is organized by the bodies of public administration, there is a concurring effort for spontaneous horizontal co-ordination among some institutions that are active in the field of drug demand reduction. Usually these activities involve joint initiatives of institutions of a similar type or link institutions that complement each other, e.g. the establishment of the Association of NGOs (ANO) that works with the Society for Addictive Illnesses and the Association of A-Clubs (which publishes the magazine *Semprefit* with a focus on the drug scene in the country) both of which have been active in the Czech Republic (and Czechoslovakia) for several decades. The mutual relationships between these institutions are reinforced by the fact that some of staff work at more than one of the institutions and that the institutions refer clients to one another.

There are different forms of horizontal co-ordination. Usually, this involves informal activities based on actual needs or which are related to the specific experiences of a given organization. Some institutions offer information, supervision, stages and training to other institutions and experts of their own initiative.

1.6 General health and welfare system in the Czech Republic

Within 10 years, the Czech Republic has succeeded in creating a relatively differentiated network of institutions which focus on the reduction of drug demand. After a period during which various institutions and programmes emerged, the focus of health and welfare policy is now shifting to securing professional quality and a client-oriented approach of the services provided, as well as ensuring the well-functioning co-ordination and integration of these services.

Primary prevention

The political changes that started in 1989 marked an important step in primary prevention. Drug issues ceased to be regarded as taboo, and a discussion and learning process was opened at both the professional and public level. The approach of professionals and the interested public has become significantly differentiated ever since. As a minimum, a formal agreement exists that the drug problem has its social, familial, psychological and biological aspects (the so-called biological-psychological-social model) and that it cannot be attributed only to a certain "antisocial" class of society or to a specific personality disorder.

Prevention programmes in the Czech Republic used to consist (and often still consist) mainly of information about the health damage caused by drugs, and of statements made by personalities esteemed by adolescents. The media usually "complement" the discussions with experts by giving dramatic portrayals of victims and often present exaggerated and fragmentary epidemiological data. A positive development may be seen in the efforts to work at the peer level (peer programmes) and through parents. Other prevention programmes include support for the development of healthy life styles, programmes for young children (early prevention), putting the prevention of non-alcoholic drugs in the context of other dependencies, and efforts to work continuously and in a co-ordinated manner.

The Czech Government set the following targets in its programme of anti-drug policy (NDC, 1998):

1. Active support for efficient prevention programmes focused on adolescents at school, in the family and in the communal environment.
2. Continuing education of intermediators (teachers, physicians, social workers etc.) who work in the sphere of prevention.

Within the concept of the government's anti-drug policy, the responsibility for prevention is therefore primarily with the Ministry of Education, Youth and Sports, which adopted the minimum programme for the prevention of addictive substances at schools and educational facilities entitled "School without Drugs". The prevention of drug abuse is included in the national programme "Healthy School" (NDC, 1999). Schoolchildren and students who are having drug-related problems, as well as their parents and teachers, usually first turn for help to one of the 104 Pedagogical and Psychological Counselling Centres (NDC, 1998) or to the Centres of Pedagogical Care or to the Pedagogic Centres that are managed by the Ministry of Education. These centres identify the pupils or students who have problems or are at risk. They provide counselling in drug-related issues. Every year, the Ministry of Education organizes a competition for grants within its "Programme for Support and Protection of Children and Youth". The scheme supports programmes aimed at the prevention of negative social phenomena and implemented by civic associations.

The primary prevention of drug addiction is implemented by health care institutions that are controlled by the Ministry of Health or are financed directly from the budget of the Ministry. These are usually included in a broader concept of healthy lifestyles and the complex prevention of other health risks. The Ministry of Health holds an annual selection process for the Programmes for Health Support. The prevention of drug abuse is one of the priorities of the scheme. The "Healthy City" projects are financed from this budget. The National Institute of Public Health and the Association of A-Clubs (which publishes the magazine *Peer Programme*) carry out long-term activities focused on the mediation of information (epidemiology, publishing activities, lectures and educational programmes). The Hygienic Service runs a Drug Information System, which is based on the continual monitoring of incidents of problem drug users, infectious diseases, acute intoxication and premature deaths (NDC, 1998). However, thus far it has not provided thorough information about the full scope of the problem. The civic association FIT IN – Parents Against Drugs issues a wide range of publications for people involved in work dealing with the drug problem. The so-called "FIT IN 2001 Initiative" (Nonina and Hlavat, 1995), in which other organizations besides FIT IN also participate, is focused on the support of safe environments for children and adolescents. Some non-governmental institutions declare prevention as their primary purpose, e.g. the Prevention and Crisis Centre in Liberec or the Foundation for Prevention and Treatment of Drug Addictions "Drop-in".

The Ministry of Defence incorporated the prevention of drug abuse into its policy for the prevention of socially pathological phenomena in the army and especially among new recruits. Its main focus is, besides educational programmes, on leisure time activities. The Ministry of Interior also has a co-ordinated comprehensive programme for the prevention of crime. In 1998, 23 local projects for the prevention of drug addiction were financed through this programme (the total amount of financial support was EUR 42,589 or CZK 1,540,000). The projects aimed at broadening the scope of leisure time activities for children and adolescents, educational/pedagogical activities and counselling, and peer programmes (NDC, 1999).

Treatment, care and re-socialization

Health care and prevention in the field of drug addiction were among the priorities of the Ministry of Health in 1998 (NDC, 1998 and 1999; Ministry of Health, 1995). In 1998, the Ministry focused on the development of programmes of early intervention, programmes for harm reduction, outpatient facilities with elements of follow-up care, centres providing day care together with intensive outpatient treatment, facilities with detoxification programmes and support for institutional care and therapeutic communities. The first methadone substitution programme (NDC, 1999), which was opened in 1997 in the General Faculty Hospital in Prague, was financed as a pilot project in the beginning. The programme was introduced with the approval of the Ministry of Health as an experiment for a total of 20 clients. The results of the first programme of this type in the Czech Republic received a positive assessment, therefore, the further development of substitution programmes was included in the concept of the government's anti-drug policy. A specialized unit for infectious hepatitis with a programme for the complex treatment of drug addictions was also created with the financial support of the Ministry of Health. The Ministry of Health is attempting to create a comprehensive and continuous system of care for drug addicts in cooperation with the Ministry of Education, Youth and Sports and especially in cooperation with the Ministry of Labour and Social Affairs. In 1998, the National Drug Commission registered 237 facilities providing treatment or counselling, which report contacts with drug users as part of their activities (NDC, 1999).

De-toxification programmes in the Czech Republic are seen as one form of therapeutic intervention. De-toxification units are established in state (governmental) medical facilities, usually at specialized inpatient wards for the treatment of addictions. After de-toxification, patients may start treatment programmes oriented on abstention or they can leave upon their own request.

Harm reduction programmes in the Czech Republic were initiated by NGOs. The first programmes focused on the exchange of needles and syringes. The first needle exchange programme was started at the Sananim Contact Centre in 1993. Needle exchange programmes also spread quickly at the regional level. NGOs remain their primary organizers. Cooperation between NGOs and state hygienic stations in needle exchange programmes proved to be very important. In many cases, it is the hygienic stations that provide NGOs with material for the replacement programmes. The majority of NGOs implementing needle exchange programmes aims to achieve the return of the used needles and syringes. In well-administered programmes, the return rate is about 90%. The needle exchange programmes are often related to street work and outreach programmes.

The Ministry of Labour and Social Affairs is administering the system of social services specifically directed at clients with drug problems. The system will eventually include the following according to the draft Act on Social Support (NDC, 1999):

1. Low-threshold contact centres and outreach work.
2. Outpatient counselling and therapeutic services.
3. Therapeutic communities.
4. Protected employment and programmes for assistance in finding jobs.
5. Shelter accommodation.
6. Social programmes for drug addicts who are undergoing substitution treatment.
7. Social programmes for active drug users who are not undergoing treatment.

While the existing offer of the facilities 1-3 listed above is quite satisfactory, the services listed under 4-7 are not available in some regions (sometimes they are not available in the entire Czech Republic). Follow-up care is the least-developed component of the system of care for drug users, because it is relatively "new" and rather cost-intensive (Hampl, 1997). The negative attitudes of the majority of the population are a setback for the creation of a system of social services for active drug users. At present, follow-up care is provided by eight therapeutic communities and by two specialized programmes (both run by NGOs) in Prague and Olomouc, which have at their disposal a follow-up treatment programme and shelter accommodation. However, the capacity of these facilities is not sufficient. At the level of district authorities, social assistance to drug addicts was provided by 150 social workers, 350 social workers for youth and 28 social assistants in 1998. About half of the social assistants also worked at the same time in contact facilities (NDC, 1998 and 1999).

Outpatient treatment services

Until the 1990s, all outpatient treatment was provided within the framework of the psychiatric departments at district health centres. Due to the prevalence of alcohol-related problems, these facilities were called "Anti-Alcoholism Counselling Centres", and then, from the 1960s onwards, "Outpatient Centres for Alcoholism and Toxicomania" (AT Centres). In the 1970s and 1980s, a network of about 170 such centres providing care throughout the country existed. Their service teams included psychiatrists, nurses and social workers. At the majority of these centres, psychiatrists were involved only part-time. These centres also had one important responsibility: to provide follow-up treatment (or after-care) to alcoholics or drug users discharged from hospitals (Csémy, 1999). In 1993, a number of 5,234 patients were treated at 160 AT Centres for problems with non-alcoholic drugs (Hampl, 1997). After 1993, many AT Centres were privatized or replaced by the newly-established treatment and contact centres. In 1998, the Czech Republic had 257 AT Centres and psychiatric or psychological outpatient centres, which reported treatment of dependencies on drugs or alcohol. Only 57%, however, treated more than 50 patients with a drug or alcohol problem per year (Hampl, 1997). In 1997, the first day care outpatient programme for milder forms of dependencies was opened in Prague. The programme is run on a trial basis (NDC, 1998).

After 1989, the first drop-in centre in the country was established. At present, most outpatient treatment services are provided by NGOs (drop-in centres, contact centres etc.) or by specialized private out-patient clinics. The new centres organized as NGOs receive funds from multiple sources. When compared to the centres that existed earlier and in which the role of psychiatrists was prominent, the new centres have more diversified teams. The approach to drugs as articulated by NGOs is that abstinence is no longer considered the only goal. Harm reduction strategies (needle exchange programmes, outreach work) represent an important part of the national drug policy, and were first initiated by these centres (Csémy, 1999).

Inpatient treatment programmes

Compared to the above-described structural differentiation in outpatient treatment services, the development of inpatient facilities has been less visible. The capacity for inpatient psychiatric treatment, which had been stable for several decades, dropped by 20% in 1990. The inpatient treatment of disorders caused by substance abuse takes place at specialized units of psychiatric hospitals (which provide about 90% of the overall treatment capacity) or at specialized wards of the psychiatric departments of general hospitals. There are specialized departments for persons addicted to drugs, although alcoholics and drug users are treated together in most of the existing programmes. The standard duration of a hospital stay is three months. The final goal of the treatment is abstinence. As far as the therapeutic approaches are concerned, most centres may be described as eclectic, that is, elements of different therapeutic schools are often used (behavioural, cognitive dynamic psychotherapy, etc.). The therapeutic team encourages the participation of family members or other close persons in the treatment and tries to establish conditions for after-care. More than one-third of patients admitted to treatment for drug dependency leave the hospital within the first seven days (Csémy, 1999).

A network of specialized facilities providing detoxification services was created in the Czech Republic. However, some regions are still in want of such facilities and in the majority there are waiting lists. According to the draft minimum network as proposed by the Ministry of Health, by the year 2002 there should be a detoxification unit at every regional hospital (NDC,

1998). Non-state institutions have started to provide short-term and medium-term care. The care is provided quite satisfactorily throughout the whole territory of the Czech Republic (NDC, 1999). In view of the growing demand and of the regional discrepancies, the capacity of some institutions was increased (Brno, Hradec Králové). There are about 250 hospital beds for the treatment of non-alcoholic dependencies (NDC, 1999). Long-term treatment and re-socialization are provided by institutions which have the form of therapeutic communities. There are about 90 beds in eight institutions within the framework of the Ministry of Labour and Social Affairs (NDC, 1998).

The treatment of drug addiction may only be carried out by accredited medical facilities. Besides public medical facilities, the treatment of drug addiction may also be carried out by private providers or by NGOs. NGOs that are not accredited as medical facilities cannot provide treatment. Such facilities provide psychosocial support and intervention, counselling and contact services. The cost of treatment of drug addicts who have medical insurance is covered by health insurance companies. If a drug addict does not have medical insurance, the necessary costs are borne by the state.

1.7 *The epidemiological development*

The misuse of illicit drugs in the countries of Central and Eastern Europe is one of the major current health and social problems (Csémy, 1997). In their review, Ne‰por and Csémy (1994) characterized four Central European post-Communist countries (the Czech Republic, Poland, Hungary and Slovakia) as countries where problems related to the use or misuse of addictive substances increased in the period after the socio-political changes. Especially striking is the rapid expansion of the use of illicit substances by youths in all of these states.

Besides a steep increase in the problems related to the drug abuse, in the last decade the problems related to the abuse of alcohol have also increased. The abuse of alcohol is very common in the Czech Republic, as is attested by the first rank held by the Czech Republic in the per capita consumption of beer worldwide. Since the 1980s, the consumption of alcohol has been increasing substantially, especially among women and adolescents.

Drug abuse and the drug abuse subculture did exist in the Czech Republic before the socio-political changes of 1989, but in a substantially different form from the current drug scene. The drug abuse subculture has been permanently present in the country, and especially in Prague, since the period of the students' unrest at the end of the 1960s. During the 1970s and 1980s, the drug subculture was perceived as a marginal part of the underground culture. During the period of the totalitarian regime there were very limited opportunities for independent research, therefore our knowledge about this population relies on studies done in the field of psychiatry (Vojtík and Bichá, 1987; Netík et al., 1991). Based on these studies, we conclude that the drug abuse communities were relatively closed, and that the most often misused drugs were pharmaceuticals containing psychoactive substances (particularly opiates or stimulants), and volatile substances.

The manufacture of drugs at home(s) became popular in the Czech drug abuse subculture, especially during the 1980s. Two types of so-called specifically "Czech" drugs spread widely and are still being produced and used among drug users: the "Braun"-opiate, in which the base is codeine, and "Pervitin" - a methamphetamine-like stimulant.

Survey of adolescents

The first important data source is represented by survey studies among the general population or the population of schoolchildren. Data from the European School Project on Alcohol and Other Drugs (ESPAD) are important because of their international comparability. The ESPAD survey was carried out in 1995 and in 1999. The results of the 1995 survey (Hibell et al., 1997) revealed that in the Czech Republic, the availability of illicit drugs is relatively easy and the extent of personal experience with drugs is higher than in other countries of CEE. Among Czech students, 23% reported experience in their lifetimes with some type of illicit drugs, while for students from Slovakia it was 10%, from Poland 9%, and from Hungary 5%. The subsequent data collection in 1999 was an opportunity to compare the development during the second half of the 1990s. The changes in the lifetime prevalence of substance use among adolescents aged 16 are shown in Figure 1. With the exception of the use of volatile solvents and anabolic steroids, a substantial increase was observed in all other major types of drugs. Similar to the changes in drug use, the attitudes of adolescents toward hazardous forms of addictive behaviour also changed, and in 1999 respondents reported more tolerant attitudes in this respect. Data on the perceived availability of drugs in society suggest that young people can get drugs quite easily in any region of the country.

Figure 1: Lifetime prevalence of addictive substance use among Czech adolescents

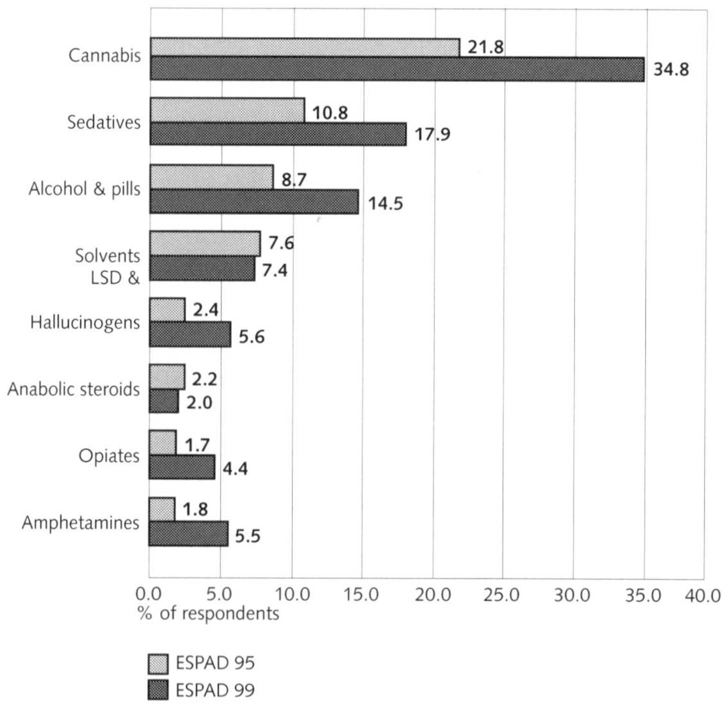

Note: Pervitin is included among amphetamines.

Source: Hibell et al., 2000.

The extent of the drug problem differs by region throughout the country. The most serious problem exists in the more industrialized and urbanized parts, especially in the capital and in the regions of Northern Bohemia and Northern Moravia (see Figure 2). For these reasons, we decided to collect data from Prague, the capital, and from the largest city in Northern Bohemia, Ústí nad Labem.

Figure 2: Lifetime prevalence of substance use by Czech adolescents by region

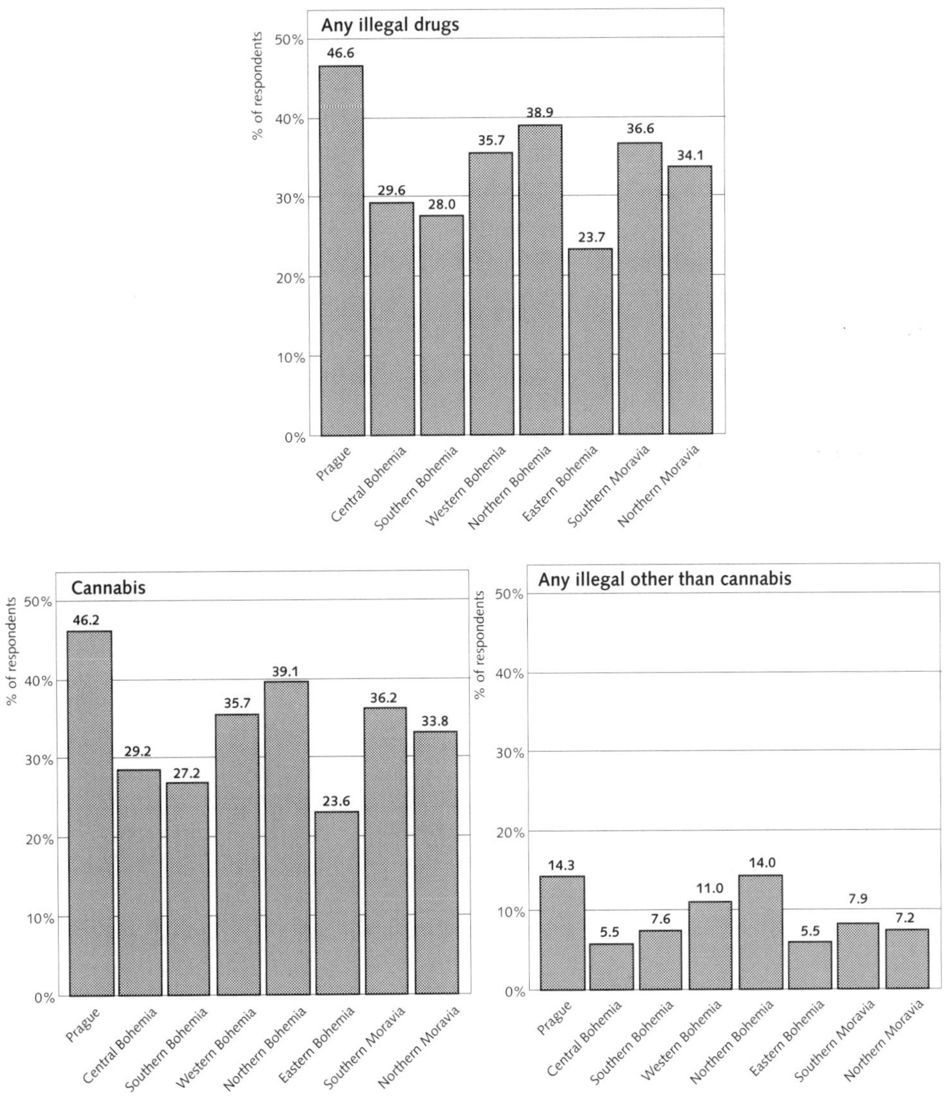

Source: Csémy et al., 1999b.

Profile of problem drug users

The surveys provide information about only one part of the drug scene. We have added the results of specific studies focused on the profile of the problem users to this data. In recent years, two studies have been conducted that focused on the patterns and context of substance use among the population of drug users in Prague. The first study was carried out in 1995, and 280 clients from five specialized treatment and contact centres in Prague were surveyed (Csémy, 1999). To illustrate the characteristics of Czech drug users, we have included the main findings in this report. Figure 3 illustrates the structure of drug preferences. The most important finding is the massive presence of Pervitin (a methamphetamine-like stimulant produced in home laboratories in the Czech Republic) as a primary drug (66.4% of all primary drugs). Heroin was reported as a primary drug by somewhat less than one-quarter of clients. These two specific substances – Pervitin and heroin – represented roughly 90% of the primary drugs used in the studied sample. As a secondary drug, heroin was reported most commonly (in 30% of cases). Approximately 22% of the respondents reported the use of Pervitin or cannabis as a secondary drug. Primary heroin users often consumed

Figure 3: Structure of drug preferences among clients of treatment and contact centres

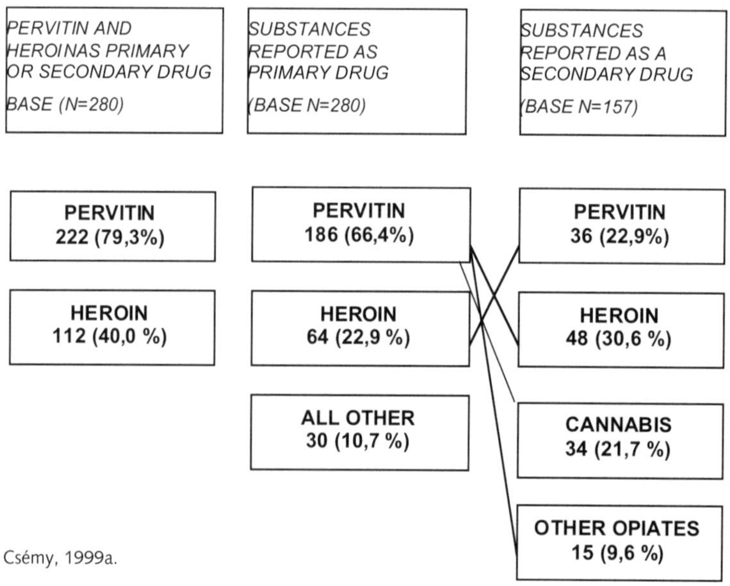

Source: Csémy, 1999a.

Pervitin as a secondary drug, while primary Pervitin users choose mostly heroin as a secondary drug, but also other opiates or cannabis (see links between the second and the third column of Figure 3). The first column of Figure 3 indicates the rate of use of Pervitin and heroin irrespective of whether it is the primary or secondary drug.

Primary drugs and the age of users

The mean age of Pervitin users was slightly lower than that of heroin users. In the group of primary Pervitin users, a sharp peak around the age of 17-18 was found, while the majority of heroin users fall into a broader age range of between 16 and 21. Both primary Pervitin and primary heroin users initiated the use of any drug at an average age of 16; female primary Pervitin users generally starting using drugs earlier than their male counterparts. The time lag between the first use of the current primary drug and the first use of any drug is larger for heroin than for Pervitin, and also larger for males than for females. In general, females tend to move to the use of their current primary drug within a rather short period of time.

Primary drug, frequency of use, routes of administration

We compared the frequency of primary drug use in the two main primary drugs by gender. The percentage of daily users is the same for males and females in the heroin subgroup (80.6% and 80.8%) as well as in the Pervitin subgroup (39.5% and 40.6). The most striking difference between the two types of primary drugs is that the daily use of heroin is double that of Pervitin.

Regarding the route of drug application, injection was found to be most prevalent. About 80% of clients reported injecting their primary drug within the past 30 days.

Problem drug users and drug dependent people in treatment systems

Currently, more than 200 centres claim to provide outpatient services for drug users. Despite the weak cooperation between existing outpatient facilities, there are some signs of vertical co-ordination. For example, an Association of NGOs was recently established that works in the field of drug addiction and aims to co-ordinate the activities of the individual NGOs. According to the most recently available data in 1998, there were over 5,000 patients registered in outpatient centres.

The capacity of inpatient psychiatric treatment, which had been previously stable for several decades, was reduced by 20% since the beginning of the 1990s. Of the psychiatric bed capacity, 11% (approx. 1,200 beds) represent specialized beds for the treatment of addictive disorders. However, the relative share of hospitalizations for addictive disorders has increased since the late 1970s, and even more sharply since 1990. In 1996, one out of four psychiatric admissions was for an addictive disorder.

Table 1: Hospital discharges for alcohol and drug use related disorders by gender between 1994 and 1998 (1994: introduction of the ICD 10 in the Czech Republic)

	Males		Females	
ICD 10	F 10 (Alcohol)	F 11-19 (Drugs)	F 10 (Alcohol)	F 11-19 (Drugs)
1994	6536	775	2146	356
1995	6821	1250	2340	513
1996	7262	1828	2602	834
1997	7564	2216	2624	1225
1998	7280	3002	2717	1531

Source: Zdravotnická statistika. Psychiatrická péãe 1994-1998. Ústav zdravotnickych informací a statistiky, Praha [Health Statistics. Psychiatric Care 1994-1998. Institute of Health Information and Statistics, Prague]

Table 1 shows a comparison of the changes in hospitalizations for alcohol-related disorders and for drug use-related disorders. It is clear that the number of cases treated for drug-related problems multiplied during the second part of the 1990s.

Table 2 shows the number of hospital discharges (only cases with a diagnosed syndrome of dependence) in 1994-1996 and the respective mean ages. Within these three years, the most rapid increase was found in opiate dependency, use of stimulants and use of multiple drugs. In these three categories, we also saw a significant decrease in the mean age. There are important differences in the average length of stay in treatment centres by type of disorder. The shortest average stay for opiate dependence was 23 days, and 31 days in the case of dependency on stimulants, while the average lengths of stays in hospitals for alcohol dependency is 42 days. Over one-third of patients admitted to treatment for drug dependency leave the hospital within the first seven days (Csémy, 1999). The treatment outcomes are affected by the high rate of persons who do not complete the treatment programme.

Table 2: Number of hospital discharges and mean age of patients by DGs of dependence (ICD 10) in 1994, 1995, and 1996 (Age range 15-64)

DG (ICD-10) / YEAR	1994 N (Mean Age)	1995 N (Mean Age)	1996 N (Mean Age)
F10.2 (Alcohol)	6907 (41.6 years)	7306 (41.6 years)	7995 (41.9 years)
F11.2 (Opiates)	90 (30.9 years)	216 (27.3 years)	538 (23.1 years)
F13.2 (Sedatives)	50 (40.8 years)	58 (38.9 years)	79 (42.7 years)
F15.2 (Stimulants)	78 (25.1 years)	248 (22.5 years)	398 (22.3 years)
F18.2 (Volatile subst.)	71 (24.8 years)	100 (24.7 years)	83 (26.1 years)
F19.2 (Polydrug use)	186 (30.5 years)	344 (27.7 years)	497 (25.9 years)

Source: Zdravotnická statistika. Psychiatrická péãe 1994-1998. Ústav zdravotnickych informací a statistiky, Praha [Health Statistics. Psychiatric Care 1994-1998. Institute of Health Information and Statistics, Prague]

A sharp increase in drug abuse in the 1990s constitutes a serious social and also health problem in the Czech Republic. In this paper, we attempt to give an overview of the response of society to the adverse health consequences of drug misuse. Many specific options for treatment have been established in recent years. The task that remains to be done is to establish a long-term, well-functioning treatment system based on the functioning treatment options.

On the whole, we may summarize that the estimated number of persons who have used illicit drugs in their life is about 250,000 to 300,000. According to the opinion of experts, the number of heavy or problem drug users including drug dependants varies between 15,000 and 30,000. The subpopulation of current drug users consists of rather young people with the majority belonging to the age group of 15-25. The most abused substances among problem users are Pervitin (methamphetamine) and heroin.

2 Organizations active in the area of drug demand reduction

2.1 The overall number of drug demand reduction institutions

The government "Concept and Programme of the Drug Policy for the Years 1998-2000" (NDC, 1998) was used as a guideline for describing the existing institutional context and for the selection of the institutions included in the study. Overviews of anti-drug programmes prepared by the National Drug Commission or by regional anti-drug co-ordinators served as additional sources. The government programme lists the organizations founded and managed by the state in accordance with the national anti-drug policy of the government. The lists of the National Drug Commission and the regional anti-drug co-ordinators include the institutions that report or declare activities related to drug demand reduction. We approached 53 institutions. Data on 49 institutions were processed (92.5% response rate). In four instances, the information was not obtained because a particular institution was either only marginally involved in drug work, refused to cooperate or the responsible person could not be contacted. Of the 49 institutions that responded, 15 were active on a national scale, 25 were active in Prague and 9 in Ústí nad Labem.

National level

In accordance with the national anti-drug programme of the Czech Government, we focused mainly on the key ministries: the Ministry of Labour and Social Affairs; Ministry of Education, Youth and Sports; Ministry of the Interior; Ministry of Defence; National Drug Commission. There is usually one official responsible for drug issues at the ministries. The official usually has lower executive authority and his or her main responsibility is the administration of the particular section of the ministry. The section is formally supervised by a head of a unit or a deputy minister who does not deal personally with drug issues and who was not present at our interviews. In cases in which the drug issues were only one of many activities of the institution at the national level, the relevant officials were not informed in detail about the drug issues in the Czech Republic and were unable to answer questions related to epidemiology and attitudes towards drug problems. The Office of the Chief Hygienist of the Czech Republic, which is responsible for the National Health Programme, and the Inspectorate for Narcotics and Psychotropic Substances are two institutions that work under the authority of the Ministry of Health. Of the 15 organizations that were surveyed, five were originally established and are still administered as local institutions in Prague, but in fact have a national outreach. They carry out their programmes, research and information activities both in Prague and on the whole territory of the Czech Republic.

By 31 December 1997, the Czech Republic had 10,299,125 inhabitants: 48.63% were men, 51.37% were women. There were 772,497 young people aged between 15-19 years and 911,757 aged 20-24 years (Statistical Yearbook of the Czech Republic, 1998). In 1998, 3,858 new problem drug users were registered, that is, 237 per 100,000 inhabitants. The increase in incidence as compared to previous years is evident not only in Prague, but in other regions as well. In 1998, 2,549 men and 2,307 women were registered as problem drug users. The average age of new problem drug users at the time of their first contact with drugs was 20.6 years (12.7% reported their first experience with drugs before 15 years of age) (The Prague City Hall, 1998). Estimates of the number of problem drug users in the Czech Republic range from 15,000 to 30,000 (NDC, 1998). For more information see section 1.3.

Local level

Prague and Northern Bohemia's Ústí nad Labem were chosen for the study in view of the importance of the institutions there and of the gravity of the drug-related problems. Prague and Northern Bohemia are among the three regions considered the most endangered by drug abuse in the Czech Republic (The Prague City Hall, 1998). The phenomena registered on the local level in these regions are:

- Increasing prevalence of non-alcoholic drugs.
- Increasing incidence of problem drug users.
- Increasing numbers of heroin users.
- Increasing numbers of intravenous drug use and risky behaviour among the registered drug users.
- Increasing crime rates related to drug use.
- Increasing numbers of confiscated drugs.
- Increasing numbers of young Roma dependent on drugs.
- Decreasing age of drug users.
- Increasing drug-related mortality rates.

Prague

The capital of Prague has a specific place in the drug scene both as a big city and as the administrative centre of the Czech Republic. On the one hand, there are factors like the availability of various types of drugs at low purchase prices, anonymity, higher local concentrations of risk population groups, a large offer of different possibilities on how to spend free time (in both a positive and negative sense), the problems of large housing projects, minority issues and other phenomena that are common for large European cities. At the same time, Prague also offers more of the positive alternatives, programmes and activities for drug demand reduction. Prague is the headquarters of the majority of national institutions and organizations dealing exclusively with drug problems. For example, the civic association SANANIM was listed in relation with the following types of programmes: school programmes, outreach work, outpatient treatment, harm reduction, after-care, parents of drug users. Some of the institutions on the list of the Prague anti-drug co-ordinator have a national scope (e.g. the five local institutions with a national scope mentioned). In our study, these institutions were included as national institutions. The majority of these institutions were established in Prague and have their headquarters there. These are gradually establishing branches outside of Prague, offering their programmes outside Prague (usually lectures and training) and are gradually extending their information and research activities to cover the whole territory of the Czech Republic (e.g. Hygienic Office of the Capital of Prague). Medical establishments in Prague are under greater pressure to admit patients from other parts of the country because they employ well-known experts, sometimes offer more differentiated care or simply because they are in Prague and deal with drug demand reduction. The National Drug Commission is implementing a new strategy for dealing with problems related to trade in illicit drugs and their use in Prague. The programme entitled "Together against Drugs" (The Prague City Hall, 1998) set priorities of anti-drug policy for the years 1998 through 2000. The aim of the anti-drug policy of the capital city is to protect citizens against the negative consequences of drug abuse and to support individuals opting for a life without drugs. Since 1995, Prague has been a member of the association "European Cities Against Drugs" (ECAD). By 1 July 1997, 568,133 men (47.2% of the total number of inhabitants) and 634,419 women (Statistical Yearbook of the Czech Republic, 1998) lived in Prague.

The study included 25 Prague institutions selected from the list of drug demand reduction institutions provided by the Prague drug demand reduction co-ordinator. The selection criteria included the importance of the institution in the drug demand reduction field (assessed by the authors of the study and by the co-ordinator), the number and type of activities offered, and the particular type of mission (institutions for the ethnic minority of Roma, parents' associations). Several institutions were included in the course of the study upon recommendation of interviewed experts.

Ústí nad Labem

According to an assessment of the drug scene, Ústí nad Labem is one of the most endangered towns in the Czech Republic. In January 1995, a local Anti-drug Commission was created in Ústí nad Labem. However, this local commission did not meet its objectives and part of its responsibilities was taken over by a programme group of the Project for Development of Social Services, which deals with drug issues (Ústí nad Labem, 1998). The group also includes service providers. According to a local survey study carried out in 1997, 40% of students at secondary schools have had experience with a drug. The figure was 24% in 1995 (op. cit.). The contact centre in Ústí nad Labem has a register of 468 clients (347 men, 121 women). Of these, 72.4% are heroin users. By 1 July 1997, the district of Ústí nad Labem had 118,717 inhabitants (48.4 % were men) (Statistical Yearbook of the Czech Republic, 1998).

The office of the anti-drug co-ordinator in Ústí nad Labem registered a total of 15 institutions including the Police Directorate and School Office. Only three of them deal exclusively with drug issues. A detoxification unit, and outpatient and short-term inpatient hospital treatment are provided by the Psychiatric Ward of the Masaryk Hospital in Ústí nad Labem and therefore are registered as organizations not dealing exclusively with drug issues. Following the recommendation of the regional anti-drug co-ordinator, all major nine institutions dealing with drugs were included in our study. Four had a regional scope, five operated inside the town.

2.2 *Drug demand reduction institutions in the Czech Republic by type of organization*

The basic characteristics of the institutions that were surveyed differed in particular by legal status, which fundamentally determined the personnel, administrative and functional framework of each organization.

Table 3: Legal status of the organizations surveyed

	National level N (%)	Prague N (%)	Ústí nad Labem N (%)	Total N (%)
Governmental or Public agency	10 (66.7)	9 (36.0)	5 (55.6)	24 (49.0)
Private	0	2 (8.0)	0	2 (4.1)
Non-profit, Voluntary org.	5 (33.3)	14 (56.0)	4 (44.4)	23 (44.9)
Total	15	25	9	49

While governmental and public organizations prevailed at the national level (the majority of these was initiated by the government and work within the framework of governmental bodies in which the government's administrative rules, possibilities and limits determine their activities), in Prague, which has the highest potential on a local level, NGOs prevailed. The limited possibilities of the smaller communities are best documented by the fact that even in districts with the biggest social problems in the Czech Republic, no private organizations are able to "make a living". Some programmes which are implemented in Prague by NGOs are missing in Ústí nad Labem, or are carried out by governmental (public) institutions. This was reflected in the organizational orientation of the institutions: institutions in which drug demand reduction was only a part of their activities prevailed on a national level and in Ústí nad Labem. Only two institutions (4.1%) were private. One of them was a privatized centre for alcoholism and toxicomania (AT centre), the other one was a PR agency that was active in drug demand reduction (lectures, publications), because it was easier to obtain money for the drug issue rather than for any other topic.

Table 4: Orientation of the organizations regarding their involvement in drug-related activities

	National level N (%)	Prague N (%)	Ústí nad Labem N (%)	Total N (%)
DDR exclusively	4 (26.7)	13 (52.0)	3 (33.3)	20 (40.8)
DDR part of other activities	11 (73.3)	12 (48.0)	6 (66.7)	29 (59.2)

Almost 41% of institutions (mainly in Prague) are specialized in drug demand reduction exclusively. Although drug co-ordinators on the local level deal with drug demand reduction exclusively, they fall under public administration (Town Hall of Prague or Ústí nad Labem) and therefore are included in the category "DDR part of other activities".

Table 5: **DDR organizations by date of establishment and area of operation**

Date of establishment	**National level** N (%)	**Prague** N (%)	**Ústí nad Labem** N (%)	**Total** N (%)
before 1948	3 (21.4)	1 (4.0)	0	4 (8.5)
1949-1970	1 (7.1)	1 (4.0)	2 (25.0)	4 (8.5)
1971-1989	0	4 (16.0)	0	4 (8.5)
1990-1995	10 (71.4)	10 (40.0)	4 (50.0)	24 (51.1)
after 1995	0	9 (36.0)	2 (25.0)	11 (23.4)
Total	14	25	8	47
Missing answer	1	-	1	2

Table 6: **DDR organizations by date of establishment and legal status**

Date of establishment	**Governmental/ public agency** N (%)	**Private** N (%)	**NGO** N (%)	**Total** N (%)
before 1948	3 (13.6)	0	1 (4.3)	4 (8.5)
1949-1970	4 (18.2)	0	0	4 (8.5)
1971-1989	3 (13.6)	0	1 (4.3)	4 (8.5)
1990-1995	9 (40.9)	2 (100)	13 (56.5)	24 (51.1)
after 1995	3 (13.6)	0	8 (34.8)	11 (23.4)
Total	22	2	23	47
Missing answer	2	-	-	2

Almost 50% of institutions were created before 1990. The first non-governmental institution (with the exception of the Red Cross) was established at the end of the year 1989. The majority of NGOs were created in 1994-1995 (five organizations per year) at a time when conditions were probably the most favourable (high demand, limited offer of drug demand reduction programmes, low competition, stimulating atmosphere) and the conditions under which NGOs could operate were already formulated. A clear legal framework for the establishment and functioning of non-governmental institutions also enabled NGOs to be financed from several sources. From 1996 on, the number of newly-established institutions dropped. As far as the date of launch of the drug demand reduction programmes is concerned, only four institutions reported that they had launched their programmes before 1989.

The majority of institutions started the programmes oriented towards drug demand reduction in the years 1993-1995.

Table 7: DDR organizations by date of start of their DDR programmes

Time	N	%
before 1980	3	6.1
1981-1989	2	4.0
1990-1992	4	8.1
1993-1995	27	55.1
after 1995	13	26.5
Total	49	100.0

2.3 *Human and financial resources*

Almost one-third (32.7%) of institutions stated that they employed one or less employees (one or more part-time contracts) in their drug demand reduction units. There was no full-time employee in the drug demand reduction programme in 20.4% of the institutions (mostly governmental or public institutions, in which drug demand reduction was only one of the activities). In various commissions and committees for drug-related issues at some ministries, external experts or officials of the ministry were nominated only formally. Ten institutions (mostly those oriented towards treatment and rehabilitation) had more than 10 employees. Slightly more than one-fourth of the institutions stated that they worked with volunteers. The following professional groups were most frequently employed: psychologists (44.9% of institutions), educators (38.8%), social workers (36.7%), physicians (34.7%), psychiatrists (28.6%), managers (12.2%), lawyers (6.1%), sociologists (4.1%) and public health professionals (2.0%). These professionals with university education were employed as full-time or part-time paid staff.

Table 8: Total budget of the studied institutions (in thousands of EUR)

Budget (in 1,000 EUR)	N	%
<5	3	9.1
6-10	2	6.1
11-20	3	9.1
21-50	3	9.1
51-100	9	27.3
> 100	13	39.4
Missing data	16	32.7

Table 9: Drug demand reduction budget of the studied institutions (in thousands of EUR)

Budget (in 1,000 EUR)	National level (15)		Prague (25)		Ústí nad Labem (9)		Total (49)	
	N	(%)	N	(%)	N	(%)	N	(%)
<5	0	0.0	4	21.1	2	22.2	6	14.6
6-10	2	15.4	0	0.0	1	11.1	3	7.3
11-20	0	0.0	3	15.8	3	33.3	6	14.6
21-50	3	23.1	3	15.8	0	0.0	6	14.6
51-100	0	0.0	5	26.3	2	22.2	7	17.1
> 100	8	61.5	4	21.1	1	11.1	13	31.7
Missing Data	2		6		0		8	

Table 10: DDR budget by status of the organization

Budget (in 1,000 EUR)	Governmental (24)		Private (2)		NGO (23)	
	N	(%)	N	(%)	N	(%)
< 5	1	5.3	0	0.0	5	23.8
6-10	1	5.3	0	0.0	2	9.5
11-20	2	10.5	0	0.0	4	19.0
21-50	4	21.1	0	0.0	2	9.5
51-100	1	5.3	0	0.0	6	28.6
> 100	10	52.6	1	100.0	2	9.5
Missing data	5		1		2	

Note: Exchange rate in 1998 1 EUR = 36.16 CZK.

The annual budgets of the institutions surveyed in 1998 ranged from EUR 830 (CZK 30,000) (Self-help Association of Patients "Pavucina") to EUR 21.8 million (CZK 790 million) (Ministry of Defence). Sixteen institutions (32.7%) did not state, or, which was more often the case, did not know the total budget of their institution. This was usually the case at state treatment facilities or at institutions which did not deal with drug demand reduction exclusively and which did not have their own separate budget.

Approximately one-third of the institutions that answered had an annual budget that was lower than EUR 50,000. However, the validity of the data is questionable, because the majority of governmental and public institutions gave estimates of their budgets and it was not possible to verify the data thus obtained. For example, the National Drug Commission stated the budget for drug demand reduction at EUR 127,000 (CZK 4.6 million), but this budget covered only the current costs of the Commission itself.

However, in 1998 the Commission allocated EUR 4.2 million (CZK 150 million) of the state budget to drug demand reduction institutions (quoted from the National Drug Commission's annual report). The Prague drug co-ordinator had EUR 440,000 (CZK 16 million) available in 1998 for drug demand reduction programmes, while the drug co-ordinator in Ústí nad Labem reported an annual budget of only EUR 8,300 (CZK 300,000). Out of 29 institutions dealing with drug demand reduction as one of their activities, only 16 (55%) stated both their total budget and their DDR budget. These institutions spent between 1% to 35% of their budget on drug demand reduction activities. Frequently, they reported allocating up to 15% for these activities (in sum 10 organizations).

Drug demand reduction programmes of the studied institutions were most frequently financed by public/governmental agencies (91.8% of institutions were financed from this source). The next most frequent sources of financing were fees and individual donations (next as far as frequency is concerned, not the volume of finances), international organizations (especially the EU Phare Programme) and the public sector. The institutions surveyed were asked about the proportion of the organization's funds devoted to DDR programmes by source in 1998 and in 1995 (or in 1996, if the institution did not exist in 1995). Yet even in 1996, six of the institutions studied did not exist. Therefore, the number is 43 for 1995.

In 1998, 91.8% of institutions were financed at least in part by public or governmental organizations. In comparison to 1995, there was a slight increase in donations from individuals. However, the share of a particular source of financing has a higher information value. For example, in 1995 three institutions reported that they received more than 25% of funding from international organizations. In 1998, it was only one institution (eight institutions, however, received between 1% and 25% from international organizations in 1998). We can assume that the financing provided by international institutions was aimed at the establishment of drug demand reduction institutions and the initialization of certain programmes. Only one governmental institution stated in 1998 that it received money from an international organization. In the same year, 30.4% of organizations received at least 25% of their budget from this source (in case of one NGO it was 25-50%). Six local Prague institutions (23%), two institutions active on the national level but based in Prague, and one institution from Ústí nad Labem were co-financed by an international institution.

Table 11: DDR organizations by sources of funding

	1995 (N=43)		1998 (N=49)	
Funds	N	%	N	%
International organization (e.g. UN, EU, OECD)	6	14.0	9	18.4
Foreign governments/agencies	2	4.7	3	6.1
Other foreign organization	2	4.6	2	4.0
Public/government agencies	37	86.0	45	91.8
Private sector	5	11.6	8	14.3
Voluntary organization	3	7.0	3	6.1
Fees and individual donations	5	11.6	10	20.4

A share of 65.1% of institutions in 1995 and 57.1% of institutions in 1998 reported that they were financed exclusively by public or governmental agencies. In 1995, 91.7% of governmental organizations and 34.8% of NGOs received more than 75% of their budget from public or governmental agencies. In 1998, these figures were 95.8% and 56.5%, respectively. It is obvious from this comparison that NGOs are receiving increasing funding from public or governmental agencies. Two NGOs secured more than 70% of their budget from fees and individual donations. Only three organizations (NGOs) stated that they received some funding from voluntary organizations.

2.4 *DDR orientation of the different types of institutions*

On the national level, the most frequently reported mission of organizations (40.0%) was policy-making (policy design, co-ordination, advice), and influencing attitudes and knowledge (20.0%), that is, various prevention and educational activities. This corresponds to the prevalence of governmental institutions at this level, which usually address drug demand reduction within the framework of a certain public sector (not exclusively). At the local level, there was a prevalence of institutions which were oriented on personal care and advice (assistance to vulnerable groups, groups at risk, drug addicts and their relatives, counselling, therapy, rehabilitation and harm reduction) and on influencing attitudes and knowledge. When comparing situations in the capital city and in the regions, it becomes obvious that on the regional level there is a relatively smaller offer (56.0% vs. 33.3%) of institutions whose mission it is to provide differentiated concrete care services and counselling. On all levels, there is a relative lack of institutions whose mission is unequivocally socially-oriented (support of social integration, family support, support of particular communities). The following table lists the missions of organizations by legal status.

Table 12: DDR organizations by mission

Mission	National Level (15) N (%)	Prague (25) N (%)	Ústí nad Labem (9) N (%)	Total (49) N (%)
Influencing attitudes, knowledge and skills	3 (20.0)	8 (32.0)	3 (33.3)	14 (28.6)
Personal care and advice	3 (20.0)	14 (56.0)	3 (33.3)	20 (40.8)
Support for communities and social institutions	1 (6.7)	2 (8.0)	1 (11.1)	4 (8.2)
Policy design, co-ordination	6 (40.0)	1 (4.0)	2 (22.2)	9 (18.4)
Intelligence, research	2 (13.3)	0 (0.0)	0	2 (4.1)

Table 13: Mission of DDR organizations by legal status

Mission	Government, public agency N (%)	Private N (%)	NGO N (%)	Total N (%)
Influencing attitudes, knowledge and skills	5 (20.8)	1 (50.0)	8 (34.8)	14 (28.6)
Personal care and advice	7 (29.2)	1 (50.0)	12 (52.2)	20 (40.8)
Support for communities and social Institutions	2 (8.3)	0 (0.0)	2 (8.7)	4 (8.2)
Policy design, co-ordination	8 (33.3)	0 (0.0)	1 (4.3)	9 (18.4)
Intelligence, research	2 (8.3)	0 (0.0)	0 (0.0)	2 (4.1)

None of the organizations analysed stated interest representation as their mission. Only one institution working as part of a public governmental organization which has a policy and co-ordinating role at the national level reported co-ordination and policy implementation as its mission in drug demand reduction. Most NGOs specified their mission in their statutes; other organizations sometimes had problems defining their mission. Many organizations defined their mission in terms of goals.

3 Drug demand reduction activities

Part 3 informs about the goals in the area of drug demand reduction of the organizations studied and about the specific activities and programmes implemented by these organizations in 1998. Responses to open questions were classified according to a key that was established afterwards.

3.1 Goals of organizations

Table 14 lists the goals of organizations in the field of drug demand reduction. Each organization was allowed to state a maximum of three goals. The table gives the number of institutions (in percentages) which reported the particular activity as one of their drug demand reduction goals (listed as number one to number three).

The most frequently stated goal in the field of DDR activity was prevention, followed by treatment, DDR activity in general, rehabilitation and after-care, co-ordination and other. Research, documentation, funding, co-ordination, policy development and legislation were reported mainly by governmental organizations.

A share of 73.5% of all institutions reported prevention (usually primary prevention) and the dissemination of information (that is, various educational events, leisure time activities and information activities for the public and especially for youth) as one of their main goals (29.8% reported prevention as a first goal). These activities usually require the lowest personnel and financial investments, are relatively easy to declare and the criteria for their evaluation are unclear. These institutions are followed, after a large gap, by institutions which state treatment and care for drug users or drug addicts as one of their main activities. It is apparent from the declared goals that approximately one-fourth of the institutions are focused on providing care to people who are at immediate risk by drugs (treatment, care, rehabilitation). The remaining part of the institutions are oriented more on the general public, providing help and support to experts, or they are active in policy advice, co-ordination and funding of drug demand reduction activities. Only one NGO (Association of NGOs) stated interest representation as its goal.

Table 14: The goals of the organizations in the field of drug demand reduction

	Legal status		DDR orient.		Level of operation			Total
	Govern-mental	*NGO/ Private*	*Excl.*	*Incl.*	*Na-tional*	*Prague*	*Region*	
	%	%	%	%	%	%	%	%
DDR (general statements)	25.0	44.0	25.0	41.4	26.7	36.0	44.4	34.7
Prevention/information	54.2	92.0	85.0	65.5	60.0	84.0	66.7	73.5
Treatment and care	29.2	44.0	65.0	17.2	13.3	52.0	33.3	36.7
Rehabilitation (after-care)	25.0	20.0	35.0	13.8	0.0	40.0	11.1	22.4
Research/Documentation	20.8	0.0	10.0	10.3	20.0	4.0	11.1	10.2
Funding/fund-raising	25.0	4.0	5.0	20.7	33.3	4.0	11.1	14.3
Co-ordination	37.5	0.0	10.0	24.1	33.3	8.0	22.2	18.4
Interest representation	0.0	4.0	5.0	0.0	0.0	0.0	11.1	2.0
Policy Development/ Legislation	16.7	4.0	5.0	13.8	33.3	0.0	0.0	10.2
Training of professionals	12.5	20.0	20.0	13.8	26.7	4.0	33.3	16.3

The prevention and providing of information was stated as a goal by more than 90% of non-governmental institutions. However, the NGOs were at the same time also more active in treatment and care. Only two institutions (both of them NGOs) indicated after-care and rehabilitation as their primary goal. Governmental and public institutions that usually work at a national level and for whom drug demand reduction represents only a part of their activities, stated as their principal goals research and documentation, funding, co-ordination of activities, policy goals and legislation. The training of professionals was largely a focus of NGOs. Treatment and rehabilitation were mainly the goals of institutions exclusively oriented on drug demand reduction.

3.2 *Drug demand reduction activities: significance and outlook*

In the context of their drug demand reduction activities, the institutions interviewed regarded treatment and care (34.5%) as the most significant, followed by prevention and information (32.6%), co-ordination (10.2%), policy development and legislation (8.2%), rehabilitation and after-care (6.1%), funding (6.1%) and research (2%). The institutions interviewed had different views on how important the individual types of activity are, depending on whether the institution was dealing with drug demand reduction exclusively or not. While the institutions dealing with drug demand reduction exclusively stressed, first of all, the importance of treatment and care, the institutions that were only partially involved with drug demand reduction, underlined the importance of prevention. In this context, the institutions dealing with drug demand reduction exclusively were planning to extend their treatment and care providing activities in the near future. There was no major difference between governmental and non-governmental institutions in this respect. Eleven institutions were planning to extend their treatment activity, eleven institutions were planning to increase their activity in prevention and four institutions intended to extend their rehabilitation and after-care. Only four institutions (8.2%) were planning to terminate drug demand reduction activity in the near future. In all four cases, this involved prevention activities (lectures and seminars).

A share of 83.7% of institutions reported that they were monitoring or evaluating the quality of professional work and the services provided. However, in most cases this was a general declaration of the evaluation of programmes (22.4%) or self-evaluation (22.4%). Feedback from clients or from other institutions was reported by four organizations (8.2%), three institutions reported using statistics on attendance or work reports, three used indicators from international organizations and another three institutions reported supervision or auditing.

3.3 *Activities of organizations in the field of drug demand reduction*

Besides stating the organizational goals in the field of drug demand reduction, the queried institutions also responded to a direct question about which specific activities they carried out in prevention, treatment, rehabilitation, etc. In some cases, these activities might be similar to the missions or aims declared earlier on. The institutions interviewed most frequently stated that in the field of DDR they were involved in prevention and in this area they also had the highest number of activities in absolute figures. The least frequently stated activity was interest representation. The frequency of the individual drug demand reduction activities reflects not only the demand for the individual activities, but often the difficulty of carrying out these activities.

Table 15: **Major DDR activities reported by organization**

	Number of institutions that reported specific activities	Per cent of the total number of institutions
Prevention	46	93.9
Treatment/care	22	44.9
Rehabilitation	15	30.6
Research	25	51.0
Funding	15	30.6
Co-ordination	21	42.9
Interest representation/protection of civic and human rights	8	16.3
Policy development	24	49.0
Training of professionals	32	65.3

The following table gives the shares of the institutions that show a particular type of activity. The institutions are differentiated with regard to whether or not they deal with drug demand reduction exclusively, by legal status and by the level of operation (values are in percentage).

Table 16: **Activities reported by DDR orientation, legal status, and level of operation**

	DDR orient.		Legal status		Level of operation		
	Excl.	Incl.	Gov.	NGO	Natl.	Prague	Reg.
Prevention	90.0	96.6	91.7	96.0	100.0	92.0	88.9
Treatment	75.0	24.1	33.3	56.0	20.0	64.0	33.3
Rehabilitation	55.0	13.8	25.0	36.0	13.3	48.0	11.1
Research	60.0	44.8	66.7	36.0	66.7	52.0	22.2
Funding	20.0	37.9	45.8	16.0	53.3	12.0	44.4
Co-ordination	35.0	48.3	58.3	28.0	60.0	24.0	66.7
Interest representation/ protection of civic and human rights	20.0	17.2	12.5	24.0	13.3	12.0	44.4
Policy development	45.0	51.7	66.7	32.0	73.3	32.0	55.6
Training	80.0	55.2	66.7	64.0	80.0	56.0	66.7

Prevention, information, education

A number of 46 of 49 institutions interviewed stated that they were implementing a programme or an activity in the field of prevention. A number of 31 institutions reported two or three prevention activities. Most frequently, the organization of lectures and seminars was reported (48 of the total of 93 preventive activities, i.e. 51.6%). Another frequently reported activity was the distribution of brochures, leaflets, films and other publishing materials (22.6%) and the operation of information services, the organization of clubs and camps (6.5%). All other prevention and information activities (development of training programmes, counselling, street work, organization of special events – concerts, sports events and public information campaigns) were not reported more frequently than three times.

A share of 60% of the lectures or seminars reported by the institutions interviewed were implemented by NGOs. By contrast, government and public organizations implemented almost 60% of the information and publishing activities but, surprisingly, no public information campaign. NGOs also more frequently organized the dissemination of information, clubs and camps. A share of 67% of information brochures, leaflets and publishing materials were published and distributed by organizations that were only partially involved in drug demand reduction. These organizations also more frequently organized sports and cultural events. Only organizations dealing exclusively with drug demand reduction organized street work and counselling. Most differentiated prevention programmes were reported by organizations working in Prague. Some prevention programmes (development of training programmes, street work, operating of information services, organization of clubs and camps) were not reported in Ústí nad Labem.

The earliest prevention programme in existence was initiated in 1970, but most of the prevention programmes were introduced after 1990. The majority of prevention activities focused on students (21%) or youth and children (19.6%), followed by the general population (12%) and professionals (7%). Activities organized by government organizations were more focused on students (28%) and youth and children (24%).

Table 17 shows the percentage of organizations differentiated according to their drug demand reduction orientation, legal status and level of operation, which deal with the given type of prevention activity. The table does not take into account whether the organizations reported one or more of these activities. The first column (N) states the total number of institutions which reported that they organize lectures and seminars, distribute information materials, etc.

Table 17: Preventive activities reported by DDR orientation, legal status, and level of operation

	N1	N2	DDR orientation		Legal status		Level of operation		
			Excl. (%)	Incl. (%)	Gov. (%)	NGO (%)	Nat. (%)	Prague (%)	Reg. (%)
Lectures/ seminars	34	48	80.0	62.1	58.3	80.0	66.7	72.0	66.7
Distribution of information materials	16	21	25.0	37.9	37.5	28.0	33.3	28.0	44.4
Training programmes	3	3	10.0	3.4	4.2	8.0	6.7	8.0	0.0
Counselling	1	1	5.0	0.0	0.0	4.0	0.0	0.0	11.1
Street work	3	3	15.0	0.0	4.2	8.0	6.7	8.0	0.0
Organization of information points, clubs, camps	5	6	5.0	13.8	4.2	16.0	6.7	16.0	0.0
Special events	3	3	5.0	6.9	4.2	8.0	0.0	8.0	11.1
Public information campaigns	2	2	5.0	3.4	0.0	8.0	0.0	4.0	11.1
Others	6	6	15.0	10.3	12.5	12.0	20.0	8.0	11.1

Note: N1 = Number of organizations reporting at least one specific activity
N2 = Number of specific activities reported by categories

Treatment and care

A number of 22 institutions reported that they were involved in treatment and care. Forty-two treatment activities were reported, of which the treatment of addictions without further specification was the most frequently reported (21.4% of all treatment activities), followed by group psychotherapy (19%), outpatient clinics (16.7%), individual counselling and therapeutic communities (both 9.5%). Only one institution reported detoxification, needle exchanges, condom distribution and methadone treatment. The following items were missing entirely: medical care, which was probably reported as "treatment", referral and after-care, employment and educational support (this type of activity was included by the majority of institutions as rehabilitation). Detoxification and methadone programmes were organized solely by state health care institutions. NGOs alone stated individual counselling, family therapy, day centres and needle exchange as their activity. NGOs most frequently organized therapeutic communities and group psychotherapy. Institutions with a national scope stated treatment but without further specification. On the local level, in Prague all of the listed activities were represented; in Usti nad Labem the treatment offer was limited to general treatment, a therapeutic community, an outpatient clinic and day centres.

Table 18: Reported therapeutic activities by DDR orientation, legal status, and level of operation

	N1	N2	DDR orientation		Legal status		Level of operation		
			Excl. (%)	Incl. (%)	Gov. (%)	NGO (%)	Nat. (%)	Prague (%)	Reg. (%)
Detoxification	1	1	5.0	0.0	4.2	0.0	0.0	4.0	0.0
Individual counselling	4	4	15.0	3.4	0.0	16.0	0.0	16.0	0.0
Treatment (general)	8	9	30.0	6.9	16.7	16.0	13.3	20.0	11.1
Therapeutic commun.	4	4	10.0	6.9	4.2	12.0	0.0	12.0	11.1
Group psychotherapy	7	8	25.0	6.9	4.2	24.0	0.0	28.0	0.0
Family therapy	2	2	10.0	0.0	0.0	8.0	0.0	8.0	0.0
Day centres	2	2	5.0	3.4	0.0	8.0	6.7	4.0	0.0
Outpatient clinic	6	7	20.0	6.9	16.7	8.0	6.7	16.0	11.1
Methadone treatment	1	1	5.0	0.0	4.2	0.0	0.0	4.0	0.0
Needle exchange, condom distribution	1	1	5.0	0.0	0.0	4.0	1.0	0.0	0.0
Other	2	3	5.0	3.4	4.2	4.0	6.7	4.0	0.0

Note: N1 = Number of organizations reporting at least one specific activity
N2 = Number of specific activities reported by categories

The oldest of the treatment activities listed above dates back to the 1970s. The first detoxification programme started in 1996, the first therapeutic community started in 1994. The methadone programme has been in operation since 1997. The institutions that were questioned regarded drug users and addicts as a target group for 40% of the above-listed activities, 25% of their activities were aimed at youth and adolescents, 20% for drug users' families and relatives, and 7.5% for groups at risk.

Rehabilitation

Fifteen of the institutions that were questioned reported that they were engaged in rehabilitation and/or after-care in the following areas: day after-care centres (30.4 % of all these activities), group therapy or group meetings (26.1%), hostels (8.7%), individual counselling and legal advice (8.7%) and in one case also assistance in social re-adaptation after treatment, and assistance in searching for employment. The following activities were missing entirely: assistance in finding housing, assistance in reintegration with families, assistance in education and motivation for education, engaging drug users in field work, work with other drug users, and mutual support. Only NGOs organized hostels, offered assistance in finding housing and searching for employment. None of these activities was carried out on a nation-wide scope. Organizations in Ústí nad Labem reported only two after-care activities, group meetings and individual counselling. Although the institutions questioned might have omitted some activities, it is clear that the need for differentiated rehabilitation and after-care is not fully saturated. This finding, which is in line with the priorities of the anti-drug policy (NDC, 1998), might reflect an underestimation of the social aspects of the issue in the past as well as the stress placed on the medical aspect of the problem.

Table 19: Rehabilitation activities reported by DDR orientation, legal status, and level of operation

	N1	N2	DDR orientation		Legal status		Level of operation		
			Excl. (%)	Incl. (%)	Gov. (%)	NGO (%)	Nat. (%)	Prague (%)	Reg. (%)
Day after-care centre	6	7	25.0	3.4	8.3	16.0	6.7	20.0	0.0
Hostel	2	2	10.0	0.0	0.0	8.0	6.7	4.0	0.0
Group therapy, group meetings	5	6	25.0	0.0	12.5	8.0	0.0	16.0	11.1
Assistance in social re-adaptation	1	1	0.0	3.4	0.0	4.0	0.0	4.0	0.0
Assistance in searching for employment	1	1	5.0	0.0	0.0	4.0	1.0	0.0	0.0
Individual counselling, legal advice	2	2	10.0	0.0	0.0	8.0	0.0	4.0	11.1
Other	4	4	10.0	6.9	8.3	8.0	6.7	12.0	0.0

Note: N1 = Number of organizations reporting at least one specific activity
N2 = Number of specific activities reported by categories

The first rehabilitation activities of the institutions interviewed started in 1971. A majority of the after-care activities was focused on abstainers, recovered clients, clients after treatment and ex-patients (38.1%), or on drug users and addicts (33%).

Research, documentation and database

Of the 33 different research activities reported by 25 institutions, 15 activities (45.5% of all these activities) involved research in general (epidemiological research, drug trends studies, rapid assessment or first treatment demand). The other 13 activities focused on collecting and publishing statistics. Four activities included conducting an evaluation (project assessment, documentation of projects) and one institution stated that it was engaged in developing methods and methodology. Research, documentation and database work was reported as one of their *important* activities by 61% of governmental organizations and by only 39% of NGOs. In Usti nad Labem, of all nine institutions interviewed, only one stated research and documentation as its main activity. Two institutions in Prague focused exclusively on research and drug-trend studies. In both cases, these were government institutions with a nation-wide scope, one of them engaged in medical research and the other in studying the issue of addictions.

Table 20: Research, documentation and database reported by DDR orientation, legal status, and level of operation

	N1	N2	DDR orientation		Legal status		Level of operation		
			Excl. (%)	Incl. (%)	Gov. (%)	NGO (%)	Nat. (%)	Prague (%)	Reg. (%)
Research (general)	13	15	30.0	24.1	41.7	12.0	46.7	20.0	11.1
Collecting, publishing statistics	11	13	35.0	13.8	25.0	20.0	20.0	32.0	0.0
Conducting evaluation	4	4	5.0	10.3	8.3	8.0	6.7	12.0	0.0
development of methods, methodology	1	1	5.0	0.0	0.0	4.0	6.7	0.0	0.0

Note: N1 = Number of organizations reporting at least one specific activity
N2 = Number of specific activities reported by categories

Ten of the research and documentation activities (32.3%) were carried out for use by the questioned institutions, six were intended for the general public and six for teachers, lecturers and students. Only two research activities (6.5% of all the research activities) were designed primarily for professionals and one for decision-makers (politicians).

Funding and fund-raising

Fifteen institutions stated that they were involved in funding and fund-raising. In the majority of cases (78.9% of the listed activities), this meant general support, subsidizing projects, the distribution of funds or providing grants. Only in one case (5.3% of all of these activities) fund-raising took the form of organizing sports or cultural events. None of the institutions reported fund-raising through contacts with donors. The majority of institutions which stated funding as one of their important activities were government or public institutions, and drug demand reduction was only one of their activities (71.4%). A share of 57% of the funding or fund-raising activities were carried out at the national level.

Table 21: Funding, fund-raising reported by DDR orientation, legal status, and level of operation

	N1	N2	DDR orientation		Legal status		Level of operation		
			Excl. (%)	Incl. (%)	Gov. (%)	NGO (%)	Nat. (%)	Prague (%)	Reg. (%)
Support general	13	15	15.0	34.5	41.7	12.0	53.3	8.0	33.3
Support for specific projects	1	1	5.0	0.0	0.0	4.0	0.0	4.0	0.0
Fund-raising, organization of events	1	1	5.0	0.0	0.0	4.0	0.0	4.0	0.0
Other	2	2	5.0	3.4	4.2	4.0	13.3	0.0	0.0

Note: N1 = Number of organizations reporting at least one specific activity
N2 = Number of specific activities reported by categories

A share of 75% of all these activities was aimed at organizations operating drug demand reduction programmes; in the remaining four cases, the funding was not limited to drug demand reduction organizations exclusively, but also covered other medical and social programmes.

Co-ordination

A number of 21 organizations reported that they were engaged in co-ordination and stated 24 activities in this field. Ten institutions reported co-ordination of the drug demand reduction programmes at the regional or national level. Eight co-ordination activities included the co-ordination of other organizations' activities within specific areas (training, prevention or therapy) and six activities within one's own organization. Three institutions interviewed were part of the existing system of co-ordination (National Drug Commission, Prague and Usti nad Labem Co-ordinators). Co-ordination as a specific activity was more frequently reported by government or public organizations than by NGOs.

Table 22: Co-ordination reported by DDR orientation, legal status, and level of operation

	N1	N2	DDR orientation		Legal status		Level of operation		
			Excl. (%)	Incl. (%)	Gov. (%)	NGO (%)	Nat. (%)	Prague (%)	Reg. (%)
Co-ordination within organization	6	6	20.0	6.9	12.5	12.0	26.7	8.0	0.0
Co-ordination of other organizations' acts	8	8	10.0	20.7	25.0	8.0	26.7	4.0	33.3
Co-ordination at the regional, national level	10	10	15.0	24.1	29.2	12.0	26.7	12.0	33.3

Note: N1 = Number of organizations reporting at least one specific activity
N2 = Number of specific activities reported by categories

Interest representation, protection of civil or human rights

Eight organizations declared that they provided interest representation or the protection of civil and human rights. A share of 75% of all listed activities were legal advice or interest representation and none of the institutions interviewed stated any activity in protecting drug users' rights. The reported activities focused on public opinion or public institutions. None of them focused on drug users. Two of the organizations involved in interest representation were government organizations and six of them were NGOs.

Table 23: Interest representation, protection of civic or human rights reported by DDR orientation, legal status, and level of operation

	N1	N2	DDR orientation		Legal status		Level of operation		
			Excl. (%)	Incl. (%)	Gov. (%)	NGO (%)	Nat. (%)	Prague (%)	Reg. (%)
Legal advice, representation	6	6	15.0	10.3	8.3	16.0	13.3	12.0	11.1
Lobbying, advocacy	1	1	5.0	0.0	0.0	4.0	0.0	0.0	11.1
Other	1	1	0.0	3.4	4.2	0.0	0.0	0.0	11.1

Note: N1 = Number of organizations reporting at least one specific activity
N2 = Number of specific activities reported by categories

Policy development and legislation

Twenty-four organizations reported involvement in policy development and legislation. Of 28 activities in the field of policy development and legislation, 20 involved the development of strategies, policy and legislation, and six involved participation in strategy, policy or development processes. The majority of these activities were implemented by government organizations (66.7%) and by the organizations that did not deal with drug demand reduction exclusively (51.7%). Almost three-fourths of these organizations were active on the national level. Activities in the field of policy development and legislation were designed primarily for the government and ministries, and for local authorities.

Table 24: Policy development and legislation reported by DDR orientation, legal status, and level of operation

	N1	N2	DDR orientation		Legal status		Level of operation		
			Excl. (%)	Incl. (%)	Gov. (%)	NGO (%)	Nat. (%)	Prague (%)	Reg. (%)
Development of strategy, policy, legislation	18	20	30.0	41.4	45.8	28.0	60.0	20.0	44.4
Participation in policy or legislation processes	6	6	10.0	13.8	20.8	4.0	26.7	8.0	0.0
Comments on existing or future programmes	1	1	5.0	0.0	4.2	0.0	0.0	4.0	0.0
Other	1	1	5.0	0.0	0.0	4.0	6.7	0.0	0.0

Note: N1 = Number of organizations reporting at least one specific activity
N2 = Number of specific activities reported by categories

Training of professionals

Thirty-two organizations (65.3%) stated the training of professionals as one of their activities in drug demand reduction. A share of 53% of the training activities was for professionals involved in drug demand reduction, 21.6% was for teachers and trainers and 17.6% for students. Only two training programmes (4%) were designed for policemen and judges and one programme was aimed at volunteers. There was no significant difference in the number of training activities between the studied groups of institutions (government organizations vs. NGOs, exclusive vs. inclusive, Prague vs. Usti nad Labem).

4 Organizations' attitudes towards the drug problem and their perception of drug demand reduction policies

4.1 Organizations' perception of the problem

Within the framework of our study an interesting task was to study the organizations' perception regarding the magnitude of the drug problem and their perception of the national drug policy in the country. The first two questions targeted the estimated number of drug users during the last year and the estimated number of drug users in the country in five years. The answers varied widely across the organizations, but when we looked into group means, the estimates were close to the opinion of the experts in epidemiology.

The average number of drug users in 1998 as estimated by 30 organization was about 255,000. For the year 2003, this number was estimated to be about 303,000. The answers ranged from 10,000 to 1,500,000 drug users. Estimates given by organizations in Prague were somewhat higher than the estimates of national organizations and institutions from Ústí nad Labem. The organizations involved exclusively in the drug field gave more conservative estimates than inclusive organizations. This more conservative estimate could be due to a better knowledge of the field by organizations working specifically with the drug-using population.

Table 25 summarizes the respective figures by status of the organization, level of operation and focus. The closeness of the averages of the estimates given by these subgroups is really surprising. The number of non-responding organizations is indicated in the second column.

Table 25: Estimates of the number of drug users in the country in 1998 and in 2003 (in thousands)

	N responding/N non-resp.	Mean (s.d.) 1998	Mean (s.d.) 2003
Status of organization			
Governmental	14/10	251 (269)	290 (316)
NGO	16/9	261 (320)	314 (404)
Level of operation			
National	8/7	247 (326)	274 (388)
Prague	15/10	288 (319)	354 (408)
Usti nad Labem	7/2	199 (214)	225 (213)
Focus of organization			
DDR Exclusive	15/5	200 (265)	202 (251)
DDR Inclusive	15/14	312 (316)	403 (428)

The summary of the expected changes could also be expressed as an averaged ratio of the estimates for 2003 and for 1998. The results are given as an expected change in percentages (See Table 26). The increase varies from 19% to 50%, and in general reflects that expectation for the next five years of DDR organizations who predict an increase in drug users by approximately one-third.

Table 26: The estimated change between 1998 and 2003

	N responding/ N non-respond.	Estimated change in %
Level of operation		
National	8/7	+19
Prague	15/10	+30
Usti nad Labem	7/2	+50
Type of organization		
DDR Exclusive	15/5	+28
DDR Inclusive	15/14	+37
Status of organization		
Governmental	14/10	+35
NGO	16/9	+29

The representatives of selected organizations were also asked about the estimated share of specific drugs in total drug use in 1998 and 2003. The mean and standard deviation of the estimates is inserted into Table 27. Two conclusions can be drawn from these figures. First, the answers quite correctly identified cannabis as the most widely-used drug, as well as the importance of the stimulants and opiates in the drug scene. Second, only small changes are expected in the next five years regarding the structure of the misused drugs. A slight decrease is only expected in the case of amphetamine misuse.

Table 27: Estimated share of specific type of drug in the total drug use in 1998 and 2003 (Values are percentages)

Drug/Year	N responding/N non-responding	Mean	Std. dev.
Opiates 1998	36/13	18	13
Opiates 2003	33/16	20	14
Cocaine 1998	31/18	5	11
Cocaine 2003	29/20	2	3
Cannabis 1998	35/14	46	26
Cannabis 2003	33/16	47	24
Hallucinogens 1998	33/16	8	8
Hallucinogens 2003	31/18	8	8
Amphetamines* 1998	36/13	26	18
Amphetamines* 2003	33/16	23	16
Other 1998	32/17	5	6
Other 2003	28/21	5	5

Note: *Amphetamines include Pervitin.

4.2 *Organizational attitudes*

Drug abuse certainly involves a complex set of attitudes, beliefs, prejudices, etc. Sensitive aspects also exist which are discussed in society from time to time (e.g. legalization of "soft drugs"). Our respondents were also asked to answer eight questions focused on the social and moral aspects of the drug-related problem. The wording of the questions was as follows:

- Taking illegal drugs can sometimes be beneficial.
- Adults should be free to take any drug they wish.
- We need to accept that using illegal drugs is normal for some people's lives.
- Smoking cannabis should be legalized.
- The best way to treat people who are addicted to drugs is to stop them from using drugs altogether.
- The use of illegal drugs always leads to addiction.

- Taking illegal drugs is always morally wrong.
- All use of illegal drugs is drug abuse.

The results were organized as profiles based on the means for the subgroups of organizations. The profiles in Figures 4 to 6 allow a comparison of the differences and similarities in the perception of the social and/or ethical aspects of drug use.

The attitudinal scale may to some extent be understood as a scale expressing the degree of conservatism on the one hand, and liberalism on the other hand.

The smallest differences between average values in the individual items are found in Figure 4, which shows the average values according to the level on which the organizations operate. Organizations active at the national level (including ministries and other institutions representing more or less the formal aspect of the state drug policy) displayed a more marked tendency towards conservatism in their attitudes than organizations operating at the local level in Prague or Ústí nad Labem.

Figure 4: Profile on attitudes towards the drug problem. Group means by level of organization

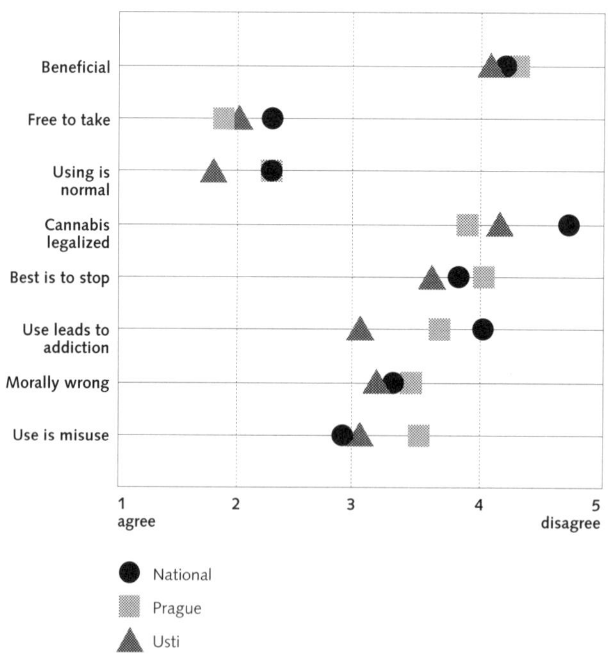

Figure 5: Profile on attitudes towards the drug problem. Group means by status of organization

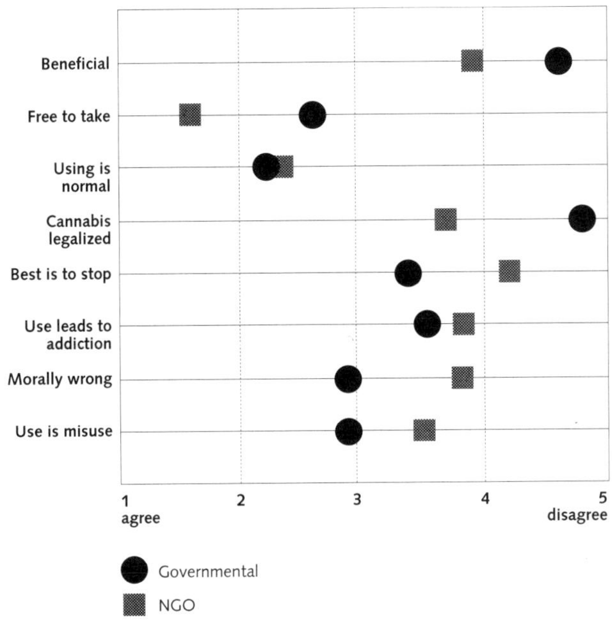

Figure 6: Profile on attitudes towards the drug problem. Group means by scope of activity of an organization

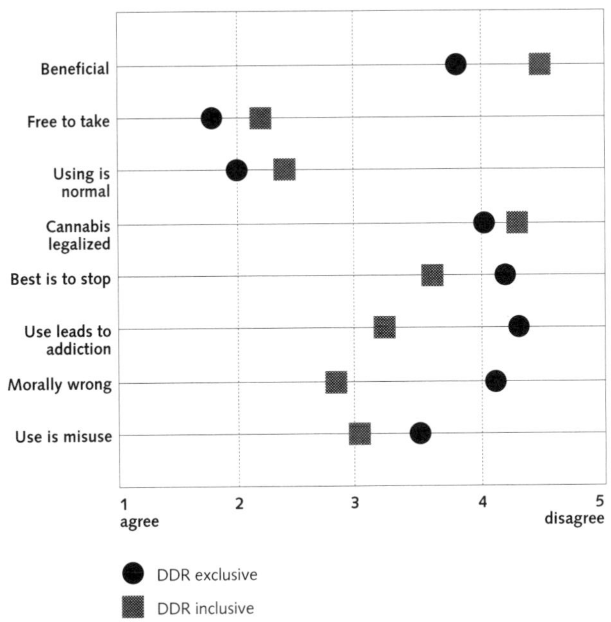

It is apparent from Figure 5 that NGOs are much more liberal in their attitudes towards drugs than governmental institutions. The biggest difference in the attitude of governmental and non-governmental organizations is in their position on the legalization of marijuana, whether or not an individual has the right to choose to use drugs as well as in the moral renunciation of drug use.
Figure 6 provides a comparison of organizations dealing exclusively with drugs and organizations which implement drug demand reduction only as part of their activities. The biggest differences are found when we look at the polarization of attitudes on the liberal-conservative continuum. It may therefore be assumed that more liberal attitudes towards drug issues are related to the intensity of contacts with the community of problem drug users. It may also be said that people who work directly with drug addicts are less prejudiced and less limited by social stereotypes, or, that they might accept certain attitudes of their clients. This is obvious when we look at the greatest differences in average values. These are related to the moral assessment of drug use, views on the beginning of drug dependency and views of the essence of drug use ("all use is misuse"). The very broad differentiation of views seen here is interesting not only from a theoretical point of view, but also because it may influence decision-making in practical issues which relate to drug policy.

4.3 *Perception of the national drug policy*

To better understand the representation of the national drug policy by the relevant organizations acting in the field, the participants were asked to express their own views on the national drug policy in two ways. In a Likert-type scale five policy orientations were offered: *health promotion, harm reduction, demand reduction, control of supply and law enforcement*. Thereafter, the respondents were asked to express the strengths and weaknesses of the national drug policy using their own formulations.

In Table 28 the results of the responses obtained on the above-mentioned Lickert scale are summarized as group means on each specific policy orientation. In fact, the differences in the means are small and the values are around the midpoint of the scale. Interpreting these findings leads us to conclude that the perception of priorities in the national drug policy expressed by the representatives of the organizations surveyed reflects a balance between preventative and repressive approaches. The group means were tested using non-parametric techniques and the only statistically significant difference was found in control supply, where the mean scale of national organizations was higher than that of the organizations from Prague and Ústi. No statistically significant differences were found in all other comparisons made.

Table 28: Perception of the orientation of the national drug policy

	All Org.	Level			Status		DDR Type	
		Natl.	Prague	Usti	Govern.	NGO	Excl.	Incl.
Health promotion	3.3	3.6	3.3	2.9	3.2	3.4	3.0	3.5
Harm reduction	3.3	3.6	3.2	3.3	3.6	3.1	3.3	3.4
Demand reduction	3.1	3.6	2.8	3.1	3.1	3.0	3.0	3.1
Control of supply	3.1	3.9	2.9	2.7	3.1	3.1	3.4	2.9
Law enforcement	3.3	3.8	3.1	3.3	3.7	3.4	3.6	3.2

The perceived strengths and weaknesses of the national drug policy were investigated using open-ended questions. Using the techniques of content analysis, categories were created, and the answers received were recorded according to these categories. The results are summarized in Tables 29 and 30. Since up to three answers were allowed, we used the multiple response technique to summarize the frequency tables.

Table 29: The perceived strengths of the national drug policy (based on multiple response analysis)

	Number of responses	Per cent of responding organizations
Awareness of the drug problem, public discussions, better understanding of the problem	8	17.8
Efficient network of organizations, effective cooperation	17	37.8
Competent, expert-based and professional	5	11.1
Prevention programmes, preventative programmes in schools, new subjects of drug prevention	13	28.9
Therapy programmes	5	11.1
Harm reduction programmes	8	17.8
Effective policy, conception, legislation	15	33.3
Supply control, law enforcement (drug market), new legal institutions for police for combating drug criminality	8	17.8
Other	6	13.3
Total number of responses	85	-

Regarding the strengths of the national drug policy, the following features were the most frequently stated:

- Efficient network of organizations, effective cooperation.
- Effective policy, conception.
- Legislation, prevention programmes, preventative programmes on schools, new subjects of drug prevention.

The organizations interviewed also had a positive perception of the awareness of the drug problem and the importance of the problem as a social issue. The perception of the strengths of drug policy showed almost no differences by type of organization; one exception is harm reduction, which as a specific topic was more frequently stated by the DDR exclusive organizations. The fact that therapeutic programmes were not reported as often as a strength may be interpreted to mean that these programmes have already become a natural part of the DDR system.

Table 30: Perceived weaknesses of the national drug policy

	Number of responses	Per cent of responding organizations
Lack of awareness of the drug problem (drug users are not recognized as patients)	4	8.7
Lack of professionals, experts	6	13.0
Ineffective programmes	4	8.7
Focus on law enforcement, repressive approach, proclamation of war on drugs	6	13.0
Lack of policy, there is no drug policy, lack of a conceptual approach, lack of a national programme of priorities, lack of programmes	33	71.7
Lack of co-ordination, there is no co-ordination, there is big chaos, incoherence of ideas, communication on the vertical level	19	41.3
Lack of research, information, no information/data on the number of drug users, absence of research institutes		
Insufficient funding, financial problems	14	30.4
Lack of evaluation, lack of control and monitoring of programmes	1	2.2
Barriers to the development of non-governmental institutions	0	0
Other	20	43.5
Total number of responses	107	-

The following areas were identified as the major weaknesses or problems of drug policy:

- Lack of policy, lack of a conceptual approach, lack of a national programme of priorities, lack of programmes.
- Lack of co-ordination, incoherence of ideas, communication on the vertical level.
- Insufficient funding, financial problems.

To a lesser extent, a lack of professionals and experts was reported as a weakness, and also the repressive approaches to solving the drug problem. No substantial differences were found in the perceived weaknesses between all types of organizations. It is interesting to note that none of the organizations reported *societal or financial barriers in the development of NGOs* as a weakness.

In the case of the first two categories (the most frequently mentioned strong and weak aspects of the national anti-drug policy), we have a partial overlap. This is due to the fact that some organizations regard, for example, the concept of anti-drug policy in general as very good, but at the same time have objections to the design or the number of the particular programmes supported. It is also necessary to take into account the concrete conditions and needs of the individual organizations. It might therefore be very well possible that some organizations comment positively on certain aspects of the anti-drug policy that are criticized by other organizations. This is well documented in the co-ordination and communication category, which is viewed as satisfactory by institutions working at the national level, while smaller institutions on the local or regional level may have completely contrary views. These results underpin the importance of clear communication and work as regards information on the vertical level for implementing the priorities of anti-drug policy. At the same time, the results imply an increasing differentiation of the institutions demonstrated by the differentiated fundamental attitudes towards the drug issue and drug policies.

5 Co-ordination

In the last part of the research questionnaire, specific attention was devoted to the co-ordination of the organizations studied. We limited this part of the analysis to organizations in Prague. The organizations were asked to report with which other organizations they cooperate as regards: *financial matters, exchange of experience, support, non-formal communication, strategic cooperation and common activities.*

Cooperation in financial matters

The question on cooperation in financial matters was divided into two parts. In the first part, the organizations reported from which organizations they received financial support. In the second part, they were asked to indicate to whom they provided support. The first part of the question was answered by 26 of 40 institutions and 12 organizations were mentioned as supporters. Among these 12 organizations, three were identified as *important financing agencies*: in the first place is the Drug Commission of the Prague City Hall (17 nominations), followed by the National Drug Commission (12 nominations) and finally the Department for Care of People with Drug-related Disorders in the Ministry of Health (eight nominations). These three organizations are responsible for drug policy at the national or municipal level, and all have specific budgets for the support of anti-drug activities. These three were nominated mostly by NGOs because NGOs do not have regular institutional funding sources like the governmental institutions do. The second question (providing financial support) was replied to by only six organizations. The only explanation of this might be that the institutions with support schemes reported this fact in the previous sections of the questionnaire (mission, activities).

Sharing experiences

The picture on the sharing of experiences is very similar for both the receiving and the providing aspects. There were seven institutions nominated by at least three other organizations as institutions providing experience. At the top of the ranking were the National Drug Commission and the Drug Commission of Prague, followed by the Department for Treatment of Addictions in Prague 8 and Sananim. It seems that the first two institutions were nominated because of consultancy on managerial issues, whereas the following two in connection with problems of treatment and prevention. Interestingly, the same organizations were also nominated frequently as those to whom experience is provided. This suggests support for the idea of reciprocity or bi-directionality of the process of knowledge accumulation.

Support

In this part, support is interpreted as non-financial support, for example, an understanding of the goals and activities of institutions. Compared to the previous aspects of co-ordination in this section, we received more replies. The same key organizations were again nominated as those providing and receiving support. Besides the organizations already mentioned, a few more organizations were nominated, and NGOs were mentioned very frequently. Compared to the exchange of financial support and experience, the focus in this section is more on cooperation at the horizontal level. Links in this type of co-ordination are typical for NGOs.

Informal communication

The pattern in this section is very similar to the pattern regarding support. Both areas were perceived by the responding organizations as being almost identical. Three major clusters were identified. The first is made up of those organizations which nominated the National Drug Commission and the National Commission of the city, the second one is around two major NGOs in Prague (Sananim and Drop-In) and the third one is represented by links to the Department for the Treatment of Addictions in Prague 8. In the first cluster, a very mixed set of organizations was found. The second cluster is dominated by organizations providing contact services for drug users (mostly NGOs). The composition of the third cluster reflects those organizations with direct involvement in outpatient and/or inpatient treatment, regardless if they are GOs or NGOs.

Strategic cooperation

The most important role in this respect was attributed to those organizations that distribute financial support, and these are the same three organizations identified in the first area of our analysis. Second place is taken by the two major inpatient treatment centres in Prague (Department for Treatment of Addictions in Prague 8 and Department for Treatment of Addictions of the University Hospital Prague – Apolinarius). Beside their capacity for inpatient treatment, these organizations also run detoxification units. The only methadone programme is administered by the Apolinarius Clinic.

Finally, a number of links again run to Sananim and Drop-In, the most influential NGOs in the field.

Common activities

Most of the common activities of NGOs are linked to the Sananim and the Drop-In projects. This could be due to their activities in the training programmes for NGOs. To a lesser extent, the same organizations reported links to the Department for the Treatment of Addictions in Prague 8. A strong association was reported between the three *managerial* organizations and the rest of the organizations studied. This is due to the fact that the organizations who receive support are obliged to submit a progress or final report and therefore might perceive the funded activity as a common activity.

Based on the analysis of cooperation, we identified the most important *players* in the field of drug demand reduction in Prague. The characteristics of these institutions are summarized in Table 31.

Table 31: Important organizations in drug demand reduction in Prague

Organization	**Level of Operation**	**Legal Status**	**DDR Orientation**
National Drug Commission	National	GO	Exclusive
Drug Commission of Prague	Prague	GO	Exclusive
Dept. for Care of People with Drug Problems of the Ministry of Health	National	GO	Exclusive
SANANIM	National	NGO	Exclusive
Dept. for Treatment of Addictive Disorders Prague 8	Prague	GO	Exclusive (+ Alcohol)
Dept. for Treatment of Addictive Disorders, University Hospital Prague	Prague	GO	Exclusive (+ Alcohol)
DROP-IN	Prague	NGO	Exclusive

As shown in the table, three of the identified organizations operate at the national level, two are NGOs and all organizations are exclusively active in the drug field. The first three institutions focus activities on the management of drug policy, the remaining four organizations are major representatives of activities in the field of treatment and prevention, but also in training and education.

6 Summary and conclusions. Recommendations for policy and research

The results discussed in this chapter are based on the data obtained from 49 institutions in Prague and Ústí nad Labem in Northern Bohemia. These areas are among those the worst affected by the drug abuse problem. The selection of the institutions was made so as to ensure a representative cross-section of the important representatives active in the field of drug demand reduction. Of 49 institutions, 20 dealt with drug demand reduction exclusively and 29 institutions dealt with drug demand reduction only as one of their activities.

The majority of the institutions studied were established in the 1990s, especially in the years 1993-1995. It seems that at the end of the 1990s, the needs and services reached a certain equilibrium and that the newly-established institutions focused mostly on strengthening and developing their organizational structures or on the development and improvement of the services they provide.

Drug demand reduction institutions have a strong representation of professionals, most frequently psychologists, teachers for people with disabilities, psychiatrists and social workers. The results suggest that human resource management is one of the major problems encountered by the organizations active in drug demand reduction. One of the reasons is, of course, the financing situation. There is a general lack of resources that society can allocate to health and social care. Moreover, there is another problem: the method of financing. Certain activities are entirely dependent on subsidies or grants, which are provided mostly for one-year periods only. Additionally, even the approved grants and subsidies reach the recipients with delays. In this situation, it is obvious that the staff of drug demand reduction institutions are professionals who, besides their professional qualification, have a strong personal commitment to the problems they deal with.

A lack of financial resources is not the only difficulty. The professional staff is faced with limited possibilities of growth and career development. In the case of state institutions, financing is relatively stable. It is provided by institutional subsidies, which include overheads. The system of financing of NGOs, which play an important role in anti-drug activities, has undergone a rapid development in the 1990s. At present, the available sources of support are generally known and the rules and conditions for applying for grants and subsidies are now sufficiently clear. As mentioned before, the short-term nature of these subsidies (usually one year) is a significant flaw. For NGOs, the uncertainty of whether or not they will receive support, or in what amount, is a circumstance that complicates their planning and makes providing activities on a long-term horizon difficult.

An analysis of the activity of the institutions observed showed three large groups of anti-drug activities. The first and most important one, is providing various forms of treatment care and counselling. The second area is influencing the attitudes and activities in primary prevention. The third area includes work on drug policies, co-ordination of anti-drug activities and support of organizations which are active in the field of drugs. While the first and second area involve both governments and NGOs, the third area involves mainly governmental institutions, especially those with a national focus. A specific role is played by the National Drug Commission at the Office of the Government of the Czech Republic, as well as by individual ministries, especially the Ministry of Health, Ministry of Labour and Social Affairs and Ministry of the Interior.

The institutions which we studied differed quite substantially as regards their perception of the drug issue. They had quite different views of the scope of the problem. According to the average of the estimates made by representatives of the studied institutions, in 1998 about 250,000 persons were using drugs in the Czech Republic. Although the range of estimates is broad, it seems that this average value is close the value stated by epidemiologists. The institutions interviewed expect an increase in the number of drug users by 30% to 40% within the next five years. As far as the share of the individual types of drugs on the drug scene is concerned, the data obtained place cannabis unequivocally in first place, followed by amphetamines (in our case represented by Pervitin) and opiates, especially heroin. These three groups of drugs represent approximately 85% of the drug scene. It is interesting that the addressed institutions do not envisage any changes in the share of the individual drugs in the drug scene.

A discussion of the strong points and weaknesses of drug policy in the Czech Republic with the staff of the institutions interviewed proved to be very difficult. This is because different types of institutions operate under different circumstances and therefore have different experiences and represent different interest preferences. The existing network of anti-drug institutions and their potential for cooperation is viewed as a strong point. A second strong point is the existing concept of anti-drug policy, which is complemented by a satisfactory basis of anti-drug institutions. In third place, prevention programmes and conditions under which these programmes are implemented were mentioned (e.g. cooperation with schools, support from the Ministry of Education etc.). Harm reduction programmes were mentioned significantly less often, but they were also rated positively. The most often quoted weaknesses of the national drug policy were vaguely formulated priorities of anti-drug policy or an insufficient implementation of the approaches approved in the concept for an anti-drug policy. Ranked second were communication problems at the vertical level and the inefficient co-ordination of anti-drug activities. The third weak point of the national anti-drug policy was stated to be problems in financing. Other topics apart from these three areas were mentioned only rarely.

Cooperation among the institutions studied was investigated from different angles. Three groups of cooperating organizations were clearly distinguishable. On the vertical level, the National Drug Commission, town halls and the Ministry of Health dominate to which all state and non-governmental institutions working in the field relate. This circle is defined by economic dependence and by the need for the management and co-ordination of activities in accordance with the priorities of the anti-drug policy. The second circle of cooperation is formed mostly by NGOs providing contact services and counselling. The narrowest circle of cooperation is between state and NGOs providing treatment. In this case, the relations are probably limited to the referral of clients, to directing clients to appropriate types of care, etc.

An analysis of the institutional context of the activities focused on drug demand reduction reveals a number of suggestions which could help to improve the quality of work in this area. We have summarized these suggestions into the following five points:

1. *Improvement of communication and sharing of information.* The present technological possibilities are not exploited sufficiently. A majority of the institutions have computer equipment which would enable them to communicate via email and to have access to the Internet. Still, important information is available only partially, is incomplete and scattered across many different places. The same applies to cross-references. There is no specialized Czech magazine in which a professional discussion on the theoretical, conceptual or practical aspects of the drug problem could take place. The web site of the National Drug Commission represents a temporary solution. However, this web site focuses mainly on mediating information to anti-drug co-ordinators. An im-

provement of co-ordination and space for the continuous exchange of expert ideas would be beneficial to the whole community.

2. *Improvement of horizontal communication on the local level.* It appeared that there are strong reservations about horizontal cooperation between governmental and non-governmental institutions. The services provided by the different organizations could complement each other. More intensive use of these services would significantly contribute not only to prevention, but also to treatment. Patients treated in a specialized state inpatient facility could, for example, be referred to an after-care programme run by an NGO.
3. *Economic stabilization of drug demand reduction institutions.* A change in the system of financing will be necessary, especially for non-governmental institutions so as to enable them to plan their activities over a longer term. Economic stability is also a prerequisite for the stabilization and the development of human resources.
4. *The dominant influence of the medical approach to drug demand reduction issues prevailed in governmental organizations.* The social aspects of prevention and re-socialization in after-care are underestimated or tackled only formally. Although there was a substantial lack of certain forms of after-care among the activities carried out by the investigated institutions, this was not viewed by the majority of them as a serious problem.
5. *The development of a system of education.* In order to maintain and improve the quality of services it is of utmost importance to have a well-conceived system of education that would secure the professional growth of experts and create conditions for a long-term professional career in the field. Our survey showed that various types of training and education are offered by a number of agencies, but there is no complex system of accredited professional education.
6. *Research.* At present, research in the area of drug demand reduction is entirely marginal. An underestimation of the importance of research for the future development of the field is a factor which restricts the development of quality. Without research, the whole drug demand reduction field does not get reliable feedback about its results and therefore it will be very difficult to set priorities for the future. Unfortunately, no mechanism has been established that would support research in this field.

In our opinion, it is possible to achieve the desired increase in efficiency in the drug demand reduction field by taking the appropriate and right decisions and by implementing these consistently. The aim of our work has been to assist this process.

References

Csémy, L. (1997) 'Prague City Report', pp. 245-277 in: Council of Europe, *Multi-city Network Eastern Europe*. Council of Europe Publishing.

Csémy, L. (1999) 'Drug Misusers and their Treatment in the Czech Republic: Changing Problems and Changing Structures', *European Journal of Addiction Research* 5 (3): 133-137.

Csémy, L. (1999a) 'The Misuse of Alcohol and Other Drugs in Adolescents: An Analysis of Risk Factors'. Unpublished Research Report, IGA MZ CR No. 2886-4. Prague: PCP.

Csémy, L. et al. (1999b) *ESPAD 99 – The European School Survey Project on Alcohol and Other Drugs: The Czech Republic*. Research Report. Prague: Psychiatrické centrum.

Hampl, K. (1997) ¤e‰ení problematiky abusu alkoholu a ostatních drog na úrovni ordinací AT Kandidátská disertaãní práce, Mûlník [Problems of Abuse of Alcohol and of Other Psychoactives and the Role of Outpatient Facilities. Unpublished Doctoral Dissertation]

Hibell, B./Andersson, B./Bjarnason, T./Kokkevi, A./Morgan, M./Narusk, A. (Eds.) (1997) *The 1995 ESPAD Report. Alcohol and Other Drug Use Among Students in 26 European Countries*. Stockholm: CAN.

Hibell, B. et al. (2000) *The 1999 ESPAD Report. Alcohol and Other Drug Use Among Students in 30 European Countries*. Stockholm: CAN.

Kalina, K./Bém, P. (1994) 'Drug Problems and Drug Policy in the Czech Republic', in: Skála, J./Kalina, K./Bém, P. (Eds.), *Substance Abuse in the Czech Republic*. Prague.

Ministry of Health of the CR (1995) *National Health Programme: Long-term Strategy*. Praha.

NDC / The National Drug Commission [Meziresortní protidrogová komise] (1998) Programme of the National Anti-drug Policy of the Government of the Czech Republic for the Period 1998-2000 [Koncept a programme protidrogové politiky vlády na období 1998-2000]. Praha: Office of the Government of the Czech Republic.

NDC / The National Drug Commission [Meziresortní protidrogová komise] (1999) Report on the Situation and Development in the Area of Drugs in the Czech Republic 1999 [Zpráva o stavu a vyvoji ve vûcech drog v ãeské republice za rok 1998]. Praha: Office of the Government of the Czech Republic.

Ne‰por, K./Csémy, L. (1994) 'Alkohol a drogy ve stfiední Evropû - Problémy a moÏná fie‰ení' [Alcohol and Drugs in Central Europe – Problems and Possible Solutions], ãasopis Lékafiû ãeskych 133 (16): 483-486.

Netík, K./Budka, I./Neumann, J./Válková, H. (1991) K osobnosti kriminálního toxikomana [Personality of the criminal drug misuser], Psychiatrtické centrum Praha, ed. Zprávy 108.

NoÏina, M./Hlavaty, L. (Eds.) (1995) ãeská republika ve svûtle drog [The Czech Republic in the World of Drugs]. Praha: KLP.

Statistická roãenka 1998 [Statistical Yearbook of the Czech Republic 1998] (1999) Praha: ãSU.

The Prague City Hall [Magistrát hl.m.Prahy] (1998) "Together Against Drugs. The Anti-drug Programme of the City of Prague", Working Document [„Spoleãnû proti drogám",

Koncepce a program protidrogové politiky hl.m.Prahy na období 1998-2000, Interní tisk]. Praha.

Ústí nad Labem (1998) Okresní úfiad Ústí nad Labem: Koncepce a program protidrogové politiky okresu Ústí nad labem na obdoví 1998-2000, interní tisk [The Authority of the Ústí nad Labem County: Anti-drug Programme of the County of Usti nad Labem, Working Document]. Ústí nad Labem.

Vojtík, V./Bfiicháãek, V. (1987) Mládeï ohroïená toxikomanií [The youth at risk of drug misuse], Vyzkumny ústav psychiatricky, edice Zprávy 80.

Zdravotnická statistika. Psychiatrická péãe 1994-1998. Ústav zdravotnickych informací a statistiky, Praha. [Health Statistics. Psychiatric Care 1994-1998. Institute of Health Information and Statistics, Prague]

Annex: List of researched organizations

A.N.O. Association of NGOs (Prague)

After-care Centre (Prague)

AT Centre Prague 4 (Prague)

Centre for Addicts (Prague)

Centre for Youth at Risk (Prague)

Centre for Youth Klicov (Prague)

Centre of Community Work (Ústi nad Labem)

CESTA – Educational and Treatment Department (Prague)

City Council Prague 12 (Prague)

City Council Ústí nad Labem (Ústi nad Labem)

Credum Centre (Prague)

Czech Red Cross (Prague)

District Administration (Ústí nad Labem)

District Hygienic Station (Ústí nad Labem)

Drak (Ústi nad Labem)

DROP-IN Foundation (Prague)

Drug Abuse Prevention Centrum (Prague)

Drug out club – Community Centre (Ústi nad Labem)

Eset Help (Prague)

FILIA Institute (Prague)

General Faculty Hospital Department for Treatment of Addictive Disorders (Prague)

Grant Agency of the Czech Republic (Prague)

Hygienic Station of the Capital Prague (Prague)

Child Club 8 (Prague)

Child-line – Telephone Help (Prague)

Life Without Addictions (Prague)

Masaryk's Hospital, Department of Psychiatry (Ústi nad Labem)

Medea Kultur (Prague)

Ministry of Defence (Prague)

Ministry of Education (Prague)

Ministry of Health – Inspectorate for Narcotic Drugs (Prague)

Ministry of Health, Department of Care for Drug Addicted People (Prague)

Ministry of Labour and Social Affairs, Department of Social Services (Prague)

Ministry of Health – The National Health Promotion Programme (Prague)

National Institute of Public Health – Drug Information Centre (Prague)

Nefrit (Prague)

Pavucina – Self Help Centre (Prague)

Prague Psychiatric Centre (Prague)

Probation Service (Prague)

Proxima Sociale (Prague)

Psychiatric Hospital, Department for Treatment of Addictive Disorders (Prague)

Regional Hygienic Station (Ústi nad Labem)

Roztoc – Association of Parents (Prague)

SANANIM, Association for Treatment and Prevention of Drug Problems (Prague)

Teen Challenge (Prague)

The City Hall of Prague (Prague)

The National Drug Commission (Prague)

Triangl (Prague)

White Light Therapeutic Community (Ústi nad Labem)

CHAPTER 3

Drug Demand Reduction in Hungary
The Two Worlds of Prevalence and Perception

Zsuzsanna Elekes and Tünde Györy

1 Policy conditions: The institutional, social and epidemiological context

1.1 *Drug policy in Hungary*

Drug consumption in Hungary was officially recognized as a social problem for the first time in the mid-1980s, at the Thirteenth Congress of the Hungarian Socialist Worker Party in 1985, where the drug problem was mentioned by high-level politicians. However, information about young people using drugs was availabe in professional circles since the end of the 1960s.

The denial of the drug problem was characteristic for the late 1960s and most of the 1970s in Hungary. It was only towards the end of the 1970s that drug-related articles were allowed to be published, and even at that time, only in few scientific journals. After more than ten years of secretiveness and mystery-making, the beginning of the 1980s brought about significant changes in the way the drug problem was viewed. As a first step, a hospital-based treatment programme for drug users was developed and pilot-tested, and received high publicity in the press. This programme instigated an extensive campaign to find solutions for the drug problem. Its elements were: publicity in the press, a series of reports on radio and TV, documentary and report films depicting the seriousness of the problem and the challenge to find a solution. A centrally managed programme was initiated to work out a model for prevention, treatment and rehabilitation, and it also provided financial support for research purposes. It was from that time on that drug consumption was regarded as an existing social problem. In 1985, the Mass Media Research Institution conducted a public opinion poll about the probability and seriousness of 20 social problems or threats. On the scale of probability, the proliferation of drugs occupied the thirteenth place. On the scale of seriousness, it ranked on the second place, preceding problems such as housing and declining living standards (Nagy, 1985).

Drug consumption has become a central issue when a whole range of other social problems, including the decrease of life expectancy, the increase of alcoholism and suicide, declining living standards and the increase of poverty, came to be better known beyond the confines of the professional world. It was also obvious that there were no simple solutions for these problems given the worsening economic conditions, without radically changing the institutional structure. At the same time, problems that were relatively less serious and demanded less financial support were addressed and diverted the public's attention from the underlying causes. Although a number of treatment institutions were established at that time, only a few measures were taken to solve the drug problem. Criminalization and the general disapproval of any kind of drugs were characteristic for this period (Rácz, 1990).

After the political transition, the government established in 1991 the Inter-ministerial Drug Committee to harmonize the activities of ministries that were involved in the fight against the drug problem, to co-ordinate international relations, and to oversee the implementation of decisions made with regard to drugs. In 1996 the parliament established a temporary committee to evaluate the activities of the Inter-ministerial Drug Committee. The committee suggested the termination of the Committee's operation, which happened in 1998. After the elections of 1998, at the beginning of 1999, the institutions of the official drug policy were reorganized and their competencies were reallocated. Since then, the co-ordinating and policy formulating body is the Drug Co-ordination Committee, which is headed by the Minister of Youth and Sport. The Committee co-ordinates the activities of other ministries in the area of drug consumption.

1.2 *Legislation*

Until the beginning of the 1970s, legal regulation of drug-related issues merely meant the ratification of international conventions and contracts. The amendment of the criminal code in 1971 referred not only to the Single Drug Convention in 1961, but also to the necessity of the increased protection of society. Preventive measures against drug trade and smuggling, and the increasing number of drug abuse cases in Hungary were hardly addressed.

A law that came into force in 1979 included not only the crime of drug abuse, but also the delinquency of creating pathological addiction, as adapted to the specific Hungarian circumstances. According to this ruling, anyone who persuades a teenaged person to use inhalants commits delinquency (ISMertetö, 1999).

According to this law, which is essentially in line with international conventions including the 1961 and 1972 UN Drug Conventions, and the 1988 UN Convention) it is a crime to "prepare, receive, keep, circulate, import, export or transit harmful drugs through the country", and an offender can be sentenced to one to five years (in the most serious case, two to eight years) of imprisonment. Furthermore, anyone can be brought to trial and convicted who "supplies a person under 18 with harmful drugs". The Hungarian Penal Code considers it an offence if someone makes arrangements for drug abuse and "prepares, receives, or keeps harmful drugs in small quantities that are not intended for circulation" (Frech, 1989). Drug consumption itself is not an offence according to the Hungarian rules, but there are quite severe punishments for keeping and receiving drugs.

A law passed in 1993, introduced higher sentences for drug trafficking and production. The same law declared drug addiction a health problem and allowed drug addicts to choose to undergo medical treatment instead of being brought to trial. An important step in drug-related legislation was the revision of the drug law in 1998. The Party of the Young Democrats, who won the elections in 1998, gave high priority to the drug problem in their election campaign. One of the first actions of the new parliament was the amendment of drug-related laws. The bill included higher fines and introduced the offence of consumption. The parliament ratified the new law in March 1999.

In the following, the sentences for different types of drug offences according to the new law of 1999 are listed:

Overview 1: Sentences for different types of drug offences

• Consumption (independent from quantity)	2 years imprisonment
• Receiving, keeping, preparing etc. small quantities	2 years imprisonment, or financial penalty, or social work
• Offering, giving small quantities	2 years imprisonment
• Receiving, keeping, preparing etc. small quantities of different kinds of drugs	5 years imprisonment
• Offering, giving more than a small quantity	2-8 years imprisonment
• Receiving, keeping, preparing etc. significant quantities	5-15 years imprisonment
• Circulating significant quantities	10-15 years or lifetime imprisonment

Source: TASZ / Hungarian Civil Liberties Union.

The law of 1999 introduced an alternative way of dealing with drug-addicted persons on condition that they can prove in the first court case that they participated in a treatment programme for drug addiction for at least six months. The law however does not require that the treatment was successful (ISMertetö, 1999).

In accordance with international conventions, the Hungarian criminal code also has a regulation that allows the court to defer prosecution of a drug-addicted person for one to two years if the sentence provided for the crime committed is less than three years of imprisonment. During this period of time the defendant stays under patron supervision, and can be sent to remedial and/or preventive treatment. The court can also order a drug addict who has been sentenced to prison to take part in a withdrawal cure while in prison. There are, however, no treatment and rehabilitation programmes in Hungarian prisons that could be offered to such drug users.

Until the beginning of the 1970s the legal regulation primarily concentrated on supply reduction and efforts concentrated on the prevention of trade and smuggling. More severe punishment and the enactment of rules concerning the consumption of drugs were a consequence of the shift towards demand reduction in legal regulation from the mid-1970s onwards. However, drug consumption itself was penalized only from 1999 onwards. There are also some harm reduction programmes in Hungary, including three needle exchange programmes (the first needle exchange centre was established in 1996). The first methadone maintenance programme started in the mid-1990s. Legal regulation concerning methadone maintenance is, however, still inadequate.

1.3 Governmental concepts and strategies

The first version of the programme dealing with the nation's answer to drug use in Hungary was prepared for discussion in 1990. In 1996 the secretariat of the Inter-ministerial Drug Committee prepared the "Draft of the multi-disciplinary drug demand reduction strategy". In 1998, the Ad-hoc Committee set up by the parliament to curb drug consumption submitted its report, and in the same year the Inter-ministerial Drug Committee prepared an outline of the National Drug Strategy. However, all these documents remained in the state of drafts.

The new government elected in 1998 established the Ministry of Youth and Sport, and within it a Deputy Under-Secretariat responsible for drug co-ordination and the Drug Co-ordination Committee that is responsible for developing the national drug strategy. In autumn 2000, following extensive discussions with experts, the Parliament accepted the "National Strategy for Curbing Drug Use". The strategy seeks to achieve a balance between demand and supply reduction. The main objectives are as follows:

1) Society should be sensitive to the effective handling of drug-related issues, and the local communities should improve their problem-solving skills in confining the drug problem (community cooperation).
2) To create adequate circumstances to enable young people to develop a productive lifestyle and to say no to drugs (prevention).
3) To help those individuals and families who are affected by drugs (social work, treatment, rehabilitation).
4) To reduce the accessibility of drugs (supply reduction) (Nemzeti Stratégia, 2000: 30).

The newly adopted National Strategy puts an emphasis on demand reduction. It is the responsibility of the Drug Co-ordination Committee to control the implementation of the strategy, and to co-ordinate the operations of the ministries and the institutions of the state in collaboration with yet to be established local Drug Conciliation Forums. There are also several professional forums (e.g. Society for Addiction, Society of Psychiatry) that work with some of the state institutions.

1.4 Financing

The operating expenditures of the national health provision will be financed through the compulsory health insurance system. The basic health provision is financed by the Health Insurance Fund in accordance with the quota, the outpatient provision is financed in accordance with the relative rate of service charges, and hospitals are financed in accordance with the costs of patients attended to, and on the basis of a given group of illnesses. Some of the demand reduction programmes operate within the framework of the health care system and are financed by the health insurance system. The NGOs involved in treatment and rehabilitation can apply for support through the health insurance system.

The Drug Co-ordination Committee also has funds at its disposal that will be distributed through a tender system for research and to programmes that are in line with the objectives of the National Drug Strategy. Besides the above-mentioned resources, local governments, various funds, and churches also contribute to financing DDR (drug demand reduction) programmes. From 2001 on, a separate budget will be available to implement the National Drug Strategy.

1.5 Epidemiology

Survey data on drug use among secondary school students

The first data on drug consumption in Hungary date from 1974. A survey in two secondary schools in Budapest (the capital city) revealed that 4.8% of the respondents had used some kind of drug at least once in their life. In 1976, the lifetime prevalence of drug consumption in a random sample of 100 convicted criminals was 43%. A survey conducted in 1983 in one of the capital's districts showed a 4.6% lifetime prevalence of glue-sniffing. According to a secondary school survey in Budapest in 1985, 6% of the 14 to 18-year-olds interviewed had tried glue-sniffing, and 9.6% had used illicit drugs (Elekes/Paksi, 1994).

The available data suggests that in the 1970s drug consumption in the form of politoxicomany developed – combining the primary drug alcohol with pharmaceutical drugs. The inhalation of volatile substances reached heights in the 1970s, and declined again in the early 1980s. The first psychostimulants (Gracidin, Centedrin, and Parkan) date back to the same period. The opiates used at that time were morphine, codeine, and hydrocodine (National Report, 1992).

A survey carried out among secondary school students in Budapest in the autumn of 1992 (sample size was 4,700) revealed that 11.6% of the 17-year-old school pupils had at least once in their life tried an illicit drug. Based on the frequency of use and the last month prevalence it was concluded that for the majority of the pupils this was occasional use or a try-out. Marijuana was the most frequently used (lifetime prevalence rate 6.4%) illicit drug, followed by glue-sniffing (3.4), use of opiates (3.1%), and amphetamines (3.1%). Another 17.2% of the secondary school pupils had, at least once in their life, tried sedatives (13.0%), sleeping pills (6.4%) or opiate pills (4.5%) available upon prescription but not received from medical doctors (Elekes/Paksi, 1994).

According to the 1995 ESPAD study, the heavy consumption of licit drugs was particularly common among 16-year-old secondary school students in Hungary: 8.3% of them took tranquillizers without prescription, but the rate of those taking tranquillizers on prescription was also a high with 7.6%; 4% took sleeping pills without prescription and 10% combined medication with alcohol. The lifetime prevalence rates of illicit drugs was lower. Marijuana and hashish seemed to be the most widespread drugs, with a lifetime prevalence rate of 4.5%, whereas opiates (meaning mainly poppy products) had a lifetime prevalence rate of 1.2%. The occurrence of other illicit drugs was under 1%. Inhalants were also prominent, with a lifetime prevalence rate of 5.8%, but other data suggest that their spread was significantly higher than two years earlier (Elekes/Paksi, 1996).

A considerable change regarding the use of illicit drugs took place between 1995-1999. The consumption of most drugs has increased in these four years. Although marijuana was among the most widespread drugs in 1995, its lifetime prevalence hardly exceeded the prevalence of opiates or sniffing. By 1999, marijuana spread faster than any other drug. Not only the lifetime prevalence of marijuana had increased, but also its last-month prevalence. The use of tranquillizers or sedatives without medical supervision also rose between 1995 and 1999 (Elekes/Paksi, 2000).

Based on different surveys in some of the counties in 1996 and on a methodological survey conducted in 1998 and prepared for ESPAD 1999, it can be concluded that the rise of illicit drug use mainly took place between 1996 and 1998. Comparing the lifetime prevalence data from research conducted in 1998 among second grade students at secondary schools in the capital with the results of the 1999 ESPAD survey shows similar data (Elekes/Paksi, 2000).

Table 1: Frequency of use in lifetime for all students (ESPAD 1995 and 1999) (Percentages)

	Lifetime prevalence rate	
	1995	1999
Any illicit drugs	5	12
Any illicit drugs other than marijuana	1	5
Marijuana, hashish	4	11
Amphetamines	0	2
LSD or other hallucinogens	1	3
Crack	0	1
Cocaine	0	1
Ecstasy	0	3
Heroin	0	1
Inhalants	6	4
Tranquillizers or sedatives by prescription	8	9
Tranquillizers or sedatives without prescription	8	10
Alcohol together with pills	10	8

Source: Elekes/Paksi, 2000.

Survey data on drug use among adults

There is no reliable survey data concerning drug consumption within the adult population. In 1986 a national survey conducted in the adult (18 years and older) population shows that 6.7% of the survey participants took medication without a medical indication, and 9.2% took sedatives. In 1990, a representative national survey of the 18 years and older population indicated that 5.5% of those interviewed had used an illicit drug. Among the illicit drugs the lifetime prevalence of marijuana and hashish was 1.0%, of morphine and opium 0.8%, and of LSD and cocaine 0.2% (Elekes/Paksi, 1994). A national survey carried out in 1997 showed that among the 18 to 65-year-old population the lifetime prevalence rate of illicit drugs was 9.5% (Kó, 1998).

Data on drug-related deaths

The first drug-related death was registered in 1969. According to police data the number of drug-related deaths between 1973 and 1988 was 55, in 1989 only 6 cases were registered, while in 1990 there were no drug-related deaths.

In 1994 the police reported 5, and the treatment system 28 death cases. However, these data are unreliable because the term 'drug-related death' was not clearly defined until 1995.

Table 2: Cases of drug-related deaths between 1995-1999

Type of drug	1995	1996	1997	1998	1999
Opiates	4	51	46	23	40
Amphetamines	2	1	1	4	1
Sedatives, tranquillizers	148	215	255	210	281
Cocaine	-	-	-	3	-
Cannabis	-	-	-	-	1
Hallucinogens	-	-	-	1	-
Inhalants	12	8	1	32	10
Polytoxicomany, other drugs	38	13	36	65	4
Total	204	288	339	338	337

Source: ISMertetö, 2000.

The data are also inconsistent after 1995 and drug mortality figures registered by the police do not correspond with data available from the health statistics. Consequently these data have to be taken with a pinch of salt.

Data on drug-related crimes

In Hungary police registers are compiled according to *main crimes*. Therefore only those drug-related crimes are registered that constituted a main crime.

Table 3: Drug-related crimes

Year	Number of investigated crimes	Number of known offenders
1995	429	455
1996	440	464
1997	943	903
1998	2068	1727
1999	2860	2582

Source: ISMertetö, 2000.

In the second half of the 1990s the number of drug-related crimes increased. This was an increase in absolute numbers that was not due to any changes of the criminal code (the relevant bill passed in 1998 and the new drug law coming into effect in 1999 could not have significantly influenced police data in 1999). Two factors have to be taken into consideration when interpreting the available data. Firstly, criminal statistics build on so-called output observations. This means that the statistics are not revised once a crime was committed but at the end of the investigations, which is approximately one year later. Therefore the real changes in data occurred a year earlier than when they appear in the statistics. Secondly, although there has been an increase, the rate of "drug-related crimes" reaches only 0.5 per cent of all the crimes solved.

Data on registered drug users

Data from health providers show that the number of registered drug users increased considerably during the 1990s. However, it is not clear if this was an actual increase or if it was due to changes in data processing, or simply because patients, who were treated and registered at several institutions in the same year, were counted double.

Table 4: Number of people treated in health institutions

1995	3553
1996	4718
1997	8494
1998	9458
1999	12765

Source: ISMertetö, 2000.

Both treatment (rehabilitation) and police data indicate an increased drug problem in the second half of the 1990s. However, when interpreting the data changes in the data registration system have to be taken into consideration, as well as the fact that the drug problem received more attention in this time period, which also contributed to an increase in the number of treated cases.

Table 5: The number of people in treatment (rehabilitation) in 1999 according to sex and type of drug

Type of drug	**Total number of patients**		**New patients (registered first time)**	
	Man	Woman	Man	Woman
Opiates	2968	889	1277	388
Cocaine	137	40	63	20
Cannabis	1433	207	868	121
Hallucinogens	218	76	87	38
Amphetamines	994	370	415	156
Sedatives, tranquillizers	648	1086	222	286
Politoxicomany	1172	1767	518	1033
Inhalants	347	78	178	38
Others	115	220	40	22
Total	8032	4733	3668	2102

Source: ISMertetö, 1999.

2 Organizations active in the area of drug demand reduction

2.1 *The overall number of Drug Demand Reduction Institutions*

In Hungary there is no central database containing information about DDR institutions. A periodical titled *Droginfo* is to compensate for the lack of information. It is the information base of "institutions, social organizations and groups involved in questions related to the drug problem". The periodical does not only compile DDR programmes but it also includes all the institutions and programmes that try to tackle the drug problem, including supply reduction programmes. *Droginfo* offers the most reliable information available on organizations active in the field of drug demand reduction with 144 listed institutions, organizations and groups in Hungary in the year 1998. However, since institutions contribute data to the periodical on a voluntary basis, the publication may not include all DDR programmes and institutions. Also the periodical does on the one hand not include ministries and research institutions and on the other hand lists certain foundations and organizations under several activities (*Droginfo*, 1998).

There are also other relevant publications in Hungary. The multi-country drug programme of Phare published the „*Living Document*" in 1997, which gave an overall picture of treatment facilities for drug users in Hungary (*Élö Dokumentum*, 1997). The Centre of Social Resources in Budapest published a survey on the situation of drug use and the services offered by organizations involved in the treatment of drug-related problems in Budapest in 1997 (*Drogproblémák kezelésével foglalkozó intézmények*, 1997).

All three publications were taken into consideration when deciding about which organizations to include in this project. Forty-six institutions operating in the field of drug demand reduction were chosen, including 41 in Budapest, and 5 in Szeged. Some of the organizations in Budapest operate on the national level, while others work only in the capital. A considerable number of the organizations deals with clients from different parts of the country. Despite the low number of organizations operating in Szeged, they were included in the sample because they are the oldest and most active organizations in the field of drug demand reduction in Hungary. Besides that, Szeged is population-wise one of the biggest towns in the country and the level of drug consumption seems to be above national average, both in town as well as in the rest of Csongrád county, of which Szeged is the capital. Beside Szeged, also Pécs lately showed increasing activities in the field of demand reduction. Related activities in other towns are more limited in scope.

There is only one source of information about territorial variation in drug consumption, i.e. the ESPAD 1995 survey conducted among secondary school students. This was the only survey that analysed differences in drug consumption by counties. The survey revealed that the lifetime prevalence of illicit drugs was the highest in Csongrád county, with 16% of 16 to 17-year-old secondary school students interviewed having tried illicit drugs at least once in their life. Budapest showed the second-highest prevalence with 12%, and the national average was 10% among the 16 to 17-year-old population. It was mentioned earlier that drug consumption has considerably increased in Hungary since 1995, but the only data available is for Budapest and the country as a whole. It is estimated that Csongrád county and Budapest are currently among the regions with the highest drug consumption rates.

2.2 *General description of Drug Demand Reduction Institutions included in this project*

Type of organization

More than half of the institutions included in this project are governmental organizations. In addition the sample includes 16 non-profit or voluntary organizations. Three organizations are private organizations, and only one organization has no legal status. (Henceforth, we will use the abbreviation "GO" for a governmental organization and "NGO" for a non-profit or private organization. The organization having no legal status will be excluded from the analyses of institutions by status of organization.)

A considerable number of organizations included in the survey were established after the political changes took place. Two thirds of them were formed in the 1990s, the first part of this decade being particularly favourable for establishing new organizations. Almost half of the institutions, mostly in the non-profit sector, were founded between 1991 and 1995. Nine organizations, 21% of the sample, were established in 1992.

Table 6: Drug Demand Reduction Institutions by type of organization

Status	National level	Budapest	Szeged	Total
Governmental	14 (58.3%)	8 (47.1%)	4 (80.0%)	26 (56.5%)
Private	1 (4.2%)	2 (11.8%)		3 (6.5%)
Non-profit	9 (37.5%)	6 (35.3%)	1 (20.0%)	16 (34.8%)
No legal status		1 (5.9%)		1 (2.2%)
Total	24 (100%)	17 (100%)	5 (100%)	46 (100%)
DDR exclusive	6 (25.0%)	7 (41.2%)	1 (20.0%)	14 (30.4%)
DDR inclusive	18 (75.0%)	10 (58.8%)	4 (80.0%)	32 (69.6%)

The establishment of organizations more or less went hand in hand with the launch of their activities in the field of drug demand reduction: 22% started these activities between 1980 and 1989, half of them between 1990 and 1995 (22% in the year 1992) and 29% of the organizations between 1996 and 1999. The proportion of institutions that have been involved in drug demand reduction programmes before 1980 is rather low.

Fourteen of the institutions are active only in the field of drug demand reduction (DDR exclusives). Out of these, six operate on the national level, seven organizations are located in Budapest, and only one is to be found in Szeged.

Mission and objectives

Most organizations included in the survey are involved in the provision of information, education, care and advice. Three institutions in Budapest mentioned support as their main activity. Among national organizations, policy design, co-ordination, and research appear to be the dominant areas of activity.

A considerable proportion of the institutions work exclusively on drug demand reduction. The majority of the organizations mentioned prevention, information, care, treatment and giving advice as belonging to their activities. Among national institutions, prevention is more frequently the main activity than care and treatment. Prevention was often on the agenda of organizations in Budapest, but the rate of treatment institutions is also high. Three of the organizations in Szeged emphasize treatment as their main activity, while one organization is involved in both prevention and research.

Table 7: Main mission of the organization (in percentages)

Mission	National level	Budapest	Szeged	GO	NGO	DDR exclusive	DDR inclusive	Total
Attitudes, knowledge	45.8	47.1	20.0	30.8	63.1	50.0	40.6	43.5
Care and advice	33.3	29.4	60.0	46.1	21.0	35.7	34.4	34.8
Support	4.2	17.6	-	3.8	15.8	7.1	9.4	8.7
Policy design, co-ordination, advice	12.5	-	20.0	11.5	-	-	12.5	8.7
Intelligence, research	4.2	-	-	3.8	-	-	3.1	2.2
Other	-	5.9	-	3.8	-	7.1	-	2.2
Total %	100.0	100.0	100.0	100.0	100.0	100.0	100.0	100.0
n	(24)	(17)	(5)	(26)	(19)	(14)	(32)	(46)

Staff

In 7 of the institutions interviewed there were no permanent paid employees. The average number of paid employees is 60 in the national institutions, 9 in organizations located in Budapest, and 45 in organizations located in Szeged. This high average number for the latter is due to the University of Medical Sciences in Szeged. The average number of staff is much lower in the field of drug demand reduction, especially in the national institutions where on average 11 employees work in this field. The number of employees involved in drug demand reduction is only slightly lower than the total number in the organizations in Budapest (the average being 9). The main reason for this is the fact that these organizations concentrate on various specialized fields of drug demand reduction. The number of the employees involved in drug demand reduction in Szeged is 34.

Hence, rather few permanent, paid employees work in the field of drug demand reduction in most of the institutions. Altogether 13 organizations employ voluntary workers, 5 of them are national institutions, 6 of them are located in Budapest, and 2 of them in Szeged. Mostly non-profit organizations employ voluntary workers. The number of voluntary workers varies but it is below 10 for most organizations. Altogether 6 of the organizations interviewed have registered members. These are all non-governmental organizations. Two thirds of the organizations questioned have full-time employees working on drug demand reduction programmes. The average rate of full-time employees is 91% at the national organizations, 63% in Budapest, and 83% in Szeged.

Nineteen institutions have part-time employees, and there are 3 institutions that have only part-time employees. The average proportion of part-time employees is 15% in national organizations, 21% in Budapest, and 11% in Szeged. Nine organizations employ voluntary workers in the field of drug demand reduction. Three of them are national organizations, five operate in the capital and one in Szeged. There are altogether 4 organizations that employ only voluntary workers. Though only private and civil organizations employ voluntary workers, the proportion of part-time workers is similar in GOs and NGOs.

Paid experts work for 36 organizations, and paid other employees work for 20 organizations. Voluntary professionals work in 9 institutions and other voluntary employees are involved in 5 organizations.

The data show that a high proportion of organizations in drug demand reduction programmes have paid employees and experts. Much fewer organizations employ voluntary experts and other voluntary workers although in absolute numbers there are more volunteers than paid employees. The number of voluntary workers is especially high in national institutions. Taking all the data into consideration it can be concluded that the majority of Hungarian organizations employs experts and paid employees. The voluntary and non-professional workers still play a smaller role in drug demand reduction programmes.

Table 8: The average number of employees according to the type and level of the organizations

Mission	National level	Budapest	Szeged	GO	NGO	DDR exclusive	DDR inclusive	Total
Paid experts	10.9	7.9	14.4	11.2	8.9	6.7	11.5	10.3
Paid other employees	10.2	1.7	38.2	15.2	7.3	6.8	14.3	12.4
Total paid employees	14.6	9.0	45.0	19.1	12.7	10.4	18.8	16.7

Mission	National level	Budapest	Szeged	GO	NGO	DDR exclusive	DDR inclusive	Total
Voluntary experts	24.7	9.2	13.0	-	16.9	24.2	7.3	15.5
Other voluntary persons	26.5	29.0	1.0	1.0	27.7	1.5	36.3	22.4
Total voluntary workers	31.7	23.7	7.0	1.0	28.6	16.7	28.2	23.6

Mission	National level	Budapest	Szeged	GO	NGO	DDR exclusive	DDR inclusive	Total
Total experts	13.5	9.3	17.0	11.2	15.9	13.1	11.4	12.3
Total other persons	16.9	8.0	38.5	15.3	20.2	7.4	20.2	17.2
Total employees	19.3	14.1	47.8	19.1	26.3	16.2	22.1	20.9

Table 9: The number of organizations where paid experts with various qualification are employed

Mission	National level	Budapest	Szeged	GO	NGO	DDR exclusive	DDR inclusive	Total
Medical	9	9	4	14	7	6	16	22
Social worker	7	7	4	11	6	5	13	18
Psychiatric	6	7	4	12	4	4	13	17
Educational	4	6	3	7	6	3	10	13
Psychology	5	4	2	9	2	2	9	11
Lawyer, legal	3	-	3	3	2	1	5	6
Sociology	3	2	1	4	1	-	6	6
Public health	3	-	-	2	1	1	2	3
Manager / Economist	2	1	0	1	2	-	3	3
Other	7	4	3	9	5	4	10	14

In the field of drug demand reduction half of the institutions included in the study mainly employed medical professionals. Psychiatrists and social workers hold the second place, and these are followed by psychologists and pedagogues. Managers and public health specialists are rare, these professions are rather found in the national institutions.

Funding

There are two problems related to the data on the total budget. Firstly, the data shows estimated amounts because the experts interviewed rarely knew the exact numbers as the budget of the organization is prepared by different departments within the organizations, and the budget is not always divided by type of activity (especially in the case of larger organizations). Secondly, the budget depends on the type of organization. Considerable funds are allocated for drug demand reduction programmes in institutions in the capital because they are specialized in this kind of activities, whereas in national organizations drug demand reduction is one of many other tasks.

Table 10: The average total budget of institutions interviewed in 1998 and the amount of money allocated to drug demand reduction (EUR)

	National	Budapest	Szeged	GO	NGO	Exclusive	Inclusive	Total budget
Total budget	34,611,810.8	38,288.4	24,684,780.2	39,013,626.3	1,656,481	41,811.6	30,074,640	21,241,505.2
Missing	6	5	1	8	4	4	8	12
Drug demand reduction	370,691.9	31,155.25	93,233.5	435,760.4	31,255.5	41,981.6	371,751.4	239,843.5
Missing	9	9	3	13	6	4	17	21
The average proportion of DDR in total budget	52%	94%	37%	59%	65%	98%	42%	64%
Missing	8	8	2	11	5	3	15	18

Note: ECU 1 = HUF 225.24 (01.01.1998).

Table 11: Number of organizations receiving funds for drug demand reduction programmes from different sources in 1995 and 1998

Source	**1995**	**1998**
Public government agencies	31	35
Private sector	9	14
Other foreign organizations	6	10
Membership fees and donation	4	8
International organizations	2	4
Voluntary organizations	1	1
Foreign governments and organizations	2	-

The data above show that state and public financing play a central role in the budget of the organizations involved in drug demand reduction. In 1995, 73% of GOs and 62% of non-profit organizations were financed at least partly by public government agencies, and in 1998 it was 80% and 75% respectively. Thirteen institutions receive only public funds. In 1995 one GO and one non-profit organization received funds from international organizations, which account for 10-20% of the budget in these institutions. In 1998 four institutions (3 GOs and 1 non-profit organization) received international funds, which accounted for 30% of the budget of the organization in the capital, and 10-20% of the budget of the other national organizations.

In 1995 one GO and one non-profit organization received money from foreign governments and organizations. The proportion of support was below 10% in all the above-mentioned budgets. Besides that, the Soros Foundation plays an important role as funding agency. In 1995 five non-profit and one governmental organization, in 1998 seven non-profit, and three governmental organizations were supported by this foreign organization. The proportion of this source in the budget is also increasing.

The private sector plays a considerable and increasingly important role in the financing of drug demand reduction programmes. In 1995 three GOs and six non-profit organizations were privately supported, accounting for 50% of the budget in three institutions. In 1998 four GOs and ten non-profit organizations received money from the private sector, which exceeded 50% of the budget in four institutions.

Voluntary organizations do not really support drug demand reduction programmes. Organizations also use membership fees and donations to fund their programmes, but these sources account only for a small fraction in the budget of these organizations. While in 1995 only four organizations covered their expenses from these fees (in one case up to 90%), this number has doubled by 1998. It has to be mentioned, however, that this way of financing remains below 10% of the total budget in most of the cases.

3 The activities of organizations in drug demand reduction

3.1 *The main goals of organizations*

For 23 organizations interviewed, the main goal was prevention and information services, followed by the general field of drug demand reduction in 15, and by treatment and care in 14 organizations. Eleven organizations stated that their main goal is training of professionals.

Examining the main goals of the organizations with regard to their operating area and legal status, it can be stated that there are no big differences between organizations working on the national level and in local areas. While treatment and care are the main goals of organizations operating in Budapest and Szeged, interest representation and policy development are the main goals of organizations working on the national level.

Drug demand reduction in general and prevention are the most common goals of NGOs, while treatment, care and rehabilitation are characteristic of the GOs' goals.

Table 12: Main goals of the organizations

Main goals	Total N = 46	National level N = 24	Budapest N = 17	Szeged N = 5	GO N = 26	NGO N = 19	Exclusive N = 14	Inclusive N = 32
Prevention/ Information	**23 (50.0%)**	12 (50.0%)	10 (58.8%)	1 (20%)	10 (38.5%)	13 (68.4%)	8 (57.1%)	15 (46.9%)
DDR (general stat.)	**15 (32.6%)**	8 (33.3%)	5 (29.4%)	2 (40%)	6 (23.1%)	8 (47.4%)	3 (21.4%)	12 (37.5%)
Treatment and care	**14 (30.4%)**	6 (25.0%)	6 (35.3%)	2 (40.0%)	11 (42.3%)	3 (15.8%)	5 (35.7%)	9 (28.1%)
Training professionals	**11 (23.9%)**	7 (29.1%)	3 (17.6%)	1 (20.0%)	7 (26.9%)	4 (21.1%)	4 (28.6%)	7 (21.9%)
Funding/Fund raising	**4 (8.7%)**	3 (12.5%)	-	1 (20.0%)	3 (11.5%)	1 (5.3%)	1 (7.1%)	9 (9.4%)
Rehabilitation (after-care)	**4 (8.7%)**	2 (8.3%)	1 (5.9%)	-	3 (11.5%)	1 (5.3%)	2 (14.3%)	2 (6.3%)
Co-ordinating	**2 (4.3%)**	1 (4.2%)	1 (5.9%)	-	2 (7.7%)	-	1 (7.1%)	1 (3.1%)
Research/ Documentation	**1 (2.2%)**	1 (4.2%)	-	-	1 (3.8%)	-	-	1 (3.1%)
Interest representation	**1 (2.2%)**	1 (4.2%)	-	-	-	1 (5.3%)	-	1 (3.1%)
Policy development	**1 (2.2%)**	1 (4.2%)	-	-	-	1 (5.3%)	-	1 (3.1%)
Other	**6 (13.0%)**	2 (8.3%)	3 (17.6%)	1 (20%)	3 (11.5%)	2 (10.5%)	2 (14.3%)	4 (12.5%)

3.2 *Drug Demand Reduction Institutions by area of activity*

Organizations were asked to describe their three main fields of activity, and to include details on the actual task, the date of the beginning of the work, and the target group. In some cases it was not possible to limit organizations to define only three activities, and the additional activities were included in the survey.

In this chapter, the percentages in the table cells indicate the positive answers given in the case of each independent and dependent variable.

Seventy-six per cent of the organizations stated that prevention/information is one of their main activities, with a significantly higher proportion of organizations operating on national level as well as NGOs. Treatment and care programmes are carried out in 44% of the organizations interviewed. While organizations in Szeged concentrate more on treatment and care programmes, organizations on the national level expressed that these programmes account for significantly smaller proportions.

Policy development/legislation is not a typical activity of the organizations interviewed. Only 15% of them mentioned that it is one of their main goals. A significant difference has been observed between GOs and NGOs. This activity is more common for GOs, with 23% of them mentioning it.

Eleven per cent of the organizations are involved in activities related to interest representation and protection of civil and human rights. There are significantly more NGOs than GOs representing the interests of drug users in Hungary.

Table 13: Main activities of organizations

Main activity	Total N = 46	National level N = 24	Budapest N = 17	Szeged N = 5	GO N = 26	NGO N = 19	Exclusive N = 14	Inclusive N = 32
Prevention/ Information	**35 (76.1%)**	21 (87.5%)	11 (64.7%)	3 (60.0%)	17 (65.4%)	17 (89.5%)	11 (78.6%)	24 (75.0%)
Training professionals	**27 (58.7%)**	16 (66.7%)	9 (52.9%)	2 (40.0%)	17 (65.4%)	9 (47.4%)	6 (42.9%)	21 (65.6%)
Treatment and care	**20 (43.5%)**	8 (33.3%)	8 (47.1%)	4 (80.0%)	14 (53.8%)	6 (31.6%)	7 (50.0%)	13 (40.6%)
Doing research/ Documentation	**19 (41.3%)**	12 (50.0%)	6 (35.3%)	1 (20.0%)	11 (42.3%)	7 (36.8%)	5 (35.7%)	14 (43.8%)
Co-ordinating	**17 (37.8%)**	10 (43.5%)	6 (35.3%)	1 (20.0%)	11 (42.3%)	5 (27.8%)	54 (30.8%)	13 (40.6%)
Funding/Fund raising	**16 (35.6%)**	11 (47.8%)	4 (23.5%)	1 (20.0%)	9 (34.6%)	6 (33.3%)	5 (38.5%)	11 (34.4%)
Rehabilitation (after-care)	**13 (28.9%)**	6 (26.1%)	5 (29.4%)	2 (40.0%)	7 (26.9%)	5 (27.8%)	6 (42.9%)	7 (22.6%)
Policy development	**7 (15.2%)**	6 (25.0%)	1 (5.9%)	-	6 (23.1%)	1 (5.3%)	1 (7.1%)	6 (18.8%)
Interest representation	**5 (10.9%)**	4 (16.7%)	1 (5.9%)	-	1 (3.8%)	4 (21.1%)	-	5 (15.6%)

3.3 *Analysis of some selected activities on an individual basis*

Prevention/Information

Seventy-six per cent of the organizations expressed that one of their main activities is prevention and information. The most popular prevention activity is giving lectures and seminars (54%). Thirty-seven per cent of the organizations interviewed stated that they are distributors of films, brochures, leaflets and other publications. Counselling is the main activity of 26% of the organizations. The running of information points, organization of clubs and camps, and the development of training programmes are done by 14%. Street work was not mentioned by the organizations at all. The reason might be that institutions do not perceive street work as an activity but as a methodology.

Significantly more national than local organizations organize lectures and seminars, distribute brochures and organize special events. Counselling and the distribution of brochures are more NGO-specific, while public information campaigns are most frequently organized by GOs.

Fifty-one per cent of the organizations working in the field of prevention programmes were involved in only one activity, and offering lectures and seminars was mentioned most frequently. Thirty-seven per cent of the organizations were involved in two activities, while three activities were carried out by only 17%.

Table 14: The most important activities in the area of prevention

Activities within prevention	Total N = 46	National level N = 24	Budapest N = 17	Szeged N = 5	GO N = 26	NGO N = 19	Exclusive N = 14	Inclusive N = 32
Lectures, seminars	**19 (41.3%)**	10 (41.7%)	7 (41.2%)	2 (40.0%)	9 (34.6%)	9 (47.4%)	7 (50%)	12 (37.5%)
Distribution of brochures	**13 (28.3%)**	9 (37.5%)	3 (17.6%)	1 (20.0%)	4 (15.4%)	9 (47.4%)	5 (35.7%)	8 (25.0%)
Counselling	**9 (19.6%)**	4 (16.7%)	4 (23.5%)	1 (20.0%)	1 (3.8%)	7 (36.8%)	3 (21.4%)	6 (18.8%)
Development of training programmes	**5 (10.9%)**	5 (20.8%)	-	-	2 (7.7%)	3 (15.8%)	-	5 (15.6%)
Running inform. points	**5 (10.9%)**	2 (8.3%)	3 (17.6%)	-	2 (7.7%)	3 (15.8%)	1 (7.1%)	4 (12.5%)
Public inform. campaigns	**3 (6.5%)**	2 (8.3%)	-	1 (20.0%)	3 (11.5%)	-	1 (7.1%)	2 (6.3%)
Special events	**1 (2.2%)**	1 (4.2%)	-	-	1 (3.8%)	-	-	1 (3.1%)
Street work	-	-	-	-	-	-	-	-
Other	**5 (10.9%)**	3 (12.5%)	2 (11.8%)	-	3 (11.5%)	2 (10.5%)	2 (14.2%)	3 (9.4%)

Target groups of the activities are mainly young people, including school pupils and students, as well as the general public and professionals working in DDR programmes. Parents and journalists were rarely mentioned as target groups, whereby significantly more NGOs than GOs target parents with their activities. Local communities have not been mentioned at all.

Table 15: Target groups of the prevention programmes

Target groups within prevention	Total N = 46	National level N = 24	Budapest N = 17	Szeged N = 5	GO N = 26	NGO N = 19	Exclusive N = 14	Inclusive N = 32
Youth, school pupils	12 (26.1%)	7 (29.2%)	4 (23.5%)	1 (20.0%)	5 (19.2%)	7 (36.8%)	5 (35.7%)	7 (21.9%)
The general public	11 (23.9%)	5 (20.8%)	4 (23.5%)	2 (40.0%)	6 (23.1%)	5 (26.3%)	4 (28.6%)	7 (21.9%)
Students	9 (19.6%)	4 (16.7%)	4 (23.5%)	1 (20.0%)	4 (15.4%)	4 (21.1%)	3 (21.4%)	6 (18.8%)
Professionals	7 (15.2%)	5 (20.8%)	1 (5.9%)	1 (20.0%)	3 (11.5%)	4 (21.1%)	3 (21.4%)	4 (12.5%)
Public authorities	3 (6.5%)	2 (8.3%)	1 (5.9%)	-	-	2 (10.5%)	2 (14.3%)	1 (3.1%)
Parents	3 (6.5%)	1 (4.2%)	2 (11.8%)	-	-	3 (15.8%)	1 (7.1%)	2 (6.3%)
Drug addicts	1 (2.2%)	-	1 (5.9%)	-	-	1 (5.3%)	-	1 (3.1%)
Journalists	1 (2.2%)	1 (4.2%)	-	-	1 (3.8%)	-	-	1 (3.1%)
Other (prisoners, soldiers)	3 (6.5%)	3 (12.5%)	-	-	2 (7.7%)	1 (5.3%)	-	3 (9.4%)

More than half of the organizations indicated that their programmes focus only on one target group, 42% have programmes for two different target groups, and there was only one organization that mentioned three target groups.

Treatment and care

Treatment and care as a main DDR activity was mentioned by 44% of the organizations. Forty-five per cent of the organizations stated that they have a treatment component, 25% offer detoxification, and 10% offer individual counselling. After-care is provided by four organizations. Two organizations have needle exchange and condom distribution programmes. None of the organizations mentioned family therapy, outpatient clinics, or methadone treatment. However, this doesn't mean that the organizations interviewed are not involved at all in any of these activities. It might be that the various institutions call these activities differently.

Table 16: Activities of organizations in the area of treatment and care

Activities within treatment and care	Total N = 46	National level N = 24	Budapest N = 17	Szeged N = 5	GO N = 26	NGO N = 19	Exclusive N = 14	Inclusive N = 32
Treatment (general)	9 (45.0%)	3 (12.5%)	5 (29.4%)	1 (20.0%)	7 (26.9%)	2 (10.5%)	3 (21.4%)	6 (18.8%)
Detoxification	5 (25%)	2 (8.3%)	1 (5.9%)	2 (40.0%)	4 (15.4%)	1 (5.3%)	1 (7.1%)	4 (12.5%)
After-care	4 (20.0%)	4 (16.7%)	-	-	2 (7.7%)	2 (10.5%)	2 (14.3%)	2 (6.3%)
Needle exchange, condom distribution	2 (10.0%)	-	1 (5.9%)	1 (20.0%)	1 (3.8%)	1 (5.3%)	1 (7.1%)	1 (3.1%)
Individual counselling	2 (10.0%)	1 (4.2%)	1 (5.9%)	-	1 (3.8%)	1 (5.3%)	-	2 (6.3%)
Group psychotherapy	1 (5.0%)	-	1 (5.9%)	-	-	1 (5.3%)	-	1 (3.1%)
Day centres	1 (5.0%)	-	-	1 (20.0%)	1 (3.8%)	-	1 (7.1%)	-
Medical care	1 (5.0%)	-	-	1 (20.0%)	1 (3.8%)	-	-	1 (3.1%)
Other	5 (25%)	3 (12.5%)	1 (5.9%)	1 (20.0%)	4 (15.4%)	1 (5.3%)	3 (21.4%)	2 (6.3%)

The few organizations offering detoxification, day centres, needle exchange and medical care operate mainly at the local level. After-care programmes are linked to organizations at the national level.

Fifty-five per cent of organizations working in the field of treatment and care are involved in only one activity, with 'treatment – general' showing the highest proportion; 22% stated that they are involved in two types of activities, while three organizations mentioned three activities.

Drug users are the typical target group of organizations working in the field of treatment and care. Only two of the organizations indicated that their approach is broader and includes other groups at risk (e.g. children from dysfunctional families). Similarly, families of drug users as well as 'other target groups' (e.g. prisoners) are mentioned only in few cases. Eighty-four per cent of the organizations treat people from only one target group, whereas 16% have two target groups.

Table 17: Target groups in the area of treatment

Target groups within treatment	Total N = 46	National level N = 24	Budapest N = 17	Szeged N = 5	GO N = 26	NGO N = 19	Exclusive N = 14	Inclusive N = 32
Drug users, addicts	16 (34.8%)	7 (29.2%)	6 (35.3%)	3 (60.0%)	11 (42.3%)	5 (26.3%)	6 (42.9%)	10 (31.3%)
Group at risk	2 (4.3%)	-	1 (5.9%)	1 (20.0%)	2 (7.7%)	-	1 (7.1%)	1 (3.1%)
Users' families, relatives	2 (4.3%)	-	2 (11.8%)	-	-	2 (10.5%)	1 (7.1%)	1 (3.1%)
Other target groups	2 (4.3%)	2 (8.3%)	-	-	2 (7.7%)	-	-	2 (6.3%)

Rehabilitation

Twenty-eight per cent of the organizations offer rehabilitation programmes. Assistance in social re-adaptation is the main activity within this category. Day after-care centres and individual counselling are offered by 23% of the organizations. Access to group therapy rehabilitation for drug users is more often provided by organizations that exclusively specialize in drug demand reduction than by organizations that are also involved in other programmes.

Table 18: Activities in the area of rehabilitation

Activities within rehabilitation	Total N = 46	National level N = 24	Budapest N = 17	Szeged N = 5	GO N = 26	NGO N = 19	Exclusive N = 14	Inclusive N = 32
Assistance in social re-adaptation	**6 (43.2%)**	3 (12.5%)	2 (11.8%)	1 (20.0%)	2 (7.7%)	4 (21.1%)	2 (14.3%)	4 (12.5%)
Day after-care centres	**3 (23.1%)**	1 (4.2%)	2 (11.8%)	-	3 (11.5%)	-	1 (7.1%)	2 (6.3%)
Individual counselling, legal advice	**3 (23.1%)**	2 (8.3%)	1 (5.9%)	-	2 (7.7%)	1 (5.3%)	1 (7.1%)	2 (6.3%)
Group therapy, group	**2 (15.4%)**	1 (4.2%)	-	1 (20.0%)	7 (7.7%)	-	2 (14.3%)	-
Engaging drug users in field work ...	**1 (7.7%)**	1 (4.2%)	-	-	-	1 (5.3%)	1 (7.1%)	-
Hostels	**1 (7.7%)**	-	1 (5.9%)	-	-	-	1 (7.1%)	-
Reintegration with their families	**1 (7.7%)**	1 (4.2%)	-	-	-	1 (5.3%)	-	1 (3.1%)
Other	**2 (15.4%)**	1 (4.2%)	-	1 (20.0%)	2 (7.7%)	-	1 (7.1%)	1 (3.1%)

Sixty-two per cent of the institutions offering rehabilitation programmes are involved in only one activity, 31% in two types of activities, and only one institution mentioned three types of rehabilitation activities.

Drug users, addicts and abstainers (clients after treatment, ex-patients) are the most important target groups of organizations working in the field of rehabilitation.

Table 19: Target groups in the area of rehabilitation

Target groups within rehabilitation	Total N = 46	National level N = 24	Budapest N = 17	Szeged N = 5	GO N = 26	NGO N = 19	Exclusive N = 14	Inclusive N = 32
Abstainers, recovered...	5 (10.9%)	1 (4.2%)	2 (11.8%)	2 (40.0%)	3 (11.5%)	2 (10.5%)	3 (21.4%)	2 (6.3%)
Drug users, addicts	5 (10.9%)	4 (16.7%)	-	1 (20.0%)	4 (15.4%)	1 (5.3%)	2 (14.3%)	3 (9.4%)
Youth, adolescents	4 (8.7%)	1 (4.2%)	3 (17.6%)	-	1 (3.8%)	2 (10.5%)	2 (14.3%)	2 (6.3%)
Methadone users	1 (2.2%)	-	1 (5.9%)	-	1 (3.8%)	-	1 (7.1%)	-

Research

Twenty-eight of the organizations interviewed are conducting research. The most frequently mentioned type is epidemiological research (68% reported research regarding drug trends, rapid assessment, and first treatment demands). It is likely that the research is based on the organizations' own patients, and that the results probably do not follow the general epidemiological rules.

Table 20: Activities in the area of research

Activities within research	Total N = 46	National level N = 24	Budapest N = 17	Szeged N = 5	GO N = 26	NGO N = 19	Exclusive N = 14	Inclusive N = 32
Epidemiological research	13 (68.4%)	7 (29.2%)	5 (29.4%)	1 (20.0%)	9 (34.6%)	4 (21.1%)	2 (14.3%)	11 (34.4%)
Running database, Information Centres	4 (21.1%)	2 (8.3%)	2 (11.8%)	-	1 (3.8%)	2 (10.5%)	2 (14.3%)	2 (6.3%)
Development of methods, methodology	3 (15.8)	3 (12.5%)	-	-	2 (7.7%)	1 (5.3%)	1 (7.1%)	2 (6.3%)
Conducting evaluation	1 (5.3%)	1 (4.2%)	-	-	-	1 (5.3%)	-	1 (2.2%)
Collecting, publ. statistics	1 (2.2%)	-	1 (5.9%)	-	-	1 (5.3%)	-	1 (3.1%)

Four organizations have information and database centres. In general, organizations conducting research expressed that they carry out only one activity from the above-mentioned range of activities. It is important to note that in this context the term target group is used for the research subject, and not for organizations that might be interested in using information from a research programme. For this reason these data are not comparable with data from the other three countries. Seven organizations conduct research within their own organization. The research subjects are mainly decision-makers, the general population and teachers.

Funding/Fund-raising

Thirty-five per cent of the organizations are involved in funding or fund-raising. Twenty-two per cent of the organizations do fund-raising for sports and cultural events as a form of DDR activity. Eleven per cent are involved in this activity in general (subsidizing projects, distributing funds, providing grants). Providing support for specific projects (publishing handbooks and the development of methodical materials) was mentioned by three of the organizations. Only one organization is in contact with donors for purposes of fund-raising.

Table 21: Activities in the area of funding and fund-raising

Activities within funding and fund-raising	Total N = 46	National level N = 24	Budapest N = 17	Szeged N = 5	GO N = 26	NGO N = 19	Exclusive N = 14	Inclusive N = 32
Fund-raising, organization of sports events...	10 (21.7%)	6 (17.3%)	(17.6%)	1 (20.0%)	6 (23.1%)	3 (15.8%)	3 (21.4%)	7 (21.9%)
Support (general)	5 (10.9%)	4 (16.7%)	1 (5.9%)	-	4 (15.4%)	1 (5.3%)	1 (7.1%)	4 (12.5%)
Support of specific projects	3 (6.5%)	1 (4.2%)	1 (5.9%)	1 (20.0%)	3 (11.5%)	-	1 (7.1%)	2 (6.3%)
Contacts with donors for fund-raising	1 (2.2%)	1 (4.2%)	-	-	-	1 (5.3%)	-	1 (3.1%)

Co-ordination

Table 22: Activities in the area of co-ordination

Activities within co-ordination	Total N = 46	National level N = 24	Budapest N = 17	Szeged N = 5	GO N = 26	NGO N = 19	Exclusive N = 14	Inclusive N = 32
Co-ordination within own organizations	**10 (21.7%)**	4 (16.7%)	5 (29.4%)	1 (20.0%)	5 (19.2%)	24 (21.1%)	2 (14.3%)	8 (25.0%)
Co-ordination of other organizations' activities	**3 (6.5%)**	3 (12.5%)	-	-	2 (7.7%)	1 (5.3%)	1 (7.1%)	2 (6.3%)
Co-ordination at regional and national level	**5 (10.9%)**	4 (16.7%)	1 (5.9%)	-	5 (19.2%)	-	1 (7.1%)	4 (12.5%)

Co-ordination is one of the typical activities of 18 organizations interviewed. In 10 of the organizations this basically means the co-ordination of activities among the different departments/branches of the organization all over the country (e.g. the DADA centre in Budapest.). There are three organizations that co-ordinate other organizations' activities within specific areas (training, prevention, therapy). Five organizations co-ordinate drug demand reduction programmes on national and regional levels. It is a typical activity of governmental organizations. The majority of organizations involved in co-ordination mentioned only one type of activity.

Interest representation/Protection of civil and human rights

The lack of interest representation of drug users in Hungary is clearly reflected in the survey. This activity was mentioned by only five of the interviewed organizations. Four of them provide legal advice and represent interests. Lobbying was not mentioned by any of the organizations. Those involved in interest representation offer their programmes mainly for one target group (80%). Out of these organizations, three offer help with legal problems of drug users.

Policy development and legislation

Fifteen per cent of the organizations stated that one of their main activities in the field of drug demand reduction is policy development and legislation. Organizations at the national level participate in developing strategy, policy or legislation more frequently than do local organizations. This activity is typically performed for the parliament and parliamentary commissions.

Training professionals

Within the field of drug demand reduction programmes, training professionals enjoys particular popularity. It was mentioned by 57%. Training professionals involved in drug demand reduction programmes is the most common activity, followed by training teachers and trainers. Volunteers and students each receive training only in four organizations. Training professionals is a typical activity at the national level, in governmental organizations and in institutions, which focus not only on DDR programmes. It seems that this number does not only refer to professionals from outside the organization, but in most cases these organizations train their own colleagues, or offer training programmes for teachers at schools. Significantly more GOs than NGOs organize training programmes for students.

Table 23: Activities in the area of training professionals

Activities within training professionals	Total N = 46	National level N = 24	Budapest N = 17	Szeged N = 5	GO N = 26	NGO N = 19	Exclusive N = 14	Inclusive N = 32
Professionals in DDR programmes	16 (34.8%)	11 (45.8%)	3 (17.6%)	2 (40.0%)	11 (42.3%)	5 (26.3%)	2 (14.3%)	14 (43.8%)
Teachers, trainers	5 (10.9%)	4 (16.7%)	1 (5.9%)	-	2 (7.7%)	2 (10.5%)	21 (14.3%)	3 (9.4%)
Volunteers	4 (8.7%)	2 (8.3%)	2 (11.8%)	-	2 (7.7%)	2 (10.5%)	-	4 (12.5%)
Students	4 (8.7%)	2 (8.3%)	1 (5.9%)	1 (20%)	4 (15.4%)	-	1 (7.1%)	3 (9.4%)
Policemen, judges, customs officers	1 (2.2%)	-	1 (5.9%)	-	1 (3.8%)	-	1 (7.1%)	-
Other	2 (4.3%)	-	2 (11.8%)	-	1 (3.8%)	1 (5.3%)	1 (7.1%)	1 (3.1%)

Training programmes are organized mainly for students and professionals involved in drug demand reduction programmes, followed by programmes for teachers and trainers. Only three organizations offer training programmes for volunteers. Policemen, judges and customs officers are trained by two organizations.

It is interesting to note that training of volunteers was mentioned only by organizations in Budapest, which are NGOs and do training programmes inclusively. It turned out that students are significantly more important as a target group for governmental institutions than they are for NGOs. Organizations with inclusive DDR programmes train professionals in DDR.

Table 24: Target groups in the area of training

Target groups within training	Total N = 46	National level N = 24	Budapest N = 17	Szeged N = 5	GO N = 26	NGO N = 19	Exclusive N = 14	Inclusive N = 32
Professionals in DDR	9 (19.6%)	5 (20.8%)	2 (11.8%)	2 (40.0%)	6 (23.1%)	3 (15.8%)	-	9 (28.1%)
Students	8 (17.4%)	5 (20.8%)	2 (11.8%)	1 (20.0%)	7 (26.9%)	1 (5.3%)	2 (14.3%)	6 (18.8%)
Teachers, trainers	6 (13.0%)	5 (20.8%)	1 (5.9%)	-	2 (7.7%)	3 (15.8%)	3 (21.4%)	3 (9.4%)
Volunteers	3 (6.5%)	-	3 (17.6%)	-	-	3 (15.8%)	-	3 (9.4%)
Policemen, judges	2 (4.3%)	1 (4.2%)	1 (5.9%)	-	2 (7.7%)	-	1 (7.1%)	1 (3.1%)

3.4 *The main activity in the field of DDR*

Organizations were asked to identify their main activity. For 37% of the organizations this is prevention. The majority of these organizations indicated prevention in general. Development of training programmes was mentioned by two organizations and counselling by one institution, all of them exclusively involved in DDR programmes.

Five organizations identified treatment and care as their main activity. These are predominantly local organizations (Budapest) rather than organizations with a nationwide operating area. Detoxification was indicated by three governmental institutions. Significantly more institutions involved in DDR programmes inclusively mentioned treatment and care activity.

Offering training programmes is the most important activity of four organizations, including two with training programmes for teachers and trainers.

Rehabilitation and after-care was mentioned by four organizations, with two of them meaning rehabilitation in general. The other two reported assistance in social re-adaptation. Only three organizations stated that research in the field of drug demand reduction was their main activity. Within this activity, running databases and information centres was reported most frequently, typically by NGOs.

Table 25: Main activity of organizations

Most important activities	Total N = 35	National level N = 21	Budapest N = 13	GO N = 22	NGO N = 13	Exclusive N = 9	Inclusive N = 26
Prevention	**13 (37.2%)**	**8 (38.1%)**	**5 (38.5%)**	**7 (31.8%)**	**6 (46.2%)**	**5 (55.5%)**	**8 (30.8%)**
Prevention in general	10 (28.6%)	7 (33.3%)	3 (23.1%)	6 (27.3%)	4 (30.8%)	2 (22.2%)	8 (30.8%)
Development of training programmes	2 (5.7%)	1 (4.8%)	1 (7.7%)	1 (4.5%)	1 (7.7%)	2 (22.2%)	-
Counselling	1 (2.9%)	-	1 (7.7%)	-	1 (7.7%)	1 (11.1%)	-
Treatment and care	**5 (14.4%)**	**1 (4.8%)**	**4 (31.8%)**	**4 (18.1%)**	**1 (7.7%)**	**-**	**5 (19.1%)**
Detoxification	3 (8.6%)	1 (4.8%)	2 (15.4%)	3 (13.6%)	-	-	3 (11.5%)
Treatment and care in general	1 (2.9%)	-	1 (7.7%)	1 (4.5%)	-	-	1 (3.8%)
Family therapy	1 (2.9%)	-	1 (7.7%)	-	1 (7.7%)	-	1 (3.8%)
Training professionals	**4 (11.5%)**	**3 (14.3%)**	**1 (7.7%)**	**3 (13.5%)**	**1 (7.7%)**	**-**	**4 (15.3%)**
Training in general	1 (2.9%)	-	1 (7.7%)	1 (4.5%)	-	-	1 (3.8%)
Training teachers, trainers	2 (5.7%)	2 (9.5%)	-	1 (4.5%)	1 (7.7%)	-	2 (7.7%)
Training prof. in DDR programmes	1 (2.9%)	1 (4.8%)	-	1 (4.5%)	-	-	1 (3.8%)
Rehabilitation and after-care	**4 (11.5%)**	**2 (9.6%)**	**1 (7.7%)**	**3 (13.6%)**	**1 (7.7%)**	**2 (22.2%)**	**2 (7.6%)**
Rehabilitation in general	2 (5.7%)	1 (4.8%)	1 (7.7%)	2 (9.1%)	-	1 (11.1%)	1 (3.8%)
Assistance in social re-adaptation	2 (5.7%)	1 (4.8%)	-	1 (4.5%)	1 (7.7%)	1 (11.1%)	1 (3.8%)
Co-ordination in general	**3 (8.6%)**	**3 (14.3%)**	**-**	**2 (9.1%)**	**1 (7.7%)**	**-**	**3 (11.5%)**
Research	**2 (5.8%)**	**1 (4.8%)**	**1 (7.7%)**	**1 (4.5%)**	**2 (15.4%)**	**1 (3.8%)**	**1 (3.8%)**
Epidemiological research	1 (2.9%)	-	1 (7.7%)	1 (4.5%)	-	-	1 (3.8%)
Running database and info centres	2 (5.7%)	1 (4.8%)	1 (7.7%)	-	2 (15.4%)	1 (11.1%)	1 (3.8%)
Funding and fund-raising	**2 (5.8%)**	**1 (4.8%)**	**1 (7.7%)**	**2 (9.1%)**	**-**	**1 (11.1%)**	**1 (3.8%)**
Support general	1 (2.9%)	-	1 (7.7%)	1 (4.5%)	-	1 (11.1%)	-
Fund-raising, organization of sports, cultural events	1 (2.9%)	1 (4.8%)	-	1 (4.5%)	-	-	1 (3.8%)
Devel. of strategy policy, legislation	**2 (5.8%)**	**2 (9.5%)**	**-**	**1 (4.5%)**	**1 (7.7%)**	**-**	**2 (7.7%)**

3.5 *Activities organizations would like to strengthen*

Table 26: Activities organizations would like to strengthen

To strengthen	Total N = 39	National level N = 21	Budapest N = 13	Szeged N = 5	GO N = 25	NGO N = 13	Exclusive N = 11	Inclusive N = 28
Prevention	**14 (35.9%)**	**7 (33.3%)**	**6 (46.2%)**	**1 (20.0%)**	**8 (32.0%)**	**5 (38.5%)**	**6 (54.6%)**	**8 (28.6%)**
Prevention in general	3 (7.7%)	2 (9.5%)	1 (7.7%)	-	1 (4.0%)	2 (15.4%)	1 (9.1%)	2 (7.1%)
Giving lectures, information	2 (5.1%)	-	2 (15.4%)	-	1 (4.0%)	-	1 (9.1%)	1 (3.6%)
Distribution of brochures	2 (5.1%)	2 (9.5%)	-	-	1 (4.0%)	1 (7.7%)	1 (9.1%)	1 (3.6%)
Development of training programmes	1 (2.6%)	-	1 (7.7%)	-	1 (4.0%)	-	1 (9.1%)	-
Counselling	2 (5.1%)	-	1 (7.7%)	1 (20.0%)	-	2 (15.4%)	1 (9.1%)	1 (3.6%)
Running information points	1 (2.6%)	1 (4.8%)	-	-	1 (4.0%)	-	1 (9.1%)	-
Public information	1 (2.6%)	-	1 (7.7%)	-	1 (4.0%)	-	-	1 (3.6%)
Other	2 (5.1%)	2 (9.5%)	-	-	2 (8.0%)	-	-	1 (3.6%)
Treatment and care	**7 (18.5%)**	**2 (9.6%)**	**2 (15.4%)**	**2 (60.0%)**	**5 (20.0%)**	**2 (15.4%)**	**2 (18.2%)**	**5 (17.9%)**
Treatment and care in general	3 (7.7%)	1 (4.8%)	1 (7.7%)	1 (20.0%)	3 (12.0%)	-	1 (9.1%)	2 (7.2%)
Detoxification	2 (5.1%)	-	-	1 (40.0%)	2 (8.0%)	-	-	2 (7.2%)
After-care, employ. support	1 (2.6%)	1 (4.8%)	-	-	-	1 (7.7%)	-	1 (3.6%)
Needle exchange, condom distribution	1 (2.6%)	-	1 (7.7%)	-	-	1 (7.7%)	1 (9.1%)	-
Rehabilitation & after-care	**6 (17.5%)**	**4 (19.1%)**	**2 (15.4%)**	**-**	**4 (16.0%)**	**2 (15.4%)**	**2 (18.2%)**	**4 (14.1%)**
In general	4 (10.3%)	2 (9.5%)	2 (15.4%)	-	3 (12.0%)	1 (7.7%)	1 (9.1%)	3 (10.7%)
Assis. in social readaptation	1 (2.6%)	1 (4.8%)	-	-	-	1 (7.7%)	1 (9.1%)	-
In reintegration with fam.	1 (2.6%)	1 (4.8%)	-	-	1 (4.0%)	-	-	1 (3.6%)
Training professionals	**6 (15.4%)**	**3 (14.3%)**	**3 (23.1%)**	**-**	**3 (12.0%)**	**3 (23.1%)**	**-**	**6 (21.5%)**
In general	5 (12.8%)	2 (9.5%)	-	-	2 (8.0%)	3 (23.1%)	-	5 (17.9%)
Professionals in DDR	1 (2.6%)	1 (4.8%)	-	-	1 (4.0%)	-	-	1 (3.6%)
Co-ordination	**2 (5.2%)**	**2 (9.6%)**	**-**	**-**	**1 (4.0%)**	**1 (7.7%)**	**-**	**2 (7.2%)**
In general	1 (2.6%)	1 (4.8%)	-	-	1 (4.0%)	-	-	1 (3.6%)
Other type of co-ordination	1 (2.6%)	1 (4.8%)	-	-	-	1 (7.7%)	-	1 (3.6%)
Doing epidem. research	**1 (2.6%)**	**1 (4.8%)**	**-**	**-**	**1 (4.0%)**	**-**	**-**	**1 (3.6%)**
Policy devel. in general	**1 (2.6%)**	**1 (4.8%)**	**-**	**-**	**1 (4.0%)**	**-**	**-**	**1 (3.6%)**
Funding, fund-raising in general	**1 (2.6%)**	**-**	**-**	**1 (20.0%)**	**1 (4.0%)**	**-**	**-**	**1 (3.6%)**

Organizations were asked which of their activities they would like to strengthen in the near future. Thirty-nine organizations answered this question: 36% would like to strengthen their *prevention* programmes, whereby among these there were significantly more institutions working exclusively on DDR programmes rather than inclusively. Significantly more organizations operating in Budapest would like to focus more on giving lectures and disseminating information than do national organizations.

Nineteen per cent mentioned *treatment and care* as activities they would like to further develop. It has to be mentioned that organizations, which are active on a local level (especially in Szeged) mentioned that treatment and care must be strengthened in the future. Significant differences with regard to detoxification were observed between organizations in Szeged, and national and Budapest-based organizations.

Six organizations would like to strengthen their training programmes and six the rehabilitation of drug users. Organizations with inclusive DDR activity expressed that they would like to strengthen their training programmes in significantly higher proportions than institutions with exclusive DDR activity.

It was interesting to note that none of the organizations mentioned interest representation of drug users as an activity they would like to strengthen.

3.6 *Activities organizations would like to terminate*

In general organizations did not want to terminate any of their activities in the near future. Twenty-four per cent of the organizations have not answered this question. The activities of distributing brochures and leaflets, treatment and care programmes in general, detoxification and making contact with donors for fund-raising will each be given up by one organization in the near future.

3.7 *Collection of information*

More than half of the organizations interviewed, the majority of them operating on local level, collect information about their clients. Organizations also had to identify their three main sources of information on drug demand reduction issues. Professional literature, special literature, and research conducted by other institutions are the main sources for 65% of the organizations. The informal network of colleagues involved in drug demand reduction programmes also works well. Thirty-five per cent of the organizations are getting information through this channel. Twenty-six per cent are informed directly by their clients. Media and the Internet are the sources for 24% of the organizations. Official statistics are used by 22% of the organizations and 7% of the organizations have other sources.

Table 27: Collection of information

Collection of information	Total N = 46	National level N = 24	Budapest N = 17	Szeged N = 5	GO N = 26	NGO N = 19	Exclusive N = 14	Inclusive N = 32
Professional literature	30 (65.2%)	18 (75.0%)	9 (52.9%)	3 (60.0%)	15 (57.7%)	14 (73.7%)	8 (57.1%)	22 (68.8%)
Informal network	16 (34.8%)	10 (41.7%)	4 (23.5%)	2 (40.0%)	7 (26.9%)	8 (42.1%)	5 (35.7%)	11 (34.4%)
Direct contact	12 (26.1%)	5 (20.8%)	5 (29.4%)	2 (40.0%)	6 (23.1%)	6 (31.6%)	4 (28.6%)	8 (25.0%)
Media, Internet	11 (23.9%)	6 (25.0%)	3 (17.6%)	2 (40.0%)	5 (19.2%)	6 (31.6%)	3 (21.4%)	8 (25.0%)
Official statistics	10 (21.7%)	5 (20.8%)	3 (17.6%)	2 (40.0%)	7 (26.9%)	3 (15.8%)	3 (21.4%)	7 (21.9%)
Other	3 (6.5%)	1 (4.2%)	2 (11.8%)	-	1 (3.8%)	1 (5.3%)	1 (7.1%)	2 (6.3%)

3.8 *Evaluation of the work in organizations*

Table 28: Evaluation of the work in organizations

Evaluation	Total	National level	Budapest	Szeged	GO	NGO	Exclusive	Inclusive
Yes	**25 (54.3%)**	**13 (54.2%)**	**10 (58.8%)**	**2 (40.0%)**	**13 (50.0%)**	**11 (57.9%)**	**8 (57.1%)**	**17 (53.1%)**
Reports	5 (20.0%)	3 (23.1%)	2 (20.0%)	-	1 (7.7%)	4 (36.4%)	4 (50.0%)	1 (5.9%)
Self-evaluation	5 (20.0%)	4 (30.8%)	1 (10.0%)	-	3 (23.1%)	2 (18.2%)	-	5 (29.4%)
Evaluation	5 (20.0%)	3 (23.1%)	1 (10.0%)	1 (50.0%)	1 (7.7%)	4 (36.4%)	-	5 (29.4%)
Profes. supervision, audit	2 (8.0%)	-	2 (20.0%)	-	1 (7.7%)	-	2 (25.0%)	-
Feedback	2 (8.0%)	-	1 (10.0%)	1 (50.0%)	2 (15.4%)		-	2 (11.8%)
Statistics	2 (8.0%)	1 (7.7%)	1 (10.0%)	-	1 (7.7%)	1 (9.1%)	-	1 (5.9%)
Indicators from international organizations	1 (4.0%)	1 (7.7%)	-	-	1 (7.7%)	-	-	1 (5.9%)
Other	3 (12.0%)	1 (7.7%)	2 (20.0%)	-	3 (23.1%)	-	2 (5.9%)	1 (5.9%)

More than half of the organizations interviewed evaluate their activities. Five organizations monitor the quality of professional work by reports (measuring the effectiveness, evaluation of the programme), self-evaluation of each activity, case-study and evaluation (using tests, surveys, analyses). Feedback (from clients, other institutions, mentors), statistics (including statistics on

Table 29: Evaluation of own activity

	Excellent	Good	Adequate	Problematic	Grossly deficient	Difficult to say	Total
As seen by yourself	**7 (15.2%)**	**22 47.8 (%)**	**11 (23.9%)**	**3 (6.5%)**	**2 (4.3%)**	**1 (2.2%)**	**46 (100%)**
National	6 (25.0%)	8 (33.3%)	6 (25.0%)	2 (8.3%)	1 (4.2%)	1 (4.2%)	24 (100%)
Budapest	1 (5.9%)	11 (64.7%)	3 (17.6%)	1 (5.9%)	1 (5.9%)	-	17 (100%)
Szeged	-	3 (60.0%)	2 (40.0%)	-	-	-	5 (100%)
GO	2 (7.7%)	11 (42.3%)	7 (26.9%)	3 (11.5%)	2 (7.7%)	1 (3.8%)	26 (100%)
NGO	5 (26.3%)	10 (52.6%)	4 (21.1%)	-	-	-	19 (100%)
Exclusive	4 (28.6%)	8 (57.1%)	-	2 (14.3%)	-	-	14 (100%)
Inclusive	3 (9.4%)	14 (43.8%)	11 (34.4%)	1 (3.1%)	2 (6.3%)	1 (3.1%)	32 (100%)
By clients	**10 (21.7%)**	**13 (28.3%)**	**8 (17.4%)**	**2 (4.3%)**	**1 (2.2%)**	**12 (21.7%)**	**46 (100%)**
National	6 (25.0%)	5 (20.8%)	4 (16.7%)	1 (4.2%)	1 (4.2%)	7 (29.2%)	24 (100%)
Budapest	4 (23.5%)	7 (41.2%)	2 (11.8%)	-	-	4 (23.5%)	17 (100%)
Szeged	-	1 (20.0%)	2 (40.0%)	1 (20.0%)	-	1 (20.0%)	5 (100%)
GO	3 (11.5%)	8 (30.8%)	7 (26.9%)	2 (7.7%)	1 (3.8%)	5 (19.2%)	26 (100%)
NGO	6 (31.6%)	5 (26.3%)	1 (5.3%)	-	-	7 (36.9%)	19 (100%)
Exclusive	3 (21.4%)	6 (42.9%)	2 (14.3%)	-	-	3 (21.4%)	14 (100%)
Inclusive	7 (21.9%)	7 (21.9%)	6 (18.8%)	2 (6.3%)	1 (3.1%)	9 (28.1%)	32 (100%)
By the public	**5 (10.9%)**	**20 (43.5%)**	**8 (17.4%)**	**4 (8.7%)**	**-**	**9 (19.6%)**	**46 (100%)**
National	5 (20.8%)	9 (37.5%)	5 (20.8%)	2 (8.3%)	-	3 (12.5%)	24 (100%)
Budapest	-	9 (52.9%)	2 (11.8%)	1 (5.9%)	-	5 (29.4%)	17 (100%)
Szeged	-	2 (40.0%)	1 (20.0%)	1 (20.0%)	-	1 (20.0%)	5 (100%)
GO	1 (3.8%)	11 (42.3%)	6 (23.1%)	3 (11.5%)	-	5 (19.2%)	26 (100%)
NGO	4 (21.1%)	8 (42.1%)	2 (10.5%)	1 (5.3%)	-	4 (21.1%)	17 (100%)
Exclusive	3 (21.4%)	6 (42.9%)	1 (7.1%)	1 (7.1%)	-	3 (21.4%)	14 (100%)
Inclusive	2 (6.3%)	14 (43.8%)	7 (21.9%)	3 (9.4%)	-	6 (18.8%)	32 (100%)
By politicians	**2 (4.3%)**	**8 (17.4%)**	**6 (13.0%)**	**3 (6.5%)**	**3 (6.5%)**	**24 (52.3%)**	**46 (100%)**
National	1 (4.2%)	5 (20.8%)	3 (12.5%)	3 (12.5%)	1 (4.2%)	11 (45.8%)	24 (100%)
Budapest	1 (5.9%)	2 (11.8%)	2 (11.8%)	-	2 (11.8%)	10 (58.8%)	17 (100%)
Szeged	-	1 (20.0%)	1 (20.0%)	-	-	3 (60.0%)	5 (100%)
GO	1 (3.8%)	6 (23.1%)	3 (11.5%)	2 (7.7%)	3 (11.5%)	11 (42.3%)	26 (100%)
NGO	1 (5.3%)	2 (10.5%)	3 (15.8%)	1 (5.3%)	-	12 (63.2%)	17 (100%)
Exclusive	2 (14.3%)	-	1 (7.1%)	2 (14.3%)	1 (7.1%)	8 (57.1%)	14 (100%)
Inclusive	-	8 (25.0%)	5 (15.6%)	1 (3.1%)	2 (6.3%)	16 (50.0%)	32 (100%)
By the media	**4 (8.7%)**	**16 (34.8%)**	**8 (17.4%)**	**2 (4.3%)**	**5 (10.9%)**	**11 (23.9%)**	**46 (100%)**
National	1 (4.2%)	9 (37.5%)	6 (25.0%)	2 (8.3%)	3 (12.5%)	3 (12.5%)	24 (100%)
Budapest	3 (17.6%)	6 (35.3%)	1 (5.9%)	-	2 (11.8%)	5 (29.4%)	17 (100%)
Szeged	-	1 (20.0%)	1 (20.0%)	-	-	3 (60.0%)	5 (100%)
GO	-	7 (26.9%)	6 (23.1%)	2 (7.7%)	4 (15.4%)	7 (26.9%)	26 (100%)
NGO	4 (21.1%)	8 (42.1%)	2 (10.5%)	-	1 (5.3%)	4 (21.1%)	17 (100%)
Exclusive	2 (14.3%)	4 (28.6%)	-	1 (7.1%)	2 (14.3%)	5 (35.7%)	14 (100%)
Inclusive	2 (6.3%)	12 (37.5%)	8 (25.0%)	1 (3.1%)	3 (9.4%)	6 (18.8%)	32 (100%)

attendance, drop-outs, work reports, and statistical information from the local level), professional supervision, and audit were each mentioned as evaluation methods by two of the organizations. Three organizations use other methods.

Reports are used by NGOs and organizations offering only DDR activities in a relatively high proportion. Feedback is the typical means of evaluation in the case of local institutions.

3.9 *Evaluation of activities by the organization*

The experts interviewed were asked to evaluate the activities of their own organization, by describing how others view the overall performance of the organization. This includes the opinion of clients, the general public, politicians and the media (see Table 29).

Twenty-nine of the experts interviewed in 46 organizations thought that their organizations' performance was on an excellent or good level. Twenty-three experts believed that their clients and the general public have a very good opinion about the work of the organization. More than half of the organizations did not know how politicians viewed the organization. Twenty respondents thought that the media have a high opinion of their organizations' performance.

4 Perceptions of the overall drug problem and policies by drug demand reduction organizations

4.1 *Organizations' perception of the overall problem*

Many of the experts interviewed were reluctant to estimate the present and future number of drug users. Twenty-six experts gave an estimate for 1998, and 23 of them for 2003. Many of them pointed out that the available data was unreliable.

The numbers estimated ranged from 20,000 to 1,000,000 for 1998, and from 25,000 to 2,000,000 for 2003. The experts at the University of Medical Sciences in Szeged and at the Nyírö Gyula Hospital in Budapest gave the highest estimates.

Table 30: The number of organizations who estimated the number of drug users within three categories in 1998 and 2003

The estimated number of drug users	**1998**	**2003**
20,000-100,000	7	4
150,000-500,000	16	12
more than 500,000	3	7
Total number of organizations giving estimation	26	23

Table 31: The average estimated number of drug users in 1998 and 2003

	1998			**2003**		
	N	**Mean**	**St.deviation**	**N**	**Mean**	**St.deviation**
			Status of the organization			
Governmental	20	264,250	227,198	17	568,235	594,910
Non-profit, voluntary	9	287,222	249,062	7	328,571	167,971
Private	2	110,000	127,279	1	100,000	-
No legal status	1	1,000,000	-	1	2,000,000	-
			Level of the organization			
National	18	288,889	267,441	14	450,714	521,487
Budapest	11	303,636	283,135	9	555,555	571,972
Szeged	3	183,333	104,083	3	916,667	946,484
			Focus of the organization			
DDR exclusive	10	375,000	248,607	9	711,111	531,964
DDR inclusive	22	242,727	257,994	17	450,588	603,134
Total	32	284,062	258,676	26	540,769	582,533

The majority of experts predicted around 300,000 drug users for 1998, which was published in the media (how this figure was calculated is, however, not known). The wide range of estimates shows that there is rather high uncertainty about the spread of drug consumption. In general most of the experts interviewed predicted an increase of consumption over the next five years. The national institutions and those in Szeged expected the strongest increase. The non-profit, voluntary organizations expected the smallest increase. Estimates of organizations with exclusive DDR programmes were significantly higher than those of other organizations. Answers to the questions about the structure of consumption are even more vague.

Table 32: The estimated average rate of types of drug in 1998 and 2003

Drug groups	**1998**	**2003**
Opiates	25.0	27.0
(number of respondents)	36	25
Cocaine	5.6	6.6
(number of respondents)	28	19
Cannabis	32.5	31.1
(number of respondents)	33	23
Hallucinogens	12.3	13.4
(number of respondents)	28	20
Amphetamines	31.0	27.3
(number of respondents)	36	23
Other drugs	10.0	9.5
(number of respondents)	19	12

The number of responding experts was low and the answers varied according to the type of drugs. Even fewer respondents were able to give estimates for 2003, which is mainly due to the scarcity of reliable data about the spread of drug consumption in Hungary.

Surveys described in the introduction mention cannabis as the dominant drug in Hungary, whereas according to the experts interviewed, the dominant drugs in Hungary also include opiates and amphetamines. It is likely that their answers were influenced by the fact that they are involved in care and treatment programmes for opiate and amphetamine users. It cannot be concluded that respondents predict a significant change in the consumption structure.

4.2 *Attitudes of organizations*

Of all the statements listed in the questionnaire, those about the occasional usefulness of the consumption of illicit drugs, and about the free drug use of adults provoked the highest rate of disagreement. Thirty-seven respondents strongly disagreed that taking illegal drugs can be beneficial, while four people agreed with it. The average scale value of this statement is 4.5. Thirty experts would not legalize smoking cannabis, while eight respondents agree to it. Twenty-seven respondents agreed with the statement "all use of illegal drugs is misuse", while 10 people disagreed.

More polarized answers were characteristic for other statements. For instance, 25 people absolutely disagreed that the consumption of illicit drugs is normal for certain people, whereas 10 people agreed. Eight respondents absolutely agreed that cannabis should be legalized, whereas 30 people absolutely disagreed. Seventeen experts totally disagree, and 12 experts totally agree with the following statement: "the best way to treat people who are addicted to drugs is to stop them using drugs altogether". Twenty-six people do not agree with the statement that says: "the use of illicit drugs always leads to addiction", but 11 totally agree with it. Twenty-one people disapproved of the statement: "Taking illegal drugs is morally wrong" whereas 14 people agreed with this statement.

Table 33: Average score on scale of attitudes about drug problems by level, status and main mission of organizations (scale value: agree=1, disagree=5)

Statement	Total	National	Budapest	Szeged	GO	NGO	DDR exclusive	DDR inclusive
Taking illegal drugs can be beneficial	4.5	4.3	4.5	5.0	4.6	4.6	4.4	4.5
Standard deviation	*1.2*	*1.3*	*1.3*	*0.0*	*1.1*	*1.1*	*1.5*	*1.1*
Freedom in taking drugs	4.3	4.5	3.8	5.0	4.5	4.0	4.0	4.4
Standard deviation	*1.4*	*1.2*	*1.7*	*0.0*	*1.2*	*1.6*	*1.6*	*1.3*
Using illegal drugs is normal	3.8	3.3	4.0	4.8	3.7	3.7	3.7	3.8
Standard deviation	*1.8*	*1.8*	*1.6*	*0.4*	*1.5*	*1.5*	*1.8*	*1.6*
Cannabis should be legalized	3.7	3.7	3.3	5.0	4.1	3.3	2.8	4.1
Standard deviation	*2.4*	*2.9*	*1.8*	*0.0*	*1.5*	*3.3*	*3.5*	*1.5*
Stop using drugs is the best way of treatment	3.3	3.4	2.9	3.6	3.1	3.4	3.4	3.2
Standard deviation	*1.6*	*1.5*	*1.9*	*1.5*	*1.5*	*1.7*	*1.8*	*1.6*
Use of drugs leads to addiction	3.7	3.8	3.5	3.6	4.1	3.4	3.5	3.7
Standard deviation	*1.7*	*1.7*	*1.9*	*1.7*	*1.5*	*1.8*	*1.9*	*1.7*
Taking illegal drug is morally wrong	3.3	3.6	2.8	3.8	3.5	3.1	3.5	3.3
Standard deviation	*1.8*	*1.7*	*1.8*	*1.8*	*1.7*	*1.9*	*1.9*	*1.9*
Use of drugs is misuse	2.3	2.2	2.3	2.4	2.3	2.0	2.6	2.1
Standard deviation	*1.7*	*1.7*	*1.8*	*1.9*	*1.7*	*1.5*	*1.9*	*1.6*

Attitudes of members of non-profit and voluntary organizations are in some cases contradictory. They are more likely to agree that marijuana should be legalized. At the same time, they more strongly agree that the use of drugs leads to addiction, illicit drug consumption is abuse, or that illicit drug consumption is something to disapprove of. The institutions involved exclusively in DDR programmes have a more liberal attitude towards drug consumption than do DDR-inclusive institutions.

4.3 *Characterization of the national drug policy*

Answers to questions about the national drug policy were strongly influenced by the fact that the interviews (conducted at the end of 1998 and beginning of 1999) coincided with the debate on stricter drug laws.

Table 34: The proportion of those who agree or do not agree with the listed characteristics of the national drug policy (in percentages)

	Rather no or definitely no	Equal	Rather yes or definitely yes	Difficult to say	Total (N)
			Health promotion		
Status of the organization					
Governmental	34.6	33.5	26.9	-	100.0 (26)
Private	66.7	33.3	-	-	100.0 (3)
Non-profit, voluntary	43.8	13.8	31.3	6.3	100.0 (16)
Chi-squares: 7.3					
Focus of the organization					
Exclusive	46.2	23.1	23.1	7.7	100.0 (13)
Inclusive	37.5	34.4	18.2	-	100.0 (32)
Chi-squares: 4.9					
Level of operation					
National	45.9	29.2	20.9	4.2	100.0 (24)
Budapest	37.6	31.3	31.3	-	100.0 (16)
Szeged	20.0	40.0	40.0	-	100.0 (5)
Chi-squares: 5.3					
Total	**40.0**	**31.1**	**26.7**	**2.2**	**100.0 (45)**
			Harm reduction		
Status of the organization					
Governmental	57.7	34.6	7.7	-	100.0 (26)
Private	66.7	-	-	33.3	100.0 (3)
Non-profit, voluntary	62.5	12.5	18.8	6.3	100.0 (16)
No legal status	100.0	-	-	-	100.0 (1)
Chi-squares: 18.7					
Focus of the organization					
Exclusive	71.5	21.4	-	7.1	100.0 (14)
Inclusive	56.2	25.0	15.6	3.1	100.0 (32)
Chi-squares: 3.3					

	Rather no or definitely no	Equal	Rather yes or definitely yes	Difficult to say	Total (N)
Level of operation					
National	50.0	29.2	16.7	4.2	100.0 (24)
Budapest	70.6	23.5	-	5.9	100.0 (15
Szeged	80.0	-	20.0	-	100.0 (5)
Chi-squares: 8.3					
Total	**60.9**	**23.9**	**10.9**	**4.3**	**100.0 (46)**
			Demand reduction		
Status of the organization					
Governmental	42.3	23.9	30.8	-	100.0 (26)
Private	33.3	33.3	33.3	-	100.0 (3)
Non-profit, voluntary	37.6	37.5	18.8	6.3	100.0 (16)
No legal status	-	-	-	100.0	100.0 (1)
Chi-squares: 28.0					
Focus of the organization					
Exclusive	42.9	28.6	14.2	14.3	100.0 (14)
Inclusive	37.5	31.3	31.3	-	100.0 (32)
Chi-squares: 5.9					
Level of operation					
National	37.5	37.5	20.8	4.2	100.0 (24)
Budapest	52.9	17.6	23.5	5.9	100.0 (17)
Szeged	-	40.0	60.0	-	100.0 (5)
Chi-squares: 9.5					
Total	**39.1**	**30.4**	**26.1**	**4.3**	**100.0 (46)**
			Control of supply		
Status of the organization					
Governmental	34.6	11.5	50.0	3.8	100.0 (26)
Private	-	33.3	66.7	-	100.0 (3)
Non-profit, voluntary	18.8	18.8	50.1	12.5	100.0 (16)
No legal status	-	-	100.0	-	100.0 (1)
Chi-squares: 8.4					
Focus of the organization					
Exclusive	21.4	14.3	57.1	7.1	100.0 (14)
Inclusive	28.1	15.6	50.0	6.3	100.0 (32)
Chi-squares: 3.6					
Level of operation					
National	20.8	20.8	50.0	8.3	100.0 (24)
Budapest	35.3	5.9	53.0	5.8	100.0 (15)
Szeged	20.0	20.0	60.0	-	100.0 (5)
Chi-squares: 5.2					
Total	**26.1**	**15.2**	**52.2**	**6.5**	**100.0 (46)**

	Law enforcement and control of drug users				
Status of the organization					
Governmental	19.2	15.4	61.6	3.8	100.0 (26)
Private	33.3	33.3	33.3	-	100.0 (3)
Non-profit, voluntary	12.5	13.8	50.1	18.8	100.0 (16)
No legal status	-	-	100.0	-	100.0 (1)
Chi-squares: 14.2					
Focus of the organization					
Exclusive	21.4	21.4	50.0	7.1	100.0 (14)
Inclusive	15.7	15.6	59.4	9.4	100.0 (32)
Chi-squares: 1.2					
Level of operation					
National	12.5	16.7	62.5	8.3	100.0 (24)
Budapest	29.4	17.6	47.0	5.9	100.0 (17)
Szeged	-	20.0	60.0	20.0	100.0 (5)
Chi-squares: 5.3					
Total	**17.4**	**17.4**	**56.5**	**8.7**	**100.0 (46)**

More than half of the organizations interviewed think that law enforcement and control of consumption are the most prominent features of the Hungarian drug policy. Sixty-one per cent of the respondents expressed their view that harm reduction is not characteristic of the national drug policy at all. Twenty-six per cent of the respondents mentioned demand reduction, and 27% health protection as part of the national drug policy.

The majority of the respondents thought that the main characteristics of the Hungarian drug policy are supply reduction, law enforcement, and the control of consumption. In their view less emphasis is put on demand reduction, harm reduction, and health protection. Non-profit organizations have contradictory opinions about health promotion as a part of the drug policy. The rate of explicit "yes" and "no" answers is higher among them. The judgement of the GOs and the inclusive organizations is more balanced, there are fewer determined "yes" and "no" answers among them.

None of the organizations working exclusively in DDR programmes perceived harm reduction as characteristic of the Hungarian drug policy. Similarly leaders of GOs didn't see harm reduction as part of the drug policy. On the other hand, most leaders of non-profit organizations thought that harm reduction was part of the Hungarian drug policy. According to GOs and inclusive organizations legal regulation is characteristic of the Hungarian drug policy, while exclusive organizations think that the control of supply is its most salient feature.

Table 35: The table summarizes the strengths of the national drug policy in the opinion of the respondents

Main strengths	Number of responses	Per cent of organizations
Awareness of the drug problem, public discussion, better understanding of the problem	13	28.3
Efficient network of organizations, effective co-operation	1	2.2
Competent, expert-based and professional	3	6.5
Prevention programmes, preventive programmes at schools, new subjects of drug prevention	6	13.0
Therapy programmes	4	8.7
Harm reduction programmes	-	-
Effective policy, conception, legislation	1	2.2
Supply control, law enforcement	5	10.9
Other	4	8.7
No strengths at all	16	34.8

Sixteen of the 46 organizations interviewed didn't see any strengths of the national drug policy because in their view a policy did not exist. Eight of the organizations interviewed mentioned at least two strong features, and only three organizations thought that the policy was strong in three or more areas. According to most experts, the main strength of the actual policy was *awareness* of the problem: "Finally the drug problem is dealt with."

Table 36: The table summarizes the weaknesses of the national drug policy in the opinion of the respondents

Main strengths	Number of responses	Per cent of organizations
Lack of awareness of the drug problem	4	8.7
Lack of professionals, experts	2	4.3
Ineffective programmes	5	10.9
Focus on law enforcement, repressive approach	4	8.7
Lack of policy, there is no drug policy	16	34.8
Lack of co-ordination and communication	16	34.8
Lack of research, information	2	4.3
Insufficient funding, financial problems	8	17.4
Lack of evaluation, lack of control and monitoring programmes	2	4.3
Barriers in development of non-governmental institutions	-	-
Other	8	17.4
No answer	5	10.9

As mentioned above, 16 experts thought that Hungary lacked a drug policy, and that it didn't exist at all. Five respondents did not mention any weakness at all. Fifteen respondents saw at least two weak areas, and nine people came up with at least three weaknesses. Most of them mentioned the lack of co-ordination and communication, and insufficient funding of programmes. Some also felt that advice from professionals was disregarded.

5 Conclusion

Since the mid-1980s there has been increased awareness of drug-related problems in Hungary although drug consumption stayed at a very low level until the mid-1990s. Drawing on available data it is assumed that a significant increase of illicit drug use took place in the second half of the 1990s. However, the results of a survey conducted among secondary school students show that in spite of the increase, illicit drug consumption is still low compared with international data. Despite the relatively low level, drug consumption is viewed as a serious social problem by politicians and the public. This is reflected in public opinion polls, attitude research, and, to some extent, changes in the law. At the beginning of the 1990s there was a considerable increase of DDR programmes and the number of NGOs in this area rose at the same time. While in the 1980s only GOs operated in the field of drug demand reduction, at the time of the survey more than half of the DDR programmes were run by NGOs. It continues to be the responsibility of the state and local governments to provide sufficient funds for these programmes. International financing played a marginal role at the time of the survey. The Soros Fund was a major supporter of institutions involved in drug demand reduction.

Activities of DDR institutions concentrate on prevention, information and counselling. More than half of the institutions participating in the survey, most of the GOs, were involved in treatment and rehabilitation programmes. However, rehabilitation plays a smaller role, which reflects the Hungarian health care system.

It proved difficult to evaluate institutions' opinion of the current drug policy. The time of data collection coincided with the approval of a new drug law by the parliament. The law provoked strong opposition from the organizations interviewed and attitudes towards drug law and drug policy were very critical. However, since the time of data collection, the National Drug

Strategy, with a strong focus on drug demand reduction, has been completed, and we believe that it is founded on wide professional consensus. We believe that, following the completion of the strategy, organizations' opinions about drug policy and institutions' attitudes changed significantly since the survey was carried out. When this paper was finalized it was not clear how the National Drug Strategy, passed by parliament in autumn 2000, would affect national DDR programmes and institutions, and what implications it would have for drug policies in general.

References

Droginfo 1998. *Drogproblémákat felvállaló intézmények, társadalmi szervezetek, csoportok információs tára.* Sziget Droginformációs Alapítvány 1998.

Drogproblémák kezelésével foglalkozó intézmények (1997) Drogproblémák kezelésével foglalkozó Budapesti intézmények helyzetének és nyújtott szolgáltatásainak felmérése. Budapesti Szociális Forrásközpont.

Elekes, Zs./Paksi, B. (1994) Adalékok a magyarországi drogfogyasztás alakulásához (Additions to the Formation of the Hungarian Drug Consumption), pp. 308-322 in Münnich, I./Moksony, F. (Eds.), *Devianciák Magyarországon* (Deviance in Hungary). Budapest: Közélet.

Elekes, Zs./Paksi, B. (1996) *A magyarországi középiskolások alkohol és drogfogyasztása* (The Alcohol and Drug Consumption of Hungarian Secondary School Students) *ESPAD Hungarian Country report.* Budapest: Népjóléti Mminisztérium.

Elekes, Zs./Paksi, B. (2000) *Drogok és fiatalok. Középiskolások droghasználata, dohányzása, és alkoholfogyasztása az évezred végén.* Ifjúsági és Sportminisztérium.

"Élö Dokumentum" (1997) "Élö Dokumentum" *Magyarországi kezelöhelyek a kábítószerfogyasztók részére.* Phare Multi-country programme Droginformációs rendszerek projekt.

Frech, Á. (1989) *A kábitószerek és a kábitóhatású anyagok visszaélésével kapcsolatos jogi szabályozás* (The Legal Regulation of Drug and Drug Dealing Related Crimes). Unpublished manuscript, Budapest.

ISMertetö (1999) *Jelentés a magyarországi kábítószer-helyzetröl.* Iifjúsági és Sportminisztérium. Kábítószerügyi koordinációért felelös helyettes államtitkárság.

ISMertetö (2000) *Jelentés a magyarországi kábítószer-helyzetröl.* Ifjúsági és Sportminisztérium. Kábítószerügyi koordinációért felelös helyettes államtitkárság.

Kó, J. (1998) Vélemények a bünözésröl. *Kriminológiai és kriminálstatisztikai tanulmányok.* OKKrI.

Nagy, L.G. (1985) 'Aggodalmak és várakozások' (Worries and Expectations), *Alkohológia* 4: 68-75.

National Report of Hungary 1992. Regional Phare Programme on Drugs. Drug Demand Reduction. Barcelona 12-15 July 1994.

Nemzeti Stratégia a Kábítószer-probléma Visszaszorításáért. *A kormány kábítószer-ellenes stratégiájának koncepcionális alapjai.* Ifjúsági és Sportminisztérium 2000.

Paksi B. (1998) 'Szenvedélybetegségek:dohányzás, alkohol- és drogfogyasztás', in: *Empirikus felmérés a népesség egészségi állapotának meghatározottságáról.* Budapest: Zárójelentés TÁRKI.

Rácz, J (1990) 'A drogfogyasztás sémájának társadalmi konstrukciója Magyarországon', *Alkohológia* 1: 28-35.

List of Organizations Interviewed

Oktatási Minisztérium	Ministry of Education
Ifjúsági és Sportminisztérium	Ministry of Youth and Sport
Honvédelmi Minisztérium	Ministry of Defence
Büntetés-végrehajtás Országos Parancsnoksága	National Headquarters of Penalty Execution*
Petöfi Radio – Drogéria	Radio Petöfi, Drug Store
Országos Pszhiátriái és Neurológiai Intézet Additológiai Osztály	National Institute of Psychiatry and Neurology, Dept. of Addictology*
Központi Honvéd Kórház Mentálhigiénés osztály	Central Military Hospital – Mentalhygiene Department*
Országos Alkohológiai és Addiktológiai Intézet	National Institute of Alcohology and Addictology*
HIETE Egészségügyi Föiskola Addiktológiai Tanszék	HIETE College of Public Health, Dept. Of Addictology*
Országos Tisztiorvosi Hivatal	National Medical and Public Health Office
Droprevenciós Alapítvány	Drug Prevention Foundation
Magyar Karitasz	Caritas Hungarica
CHEF-HUNGARY Általános Egészségnevelési és Oktatási Alapítvány	Comprehensive Health Education Foundation Hungary
Felnöni Erösen Szabadon Közalapitvány	Growing up Strong and Free Foundation
Egészségvirág Egyesület	Flourishing Health
ORFK Bünügyi Föigazgatóság – Bünügyi Föosztály (DADA)	National Police Headquarters – Crime Prevention Department (DADA)
UNICRI-MKM Integrált Prevenciós Project	UNICRI-Ministry of Culture and Education Prevention Project
Budapesti Szociális Forrásközpont	Regional Research Centre of Budapest
Józan Élet Egészség és Családvédö Szövetség	"Sober Life", National Association for Health and Family Protection
Sziget Droginformációs Alapítvány	Island Drug Information Fund
Mentálhigiénés Programiroda	Office for Mentalhygienic Projects
Társaság a szabadságjogokért	Hungarian Civil Liberties Union
Soros Alapítvány	Soros Foundation
Heim Pál Gyermekkórház Mentálhigéniai szakrendelés	Heim Pál Hospital, Ambulance Mentalhygiene for Children
Erzsébet Kórház Krízisintervenciós Osztály	Erzsébet Hospital, Department of Crisis Intervention*
Szent Imre Kórház Pszichiátriai Rehabilitációs Osztály	Szent Imre Hospital, Department of Psychiatry and Rehabilitation*

Szent Imre Kórház Drogambulancia	Szent Imre Hospital, Drug Outpatient Centre*
Emberbarát Alapitvány	Philantropic Foundation
Szenvedélybetegsegítö szolgálat	Assistance Service for Addicts*
Fövárosi ÁNTSZ Mentálhigéniás Csoport	Budapest Medical and Public Health Office, Dept. of Mentalhygieny Medicaland*
Narconon Alapítvány	Narconon Hungary Foundation
BRFK Megelözési Osztály Drogmegelözési Szolgálat (DADA)	Budapest Police Headquarters – Department of Drug Prevention (DADA)*
Kapocs	Self-Help Service
Kék Pont Drogkonzultációs Központ	Blue Point Drug Consultation Centre
Fövárosi Önkormányzat – Drogpolitikai Iroda	Drug Policy Office of Budapest Community*
Nyírö Gyula Kórház Addiktológiai Osztály	Nyírö Gyula Hospital – Dept. of Addictology*
Nyírö Gyula Kórház Jász u.-i Drogambulanciája	Nyírö Gyula Hospital Drug Outpatient Centre of Jász utca*
Dr. Farkasimszky Terézia Ifjúsági Drogcentrum	Dr Farkasinszky Terézia Drugs Centre for the Youth*
SZITI Kulturális és Mentálhigiénés Egyesület	SZITI Association of Culture and Mentalhygiene*
Szent Györgyi Albert Orvostudományi Egyetem Pszichiátriai Tanszék	Szent-Györgyi Albert Medical University, Dept. of Psychiatry
Drog-Stop Budapest Egyesület	Drug-Stop Budapest Association*
Budapesti Közgazdaságtudmányi és Államigazgatási Egyetem Viselkedés Kutató Központ	Budapest University of Economics, Behaviour Research Centre
Drogtájékoztató Központ	Drug Information Centre
Szeged Városi Kórház, Pszichiátriai és Addiktológiai Osztály	Municipal Hospital Szeged, Psychiatry & Addictology Ward
Református Egyház Kallódó Ifjúságot Mentö Misszió	The Hungarian Reformed Protestant Church's Mission to Rescue Troubled Youth
Polgármesteri Hivatal Szeged, Szociális, Családvédelmi és Egészségvédelmi iroda	Family and Health Protection Office of Szeged Community*

Note: * Not an official translation.

CHAPTER 4

Institutional Responses to Drug Problems in Poland
On the Crossroads

Robert Sobiech and Joanna Zamecka

1 Policy conditions: The institutional, social and epidemiological context

1.1 Introduction

The use of illicit drugs in Poland occurred throughout the entire period of the 20th century. The first systematic collection of information revealing the problem was published in the early 1920s. The recognition of the drug problem led to the development of counteracting measures such as the regulation of the drug supply, the creation of special wards for drug addicts and the formation of the first advisory institution. After World War II, drug abuse was defined almost exclusively as a medical problem and most efforts were focused on the treatment of drug addicts. In the mid-1970s, the drug abuse problem ceased to be an area solely of medical interest and became a public issue that attracted the attention of other professions (mainly representatives of law enforcement agencies) and the government itself. However, due to the tight political control of the Communist government, the problem continued to spread without any wide public awareness and was often treated as a propaganda instrument used to strengthen the ideological consensus (Sobiech, 1991).

The real discovery of the drug problem took place in the 1980s when many other social problems also appeared on the public agenda. It turned out that the phenomenon of drug abuse not only existed in Poland, but was also rising very fast in other countries and becoming increasingly popular among the youngest generations. From the very beginning, the perception of the problem and the policies proposed emphasized the medical and social aspects. Medical doctors, psychologists and psychiatrists played an important role in shaping the first definition of the problem as well as in influencing the first legislative attempts at regulation. After the introduction of martial law in 1981, the drug problem became part of the official government agenda, orchestrating "the law and order" campaign. Despite the Communist government's attempt to control the problem through repressive measures, a predominant approach was to identify the drug problem in terms of illness and psychological disorder.

The problem's discovery in the early 1980s was associated with the establishment of special therapy centres for drug addicts, the rise of the first voluntary and professional associations, the first large-scale research projects, an increase in media coverage, and books and brochures published. Public debates on the problem concentrated on such issues as: illegal cultivation of opium poppy, models of therapy (including the need for decriminalization) and the lack of public awareness. With the passage of time, a growing emphasis was put on the connection between drug addiction and organized crime. The drug problem was also utilized in political agendas, which stressed the role of repressive measures in policy planning and implementation. Therefore, in the late 1990s one of the leading topics of public discussion was to offer a justification for repressive policies. The penalization of the possession of drugs became a central issue.

1.2 Legislation

The discovery of the problems at the beginning of the 1980s led to the preparation of "the Act on the Prevention of Drug Dependence". The Act was passed by the Polish parliament on 31 January 1985. The drug problem was defined in medical terms and particular emphasis was placed on prevention and treatment. The Act created a basis for policy development describing the competencies of the state administration as well as the responsibilities of non-governmental organizations. The Ministry of Education, for example, was responsible for the development and delivery of health promotion programmes, while the Ministry of Health was responsible for the treatment, rehabilitation and social reintegration of drug users. The Ministry of Justice (in consultation with the Ministry of Health) was responsible for assistance to detained drug users. According to the law, the activities of the relevant ministries were co-ordinated within the Governmental Programme on the Prevention of Drug Dependency. Each year the Programme was to be developed by the Commission on Drug Prevention and to be accepted by the Council of Ministers.

In the mid-1990s, existing legislation became the subject of criticism from different interest groups, several professionals and politicians. It was claimed that due to the changed conditions of the drug problem and the implementation of the administrative reform, there was a need for an amendment of the 1985 regulations. Lobbying for new legislation was accompanied by a shift in the manifestation of the punitive approach adopted by right-wing parties. The above-mentioned factors resulted in the adoption of the Act on Counteracting Drug Addiction in 1997.

Despite the arguments put forward by advocates of a drug control approach, the new Act put the emphasis on drug demand policies, stressing the role of prevention and treatment (for example, the new legislation preserves the rule of voluntary treatment, provides access to treatment for drug addicts in prisons and detention centres). However, the significant increase in penalties related to drug offences was a consequence of the new law (e.g. production, distribution, encouragement of drug use). Moreover, for the first time the law penalized the possession of illicit drugs (except for small quantities).

The Act established the Council for Counteracting Drug Dependence under the Prime Minister and committed the Council of Ministers (a particular role was assigned to the Ministry of Health) to develop a National Programme for Counteracting Drug Addiction.

The administrative reform launched in 1997 ensued the delegation of many responsibilities (mostly in areas of prevention and treatment) from the state administration to local government institutions. The Act also stressed the role of non-governmental organizations, self-help groups and social networks. Policies addressing the drug problem (described in the Act as "counteracting drug addiction") focused on education and prevention, medical treatment, rehabilitation and re-adaptation of addicted persons, supervision over substances with addiction-forming liability, combating the illicit trading, production, processing and possession of drugs, and the supervision of the cultivation of plants.

The promotion of mental health and a healthy lifestyle as well as information on the harmful effects of drug use became a substantial part of the policy. It was recommended that prevention programmes (under the supervision of the Ministry of Education and Ministry of Health) be included in schools, university and vocational training curricula. The Act of 1997 obliged public television to provide information on the negative effects of drug use. A number of state agencies (Ministries of National Education, Health and Social Welfare and others) were obligated to develop and conduct preventive and educational programmes. The above-mentioned tasks could be also commissioned to local governments.

According to the Act of 1997, any health service institution or individual physician could provide treatment and rehabilitation. The 16 voivodships (regions) of Poland are granted a licence for supplying treatment and rehabilitation programmes to other organizations under certain conditions defined by the Ministry of Health. Only public health institutions with special licences were entitled to provide so-called substitution treatment (e.g. treatment using narcotic drugs or psychotropic substances). The treatment and rehabilitation provided to drug addicts were free of charge and available throughout the country.

The 1997 legislation provided for a more balanced approach which combined demand reduction measures with instruments to reduce the supply. It also created a platform for cooperation between state, local governmental and non-governmental organizations.

However, over the next few years a gradual shift towards a "supply reduction" attitude among politicians and certain circles of experts became apparent. The issue of penalization of drug possession became a leading theme in the draft legislation discussed in Polish parliament in 2000. On 21 September 2000, the amendment to the 1997 Act was voted for by a majority of MPs (375 MPs voted in favour, 18 against[1]). For the first time in the history of the problem, the amendment introduced a penalization of the possession of any illicit drug, including small quantities (up to three years imprisonment). The draft legislation also introduced more severe sanctions for drug distribution. In mid-October, the amendment was approved by the Senate (the upper house of parliament). The new Act was also approved by the President and went into force in November 2000. Overwhelming support for the politicians was accompanied by very little attention from the media. There was no public debate. Only a few protests by some experts appeared in the media. One may claim that a repressive policy had been successfully legitimized by public opinion.

1.3 *Government concepts and strategies*

Before 1990, government policy relating to the drug problem was described in the Programme for the Prevention of Drug Addiction drafted by the Committee for the Prevention of Drug Addiction. The Programme had to be approved by the Council of Ministers.

In 1993, the Minister of Health and Social Welfare set up the Bureau for Drug Addiction. The Bureau was a state agency responsible for "the supervision and implementation of tasks concerning the treatment, rehabilitation and social reintegration of drug abusers [...] health promotion and preventive programmes addressed to young people".[2]

The Bureau cooperates with the state administration and local governments, offering support and providing information on the problem. Among the numerous activities undertaken by the Bureau are: the development of a national strategy for drug prevention, the development of a training system, the monitoring of specific projects and the partial funding of drug prevention projects.

In 1993, the Bureau developed the first National Programme for the Prevention of Drug Addiction, which focused on health promotion, the prevention of drug addiction in high-risk groups, treatment, rehabilitation and social reintegration as well as on training for professionals.

In the mid-1990s, some elements of government policy were also presented in the National Health Programme (Ministry of Health and Social Welfare, 1996). The programme, which specified health policy priorities, defined a special task devoted to "reducing the abuse of other psychoactive substances and drug abuse-related health damage". It was assumed that by the end of 2005 there would be a reduction in drug demand, limited access to psychoactive substances, and general access to treatment and rehabilitation programmes. A special emphasis was put on reducing mental disorders (like withdrawal symptoms, psychoses) and somatic diseases (AIDS, viral hepatitis B) related to the use of drugs. In order to achieve these objectives the programme recommended several actions. Drug policy should be aimed at managing psychoactive substances and harmonizing legislation.

An emphasis should be placed on promoting the dissemination of reliable information on psychoactive substances at all types of schools as well as on the development of preventive programmes in mass media. The increased involvement of the police and customs was intended to result in a reduction of the supply of psychoactive substances. The programme assumed that health service workers, teachers, policemen and penitentiary personnel would be trained in the early identification of drug-related problems, and in developing skills essential for working with persons experiencing such problems. Training would also include primary health care medical personnel. It was expected that effective detoxification programmes, the treatment and rehabilitation of drug abusers and addicts would be implemented, as well as programmes reducing health damage such as methadone programmes, and needle and syringe exchange programmes. The task of creating the programmes was assigned to the Ministry of Health and Social Welfare, the Ministry of National Education, the Ministry of Internal Affairs and Administration, the Ministry of Justice and the General Headquarters of the Police.[3]

In 1999, the first fully-developed strategy for the drug problem was formulated and accepted by the Polish government. The main role in the area of drug demand reduction was assigned to the Bureau for Drug Addiction. A number of responsibilities were also delegated to non-governmental organizations. In the field of supply control there were two leading institutions: the National Police Headquarters Bureau for Combating Drug-Related Crime and the Customs Inspectorate.

The National Programme for Counteracting Drug Addiction in Poland defined 10 goals to be achieved in the period of 1999-2000:[4] The programme stressed improving access to preventive activities targeting children and teenagers, improving access to medical services and rehabilitation, increasing the efficiency of the rehabilitation of drug addicts, improving the standards in the area of rehabilitation and social reintegration of drug addicts. Other goals concerned harm reduction, development of early identification methods of the problem, increasing the effectiveness of combating illegal trade, strengthening structures and policy co-ordination at the national, regional and local levels, the development of monitoring activities for programmes to reduce drug demand and fostering international cooperation in the area of demand and supply reduction.

The programme implementation put special emphasis on the following areas: the development of local programmes and initiatives, the co-ordination between the central administration, local governments and NGOs, the monitoring of activities, the development of training programmes, the necessary amendments of existing legal regulations, the control of compounds, the development of research, studies and databases, and fostering international cooperation.

In order to meet the above-mentioned objectives it was proposed to establish a structure comprising the following levels: Activities designed within the programme were expected to be conducted in such areas as prevention, early intervention, treatment, rehabilitation, social reintegration, harm reduction and self-help. Some activities would take place at in-patient addiction therapy wards, newly established competence centres (responsible for training curriculum development, supervision of projects' implementation) as well as at existing training centres.

The programme expected financial support and services for drug addicts and their families to be provided within the framework of the state social welfare system. Under the existing health service system, treatment and rehabilitation were the responsibilities of the local authorities, while social reintegration remained under the auspices of the central administration. The National Programme also describes the strategies for other sectors, e.g. supply control and the reduction of illegal plantations, the strengthening of trade control of legal drugs and combating the illegal trade of narcotics and psychotropic substances.

The important part of the institutional response is the cooperation with corresponding organizations from other parties involved. Numerous activities have been undertaken at different levels (state, regional, local, NGOs). In many cases joint programmes and the participation in international projects enrich experience and provide examples of good practice. For example, the Bureau of Drug Addiction cooperates with leading international organizations such as the World Health Organization (for example, Programme of Substance Abuse), the United Nations Drug Control Programme, Council of Europe (the Pompidou Group), and the EU Phare Programme. In the light of Poland's accession to the European Union, one of the important factors is the alignment of national standards with EU regulations.

1.4 *Financing*

The Act on Counteracting Drug Addiction sets out drug-preventive tasks for both the central government and the local government agendas.[5] At the central government level, preventive obligations are imposed on some of the ministries, and at the local level, such obligations are mandatory for each of the three levels of self-government (voivodship, district, communal) as their own tasks. In fact, in Poland there are two types of drug prevention fund-allocating centres: first, at the national and second, at the local level.

At the national level some ministries are involved in drug prevention policy by law (Ministry of Health, Ministry of National Education, Ministry of National Defence, Ministry of Internal Affairs and Administration, Ministry of Foreign Affairs, Ministry of Finance and Ministry of Agriculture and Food Economy) and they receive their financial resources directly from the state budget. The resources planned for 1999, 2000 and 2001 are presented in the National Programme for Counteracting Drug Addiction 1999-2000.[6]

At the local level, mandatory preventive activities are financed primarily by the local governments' budgets. Moreover, communal authorities have the opportunity to develop their own drug demand reduction projects and may apply to the Ministry of Finance for allocations in the form of a grant-in-aid from the state budget. A DDR (drug demand reduction) activity at the communal level can also be financed by the state budget if it is a task commissioned to the local government by the state administration.

Since the beginning of the 1980s, some of the governmental DDR tasks have been commissioned to NGOs. In Poland there are almost 100 NGOs involved in preventive activities at the central and the local level. Their DDR activities are subsidized by the agencies of the Ministry of Health, Ministry of National Education, Ministry of Labour and Social Policy, as well as by the provincial administration and the local body of self-government.[7]

The Bureau for Drug Addiction is a central agency of the Ministry of Health and was established in 1993 for the purpose of implementing ministerial drug prevention policy. The Bureau has its own budget (received via the Ministry of Health) for commissioning DDR tasks to NGOs, both at the national and at the local level. The National Programme for Counteracting Drug Addiction states that *"the Bureau orders the implementation of programmes aiming to improve efficiency and effectiveness of prophylactic, rehabilitation and post-rehabilitation tasks. The conducted programmes are the ones that are supported by local authorities and the community and which are relevant for the directions set by the Ministry of Health"*. In 1998, the Bureau subsidized the DDR activities of 45 NGOs operating at national and local levels. The types of drug demand reduction activities that will be particularly financed in the future, as well as the rules of application for subsidies have recently been defined in more precise terms by the Bureau.[8]

Medical intervention, detoxification and rehabilitation are offered to drug dependants as an unpaid service (free access to these services is guaranteed by the law even for dependants who have no health insurance). The services are provided by the public and private health care units, non-profit organizations and professionals with medical and non-medical backgrounds. From 1999 on, their work has been financed by the State Health Services (from its receipts of insurance premiums) on the basis of contracts between them and the State Health Services. Substitution treatment is offered only by public health care services. Re-adaptation is conducted by governmental institutions and is financed with state funds. Re-adaptation is a type of activity conducted by NGOs and, just like their other DDR activities, is financed by NGO budgets obtained from all types of potential sources (public, private, national, international, etc.).

1.5 Co-ordination

Until 1990, the task of resolving the drug problem had been defined in the governmental Programme for Counteracting Drug Addiction prepared by the Commission for Counteracting Drug Addiction and was adopted every year by the cabinet.

In 1993, the National Programme for Counteracting Drug Addiction was prepared by the Bureau for Drug Addiction and passed by the Ministry of Health. The dominant role of the Ministry of Health and its agency, the Bureau, in shaping the national strategies for tackling the drug problem is also evident in the current National Programme for Counteracting Drug Addiction 1999-2000 prepared by the Bureau and adopted by the cabinet. The Programme defines national policies in the areas of drug demand reduction and harm reduction, and also in the sphere of supply reduction. The Programme is based on the Act for Counteracting Drug Addiction, which was passed in 1997 by parliament and replaced the older one from 1985. There were attempts to adopt the new legislation to the reforms in the fields of state administration and health service, and to create a new division for the competencies relating to DDR activities. Only part of those competencies are left to central institutions of the state administration and the remaining, particularly educational and preventive activities, are assigned to local self-governments.

According to the National Programme of Counteracting Drug Addiction 1999-2000, the Bureau for Drug Addiction is the body that gives direction and controls the fulfilment of the tasks in the fields of environmental prevention, rehabilitation and social re-adaptation of drug dependants. The Bureau cooperates with Voivode Plenipotentiaries (16 voivodship authority plenipotentiaries) for Drug Addiction in helping and supporting their activities at the local level. The scope of the tasks implemented by the Bureau is very wide and shows that the Bureau plays the role of a central DDR co-ordinator. The main tasks assigned to the Bureau are: creating a national strategy for counteracting drug addiction; co-ordinating drug demand reduction activities at the national level; supervision of institutions conducting DDR activities; financing a part of DDR programmes; issuing recommendations to institutions and people conducting preventive, rehabilitative, re-adaptive and instructive activities; cooperating with other departments; cooperating with local public administration units and representatives of local authorities in finding solutions to drug addiction problems; supporting actions conducted by nation-wide and local organizations such as: associations, foundations, religious associations, churches and other social initiatives; supporting and initiating training programmes for individuals working in the field of prophylactics and rehabilitation; cooperating with international organizations in order to establish standard forms and methods for counteracting drug addiction, as well as limiting the damaging effects of addiction.

The DDR activities are also co-ordinated and supervised at the local level by the voivodship self-governments. They are supposed to create their own local Voivodships Programmes for Counteracting Drug Addiction. Some of the local DDR institutions are public; they are usually incorporated into national organizations and operated as the branches of governmental institutions, but local authorities also initiate such organizations. Local NGO DDR organizations are initiated by various bodies: associations, foundations, churches, youth organizations, etc. and are operated at the local level.

As has been stated, in Poland there are almost 100 NGOs involved in DDR activities both at the national and the local level. Four of the biggest non-governmental DDR organizations that operate at the national level are: Stowarzyszenie MONAR (Association MONAR), Stowarzyszenie Katolicki Ruch Antynarkotykowy KARAN (Association KARAN Anti-drug Catholic Movement), Polskie Towarzystwo Zapobiegania Narkomanii (Polish Society of Drug Abuse Prevention) and Towarzystwo Rodzin i Przyjaciół

Dzieci Uzale˝nionych "Powrót z U" (Association of Families and Friends of Drug Dependent Children "Return from U"). They provide a wide range of services to different target groups and they accomplish DDR aims by creating and co-ordinating their networks of counselling centres, therapeutic clubs, long-term treatment centres, group therapy, re-adaptive settlements, half-way flats, street workers and so on.

There are only few professional organizations in the DDR field in Poland (organizations that engage professional staff only) like, for example, Pracownia Profilaktyki Mlodzie˝owej "Pro-M" Instytutu Psychiatrii i Neurologii (Youth Prevention Unit "Pro-M", Institute of Psychiatry and Neurology), Centrum Metodyczne Pomocy Psychologicznej MEN (Methodical Centre of Psychological Assistance, Ministry of Education) and Stowarzyszenie "Pomoc socjalna" (Society "Social Assistance"). These three organizations operate at the national level. The first one is involved in DDR activities, among others, but the latter two are involved in DDR activities exclusively.

A central database of Polish DDR organizations and DDR programmes does not exist yet, except for those financed by the Bureau for Drug Addiction, but it is neither complete nor comparable. The Methodical Centre of Psychological Assistance gathers and evaluates some DDR programmes, but these are implemented at all types of schools across the country, therefore its database is also not complete.

A first step in creating a central database of DDR organizations and DDR programmes was recently taken by the Bureau for Drug Addiction. It established its own Department of Research and Analysis in 1999, whose role would be to create an informative system using standard methods for the monitoring of the Polish drug abuse scene.[9] The main goal of the Department in the area of DDR is the constant monitoring of activities in the field of prophylactics, treatment, rehabilitation and harm reduction. A centralized collection of data will be started as from 2000.

1.6 Epidemiology

The number of illicit drug-dependent individuals in Poland has been defined traditionally by using health service data and calculating the rate of patients hospitalized for such dependence per 100,000 citizens (Sieroszwaski, 1999). The data from last decade shows a constant growth tendency; the rate nearly doubled: from 7.34 in 1990 to 15.78 in 1998 (Table 1). There is also a considerable territorial differentiation of drug addiction. It ranges from 16.1 in some parts of Poland to 31.1 in the south-west and north country districts, and in some big cities in Central Poland: Warsaw, Lublin and Lodz.

Table 1: Patients (clients) admitted to residential treatment due to drug addiction in 1990-1996 (ICD IX: 304, 305.2-9) and in 1997-1998 (ICD X: F11-F16, F18, F19)

	Number of patients	Per 100,000 citizens
1990	2803	7.34
1991	3614	9.42
1992	3710	9.66
1993	3783	9.82
1994	4107	10.65
1995	4223	10.94
1996	4772	12.35
1997	5336	13.81
1998	6100	15.78

Source: Institute of Psychiatry and Neurology.

In recent years, researchers have started to apply various methods of combining data from survey and snowball studies with the treatment and police statistics (Moskalewicz and Sieroslawski, 1995; Sieroslawski and Zielinski, 1996). The number of drug-dependent individuals estimated by using one of these methods (capture-recapture) ranged from 20,000 to 40,000 in 1993 and from 29,000 to 48,000 in 1997, while by using other methods of estimation (benchmark) it ranged from 36,000 to 60,000 in 1997 (Sieroslawski, 1999).

The data on patients admitted to residential treatment due to drug addiction in Poland shows that the number of such patients is constantly increasing and in 1998 it was two times as high as in 1990 (Table 2). This rise is explained not only by the higher prevalence of drug dependence itself, but also by the improved access to treatment provided to potential clients and by the increasing number of organizations that have been sending in their data since 1996.[10] It is probably also the reason why percentages of first-time admissions to residential treatment constantly increased in the second half of the 1990s.

Table 2: Patients (clients) admitted to residential treatment due to drug addiction in 1990-1996 (ICD IX: 304, 305.2-9) and in 1997-1998 (ICD X: F11-F16, F18, F19) by the type of contact

Type of contact	1990	1991	1992	1993	1994	1995	1996	1997	1998
First-time admitted	1260	1593	1547	1505	1693	1759	1980	2438	3115
All persons admitted	2803	3614	3710	3783	4107	4223	4772	5336	6100
Percentage of first-time admissions	45.0	44.1	41.7	39.8	41.2	41.7	41.5	45.7	51.1

Source: Institute of Psychiatry and Neurology.

Drug dependency prevails in agglomerations and it is better monitored by researchers there (Sieroslawski and Zielinski, 1998; Sieroslawski, 1999). Health services and treatment data collected in Warsaw indicated a decrease in the number of drug dependent persons in the 1990s using intravenously "kompot" – an opiate produced illegally by the addicts themselves from the poppy straw. In 1995, it was used by 34.9% of addicts within the last month before their hospitalization, while in 1998 by 14.3%. Nonetheless, opiates are still the major illicit drug of abuse because of the increased consumption of a heroin type called "brown sugar" (which is not taken intravenously from the very beginning, but only after some time of use). In 1995 it was used by only 0.2% of the addicts but in 1998 by 55.4%. Other illicit drugs are more rarely a basic substance, determining the type of dependence: amphetamine for 14.6% of addicts, marijuana for 8.5% and the rest for 5.2%.

From 1995 on, the drug usage habits have changed. Both the intravenous application of drugs and the sharing of syringes have become less frequent (Sieroslawski, 1999). These changes have had positive consequences: health complications such as various dangerous infections or even death cases caused by drug overdoses are less frequent. Therefore, HIV dissemination among intravenous drug users is showing a tendency to decline. Cases of HIV among the dependants examined (75%-83%) decreased from 43.6% in 1995 to 26.5% in 1998.

Table 3 shows the number of HIV cases among intravenous drug users reported in Poland in 1988-1999 and the HIV rate per 100,000 members of the population. After a rapid rise in1989-1991, the rate has declined since 1992 and is still relatively low.

Table 3: HIV cases among IDUs reported in Poland in 1988-1999

Year	**Number**	**Rate per 100,000 population**
1988	12	0.03
1989	411	1.08
1990	653	1.71
1991	405	1.06
1992	326	0.85
1993	205	0.53
1994	259	0.67
1995	320	0.83
1996	343	0.89
1997	312	0.81
1998	315	0.81
1999	332	0.86

Source: National Institute of Hygiene.

Table 4: Patients (clients) admitted to residential treatment due to drug addiction in 1990-1996 (ICD IX: 304, 305.2-9) and in 1997-1998 (ICD X: F11-F16, F18, F19) by the type of substance abused

Type of substance	**1990**	**1991**	**1992**	**1993**	**1994**	**1995**	**1996**	**1997**	**1998**
304.0 and 304.7 Morphine type	2163	2821	2897	2791	2996	3083	3257	x	x
304.1 Barbiturate type	99	188	103	130	82	67	81	449	509
304.2 Cocaine	2	2	4	-	2	2	4	46	45
304.3 Cannabis	1	5	1	6	14	19	18	70	110
304.4 Amphetamine t.	14	2	20	39	65	92	97	204	367
304.5 Hallucinogens	5	1	8	9	10	4	14	70	75
304.6 Other (incl. inhalants)	199	222	201	228	321	317	435	535	564
304.8 Combination (excl. morphine type)	167	196	124	93	90	115	169	x	x
304.9 Unspecified	137	159	128	135	147	110	209	x	x
304 No date in 4th digit	16	18	224	352	380	414	488	x	x
Total	2803	3614	3710	3783	4107	4223	4772	5336	6100

Source: Institute of Psychiatry and Neurology.

A new classification of diseases that has been obligatory in Poland since 1997 makes the data on the type of substance abused by patients not fully comparable. Table 4 shows that in the past few years there has been a growing tendency of abuse in all selected substances, but particularly in barbiturates, amphetamines and cocaine. Data from 1997 and 1998 show the share of each selected substance by drug dependence of all hospitalized patients (Table 5).

The predominance of morphine substances is constant, but the share was somewhat smaller in 1998 compared to a year before. The share of some of the other substances is more or less stable or a bit higher than in the case of amphetamine substances (a rise from 3.8% in 1997 to 6.0% in 1998) and cannabis (a rise from 1.3% in 1997 to 1.8% in 1998).

Table 5: Patients (clients) admitted to residential treatment due to drug addiction in 1997-1998 (ICD X: F11-F16, F18, F19) by the type of substance abused

Year	**1997**		**1998**	
Type of substance	No. of patients	%	No. of patients	%
Opiates	2313	43.3	2569	42.3
Tranquilizers	449	8.4	509	8.3
Cocaine	46	0.9	45	0.7
Cannabis	70	1.3	110	1.8
Amphetamine	204	3.8	367	6.0
Hallucinogens	70	1.3	75	1.2
Inhalants	535	10.0	564	9.2
Mixed and unspecified	1649	30.9	1861	30.5
Total	5336	100.0	6100	100.0

Source: Institute of Psychiatry and Neurology.

The gender structure of drug dependants admitted to residential treatment was stable in Poland for years and has not changed lately (Table 6). Almost three-fourths of drug-dependent inpatients are males.

Table 6: Patients (clients) admitted to residential treatment due to drug addiction in 1997-1998 (ICD X: F11-F16, F18, F19) by gender

Year	**1997**		**1998**	
Gender	No. of patients	%	No. of patients	%
Male	3936	73.8	4519	74.1
Female	1400	26.2	1581	25.9

Source: Institute of Psychiatry and Neurology.

The age structure of drug-dependent inpatients in 1998 differed somewhat from the age structure in 1997 (Table 7). The shares of the youngest (below 15 years old) and the oldest (over 45 years old) were more or less stable. The percentage of inpatients 16-24 years old increased while the percentage of inpatients of 25-44 years old decreased.

Table 7: Patients (clients) admitted to residential treatment due to drug addiction in 1997-1998 (ICD X: F11-F16, F18, F19) by age

Year	**1997**		**1998**	
Age	No. of patients	%	No. of patients	%
- 15	190	3.6	221	3.6
16-19	811	15.2	1130	18.6
20-24	1303	24.5	1649	27.1
25-29	969	18.2	1026	16.9
30-34	789	14.8	733	12.1
35-39	536	10.1	522	8.6
40-44	367	6.9	374	6.1
45 +	357	6.7	427	7.0
Total	5322	100.0	6082	100.0
Missing data	14		18	
All patients	5336		6100	

Source: Institute of Psychiatry and Neurology.

Table 8 shows the number of deaths from drug overdoses reported by the police in the past few years. The police does not register the type of dependence or the socio-demographic characteristics of the deceased. It is hard to find any tendency in the mortality rates. The same situation exists as regards deaths connected with the alcohol dependence syndrome, the rates of which were 1.9 in 1990, 4.3 in 1995 and 3.7 in 1996 and for deaths caused by suicide and self-injury, the rates of which were 13.0 in 1990, 14.3 in 1995 and 14.1 in 1996.[11]

Other police data reveal a less optimistic picture: an increasing trend of criminal activities breaking the law under the Act on the Prevention of Drug Dependence and a relatively high share of young people involved.[12] The number of drug-related crimes rose from 7,915 in 1997 to 16,432 in 1998. During the first quarter of 1999, juveniles committed 815 such crimes, while during the same period of 1998 the figure was 622. In 1998, police estimated the number of drug consumers in Poland to be 60,000 and about 18,000 of them were defined as addicts. The two largest categories of drug users identified by the police were 8 to 20-year-old (15%) and 21 to 24-year-old people (13%). Juveniles were the third-largest category of drug users involved in crime (11%).

Table 8: Deaths from overdoses in Poland reported by the police in 1991-1999

Year	Number	Rate per 100,000 population
1991	130	0.34
1992	167	0.44
1993	150	0.39
1994	151	0.39
1995	177	0.46
1996	157	0.41
1997	143	0.37
1998	179	0.46
1999	120	0.31

Source: Police Headquarter Warsaw.

Table 9 shows the police data of offences of drug laws in Poland between 1990 and 1999. The total number of offences is steadily growing, but their structure has changed. In 1999, the cases of illegal cultivation of poppy and hemp declined sharply. The number of cases of illegal drug production, the manufacture and/or storing of instruments for the illegal production of drugs, illegal drug selling, illegal promotion of drug use and the giving away of drugs, and the production, smuggling and trafficking in precursors decreased slightly in 1999 compared with the corresponding cases registered in 1998. Between 1998 and 1999 there was a considerable rise in the number of drug possession cases (partially connected with a new drug law implemented in 1997). A rising tendency was also seen in some offences such as drug trafficking (import, export or transit) and the illegal picking of poppy milk, poppy straw, opium and hemp.

In the first six months of 1998, there were 8,692 offences against drug laws (while there were 2,753 offences in the same period of 1997), which results in a 315.7% rate of growth; with the share of juveniles in 1998 being much higher than in 1997 (451% rate of growth).[13]

Table 9: Offences against drug laws 1990-1999

	Year									
Type of offence	1990	1991	1992	1993	1994	1995	1996	1997	1998	1999
Illegal cultivation of poppy or hemp	382	1712	1631	3577	3040	2780	2634	2518	1195	615
Illegal production of drugs	557	589	521	1280	387	392	459	701	574	361
Production or storing of instruments for illegal drugs production	34	60	94	123	85	97	135	116	190	143
Drug trafficking (import, export or transit)	1	6	23	21	20	69	97	148	252	406
Selling of illegal drugs	10	24	45	207	107	215	397	847	1957	1714
Giving of illegal drugs and drug use promoting	121	77	128	249	361	731	3058	3507	10762	10305
Production, smuggling or trafficking in precursors									88	61
Drugs possession								32	1380	1896
Illegal picking of poppy milk, poppy straw, opium or hemp								26	112	113
Conquest in purpose of appropriation of poppy milk, poppy straw, opium or hemp								9	22	14
Total	1105	2468	2442	5457	4000	4284	6780	7915	16432	15628

Source: Police Headquarter Warsaw.

After a steep increase in 1993, the number of people convicted by a court for drug law offences steadily decreased every year (Table 10), although the number of drug law offenders sentenced to imprisonment has constantly increased (Table 11).

Table 10: Court convictions for Drug Law Offences (DLOs) in Poland

Year	**Overall number of persons convicted (all offences)**	**Persons convicted for drug law offences**	**DLOs as % of All Persons Convicted**
1989	93,373	591	0.63
1990	106,464	231	0.22
1991	152,333	421	0.28
1992	160,703	993	0.62
1993	171,622	2,235	1.30
1994	185,065	1,862	1.01
1995	195,455	1,864	0.95
1996	227,731	1,739	0.76
1997	210,600	1,457	0.69

Source: Ministry of Justice.

Table 11: Drug law offenders sentenced to imprisonment in Poland

Year	**Number**
1989	76
1990	30
1991	32
1992	72
1993	97
1994	97
1995	100
1996	141
1997	165

Source: Ministry of Justice.

Some important information about the drug scene in Poland is contained in the ESPAD survey published in 1995 (Hibel et al., 1997). Poland participated in this type of data collecting for the first time. The results of the survey indicate drug use among the population of 15 to 16-year-old students.

The data from 1995 show that Polish students' knowledge about various types of illicit drugs was as follows: 83% of them had heard about *marihuana or hashish* and *cocaine*, 82% about *heroin*, 75% about *amphetamines*, 70% about *tranquilizers or sedatives*, 41% about LSD, 19% about *ecstasy* and 14% about *crack and methadone*. Eighty-two per cent of Polish students never used any of the illicit drugs selected in the survey. The proportion of students who had tried drugs ranged for all countries investigated from 2% among girls to 44% among boys. The figures for Polish students were moderate: 12% of boys and 5% of girls had had experience with *marihuana or hashish*, 5% of boys and 3% of girls with any *illicit drugs other than marihuana or hashish*, 6% of boys and 8% of girls with *alcohol with pills*, 11% of boys and 8% of girls with *inhalants*. However, in Poland the highest prevalence of illicit use of *tranquilizers and sedatives* was reported: 18% of all students (11% of boys and even 25% of girls).

Tranquilizers and sedatives were the most important introductory drugs in Poland, while in all other investigated countries (except Lithuania) *marihuana or hashish* were the introductory substances. Three per cent of Polish students tried *tranquilizers and sedatives* at the age of 13 or younger (of the other illicit drugs only *marihuana* and *inhalants* were used at this age by 1% of students). In Poland one also finds the highest proportion (40%) of young people who reported that these substances were "easy" or "fairly easy" to obtain, while other illicit drugs were defined as not so easy to obtain (*marihuana and hashish* by 18%; *amphetamines* by 13%; *LSD, other hallucinogens* and *cocaine* by 11%, *heroin* by 10%, *ecstasy* by 6% and *crack* by 5%).

Poland was one of the countries with the highest proportion of students who perceived the great risk of illicit drug use. The proportion of Polish students who perceived a high risk in the regular use of drugs ranged from 90% in the case of *inhalants* to 95% in the case of *cocaine or crack,* and the proportion of those who perceived one-time or two-time drug usage as a high risk ranged from 55% in the case of *inhalants* to 67% in the case of *cocaine or crack.* Students also reported that some, most or all of their friends use different illicit drugs: 22% of students reported that their friends smoke *marihuana or hashish;* 16% that their friends take *tranquilizers or sedatives* and *inhalants;* 10% that their friends use *amphetamines;* 8% that their friends take *LSD or other hallucinogens* and *anabolic steroids;* 4% that their friends use *cocaine or crack, ecstasy* and *heroine.*

According to the Chief Central Statistic Office database, in 1995 the 16-year-old population in Poland consisted of 656,276 people (as of 31 December 1995) and in 1999 it consisted of 696,623 people (as of 31 December 1999).

The data from the ESPAD'99 survey has not been published yet except for the two tables presented in the chapter on the epidemiological situation in Poland that were included in the "Information of the Bureau for Drug Addiction".[14] Table 12 shows the lifetime experience (at least one-time usage) of the different types of drugs reported in the ESPAD'95 and ESPAD'99 surveys of junior students (ca. 16-year-old) and senior students (ca. 18-year-old) of secondary schools.

In 1995, the highest shares of all students surveyed had had an experience with *tranquilizers and sedatives, marihuana or hashish* and *inhalants.* By comparing two selected groups of students, one may state that older students had some lifetime experience with *marihuana or hashish* (7%), *tranquilizers and sedatives* (2.8%) and *LSD or other hallucinogens* (0.8%) more frequently than younger students. In contrast, younger students more frequently than older students had had lifetime experience with the rest of the selected substances (except for *cocaine* that was experienced by the same percentages of younger and older students). The younger students' lifetime experience with *inhalants* is considerably higher than in the case of the older students.

Table 12: Lifetime experience (at least once) with drugs. Percentages of junior students and senior students of secondary schools in Poland. Research data from the ESPAD'95 and ESPAD'99 surveys

	Junior, 16-year-old students		Senior, 18-year-old students	
Type of substance	1995	1999	1995	1999
Tranquilizers or sedatives	18.5	18.3	20.8	20.8
Marihuana or hashish	10.1	15.1	17.1	22.4
Inhalants	10.4	9.1	7.9	5.4
Amphetamine	2.9	7.4	2.8	10.5
LSD	1.9	4.0	2.7	3.5
Crack	0.5	1.0	0.4	0.8
Cocaine	0.8	1.9	0.8	1.8
Heroin	0.8	5.7	0.6	6.8
Ecstasy	0.8	2.8	0.6	2.7
Anabolic steroids	2.8	3.4	4.0	2.6

Source: Bureau for Drug Addition.

In 1999, the ranking of substances experienced by the largest percentages of students differed somewhat from that in 1995, but only for the older students: *amphetamine* replaced *inhalants* as the substance mostly experienced (together with *tranquilizers and sedatives* and *marihuana or hashish*). The list of substances more frequently experienced by older students than by younger students also changed. In 1999, older students had lifetime experience with *marihuana or hashish* (7.3% more), *amphetamine* (3.1%), *tranquilizers and sedatives* (2.5%) and *heroine* (1.1%) more frequently than younger students. Still, younger students had lifetime experience with the rest of the selected substances more frequently than older students. However, the younger students' life experience with *inhalants* is considerably higher than in the case of older students (that difference is even bigger than in 1995).

Among all students, the highest percentages had lifetime experiences with *tranquilizers or sedatives*; that high percentage decreased a little bit in 1999 in case of younger students, but remained stable among older students. In 1999, most of the rest of the selected substances were used by higher percentages of all surveyed students than in 1995, and the increase was much higher for such substances as *heroin, amphetamines, marihuana and ecstasy*. The second survey shows that the largest increase in lifetime experience with drugs of both junior and senior students relates to the same three types of substances, but in an order that is a bit different for each group of students. The junior students' lifetime experience with drugs increased mostly in cases of *marihuana and hashish* (5% more), *heroin* (4.9%) and *amphetamine* (4.5%), while senior students' lifetime experience with drug increased mostly in cases of *amphetamines* (7.7% more), *heroin* (6.2%), and *marihuana and hashish* (5.3%); thus this increase was comparatively higher for older students than for younger students.

Only in case of *inhalants* did the percentage of students who had at least once used that kind of drug decline for each group. Still, the percentage of younger students with this type of experience is much higher than among older students. In 1999, less people had had experience with *LSD or other hallucinogens* (2.1% less), *inhalants* (1.3%) and *tranquilizers and sedatives* (0.2%) among younger students than in 1995, while in the case of the older students, less people had had experience with *inhalants* (2.5% less) and *anabolic steroids* (1.4%) than in 1995.

Marihuana and hashish were more prevalent among young people in 1999 than 1995. It is visible not only in lifetime usage, but also in data for usage during the last 12 months and usage during the last 30 days (Table 13). The increase of all selected types of marihuana or hashish usage was a little bit higher for the older students than for younger students.

Table 13: Usage of marihuana or hashish. Percentages of junior and senior students of secondary schools in Poland. Research data from the ESPAD'95 and ESPAD'99 survey

	Junior, 16-year-old students		Senior, 18-year-old students	
Usage of marihuana or hashish	1995	1999	1995	1999
Lifetime use	10.1	15.1	17.0	22.4
Use during last 12 months	6.9	12.3	10.0	17.3
Use during last 30 days	3.1	7.4	3.3	8.6

Source: Bureau for Drug Addition.

2 Organizations active in the area of drug demand reduction

2.1 *The overall number of drug demand reduction institutions*

One idea for the selection of the organizations to be included in the study was to limit their number to 50 organizations. Initially, we identified and listed organizations operating at the national level, and later on added the local organizations. Since no official records of DDR organizations in Poland existed, we identified them using many different sources of information. We decided that the study would cover all existing national level organizations; the remaining ones were selected from a large collection of organizations acting at the local level. Ultimately, we included 38 organizations operating at the national level and identified 12 organizations operating at the local level.

National organizations include 12 governmental public agencies involved in DDR activities: the Chancellery of the President of the Polish Republic, some ministries (Ministry of Education, Ministry of Labour and Social Policy, Ministry of Foreign Affairs, Ministry of National Defence) and ministerial agencies such as the Bureau for Drug Addiction affiliated to the Ministry of Health and Social Assistance, some institutes like the National Institute of Hygiene, the Institute of Psychiatry and Neurology and its special department Youth Prevention Unit "pro-M", Headquarters of the Police and Headquarters of the Penitentiary Services. The majority of these organizations dealt with drug problems inclusively. The remaining 26 national organizations, except for one private entertainment organization, were non-governmental organizations. There were mainly societies and associations, seven of them were established as organizations with exclusive DDR orientation (for example the well-known "MONAR" Association, the Society of Families and Friends of Drug Dependent Children "Return from U" and the Polish Society of Drug Abuse Prevention with their regional branches). The rest of the non-governmental, national level organizations focused their activities not only on drug demand reduction, but also conducted their operations in other areas working to reduce the risk of young people and involving a different form of social pathology. This group included such organizations like the Society of Social Prevention "KUZNIA", the Association "KARAN" Anti-drug Catholic Movement, the Society of Psychoprophylactics, the Polish Society of Health Education. Unfortunately, during the research period, one organization operating at the national level refused to participate in the survey, therefore in the end we had 37 organizations at this level.

The remaining 12 local level organizations were located in the city of Lodz, which is one of the biggest agglomerations in the country. Lodz is in central Poland and has a concentration of acute social problems (unemployment, poverty, industry transformation). It also turned out that according to some indicators, the scope of the drug problem in the region of Lodz is comparable to the national average. In Poland, the regional indicators of patients admitted in 1997 to residential treatment due to drug addiction varied from 3.6 to 32.1 persons per 100,000 inhabitants. Lodz and its surroundings represented the region of Poland where there were 16.1 to 24.0 patients per 100,000 citizens. We assumed that the counteracting activities relating to the drug problem in such an area would reflect the predominant activities undertaken in other parts of the country. We selected 12 of all organizations operating in Lodz. Therefore, one has to bear in mind that they are only a selection of local organizations (in Poland there are more than 200 organizations involved in DDR activities) and they are not a representative sample of the region.

2.2 *The number of drug demand reduction institutions by type of organization*

Nearly two in three organizations surveyed, both at the national and at the local level, defined themselves as non-profit and one in three as public organizations (Table 14). Only two organizations identified themselves as private enterprises.

Table 14: Legal status and the level of operation

	Number of organizations					
	All Investigated		National Level		Local Level	
Status	n	%	n	%	n	%
Governmental	16	32.7	11	29.7	5	41.7
Private firm, enterprise	2	4.1	1	2.7	1	8.3
Non-profit	31	63.3	25	67.6	6	50.0
Total	49	100.0	37	100.0	12	100.0

Although DDR was one of the many other activities for two of each three surveyed organizations, there are considerable differences in the organizational domain of activity between the organizations operating at the national and local levels (Table 15). While for most national-level organizations, DDR was just part of a more or less wide spectrum of many other kinds of activities, for most of the local level organizations DDR was their exclusive activity.

Table 15: Exclusive/Inclusive orientation and the level of operating

	Number of organizations					
	All Investigated		National Level		Local Level	
Specializing in DDR	n	%	n	%	n	%
Exclusively	17	34.7	10	27.0	7	58.3
Inclusively	32	65.3	27	73.0	5	41.7
Total	49	100.0	37	100.0	12	100.0

The status of organizations also differed by type of involvement in DDR activity. Drug demand reduction was for only 25% of governmental organizations their exclusive work, while it was such for 39% of non-profit organizations. The share of the latter (71%) was the largest of all investigated organizations that conducted drug demand reduction activities exclusively.

Certain characteristics of organizations determine their general missions (Table 16). Three-fourths of national organizations, but only one-fourth of local organizations defined their work as *personal care and advice*. This mission was chosen by half of the organizations with exclusive DDR orientation, and nearly half of the NGOs. The larger number of national level organizations conducted the mission of *influencing attitudes, knowledge and skills*, which was chosen by only one local-level organization. It is also conducted by a larger fraction of organizations with inclusive DDR orientation than by organizations with an exclusive orientation. Only organizations operating at the national level perceived their most important mission as providing *support for communities and social institutions*.

The mission of drug demand reduction was identified by 32 organizations with inclusive orientation and only by these. More than half of such organizations defined their DDR mission as *prevention: education, information, and training*, while one-third conducted *personal care, treatment and advice*. This latter mission was more frequently given at the local level than at the national level. The status of an organization did not modify the order of preference. Only a few organizations operating at the national level perceived their DDR missions differently than the two mentioned above.

Table 16: Mission and other characteristics of the organization

	Number of Organizations						
	Legal status		DDR orientation		Level of operation		Total
	Govern.	NGO/ Private	Excl.	Incl.	National	Local	
Mission	N=16	N= 33	N=17	N=32	N=37	N=12	N=49
Influencing Attitudes	3	11	4	10	13	1	14
Personal care and advice	5	15	9	11	11	9	20
Support for communities	1	4	3	2	5		5
Policy design, cooperation	1		1		1		1
Intelligence – research	1			1	1		1
Other	5	3		8	6	2	8

A limited number of the researched organizations were able to specify their annual total budget: 27 organizations operating at the national level and 9 organizations operating at the local level (Table 17). National level organizations' annual budgets ranked from EUR 2,000 to more than EUR 100,000, while in the case of local level organizations the range was much narrower and varied from EUR 2,000 to 100,000. More than half of the local organizations had a budget estimated at over EUR 50,000 and less than EUR 100,000. The total budget of large divisions of national organizations was higher than EUR 100,000.

Table 17: Total budget and the level of operation

	Number of organizations					
	All Investigated		National Level		Local Level	
Annual total budget (Euro)	n	%	n	%	n	%
Up to 10,000	4	11.1	2	7.4	2	22.2
10,001-50,000	5	13.9	3	11.1	2	22.2
50,001-100,000	10	27.8	5	18.5	5	55.6
More than 100,000	17	47.2	17	63.0		
Total	36	100.0	27	100.0	9	100.0

Only 34 of all investigated organizations were able to specify their annual budget for DDR (Table 18). The budget of nearly one-third of all investigated organizations is less than EUR 50,000. The richest local level organizations had budgets ranking from EUR 50,000 to EUR 100,000. Only organizations operating at the national level (each third of them) had a total annual budget of more than EUR 100,000.

Table 18: Annual budget spent on DDR and the level of organizational operating

	Number of organizations					
	All Investigated		National Level		Local Level	
Annual budget on DDR (Euro)	n	%	n	%	n	%
2,000-10,000	6	17.6	3	12.0	3	33.3
10,001-50,000	6	17.6	4	16.0	2	22.2
50,001-100,000	9	26.5	5	20.0	4	44.4
more than 100,000	13	38.2	13	52.0		
Total	34	100.0	25	100.0	9	100.0

All investigated organizations were asked to specify the sources of their DDR budgets in 1995 and 1998. Table 19 presents the average proportions of funds received from each selected source by those organizations that answered the question "number of organizations". In 1995, organizations that received almost all of their DDR funds from public or governmental agencies formed a majority, 27 of them even the full amount of their budget. Other sources – except for *foreign governments or agencies* – provided average funds ranging from one-tenth to one-quarter to only a few organizations. In 1998, the major part of organizations received on average a large proportion of their DDR funds from public or governmental agencies, 25 of them even their full budgets. All other selected sources provided the smallest average proportion of DDR budget (ranging from 2 to 18%), but for a slightly larger number of organizations than before.

Forty-three of the investigated organizations: 31 from 37 national organizations and all 12 local organizations provided the information about the total number of their employed staff and the number of their staff involved in DDR. The total number of persons at organizations participating in the survey was 27,040. Most of them (26,933) worked at the national level and only 107 at the local level. Organizational staff ranked from 2 to 20,000 employees. Local organizations had rather small staffs: more than half of those organizations had a staff of up to 10 people, while only one-fourth of national organizations worked with such small staffs. A high share of national level organizations employed more than 50 people.

Table 19: **Sources of funds and the proportion of organizations' funds devoted to DDR in 1995 and 1998**

	Proportion of DDR budget in 1995		1998	
Sources	%	Number of Organizations	%	Number of Organizations
International Organizations	17.0	3	18.4	8
Foreign Governments / Agencies			2.0	1
Other Foreign Organizations	20.0	1	18.0	2
Public / Government Agencies	92.6	38	84.5	44
Private Sector	10.3	3	16.3	8
Voluntary Organizations	13.5	4	9.1	4
Fees / Individual Donations	24.6	5	12.5	12

The number of DDR personnel in those organizations that responded to the questionnaire was 1,675 people. Most of them (1,570) worked at the national level. The rest of them (105) worked at the local level. The DDR staffs of the investigated organizations ranged from 1 to 400. More than half of all organizations both at the national and the local level had DDR units of up to 10 people (Table 20). Only several national organizations had DDR staffs larger than 50 employees.

Table 20: **Staff involved in DDR and the level of organizational operation**

	Number of organizations					
	All Investigated		National Level		Local Level	
Number of DDR Staff	n	%	n	%	n	%
Up to 10	24	55.8	17	54.8	7	58.3
11-20	7	16.3	3	9.7	4	33.3
21-50	5	11.6	4	12.9	1	8.3
More than 50	7	16.3	7	22.6		
Total	43	100.0	31	100.0	12	100.0

The majority of the investigated organizations, i.e. 32 of 37 national level organizations and all 12 local level organizations, were able to estimate the number of their paid professionals. More than half of the former and three-fourths of the latter employed from 1 to 10 professionals. More than 50 professionals were employed only by national organizations.

Not all organizations, i.e. only 28 of 37 national organizations (but almost all local organizations), were able to define the percentage of their professional paid staff. About half of the national organizations employed only paid professionals and one-third of such organizations had staffs consisting of up to half of paid professionals. Only a few national organizations did not employ any paid professional. At the national level, nearly half of the organizations engaged more than 50% professional paid staff, but not the entire staff. One-third of local organizations had staffs consisting of up to half of paid professionals.

Among 1,003 employees (that had an academic degree or a professional licence) mentioned by the investigated organizations, 904 people worked at the national level and 99 people at the local level. The two largest categories were psychologists and educators (Table 21). Taken together, they represent more than three-fourths of all professionals employed by national organizations and more than one-third of all professionals employed by local organizations. The number of professionals with psychiatric and medical backgrounds is relatively large at the local level, by contrast to their marginal presence in the staff of organizations operating at the national level. The rest of the professional backgrounds represented only a very small proportion, ranking from 0.22% to 2.77% at the national level and from 2.02% to 5.05% at the local level. Considerably large – especially at the local level – was the category of professionals with backgrounds other than those named in the questionnaire.

Table 21: Professionals and the type of their background

	Number of professionals in organizations					
	All Investigated		National Level		Local Level	
Type of background	n	%	n	%	n	%
Medical training	33	3.29	25	2.77	8	8.08
Psychiatric training	38	3.79	24	2.65	14	14.14
Legal training	14	1.40	12	1.33	2	2.02
Public health training	2	0.20	2	0.22		
Social worker training	7	0.70	6	0.66	1	1.01
Psychology training	391	38.98	372	41.15	19	19.19
Educational training	340	33.90	321	35.51	19	19.19
Sociology training	12	1.20	7	0.77	5	5.05
Management training	4	0.40	2	0.22	2	2.02
Other	162	16.15	133	14.71	29	29.29
Total	1003	100.00	904	100.00	99	100.00

Volunteers were engaged in DDR activities in nearly half of all organizations. A large share of all organizations involving volunteers and of such organizations operating at the national level engaged more than 10 to 20 volunteers. Local organizations that hired volunteers had mainly up to 10 volunteers. Organizations engaging more than 50 volunteers operated only at the national level (one-third of these organizations).

The proportion of professional paid staff and volunteers differs in each organization: 21 out of 23 organizations engaging volunteers were able to define the percentage of volunteers involved in DDR activity. The larger share of such organizations (1 out of 3) engaged more than 50% and less than 75% volunteers. Only five local organizations had volunteers and they composed no more than three-fourths of the staff. More than 75% of volunteers were involved in DDR work in only one-fourth of the national organizations.

2.3 *The development of drug demand reduction institutions*

The development of DDR institutions can be described by presenting the date of foundation and the date it started its DDR activity for each organization. One national level organization was not able to specify the time of its establishment. The oldest organizations operating at the national level engaged in DDR activity (but not from the beginning) were founded in 1910 (the first one) and in 1918 (the second one) when Poland became independent after World War I. The rest of the organizations operating at the national level (except for one that was unable to indicate the date of the start of its DDR activity) were established after World War II. Looking at the investigated organizations' date of founding, it becomes clear that most of them, even those that operated for many years (but obviously not exclusively in the field of DDR), initiated their DDR activities only relatively recently (Table 22). The local organizations were relatively younger than most of the national level organizations.

Half of all investigated governmental organizations were founded before 1979. They started to develop after 1989. The development of non-profit organizations started a little bit earlier – from the beginning of the 1980s – and after 1989 an increase in the founding of such organizations was seen. From that time on, half of all NGOs emerged. All organizations conducting DDR activity exclusively were founded in the 1980s: more than 40% in 1980-1989 and the rest after 1989. A large number of organizations working on the drug demand problem inclusively (about 40%) were founded before 1979 and nearly the same percentage emerged after 1989.

Table 22: Founding year and the level of operating

	Number of organizations					
	All Investigated		National Level		Local Level	
Founding year	n	%	n	%	n	%
1918-1979	12	25.5	12	33.3		
1980-1989	14	29.8	10	27.8	4	36.4
after 1989	21	44.7	14	38.9	7	63.6
Total	47	100.0	36	100.0	11	100.0

A number of Polish organizations started their preventive activities directly after World War II, but most began their DDR activities in the 1980s and in the first half of the 1990s. The oldest investigated organizations operating at the local Lodz level and engaged in DDR activity were founded in 1982. An increasing number of national organizations was registered between 1985-90 and of local organizations in 1991-95 (Table 23). In general, the years 1980-1994 were the time many organizations initiated their DDR activities also at the national level.

Table 23: The year of starting DDR activities and the level of operation

	Number of organizations					
	All Investigated		National Level		Local Level	
Starting year	n	%	n	%	n	%
1946-1984	10	20.4	8	21.1	2	18.2
1985-1990	16	32.7	14	36.8	2	18.2
1991-1994	15	30.6	10	26.3	5	45.5
after 1995	8	16.3	6	15.8	2	18.2
Total	49	100.0	38	100.0	11	100.0

One out of three governmental organizations started their DDR activities in 1985-1990, and the same number after 1995. Non-profit organizations initiated their DDR activities mainly in 1985-1994 (Table 24). The period between 1991 and 1994 was the time when the highest percentage of organizations working exclusively on the drug demand problem started their activities in that area. The biggest share of organizations dealing with the problem inclusively started their DDR activities in 1985-1990.

Table 24: The year of starting DDR activities and the legal status of the organization

	Status of the organization					
	Governmental, public		Private firm, enterprise		Non-profit, voluntary	
Starting year	n	%	n	%	n	%
1946-1984	4	25.0			6	19.4
1985-1990	5	31.3			11	35.5
1991-1994	2	12.5			11	35.5
after 1995	5	31.3	2	100.0	3	9.7
Total	16	100.0	2	100.0	29	100.0

Generally speaking, the so-called "Solidarity times" in the early 1980s and the subsequent period of democratic society rebuilding after 1989 were the most important periods for the emergence of DDR institutions and for DDR activity innovations and development. The slowdown in the growth of NGOs after 1995 may be interpreted as the fulfilment of existing demands, but it also resulted from a lack of favourable conditions for their development.

2.4 *Non-governmental organizations in the area of drug demand reduction*

The grass-roots discovery of the drug problem in Poland suggests that the social movements of the early 1980s would lead to the creation of a stable system of non-governmental organizations. This hypothesis is supported by the results of our research. Non-governmental organizations played a major role in demand reduction policy. The data gathered reveal that the majority of organizations active in the area of drug demand reduction come from the non-governmental sector (31 organizations); 16 organizations come from the public sector. There were only 2 firms from the private sector.

A significant number of the organizations (23.9%) were established before the official recognition of the problem (1980). These were mainly government agencies. Almost 50% of ministries and agencies interviewed were set up before 1980. Only 4 out of 29 NGOs (13.8%) were created at that time. However, the bulk of Polish organizations (almost half of all NGOs and one-third of government agencies) were created during the period of transition.

The information on the dates of commencing DDR activities sheds some light on institutional response development. Before the mid-1980s, 20% of all NGOs and 25% of governmental agencies launched their demand reduction programmes. The parallel development took place during the period of 1985-1990 (around 35% of public sector and third-sector organizations initiated their activities). At the beginning of the 1990s, a phase of rapid growth of activities of NGOs set in (35.5% of all non-governmental organizations launched their programmes). The last period, which started in 1994, was marked by the development of governmental programmes. It is worth mentioning that almost 40% of Polish NGOs were exclusive organizations, whereas exclusive organizations consisted of 25% of all governmental bodies in the field of drug demand reduction.

Our research also provided information on the activities performed. It turned out that prevention and information programmes were conducted by almost all governmental (81%) and non-governmental (96.8%) organizations. The main difference concerned treatment and care activities. This area was dominated by non-governmental organizations. The majority of NGOs (64%) was involved in the provision of treatment and care services, compared to 31% of government agencies. The less marked difference was observed in the field of rehabilitation/after-care programmes (35% of NGOs and 25% of GOs). Another area of interest of governmental organizations was policy development and participation in the legislative process. A share of 81% of public agencies and ministries declared their involvement in the above actions.

The striking characteristic of Polish GOs and NGOs seems to be a similarity in the commitment to perform the remaining activities. We observed similar proportions in both types of organizations, which conducted research (68% of GOs and 58% of NGOs), provided funding or raised funds (25% of GOs and 22% of NGOs), co-ordinated other organizations' activities (68% of GOs and 61% of NGOs) or conducted training for professionals (68% of GOs and 74% of NGOs). The differences in organizational interests were also observed in the information about their most important missions.

The comparison of organizational capacities showed another striking similarity between governmental and non-governmental organizations. Although there was a major difference between the average number of staff working in governmental and non-governmental organizations (Table 25), as far as drug demand reduction programmes were concerned, there was almost the same number of staff (42 persons in GOs and 36 persons in NGOs).

The same relation emerged in the figures concerning budgets. The average budget of ministries and government agencies (21,915,178 EUR) was almost three times higher than the average budget of an NGO (830,196 EUR). In the case of budgets for drug demand programmes, there were no significant differences between the two types of organizations (EUR 269,750 in GOs; EUR 218,646 in NGOs). NGOs seem to be more concentrated on drug problems than their governmental counterparts. Almost 90% of NGOs' budgets were spent on drug demand reduction programmes. The same indicator for governmental organizations was 51%.

Table 25: Organization capacities and legal status

Legal status	Staff total	Staff DDR	Budget total (EUR)	Budget DDR (EUR)	DDR budget percentage
Governmental agency	14,680	42	21,905,718	269,750	51
Private firm, enterprise	37	37	104,183	104,183	100
Non-profit	51	36	830,196	218,646	87
Total	4,813	38	4,302,449	220,931	82

The data gathered revealed interesting differences in the self-perception of organizations' own images. It turned out that the self-evaluations of the non-governmental organizations were more positive than the appraisals of government agencies' staffs. The most visible contrast was revealed in the images as perceived by the organizations' clients (see Table 26). Significant differences were also noted in the case of images by respondents themselves and as perceived by the public. It is worth noting that representatives of both types of organizations shared a common belief according to which a more positive opinion on their performance was expressed by politicians and the media.

An astonishing difference was revealed in the evaluation of organizations' activities and in gathering systematic information on organizations' clients. In contrast to an assumption considered likely, it turned out that NGOs more often conducted evaluations of their performance (80% of all NGOs) than government agencies. A similar difference took place in the case of information gathering on clients, where organizations from the third sector collected the relevant data more often than public administration institutions. This situation seems to result from NGOs' dependence on outside subsidies (evaluation is a convincing evidence of their effectiveness). It also reflects NGOs' direct contacts with their target group.

Table 26: Organizational image and legal status (means on scale 1-5)

Legal status	Image seen by yourself	Image seen by clients	Image seen by public	Image seen by politics	Image seen by media
Governmental agency	3.66	3.66	3.40	4.16	4.55
Private firm, enterprise	5.00	5.00	5.00	5.00	5.00
Non-profit	4.12	4.33	4.20	4.66	4.65
Total	4.02	4.14	4.00	4.46	4.64

3 Drug demand reduction activities

3.1 *The goals of the organizations in the field of DDR*

Almost all organizations operating at the local level but three-fourths of national organizations defined three goals as requested in the questionnaire. In the survey, a total of 135 goals were given (Goal 1, Goal 2 and Goal 3 accordingly in the questionnaire). The most conducted goal was *prevention/ information*, which was identified 58 times. Other goals were indicated less frequently: *treatment and care* (27); *training of professionals* (13); *rehabilitation/ after-care* (13) and some only a few times like *drug demand reduction, co-ordination, research/documentation* and *policy development/legislation*. Two categories of goals: *funding/fund-raising* and *interest representation* did not attract the attention of any organization. The majority of national organizations and most organizations of all types of legal status as well as those accounting for the highest share of organizations with an exclusive and inclusive DDR orientation, defined *prevention/information* as their primary DDR goal. The only exception was the high share of organizations operating at the local level that conducted *treatment and care*.

The particular characteristics of the organizations do not seem to influence the indications of goals significantly when analysing only Goal 1 (Table 27). The goal of *prevention/ information* was chosen mainly by national organizations and by organizations of all types of legal status and all types of DDR orientation. The only exception is the local level in which case the most frequently conducted goal was *treatment and care*. Governmental organizations, organizations with inclusive DDR orientation and organizations operating at the national level identified a slightly wider range of goals than non-profit and private organizations, organizations with exclusive DDR orientation and organizations operating at the local level.

Table 27: Goals in the field of DDR by characteristic of an organization

	Number of organizations						
	Legal status		DDR orientation		Level of operating		**Total**
Types of goals	Govern-mental N=16	NGO/ Private N= 31	Excl. N=17	Incl. N=32	National N=37	Local N=12	N=49
Drug demand reduction (in general)	1	2	2	1	2	1	3
Prevention/ Information	6	16	8	14	19	3	22
Treatment and Care	4	8	4	8	6	6	12
Rehabilitation (After-care)		2		2	2		2
Research/ Documentation	1	1	2		1	1	2
Funding/ Fund-raising							
Co-ordination	2			2	2		2
Interest Representation							
Policy Development/ Legislation	1			1		1	1
Training of Professionals	1	2		3	3		3
Other		2	1	1	2		2

Other characteristics of organizations influenced their preference for certain goals to a certain extent. The total budget of organizations influenced the selection of DDR goals in the sense that the richer the organization, the wider the spectrum of goals. Organizations with relatively small budgets (up to EUR 10,000) indicated only few types of goals with prevention clearly being the dominant goal. Organizations with budgets of more than EUR 50,000 showed a preference for this goal too, but they also indicated many other goals. Taking into consideration the DDR budgets, one may notice the same as in the case of the total budget, i.e. the richer the organization, the wider the spectrum of goals. However, the goals differ slightly when considering the specific allocations of the DDR budget, i.e. the most frequently indicated goals by organizations with DDR budgets of up to EUR 10,000 were treatment and prevention. The largest number of organizations with larger DDR budgets also conducted the two dominating goals, but with contrary preferences.

The share of paid professional staff varies slightly in the investigated organizations. The number of paid professionals influenced the goal differentiation: the higher the percentage of paid professional staff, the wider the spectrum of goals indicated by the organization. Most of the organizations employing paid professional staff conducted the goal of *prevention/information,* while most organizations without any paid personnel conducted the goal of *treatment and care*. Organizations whose staffs consisted only of paid professionals defined their goal as *treatment and care* relatively rarely and identified many other goals instead.

3.2 *Drug demand reduction institutions – area of activities*

The main DDR activities in which investigated organizations were involved are summarized in Table A (see Annex). All organizations together indicated 471 different types of DDR activities (Activity No. 1, No. 2 and No. 3 presented together). National organizations indicated a total number of 352 such activities, and local organizations indicated a total number of 119 activities. A list of activities (ranked by the decreasing number of activities selected by all investigated organizations in each of the nine selected fields) reads as follows: *prevention/information* was indicated 117 times; *training of professionals* (79); *co-ordination* (60); *treatment and care* (49); *policy development* (48); *research/ documentation* (38); *rehabilitation/after-care* (35); *interest representation* (28) and *funding/fund-raising* (17). This order of activities is in the case of national level organizations nearly the same: *prevention/information* (87); *training of professionals* (62); *co-ordination* (45); *policy development* (42); *treatment and care* (29); *research/ documentation* (29); *rehabilitation/after-care* (24); *interest representation* (18) and *funding/fund-raising* (16). However, in the case of local level organizations, the order is somewhat different than in the case of all investigated organizations. It is as follows: *prevention/information* (30); *treatment and care* (20); *training of professionals* (17); *co-ordination* (15); *rehabilitation/after-care* (11); *interest representation* (10); *research/documentation* (9); *policy development* (6) and *funding/fund-raising* (1).

National organizations showed a relative higher interest in DDR activities focused on policy development, research, funding and fund-raising compared to local organizations. By contrast, local organizations were more interested in DDR activities addressing clients – like treatment and care, rehabilitation, after-care and interest representation – than national organizations. The organizations investigated were involved in a range of DDR fields. Their involvement varied from one to eight fields of all nine fields selected in the questionnaire (Table 28). Most organizations and the majority of both national and local organizations conducted DDR activities in five fields. Only one-eighth of the national organizations, but one-fourth of the local organizations, were involved in the top eight fields.

Table 28: Organizational involvement in the varying number of DDR fields

	Organizations					
Total number of DDR fields in which an organization is involved	All Investigated N=49		National Level N=37		Local Level N=12	
	n	%	n	%	n	%
1	1	2.0	1	2.7		
2	2	4.1	2	5.4		
3	9	18.4	7	18.9	2	16.7
4	9	18.4	7	18.9	2	16.7
5	12	24.5	8	21.6	4	33.3
6	4	8.2	3	8.1	1	8.3
7	6	12.2	6	16.2		
8	6	12.2	3	8.1	3	25.0
Total	49	100.0	37	100.0	12	100.0

The mean number of fields for all investigated organizations was 4.9, while it was 4.8 for national organizations and 5.3 for local organizations. The mean number for organizations with exclusive DDR orientation was 5.4, but for organizations with inclusive DDR orientation it was 4.7. The legal status of organizations also differed as regards the mean of the fields: it was 4.8 in case of governmental organizations, 5.0 in the case of private firms and 5.1 in the case of non-profit organizations.

The organizations investigated started their DDR activities at different times (Table B in the Annex). From 1946 to1984, the organizations started most of their activities in the area of *prevention/information* and *rehabilitation/after-care*. In 1985-1990, organizations initiated the largest number of activities in the area of *prevention/information* and the least in the area of *training of professionals*. In 1991-1994, the field of *prevention/information* was again the type of activity most frequently initiated by organizations, but activities in the area of *training of professionals* ranked second in that period. After 1995, most activities initiated by organizations were in the area of *prevention/information* and the next-largest number of activities was in the area of *training of professionals*.

A look at the characteristics of the organizations, namely, their level of operation, legal status, exclusive/inclusive orientation, percentages of professional paid staff, background of professional paid staff and percentage of volunteers, shows that organizational involvement in selected types of DDR activity differed somewhat with these features. Although the involvement in DDR activity in the field of *prevention/information* was predominant for most types of organizations, the proportions of organizations conducting activities in other fields changed with their organizational characteristics.

The largest part of all investigated organizations was involved in DDR activities in the field of *prevention/information, training of professionals* and *co-ordination* (Table 29). Most of the national organizations were involved in DDR activities in the field of *prevention/information, training of professionals* and *co-ordination.* Most of the local organizations were involved in DDR activity in the field of *prevention/information, treatment and care, rehabilitation/after-care* and *training of professionals.* This data shows that national organizations preferred creating and organizing a base for developing DDR policy, while local organizations were more interested in activities addressing concrete clients and their problems.

None of the studies of the characteristics of organizations changed the dominant position of DDR activity in the field of *prevention/information.* Almost all organizations regardless of their status, DDR orientation, DDR budget or type of staff declared their involvement in that field. Rather, in the selected characteristics, a differentiated organizational involvement was revealed in the other eight DDR fields.

Table 29: Different types of DDR activity fields and the level of operation

	Organizations					
	All Investigated N=49		National Level N=37		Local Level N=12	
Type of DDR activity field	n	%	n	%	n	%
Prevention / Information	45	91.8	34	91.9	11	91.7
Treatment and Care	26	53.1	16	43.2	10	83.3
Rehabilitation / After-care	22	44.9	14	37.8	8	66.7
Research / Documentation	23	46.9	17	45.9	6	50.0
Funding / Fund-raising	12	22.4	11	29.7	1	8.3
Co-ordination	32	65.3	25	67.6	7	58.3
Interest Representation	16	32.7	9	24.3	7	58.3
Policy Development	29	59.2	24	64.9	5	41.7
Training of Professionals	37	75.5	28	75.7	9	75.0

Except for involvement in *prevention/information*, the largest numbers of governmental organizations were active in DDR activities in the field of *policy development*, *rehabilitation/after-care*, *co-ordination* and *training of professionals* (Table 30); all private firms and enterprises were involved in DDR activities in the field of *co-ordination* and *training of professionals* and the majority of non-profit organizations were most of all involved in DDR activities in the field of *training of professionals* and *treatment and care*.

Table 30: Different types of DDR activity fields and the status of organizations

	Number of organizations with status:					
	Governmental, public, N=16		Private firm, enterprise, N=2		Non-profit, voluntary, N=31	
Type of DDR activity field	n	%	n	%	n	%
Prevention / Information	13	81.3	2	100.0	30	96.8
Treatment and Care	5	31.2	1	50.0	20	64.5
Rehabilitation (After-care)	4	25.0			11	35.5
Research / Documentation	11	68.8	1	50.0	18	58.1
Funding / Fund-raising	4	25.0			7	22.6
Co-ordination	11	68.8	2	100.0	19	61.3
Interest Representation	4	25.0			12	38.7
Policy Development / Legislation	13	81.3	1	50.0	15	48.4
Training of Professionals	11	68.8	2	100.0	24	74.4

Table 31 shows that the largest number of organizations specializing in DDR exclusively (except for the involvement in *prevention/information*) were mostly interested in conducting DDR activities in the field of *training of professionals*, *treatment and care* and *co-ordination*, while most organizations working in DDR inclusively were involved in DDR activities in the field of *training of professionals*, *co-ordination* and *policy development*.

The DDR budget changes the ranking of activities developed by the organizations in the different areas. Except for their involvement in *prevention/information*, more than half of organizations with very small budgets of up to EUR 10,000 conducted *co-ordination*, *training of professionals*, *policy development/legislation* and *treatment and care*, while organizations with budgets of more than EUR 100,000 conducted mainly *policy development/legislation*, *co-ordination*, *training of professionals* and *research/documentation*. The richer organizations were more interested in developing DDR policies and research than organizations with lower budgets that focused on helping people.

Table 31: Different types of DDR activity fields and exclusive/inclusive orientation

	Organizations specializing in DDR activity			
	Exclusively N=17		Inclusively N=32	
Types of DDR activity field	n	%	n	%
Prevention / Information	16	94.1	29	90.6
Treatment and Care	11	64.7	15	46.9
Rehabilitation / After-care	10	58.8	12	37.5
Research / Documentation	10	58.8	13	40.6
Funding / Fund-Raising	3	17.6	8	25.0
Co-ordination	11	64.7	21	65.6
Interest Representation	9	52.9	7	21.9
Policy Development	9	52.9	20	62.5
Training of Professionals	12	70.6	25	78.1

The investigated organizations differed by the percentages of paid professional staff. Most of them conducted activities in the area of *prevention/information*. But the other fields of DDR activities conducted by each selected category of organization were different depending on the size of the paid professional staff. Except for their involvement in *prevention/information*, the largest numbers of organizations that did not employ any professional paid staff were involved in DDR activities in the field of *rehabilitation/after-care, treatment and care* and *training of professionals*, while organizations employing only professional paid staff conducted DDR activities in the field of *policy development*, *training of professionals*, *co-ordination* and *research/documentation*. Moreover organizations with shares of up to half of paid professional staff focused more on activities directed at their clients such as treatment, rehabilitation and interest representation. The share of those fields of activity in the case of such organizations is considerably higher than in the case of organizations with a prevalence of paid professional staff.

The background of paid professional staff does not change the organizational activity field preference, but has an effect on a portion of organizational involvement in DDR activity. Both categories of employees improved the higher level of DDR services and organizations' professionalism, but educators seemed to be a more important group than psychologists. Generally speaking, the percentage of organizations that employed educators and were involved in each field of DDR activity is higher than in case of organizations employing psychologists. Most organizations that employed professional paid staff with an educational background were involved in DDR activities in the field of *prevention/ information* (96%), *training of professionals* (82%) and *co-ordination* (78%).

The largest numbers of organizations engaging volunteers were involved in DDR activity in the field of *prevention/information*, but also in *training of professionals*, *rehabilitation/ after-care* and *co-ordination*.

In the field of *prevention/information/education* the different activities were indicated 117 times (Activities No. 1, No. 2 and No. 3 presented together in Table A in the Annex). This field is the most preferred one among all activities indicated in the nine fields selected in the study. Activities in such fields were conducted by 45 of 49 investigated organizations, by 34 national organizations and by 11 local organizations.

The earliest preventive activities started in 1975 at the national level and in 1982 at the local level. The largest share of all activities indicated in that field started in the years 1985-1990 and 1990-1994 (Table B in the Annex). Nonetheless, the relative position of the activities in the field of *prevention/information* as compared to activities in all nine selected fields was constantly first in the rankings of activities started in each period of time.

Table 32: Conducted activity in the field of prevention/information/education and the level of operation

	Number of activities (Activity 1, Activity 2 and Activity 3)					
	Total		National Level		Local Level	
Type of activity	n	%	n	%	n	%
Lectures, seminars	46	39.3	27	30.3	19	67.9
Distribution of brochures, leaflets, etc.	16	13.7	15	16.9	1	3.6
Development of training programmes	19	16.2	18	20.2	1	3.6
Counselling	7	6.0	6	6.7	1	3.6
Street work, running information points, etc.	4	3.4	4	4.5		
Special events	2	1.7	1	1.1	1	3.6
Public information campaigns	8	6.8	5	5.6	3	10.7
Other	15	12.8	13	14.6	2	7.1
Total	117	100.0	89	100.0	28	100.0

The particular characteristics of the organization did not change the dominant position of the preventive activities. They were conducted by 81% of governmental organizations, by all private firms and by 97% of non-profit organizations. Activities in the field were conducted by 94% of organizations with exclusive DDR orientation and by 91% of organizations with inclusive DDR orientation.

The most frequently mentioned activity in the prevention field was conducting *lectures and seminars*, which was indicated 27 times: 18 times by national organizations and 9 times by local organizations. All other kinds of activities in the field were mentioned mainly by organizations operating at the national level (Table 32). Two activities were most frequently indicated: *developing training programmes* and *distribution of information material*. The remainder of the activities were conducted rarely. Neither the status of organizations nor the organizational exclusive/inclusive orientation differentiated their preference of particular activities in the field described above.

In the field of *treatment and care* different activities were indicated 49 times (Activities No. 1, No. 2 and No. 3 presented together in Table A in the Annex). Activities in that field were conducted by 26 out of 49 investigated organizations, by 16 national organizations, and by 10 local organizations.

The earliest treatment activities took place in 1978 at the national level and in 1982 at the local level. The largest number of all activities indicated in the field started in 1991-1994 and the lowest number was developed after 1995 (Table B in the Annex). It appears that treatment provision has decreased in importance over time, given the observed decline in newly initiated activities. It is unclear whether this has been due to a decreased interest of organizations to initiate care and treatment activities compared to other demand reduction actions, or whether existing demands have already been sufficiently met and that there is therefore no need to start up this type of activities.

NGOs were considerably more interested in treatment activities than public agencies. That kind of work was conducted by only 31% of governmental organizations, but by 65% of non-profit organizations.

Treatment and care activities were conducted by one out of two organizations with DDR budgets of up to EUR 10,000 and by 39% of the organizations with DDR budgets of more than EUR 100,000. *Treatment and care* activities were conducted by 33% of organizations that did not employ any professional paid staff, by 64% of organizations with up to half professional paid staff, and by 88% of organizations with more than half of professional paid staff. Two-thirds of all organizations that engaged any volunteers conducted some type of activity in this field. This situation might, to some extent, have been caused by the popularity of concepts of de-institutionalization and de-professionalization adopted in Poland by MONAR and other NGOs in the early 1980s.

The most frequent activities conducted in this field were: *individual counselling* (7); *treatment (general)* (7); *therapeutic community* (5); and *family therapy* (5).

In the field of *rehabilitation/after-care* different activities were indicated 35 times (Activities No. 1, No. 2 and No. 3 are presented together in Table A in the Annex). This field turned out to be one of the least popular types of action. Rehabilitation activities were carried out by 22 of 49 investigated organizations, by 14 national organizations and 8 local organizations.

The earliest activities in the field of *rehabilitation/after-care* started in 1980 at the national level and in 1982 at the local level. The largest number of all activities indicated in this field started before 1984 and the lowest number after 1995 (Table B in the Annex).

More organizations with exclusive DDR orientation (59%) than organizations with inclusive DDR orientation (38%) developed rehabilitation programmes. They were also more often provided by organizations with relatively high budgets. Rehabilitation was only conducted by 17% of organizations with a DDR budget of up to EUR 10,000, by half of organizations with DDR budgets of EUR 10,000- 50,000, by 78% of organizations with DDR budgets of EUR 50,000-100,000, and by 46% of organizations with a DDR budget of over EUR 100,000.

Rehabilitation/after-care focused mainly on: *group therapy, group meeting* (11); *assistance in social re-adaptation after treatment* (5); and *hostels* (4).

In the field of *research/documentation/database development* different activities were indicated 38 times (Activities No. 1, No. 2 and No. 3 are presented together in Table A in the Annex). Research activities were conducted by 23 out of 49 investigated organizations. It is worth noting that 82% of all activities in the fields mentioned in the study were conducted by organizations operating at the national level.

The largest number of all activities indicated in the field started in 1985-1990 (Table B in the Annex).

Governmental organizations were more interested in these types of activities than NGOs. Activities in the field were carried out by 69% of governmental organizations and only by 39% of NGOs.

Research/documentation/database development were usually performed by organizations with higher budgets and a high rate of professional staff. These activities were not conducted by organizations that did not employ any professional paid staff. The largest involvement in the field was represented by organizations employing only professional paid staff.

Besides *research* (15 cases) that was the most popular form of action, respondents mentioned *conducting evaluation* (7); *development of methods* (7); *running database centres* (5) and *collecting, publishing statistics* (4).

Funding/fund-raising were only indicated 17 times by all investigated organizations as a DDR activity (Activities No. 1, No. 2 and No. 3 are presented together in Table A in the Annex). Only 12 out of 49 investigated organizations conducted *funding/fund-raising* activities. This type of activity was carried out by 11 national organizations and only by one local organization.

Funding/fund-raising appear to be quite new phenonema. At the national level, the earliest funding activities started in 1989. The largest number of all activities indicated in the field of *funding/fund-raising* started both in 1985-1990 and after 1995 (Table B in the Annex).

An amazing high number of organizations declares to be involved in *co-ordination activities*, i.e. they were indicated 60 times by all investigated organizations (Activities No. 1, No. 2 and No. 3 are presented together in Table A in the Annex). *Co-ordination* activities were conducted by 32 out of 49 investigated organizations, by 25 national organizations and by 7 local organizations.

Co-ordination seems to be a relatively new field. The earliest co-ordination activities started in 1989 at the national level and most actions started in 1991-1994 (Table B in the Annex).

Co-ordination was developed by 69% of governmental organizations and by 61% of non-profit organizations. The DDR budget was barely influenced by the organizational commitment in this field. Co-ordination was conducted by 83% of organizations with a DDR budget up to EUR 10,000 and by 77% of organizations with a DDR budget of more than EUR 100,000.

The main forms in the field of *co-ordination* were: *co-ordination of other organizations' activities within special areas* (20); *co-ordination at the regional, national level* (17); *co-ordination of activities within one's own organization* (13) and *co-ordination of special events* (10).

Interest representation/protection of civil and human rights turned out to be among the least popular activities, since they were only indicated 28 times (Activities No. 1, No. 2 and No. 3 are presented together in Table A in the Annex). Activities in the field were carried out by 16 out of 49 investigated organizations, by 9 national organizations and by 7 local organizations.

The earliest activities were initiated in 1981 and the largest number of activities indicated in this field was started in 1985-1990 (Table B in the Annex). No activities have been initiated in the field since 1995.

Interest representation/protection of civil and human rights activities were most common among NGOs with exclusive DDR orientation. They were conducted by 39% of non-profit organizations and by 53% of organizations involved in DDR exclusively.

The activities focused on: *legal advice, representation* (13), *protecting drug users' rights* (9) and *lobbying, advocacy* (5).

Considerable interest was observed in the field of *policy development and legislation*; they were indicated 48 times (Activities No. 1, No. 2 and No. 3 presented together in Table A in the Annex) and were conducted by 29 of 49 investigated organizations, by 24 national organizations and by 5 local organizations.

The earliest activities were started in 1978 at the national level and in 1995 at the local level. The largest number of all activities indicated in the field started in 1985-1990 (Table B in the Annex).

Organizational involvement in the field was higher at the national level as well as in the case of governmental institutions with inclusive DDR orientation. National organizations carried out 88% of all activities indicated in that field.

The conducted policy development actions were: *participation in strategy* (22); *comments and opinion of existing and future programmes, solutions* (15) and *development of strategy, policy, legislation* (11).

Training of professionals was indicated 79 times (Activities No. 1, No. 2 and No. 3 are presented together in Table A in the Annex), and turned out to be the second-popular type of set of activities carried by the investigated organizations. Activities in the field were carried out by 37 of 49 investigated organizations, by 28 national organizations and by 9 local organizations. Organizations operating at the national level conducted 80% of all activities indicated in the field.

The largest number of all activities indicated in a field started in both 1985-1990 and 1991-1994 (Table B in the Annex). Interest in developing skills and knowledge significantly increased since 1985.

The training of professionals was conducted by 69% of governmental organizations and by 79% of NGOs. They were conducted irrespective of sizes of budgets or the exclusive or inclusive involvement in drug demand reduction.

3.3 *The most important activities for organizations*

The largest number of all investigated organizations and the biggest share of national level organizations indicated *prevention/information* as their most important DDR activity (Table 33). The next most important activity conducted by national organizations was the *training of professionals*. At the local level, the majority of organizations pointed out treatment and care as the most important domain of activity. This dissimilarity once again underlines the observation that local organizations understand their work as being directed mainly at helping people with problems. The rest of the characteristics also correspond with the suggestions mentioned above stating that local NGOs with an exclusive DDR orientation were more focused on the problems of clients than on developing the appropriate conditions for a healthy social life of the general population. Moreover, those organizations were usually engaged in a relatively lower number of selected fields of DDR activities defined as the most important ones than organizations with opposite features.

The percentage of professional paid staff seems to influence decisions regarding preferences for DDR activities. The higher the share of professional paid staff, the wider the spectrum of activities defined as the most important. The majority of organizations without any professional paid staff preferred to develop prevention programmes. The largest number of organizations with a staff consisting of a certain percentage of paid professionals chose prevention and treatment. Most organizations that employed only professional paid staff, preferred co-ordination. The type of professional background did not significantly vary the activity conducted as indicated.

Table 33: The most important DDR activity

	Number of organizations						
	Legal status		DDR orientation		Level of operating		**Total**
The most important type of DDR activity	Govern-mental N=16	NGO/ Private N= 32	Excl. N=16	Incl. N=32	National N=37	Local N=11	N=48
Prevention/ Information	3	15	7	11	16	2	18
Treatment and Care	4	10	7	7	5	9	14
Training of Professionals	3	3		6	6		6
Co-ordination	5		1	4	5		5
Rehabilitation/ After-care		3	1	2	3		3
Research/ Documentation	1			1	1		1
Funding/ Fund-raising		1		1	1		1

3.4 *Conducted activities to be intensified in the near future*

Three of the organizations operating at the national level did not express any intention of increasing DDR activities in the future. This is one of the reasons why the influence of certain organizational characteristics is presented separately here. Most of the organizations that responded to this question had plans to intensify their preventive activities (Table 34). Only the field of *interest representation* failed to attract the attention of any organization. The largest number of all investigated organizations and of national organizations intended to develop preventive activities in the future. In contrast, local level organizations most frequently indicated *treatment and care* as an activity they would like to increase in the future (similar to the preference assigned to the most important DDR activity for organizations). It seems that local level organizations are more focused on continuing activities that they had already been undertaking in the field of prevention, treatment and rehabilitation than on developing new ones. National level organizations, except those that conducted *prevention,* were planning to develop all DDR activities selected in the questionnaire excluding interest representation, and particularly, the *training of professionals* in the future.

The preference shown for DDR activities that had to be intensified in the future varied slightly by legal status of the organizations (Table 35). Non-profit organizations perceived a constant need for developing prevention, treatment and research. The ranking of preferred DDR activities for non-profit organizations was only slightly different. Except for prevention, these organizations planned to expand the training of professionals, treatment and rehabilitation work.

Table 34: The type of preferred DDR activity to be intensified in the near future and the level of operating

	Organizations					
Type of DDR activity to be intensified in the near future	All Investigated		National Level		Local Level	
	n	%	n	%	n	%
Prevention / Information	20	43.5	17	50.0	3	25.0
Treatment and Care	8	17.4	2	5.9	6	50.0
Rehabilitation / After-care	4	8.7	2	5.9	2	16.7
Research / Documentation	3	6.5	3	8.8		
Funding / Fund-raising	1	2.2	1	2.9		
Co-ordination	2	4.3	2	5.9		
Interest Representation						
Policy Development	1	2.2	1	2.9		
Training of Professionals	7	15.2	6	17.6	1	8.3
Total	46	100.0	34	100.0	12	100.0

185

Table 35: The type of preferred DDR activity to be intensified in the near future and the legal status of organizations

	Organizations					
Type of preferred DDR activity to be intensified in the near future	Governmental, public		Private firm, enterprise		Non-profit, voluntary	
	n	%	n	%	n	%
Prevention / Information	4	26.7	1	50.0	15	51.7
Treatment and Care	4	26.7	1	50.0	3	10.3
Rehabilitation / After-care					3	10.3
Research / Documentation	3	20.0				
Funding / Fund-raising					1	3.4
Co-ordination	2	13.3				
Interest Representation						
Policy Development					1	3.4
Training of Professionals	2	13.3			5	17.2
Total	15	100.0	2	100.0	29	100.0

In contrast to the most important activity preferences, organizations specializing in DDR exclusively planned to considerably widen the spectrum of their different types of activities in the future than organizations with inclusive DDR orientation (Table 36). The majority of organizations in the first category intended to further develop prevention activities, but the remaining organizations desired to intensify all other types of activities excluding interest representation. Organizations belonging to the second category preferred to intensify four types of activities in the future.

The conclusion may be drawn that organizations with an exclusive DDR orientation perceived the need to broaden their DDR offers, while organizations with inclusive DDR orientation tended to prefer a greater degree of specialization.

Table 36: The type of preferred DDR activity to be intensified in the near future by exclusive/inclusive orientation of organization

	Organizations specialising in DDR activity			
Type of preferred DDR activity	Exclusively		Inclusively	
to be intensified in near future	n	%	n	%
Prevention / Information	17	48.6	3	27.3
Treatment and Care	3	8.6	5	45.5
Rehabilitation / After-care	2	5.7	2	18.2
Research / Documentation	3	8.6		
Funding / Fund-raising	1	2.9		
Co-ordination	2	5.7		
Interest Representation				
Policy Development	1	2.9		
Training of Professionals	6	17.1	1	9.1
Total	35	100.0	11	100.0

Most organizations with professional paid staff having a psychological background were planning on intensifying prevention activities in the future. The share was the highest among organizations with professional paid staff having an educational background who also wanted to develop activities in that field. However, the next largest number of the first category of organizations expressed the desire to intensify treatment, while the next largest number of the second category of organizations desired to intensify training of professionals. Organizations hiring educators indicated a slightly different type of DDR activity to be intensified in the near future than organizations that hired psychologists.

4 Perception of the problem and policy

According to numerous conceptions, an important part of any social problem is its subjective definition. Trying to understand the problem "[...] we must consider [...] the varying definitions of the problem by various groups that have an interest in it, because the definitions themselves play a role in giving a problem the form that it has in society [....] the definition usually contains [...] suggestions on how it may be solved" (Becker, 1966: 10).

Therefore, besides the attempt to describe the institutional environment of the drug problem, our research goal was focused on respondents' opinion concerning the nature of the problem and national policy. We assumed that a problem's perception and the visions developed for the type of organizational setting could determine effective counteractions. Therefore, by identifying subjective opinions, we would arrive at a better understanding of the institutional response to the problem.

4.1 *Perception of the problem*

One of the most interesting elements of our respondents' definition was their assessment of the scope of the drug problem. Representatives of selected organizations were asked to present their own estimations of the number of drug users in their country in 1998. We assumed that this estimation would reflect both existing knowledge about the problem and could also be treated as an indicator of perceived threats.

Table 37: Estimated number of drug users in 1998

Estimated number	**Frequency**	**Per cent**
Less than 100,000	9	18.4
100,001-500,000	20	40.8
More than 500,000	7	14.3
Hard to say, no answer	13	26.5
Total	49	100.0

The data included in Table 37 shows a wide discrepancy between the respondents' assessments. The estimates varied from 10,000 to 9 million users. It is worth noting, however, that more than 40% of those interviewed defined the number of drug users within the range of 100-500,000; 14% of the respondents expressed the opinion that the number of users exceeded 500,000. It is also worth mentioning that almost one quarter of our respondents refused to make such an assessment (stressing the complexity of the problem or the difficulties in accessing the reliable statistics etc.).

Simultaneously with the assessment of the current situation, respondents were asked to provide their estimations of the development of the drug problem over a 5-year horizon (Table 38). Only 15% of our experts were convinced that they would be dealing with the same or even a lower number of drug users in 2003. According to forecasts made by the majority (85%), the number of users would increase.

A share of 27% of the interviewed persons forecasted an increase of less than 50%. Almost 40% of respondents anticipated a 50-100% rise and 18.2% of respondents expected the number of drug users to more than double (Table 39).

Table 38: Estimated number of drug users 2003

Estimated number	Frequency	Per cent
Less than 100,000	4	8.2
100,001-500,000	17	34.7
More than 500,000	12	24.5
Hard to say, no answer	16	32.7
Total	49	100.0

Table 39: Forecast of drug users in 2003

Forecast	Frequency	Per cent
Decrease or stabilization	5	10.2
Increase (101-149%)	9	18.4
Increase (150-200%)	13	26.5
Increase more than 200%	6	12.2
Total valid	33	67.3
Missing	16	32.7
Total	49	100.0

It turned out that the above-described opinions differed according to type of organization. Representatives of governmental organizations usually came up with higher estimates of drug users than representatives of non-governmental organizations. It is worth mentioning that respondents from the public sector very often refused to make estimates (37.5% of all government and public agencies and 22% of non-governmental organizations). Similar phenomena appeared in the case of organizations, which operated at the national level. They more often provided higher estimates of drug users and were also more willing to give estimates.

The closer the contact with drug users and their problems, the lower the estimated number of drug users. Table 40 shows that organizations engaged in the treatment and care field produced different definitions of the problem's scope. Lower estimates also came from organizations that conducted research. However, more than 30% of them did not provide any data. A similar proportion appeared in organizations which conducted different forms of evaluations or gathered information on their clients. It seems that the perception of the problem also depends on everyday experience. The direct contacts with drug users usually resulted in narrowing the scope of the problem. The same attitude (adopted by organizations involved in research or running their own databases) seems to be shaped by access to reliable sources of information.

Table 40: Estimated number of drug users in 1998 and involvement in treatment/care activities

Estimated number of drug users 1998		Treatment/care yes	no	Total
less than 100,000	N	6	3	9
	%	23.1	13.0	18.4
100,001-500,000	N	11	9	20
	%	42.3	39.1	40.8
More than 500,000	N	2	5	7
	%	7.7	21.7	14.3
Hard to say, no answer	N	7	6	13
	%	26.9	26.1	26.5
Total	N	26	23	49
	%	100.0	100.0	100.0

Opinions on the problem's development revealed interesting differences between the organizations. Non-governmental organizations were predominant among those forecasting sharp increases in the number of drug users. Almost half of them anticipated an increase of 50-100% over the next five years, while another 22% of non-governmental organizations anticipated an increase of over 100%. Expectations of a stabilization or a decrease were expressed mostly by organizations conducting research and those involved in policy development. Forecasts predicting an alarming rise were made mostly by organizations established in the 1980s.

4.1.1 Perception of the structure of supply

Another research objective was the attempt to reconstruct opinions on the nature of the problem. Respondents were asked to express their opinions on the prevalence of drugs in Poland. In order to avoid problems with drug consumption (e.g. the use of different drugs by the same person), a question on the current and future structure of the drug supply was used. It is worth stressing that it posed some difficulties for a number of respondents. About 11-17 respondents refused to come up with estimates (in the case of cocaine only 28 persons provided assessments).

According to our respondents, three drugs dominated the Polish market in 1998: opiates (28%), cannabis (28%) and amphetamines (24%). The share of hallucinogens was estimated at 7.3% of the total market, cocaine was less popular (4.4%). It is worth noting that only a slightly different structure of supply was predicted over the 5-year horizon.

Table 41: Opiates – estimates 1998

Share in total market	N	Per cent	Valid per cent
up to 10%	10	20.4	27.8
11-20%	7	14.3	19.4
21-40%	10	20.4	27.8
more than 40%	9	18.4	25.0
Total	36	73.5	100.0
Missing	13	26.5	
Total	49	100.0	

OPIATES

The mean values do not reflect the existing dispersions among the respondents' opinions (Table 41). For example, 28% of the interviewed persons estimated that opiates constituted up to 10% of all drugs consumed by Polish drug users. Almost 20% of the interviewed persons estimated the proportion as 10-20%, and 27% as 20-30%, while the remaining percentage of the respondents (25%) saw it as higher than 30%. As regards opiates, no significant change was expected (Table 42). The share of opiates in 2003 is estimated at 26% (28% in 1998). According to the vast majority of respondents (81%), the use of opiates would decrease or remain at the same level.

Table 42: Opiates – forecast

Forecast	N	Per cent	Valid per cent
Decrease or stabilization	27	55.1	81.8
Increase (1-49%)	4	8.2	12.1
Increase (50-100%)	1	2.0	3.0
Increase more than 100%	1	2.0	3.0
Total	33	67.3	100.0
Missing	16	32.7	
Total	49	100.0	

CANNABIS

A similar situation appeared in the case of cannabis. One-fourth of the respondents estimated its share at 10% or less, around 16% declared that cannabis accounted for between 11-20%, and almost 20% estimated its scope as higher than 40% of the total market. According to 61% of organizations, there were no significant changes expected for the period 1998 through 2003. Almost 40% of respondents expected a rise in cannabis supply and 20% of them anticipated a significant rise (e.g. more than 50%) in comparison to 1998.

AMPHETAMINES

The more coherent interpretations concerned amphetamines. The majority of respondents (70%) estimated that amphetamines accounted for between 10-40% of the total market in 1998. No major change in amphetamine consumption was expected for the next five years. However, almost 25% of respondents forecasted a sharp increase (50-100%) and the remaining 13% expected a moderate increase.

COCAINE AND HALLUCINOGENS

Cocaine and hallucinogens were characterized as relatively seldom drugs in Poland. A share of 92% of the respondents estimated that cocaine represented less than 10% of the total supply (60% declared that its share did not exceed 5%). According to 74% of the respondents, hallucinogens constituted up to 10% of the Polish drug market. Different beliefs emerged in the case of forecasts. A share of 66% of the interviewed persons anticipated a significant increase in cocaine consumption. The same rise in the use of hallucinogens was expected by 27% of the organizations. It seems that the phenomenon of hallucinogens, and especially cocaine consumption, is hardly recognized and posed more interpretation problems than the consumption of other drugs like opiates or cannabis. Almost 50% of the respondents could not formulate any forecasts regarding cocaine and hallucinogen consumption.

4.2 *Attitudes towards the problem*

The research also provided remarkable information on the attitudes regarding the nature of the drug problem and related countermeasures. We were interested in reconstructing the dominant approaches to the drug problem adopted by representatives of organizations. Respondents were asked to provide their opinions on the tolerance of drug consumption, consequences of drug use and on some policy options.[15]

A striking feature of the data gathered was the relatively narrow range of the respondents' agreement with the opinions stated (Table 43). The only instances of consent related to cannabis legalization, abstinence from drugs as a precondition for effective therapy and in the case of the opinion that "All use of illegal drugs is misuse". In all remaining cases, we discovered divergences.

Table 43: Opinions on the nature of the problem and approved counteractions (means on scale 1-5)

	N	Mean	Std. Deviation
Taking drugs can be beneficial	49	4.14	1.44
Adults should be free to take drugs	49	3.41	1.81
Using drugs is sometimes normal	49	3.63	1.65
Cannabis should be legalized	49	4.65	0.93
Best treatment is not to use drugs	49	1.61	1.22
The use of drugs always leads to addiction	49	2.71	1.66

Illegal drugs were generally perceived as a dysfunctional element of a social system. A widespread disapproval (73%) was expressed in the case of the opinion that "Taking illegal drugs can sometimes be beneficial". Almost 70% of the respondents strongly disapproved that view. A similar share (80%) supported the belief that abstinence is a precondition for successful treatment. A share of 73.5% interviewed persons declared their strong approval, and a share of 10.2% partly supported the above belief.

For the majority of respondents (77.5%) any use of drugs is a misuse. Conservative attitudes to the problem were also revealed in the opinions on legalization relating to soft drugs, e.g. in case of cannabis legalization. In this case 85.7% of respondents strongly disapproved of the concept. Only 3 out of 49 persons interviewed supported the idea of legalization.

It is worth noting, however, that the conservative views discovered in the above-mentioned opinions only partially corresponded with other beliefs. For example, a similar split in respondents' opinion was revealed in the case of agreement on adults' free will to take illicit drugs (56% disagreed, 36% agreed), the approval that using illegal drugs is normal for some people's lives (61% disagreed, 33% agreed) or the opinion that "Taking illegal drugs is always morally wrong" (49% disagreed, 37% agreed). One of the most controversial questions concerned the view that the use of illegal drugs always leads to addiction. Almost half of the respondents – 38.8% – disagreed (including 24.5% who expressed a strong disagreement).

One may assume that we are dealing with two interrelated sets of definitions. The first one places the emphasis on the pragmatic aspects of the problem and results in beliefs of the negative consequences of drug use. Due to such dysfunctional effects on society and individuals, drug use should be penalized and the only successful therapy is complete abstinence. The second interpretation seems to define the drug problem from a moral perspective, stressing adults' rights to make free choices, and a limited degree of tolerance for taking some kinds of drugs. According to this perspective, some forms of drug use do not automatically create a social problem.

The data gathered did not provide a convincing explanation of the factors which had shaped respondents' interpretations. It turned out that the above opinions were not determined by the type of organizational structures or by the activities performed. There were no differences between governmental and non-governmental organizations, and there were minor discrepancies between the opinions of exclusive and inclusive organizations.

Only a few of the differences provide plausible explanations. One of them is the difference between organizations, which conducted research and other institutions. Those conducting research more often advocated liberal positions (e.g. wider support for views on the benefits of taking drugs, tolerance for drug use). The same relationships were observed in the case of organizations involved in policy or legislation development.

4.3 *Opinions on national policy*

One of the research objectives was to reconstruct organizations' views on the current national policy on the drug problem. We assumed that opinions about priorities of the national policy would characterize policy itself as well as shed some light on the interpretations provided by drug demand reduction organizations. We were interested to what extent the national policy is perceived as focused on the following dimensions: health promotion, harm minimization, demand reduction, control of supply, and law enforcement and control.

The data gathered in Table 44 shows that the Polish policy on drug problems does not have any specific emphasis. The mean values of all answers revealed that none of the above options met with unanimous support. Only demand reduction and health promotion were indicated more often than other characteristics.

Table 44: Opinions on focus of national policy (means on scale 1-5)

	N	Mean	Std. Deviation
Health promotion	49	3.00	1.22
Harm reduction	49	2.80	1.00
Demand reduction	48	3.04	1.20
Control of supply	48	2.73	1.18
Law enforcement	48	2.19	1.12
Valid N	47		

An analysis of the data gathered revealed that almost one-third of the respondents agreed that the current policy was oriented on health promotion and around 40% stressed the demand reduction focus. A share of 24% agreed that the national policy is based on harm reduction and 30% on control of supply. Only six persons (12%) claimed that the policy was law enforcement oriented. It seems that the national policy has not been perceived as a specific counteraction based on an agreed-on conception. The data gathered suggests that the policy interpretation was formulated on a common understanding of undesired courses of action, rather than on the unified approval of the policy thrust.

The evidence suggests that opinions on national policy resulted from a general attitude towards state policy rather than being based on a detailed analysis of the particular policy goals. It turned out that representatives of governmental organizations and agencies more often agreed with every characteristic of a policy provided in our research than respondents from non-profit or voluntary organizations. The same overall support emerged in the case of organizations operating on the smallest budgets (Tables 45-46).

Table 45: Opinions on national policy and legal status (means on scale 1-5)

Legal status	Health promotion	Harm reduction	Demand reduction	Control of supply	Law enforcement
Governmental agency	3.38	3.19	3.38	3.06	2.63
Private firm, enterprise	3.50	1.50	4.00	2.50	2.00
Non-profit	2.77	2.68	2.80	2.57	1.97
Total	3.00	2.80	3.04	2.73	2.19

Table 46: Opinions on national policy and organizations' budgets (means on scale 1-5)

Total budget (EUR)	Health promotion	Harm reduction	Demand reduction	Control of supply	Law enforcement
up to 10,000	3.53	2.88	3.65	3.06	2.59
10,001-50,000	3.00	2.20	2.40	2.60	2.00
50,001-100,000	2.80	2.90	2.70	2.00	1.67
more than 100,000	2.59	2.82	2.81	2.82	2.12
Total	3.00	2.80	3.04	2.73	2.19

Lack of a coherent image seemed also to determine the perception of the strengths and weaknesses of the national policy (Tables 47-48). The most frequently mentioned advantages were related to drug demand reduction activities. Opinions which stressed the importance of prevention and therapy programmes constituted more than 30% of all opinions. Another frequently mentioned group of strengths was the recognition of the drug problem by vast categories of Polish society. The third category of policy advantages emphasized co-ordination and effectiveness of counteractions. Only less than 10% of all choices concerned control of supply or law enforcement activities.

It is worth stressing that the number of responses showing policy weaknesses (128) was bigger than the number of indications of policy achievements (89) provided by our respondents. The main concern for the interviewees was the lack of a coherent policy on the problem (lack of vision, lack of a national programme). For a number of respondents, the main weaknesses were financial problems (insufficient funding, lack of stable financial support). Another group of weaknesses emphasized the lack of effective co-ordination and the lack of available communication channels at the vertical level.

Table 47: The main strengths of the national policy

	Count	Per cent of Responses
1 Awareness of the drug problem, public discussions, better understanding of the problem	18	20.2
2 Efficient network of organizations, effective cooperation	9	10.1
3 Competent, expert-based and professional	4	4.5
4 Prevention programmes, preventative programmes for schools, new subjects of drug prevention	22	24.7
5 Therapy programmes (new treatment and care centres, therapeutic communities	11	12.4
6 Harm reduction programmes	2	2.2
7 Effective policy, conception, legislation, (variety of programmes, openness to change	11	12.4
8 Supply control, law enforcement (legislation and control), repression, relatively good control of supply (drug market), new legal institutions for police (controlled purchases, secret parcels) for combating drug criminality	8	9.0
9 Other	1	1.1
10 No strengths at all	3	3.4
Total responses	89	100.0

Table 48: Main weakness of the national policy

	Count	Per cent of Responses
1 Lack of awareness of the drug problem (drug users are not recognized as patients)	13	10.2
2 Lack of professionals, experts	5	3.9
3 Ineffective programmes	12	9.4
4 Focus on law enforcement, repressive approach, proclamation of war on drugs	6	4.7
5 Lack of policy, there is no drug policy, lack of a conceptual approach, lack of a national programme of priorities, lack of programmes	34	26.6
6 Lack of co-ordination, there is no co-ordination, there is big chaos, incoherence of ideas, communication on the vertical level	14	10.9
7 Lack of research, information, no information/data on the number of drug users, absence of research institute	2	1.6
8 Insufficient funding, financial problems	27	21.1
9 Lack of evaluation, lack of control & monitoring of programmes	2	1.6
10 Barriers to the development of non-governmental institutions	7	5.5
11 Other	6	4.7
Total responses	128	100.0

5 Conclusions

The late 1990s seem to be a period of major transition for Polish drug policy. The national policy developed in the early 1980s as a demand reduction policy has been gradually shifting towards a supply control approach. However, most official government programmes still place their principal emphasis on the demand side, though the latest legislative changes suggest that a supply reduction approach is becoming more and more accepted among politicians as well as among the general public. One of the possible consequences of the increasing popularity of a repressive policy is the emergence of various forms of legitimization of a new definition of the problem.

The influence of the supply control perspective can be also observed within institutions covered by our research (strong disapproval of cannabis legalization, widespread belief that drug use cannot be beneficial). It is worth noting that national policy is still perceived by the majority of organizations as oriented on health promotion or demand reduction rather than having a focus on law enforcement or supply control.

The above beliefs seem to be supported by the type of organizational setting. Prevention and therapy are the dominant forms of activities especially in the case of NGOs. They are also the "oldest" activities, initiated in some cases even in the late 1970s. A focus on demand reduction is closely linked to the prevailing categories of professionals in the organizations surveyed, e.g. psychologists and specialists with an educational background. Their perceptions of the problems and methods applied seem to reinforce the policy perspective adopted at the beginning of the 1980s.

A very important characteristic is the key position of non-governmental organizations. Not only have they played a key role in the problem's definition in the past, but have also become a main service provider at the local level. NGOs' activities focus on prevention/information activities and providing treatment. The less important part of their activities is devoted to policy development. Policy development (and to some extent co-ordination) seems to remain the domain of government agencies.

The data gathered proves that the organizational system is rather well developed both in terms of past experiences and existing resources. Only a small proportion of all activities were initiated in the last five years. Almost half of the organizations employed more than 10 persons, which suggests that the current system is relatively well protected from current economic and political turbulence.

Besides their role in policy formulation, state administrations are also a major source of funding for drug demand programmes. In the last three years, a slight increase in the use of other funding sources has been observed. In 1998, 85% of organizations used financial resources from government agencies. Relying on state subsidies seems to be a barrier to NGOs' development, especially bearing in mind the current shift towards supply control policy and a possible change in the thrust of state subsides.

A closer look at organizations' budgets reveals that financial dependence on the government is only part of the general picture. On the one hand, there is a wide gap when comparing governmental and non-governmental organizations' overall budgets. On the other hand, there are no significant differences between NGO and GO budgets when resources allocated to drug demand reduction are taken into account. The same association applies to the number of staff employed. It seems that the involvement of government agencies is to some extent forced by the legal requirements rather than reflecting actual organizational interests. The NGOs' focus on the implementation of programmes (therapy, care and rehabilitation) is linked to a relatively low influence on policy design.

It is necessary to stress that the conclusions drawn above reflect the situation of the organizational response in the area of drug demand reduction only. In order to formulate policy recommendations, it is necessary to refer to similar research concerning the "supply control" side. However, even without such a detailed diagnosis, one may assume that a possible shift towards supply control policy could lead to significant changes in the current system and reduce the role of non-governmental organizations in the area of drug demand reduction. Therefore, the organizational response of the late 1990s described in this report might undergo considerable changes in the near future.

Notes

1 http://www.sejm.gov.pl:8009/proc3/opisy/631.htm
2 http://www.medianet.pl/~bdsnark/
3 According to the 1997 Act, the following institutions were responsible for the implementation of government policy. The Ministry of Health and Social Welfare, Pharmacy Department of the Ministry of Health and Social Welfare, Youth and Education Department at the Ministry of National Education, Social-Educational Department at the Ministry of National Defence, the Ministry of Foreign Affairs, the Ministry of Internal Affairs and Administration, the Ministry of Finance, Social Welfare Department at the Ministry of Labour and Social Policy, Department for the Development of Agriculture at the Ministry of Agriculture and Food Economy, Organized Crime Bureau of the General Public Prosecutor's Office of the Ministry of Justice, the Bureau for Combating Drug-Related Crime of the National Police Headquarters, Chief Inspector of Financial Information, Chief Inspectorate of Banking Supervision (National Bank of Poland), Prevention and Customs Supervision Department of the Central Board of Customs, Customs Inspectorate, the Office of State Protection, the Frontier Guard.
4 http://www.medianet.pl/~bdsnark/
5 *Ustawa o zapobieganiu narkomanii z 24 kwietnia 1997 roku.* [Law on Counteracting Drug Addiction from 24 April 1997]
6 *Krajowy Program Przeciwdzia_ania Narkomanii na lata 1999-2001,* 1998, Biuro ds. Narkomanii [National Programme for Counteracting Drug Addiction 1999-2000]
7 This information and the other information presented in this part of the report are taken from the document "National Programme for Counteracting Drug Addiction 1999-2000".
8 *Informator Biura ds. Narkomanii na rok 2001,* 1999, Biuro ds. Narkomanii [Bureau for Drug Addiction Directory for 2001].
9 Information on the Bureau for Drug Addition, http://www.medianet.pl/~bdsnark/
10 This data and other pieces of information and conclusions about drug epidemiology are presented in the chapter: *Epidemiological situation of drug addiction,* in: *Krajowy Program Przeciwdzia_ania Narkomanii na lata 1999-2001,* 1998, Biuro ds. Narkomanii [National Programme for Counteracting Drug Addiction 1999-2000]
11 Rocznik statystyczny GUS 1999 [Yearbook of 1999, Chief Central Statistic Office].
12 Komenda Glówna Policji, Biuro do Walki z Przest´pczoÊcia Narkotykowa, 1999, *Informacja o stanie zagrozenia narkonania,* in: Problemy narkomanii, Biuletyn 3/99
13 *Informator Biura ds. Narkomanii na rok 2001,* 1999, Biuro ds. Narkomanii [Bureau for Drug Addiction Directory for 2001]
14 Information on the Bureau for Drug Addition, http://www.medianet.pl/~bdsnark/
15 Respondents were asked to react to the following statements:
1. Taking illegal drugs can sometimes be beneficial
2. Adults should be free to take any drug they wish
3. We need to accept that using illegal drugs is normal for some people's lives
4. Smoking cannabis should be legalized
5. The best way to treat people who are addicted to drugs is to stop them using drugs altogether
6. The use of illegal drugs always leads to addiction
7. Taking illegal drugs is always morally wrong
8. All use of illegal drugs is misuse

References

Becker, Howard S. (1966) 'Introduction', in: Howard S. Becker (Ed.), *Social Problems. A Modern Approach*. New York: John Wiley and Sons, Inc.

Hibel, B. et al. (Eds.) (1997) *The 1995 ESPAD Report. Alcohol and Other Drug Use Among Students in 26 European Countries*. Stockholm.

Ministry of Health and Social Welfare (1996) *National Health Programme, 1996-2005*. Warszawa.

Moskalewicz, J./ Sieroslawski, J. (1995) 'Zastosowanie nowych metod szacowania rozpowszechnienia narkomanii' [Application of New Methods of Estimating Drug Abuse Prevalence], *Alkoholizm i Narkomania* 4/21.

National Programme for Counteracting Drug Addiction 1999-2000

Sieroslawski, J. (1999) 'Na polskiej scenie', *Âwiat Problemów* 7-8.

Sieroslawski, J./ Zielinski, A. (1996) 'Comparison of Different Estimation Methods in Poland', in: G.V. Stimpson et al. (Eds.), *Estimating the Prevalence of Problem Drug Use in Europe*. Luxembourg.

Sieroslawski, J./ Zielinski, A. (1998) DoroÊli warszawiacy a substancje psychoaktywne, *Alkoholizm i Narkomania* 1/30.

Sobiech, R. (1991) 'Conceptual Aspects of the Response to Drug Abuse in Poland', in: J. Kwasniewski J./ Watson, M. (Eds), *Social Control and the Law*. New York/Oxford: Berg.

Annex

Table A: Distribution of DDR activities conducted in different types of fields by the level of organizational operating

Type of DDR activity field		Number of organizations								
		Activity 1			Activity 2			Activity 3		
		Total	National Level	Local Level	Total	National Level	Local Level	Total	National Level	Local Level
		n	n	n	n	n	n	n	n	n
Prevention / Information	[117]	45	34	11	42	32	10	30	21	9
Treatment and Care	[49]	26	16	10	15	9	6	8	4	4
Rehabilitation (After-care)	[35]	22	14	8	8	6	2	5	4	1
Research / Documentation	[38]	23	17	6	11	8	3	4	4	
Funding / Fund-raising	[17]	11	10	1	5	5	1	1		
Co-ordination	[60]	32	25	7	18	13	5	10	7	3
Interest Representation	[28]	16	9	7	8	5	3	4	4	
Policy Development	[48]	29	24	5	15	14	1	4	4	
Training of Professionals	[79]	37	28	9	24	19	5	18	15	3
Total	[471]	241	177	64	146	111	35	84	64	20

Table B: Different types of DDR activity by the date of starting

Type of DDR activity	**Number of DDR activity (Activity 1, Activity 2 and Activity 3 counted together) starting by organizations in:** 1946-1984		1985-1990		1991-1994		after 1995		Total	
	n	%	n	%	n	%	n	%	n	%
Prevention / Information	24	24.2	36	23.7	36	23.4	21	31.8	117	24.8
Treatment and Care	12	12.1	15	9.9	19	12.3	3	3.7	49	10.4
Rehabilitation (After-care)	13	13.1	11	7.2	9	5.8	2	3.1	35	7.4
Research / Documentation	10	10.1	12	7.9	11	7.1	5	6.3	38	8.1
Funding / Fund-raising	3	3.0	5	3.3	4	2.6	5	6.3	17	3.6
Co-ordination	8	8.1	18	11.8	24	15.6	10	16.2	60	12.7
Interest Representation	6	6.1	12	7.9	10	6.5	1.6	28	5.9	21.4
Policy Development	12	12.1	15	9.9	13	8.4	8	18.3	48	10.2
Training of Professionals	11	11.1	28	18.4	28	18.2	12	17.3	79	16.8
Total	99	100.0	152	100.0	154	100.0	66	100.0	469	100.0

List of researched organizations

President of Poland, Chancellery of the President

National Institute of Hygiene, Department of Health Promotion

Ministry of Foreign Affairs

Ministry of Labour and Social Policy, Department of Social Assistance

Ministry of National Defence, Social and Educational Department, Section of Social Analysis and Education

Ministry of Education

Headquarters of Penitentiary Services

National Police Headqarters, Central Narcotics Bureau

Bureau for Drug Addiction

Agency for Professional Advice "AD"

The Polish Scouting and Guiding Association

Warsaw Charity Society

Society of Social Prevention

Polish Society of Drug Abuse Prevention

Society of Families and Friends of Drug Dependant Children, "Return from 'U' "

Society of Psychoprophylaxis

Association of Professionals in Psychotherapy and Psychoeducation for Drug Dependent Persons

Association "Solidarity plus"

Polish Psychological Society

Polish Foundation for Humanitarian Assistance

Association MONAR

The Committee for Protection of Children's Rights

The Committee on Alcohol and Drug Education

Stefan Batory Foundation

Polish Foundation of Good Templars

Center of Psychological Assistance

Nation-wide Help-Line

Youth Prevention Unit "Pro-M", Institute of Psychiatry and Neurology

Institute of Psychiatry and Neurology

Association KARAN, Antidrug Catholic Movement

Catholic Councelling Center

Association of Polish Scouts

Polish Society of Health Education

Polish League "Soberity"

Foundation "Praesterno"

Society "Social Assistance"

Whitsuntide Church

Society of Volunteers against AIDS „Be with US"

Regional Center for Social Policy

Polish Society of Drug Abuse Prevention

Society for Counteracting Drug Addiction

Department of Combating Drug Related Crime, Police Headquarters

Health Center, "Monar" Association

Independent Public Medical Care Centre, Municipal Preventive and Therapeutic Centre for Drug Endanger

Children and Youth Centre for Preventive Treatment and Development PROM

Health Center, Central Hospital

Drug Dependance Therapy Center

Dermatology Health Center

Counselling Centre "MONAR"

CHAPTER 5

The Institutional Response to Drug-Related Problems in Slovenia

Balancing Between Harm Reduction and Abstinence Approaches

Bojan Dekleva and Renata Cvelbar Bek

1 Policy conditions: The institutional, social and epidemiological context

1.1 Introduction

In Slovenia, the problem of illegal drug use became a challenge relatively late. In 1963, the abuse of analgesics was a problem in the whole territory of former Yugoslavia, and by 1967 cannabis and LSD use had also become widespread.[1]

The first "formal" attempt to tackle the problem of drug demand reduction was in 1987 with the creation of a draft Action Programme for the Prevention and Elimination of Drug Abuse by the Ministry of Health.[2] Because the scale of the problem was unknown, the draft Programme talked about the "impression of the police and health workers that the abuse of illegal drugs had increased".[3] The draft was never adopted by the National Assembly and therefore never enforced.

In 1992, the Social Democratic Party prepared a strategy called the "National Programme for the Prevention of Drug Abuse",[4] which later became the action plan for the National Committee for Drug Abuse Prevention.

The creation of a drug demand reduction policy was at the beginning significantly influenced by psychiatrists, and until 1995 psychiatric treatment was the only formally available treatment in the country for drug addicts, although other types of treatment already existed. Public opinion has traditionally tended to be prohibitive and repressive.

The approach to drug demand reduction changed gradually throughout the 1990s. There were a number of different influencing factors:

- New NGOs in the field were established and became very active.
- The influential self-help movement of concerned parents of drug addicts.
- The fear of an AIDS/HIV epidemic.
- Contacts with international organizations.

Since 1995, the government has become more concerned with drug demand reduction policy.

The milestone of governmental policy on drug demand reduction was the adoption of the methadone treatment programme in 1995. This step formally legalized harm reduction programmes in Slovenia.

After 1995, psychiatrists and medical doctors still dominated the field. However, other professionals, as for example psychologists and social workers, have been gaining more and more influence ever since. Moreover, the influence of NGOs has been growing.

The main field of tension at the end of the 1990s was still between the so-called "medical programmes" and "social rehabilitation programmes" or between methadone treatment programmes and drug-free and other programmes. However, this is more a discourse among professionals than a public discourse.

The question of decriminalization and discussions about the legalization of cannabis have sporadically appeared on the agenda in the past decade. Thus far, there has not been any political action or any serious civil activity towards achieving this aim. The general public is concerned mainly about the scale of the problem and the side-effects of illegal drug use such as crime and the spread of AIDS/HIV.

1.2 Legislation

Slovenia has ratified:

- The Single Convention on Narcotic Drugs of 1961,[5]
- The Convention on Psychotropic Substances of 1972,[6] and
- The United Nations Convention against Illicit Traffic in Drugs and Psychotropic Substances of 1988.

The principal legal acts dealing with drug related problems in Slovenia are the Crime Code[7] and the Act on Illicit Production and Trafficking of Drugs[8]. In the Crime Code, production, trafficking and the possession of drugs are defined as offences against "the health of human beings". The production and trafficking of illegal drugs, and also enabling others to use drugs, is a crime and the penalty imposed is imprisonment from one to ten years. The possession of drugs is also an offence. Compulsory treatment of drug addicts who commit a serious crime is a part of the Crime Code as well.

In 1995, the government started work on legislation concerning the prevention and treatment of drug addicts. The Prevention of the Use of Illicit Drugs and Dealing with Consumers of Illicit Drugs Act was adopted in 1999.[9] It is the first and only act regulating demand reduction policy in Slovenia. It defines measures for the prevention of illegal drug use and measures for the treatment of illegal drug addicts. It defines for the first time the different institutions responsible for drug demand reduction and how responsibility for financing is distributed. It also defines the role of non-governmental organizations in the field of drug demand reduction. Activities of non-governmental organizations may encompass educational activities, prevention and harm reduction activities. They may provide abstinence programmes, social rehabilitation and reintegration. They may also provide other activities in accordance with the law and the National programme.

Non-governmental organizations: legal framework

The first non-governmental organizations in Slovenia were established at the end of the 19th century.

Civil society in Slovenia is presented through different associations, non-governmental, non-profit organizations. The legal basis of non-governmental organizations is set out in:

- Article 42 of the Constitution of the Republic of Slovenia[10]
- the Act on Associations[11]
- the Act on Foundations[12]
- the Act on Institutions[13]

Slovene legislation generally does not operate with the term non-governmental organizations. The legal status of non-governmental organizations in Slovenia varies and it can be chosen when an NGO is established. The status of an NGO can be an association (Non-profit voluntary organizations established according to the basic principles of voluntarism and independence. They are public.), a foundation (A legal private entity whose aim is charity.) or an institution (Non-profit organizations established for the purpose of educational, research, cultural, health, social care, child care activities. Institutions can be private or public.).

The role of NGOs is also defined in other special laws (lex specialis) as for example in The Act on Social Protection[14]. NGOs are free to choose what kind of activities they perform. The activities are registered.

The legal basis for some of the NGOs' drug-related activities have been unclear up to now. There were different interpretations of their, e.g. low threshold activities (such as needle exchange), and sometimes there have been threats that their activities would be prosecuted for being related to the possession of illegal drugs or for enabling drug abuse.

NGOs seeking financing from the state or municipal budgets have to meet certain criteria. The criteria are defined in specific laws. For instance, in the case of funding from the Ministry of Labour, Family and Social Affairs the criteria consist of: registration in the field of social or health care; at least one professional working in the project who has passed the state exam in the field of social care; available and adequate premises where the programme should take place, and co-financing from other sources. Programmes that seek financing from the state budget and whose aim is to help resolve social problems in connection with drug abuse have to be verified by the Council for Drugs (Drug Council established by the Ministry of Social Affairs).

The medical treatment of drug addiction is licensed by the Ministry of Health. Health treatment can be provided only on the authorization of the Health Council. According to the Prevention of the Use of Illicit Drugs and Dealing with Consumers of Illicit Drugs Act, methadone treatment is a health treatment and can be provided only by authorized institutions for this reason.

As described above, there are two authorities that supervise and license drug demand reduction programmes: the Council for Drugs and the Health Council.

Detoxification in a hospital, according to the Prevention of the Use of Illicit Drugs and Dealing with Consumers of Illicit Drugs Act, is also considered as health treatment. There is no legal limit to the number of beds at a centre for detoxification, it is limited only by the amount of funds available.

NGOs are not eligible for insurance money as yet. The health insurance finances only the services of the public health institutions and private health clinics.

1.3 *Governmental concepts and strategies*

No comprehensive formal governmental strategy on drug demand reduction exists to date. The governmental policy is a compilation of specific policies of the specialized ministries. The Prevention of the Use of Illicit Drugs and Dealing with Consumers of Illicit Drugs Act demands that the government adopts the National Programme on the Prevention and Reduction of the Illegal Use of Drugs. Therefore, it is expected that a national strategy will be prepared in the near future.

For the time being, the different ministries define the priorities.

The main ministries responsible for drug demand reduction are the Ministry of Health and the Ministry of Labour, Family and Social Affairs. The division of responsibilities among them is quite clear, especially when speaking about financing. It is defined by the Prevention of the Use of Illicit Drugs and Dealing with Consumers of Illicit Drugs Act.

The Ministry of Health is responsible for programmes operating in the medical institutions, whereas the Ministry of Labour, Family and Social Affairs is responsible for programmes dealing with social rehabilitation, after-care and prevention. These are mainly implemented by NGOs and by some Centres for Social Work.

Governmental policy has been influenced by various international programmes, for example, the PHARE programmes, and the Council of Europe (Pompidou Group) Programme on Drug Demand Reduction for Central and Eastern Europe. Especially influential were study visits for civil servants organized under PHARE to the Netherlands and the United Kingdom.

NGOs play an important role in the creation of the governmental policy. International NGOs, as for example, the Italian NGOs, have played an important role in the creation of Slovene NGOs.

Drug demand reduction activities and policy in Slovenia are a combination of various initiatives and a consequence of the different movements, which were influenced mainly by Western European drug demand reduction policies.

Intuitively, we have identified three trends in professional interests and orientations which influence governmental concepts and are also supported by governmental actions.

The development of harm reduction programmes

The first significant step towards a drug demand reduction policy was made at the end of the 1980s with the introduction of methadone treatment in the

Vojnik psychiatric hospital. Subsequently, the drug users' NGO, "Stigma", was founded in 1991 and in 1994, methadone treatment was legalized. The introduction of methadone treatment significantly influenced the later establishment of harm reduction programmes and outreach programmes provided by NGOs and, of course, centres for methadone treatment. The governmental system of regional (methadone) A and B centres represents the most developed, staffed, institutionalized and continuously funded system of drug demand reduction.

The development of therapeutic communities

At the beginning of the 1990s, experts and the public became increasingly aware of the need for developing drug-related treatment programmes. An NGO "Social Forum" was founded in 1994, which gathered experts dealing with different types of addiction from the different fields. It was an association of mainly professionals dealing with alcohol addiction who became aware of the problems of illicit drug addiction. They started working with parents of drug users and supported the foundation of the first self-help groups of parents. Those groups and the association made a significant impact on the foundation of therapeutic communities in Slovenia, e.g. Project Man and Communita Incontro.

The development of educational and school-based prevention

Primary prevention in Slovenia started in the mid-1980s, before the outbreak of illicit drug use, such as the *School for Life Programme,* which was mainly focused on sex education. At the end of the 1980s, another preventive programme, called *Youth Workshop* was "imported" from the Republic of Serbia and logistically further developed in Slovenia. It is based on voluntary workers who organize and lead workshops (primarily) at elementary schools (for pupils aged 13-15). These workshops became widely recognized and expanded in the middle of the 1990s across all of Slovenia. Nowadays, the workshops are implemented in about 40-50 of the 160 Slovene local communities. The workshops also served as models for training many professional workers, mainly in the field of education.

In the second half of the 1990s, a few other prevention programmes and ideas arrived in Slovenia, some of them with foreign financial support. A few of the handbooks on the models of peer-based social learning and interactive and humanistic approaches have been published.

Besides the model of the *Youth Workshop*, which is not presented as a specifically DDR (drug demand reduction)-oriented programme, there is another network, *Healthy Schools*, which also offers models and programmes with different orientations, among which are some specifically drug-oriented. Two other programmes were brought to Slovenia by the organizations TACADE and the SOROS Foundation.

1.4 *Financing*

Activities are financed from four sources: the national budget, local budgets, health insurance and donations. Detoxification, methadone treatment and treatment in hospitals and health centres are financed from the national insurance scheme, whereas all other activities are financed mainly from the national budget with the exception of activities at local level, which are usually financed from local budgets as well. It is generally recognized that donations do not form a significant part of the financing.

The figures on financing are not very clear except for the fact that funding increased significantly in the last eight years. For example, in 1993 the budget of the Ministry of Labour, Family and Social Affairs for financing the drug demand reduction programmes of NGOs was 2,000,000 SIT (10,000 EUR). In 1998, it exceeded 100,000,000 SIT (500,000 EUR). The Ministry of Health and the Ministry of Labour, Family and Social Affairs have special budgetary chapters for drug programmes.

Financing is twofold: direct and indirect. The majority of the medical treatment programmes are financed by the Health Insurance Institute. The NGOs that run therapeutic centres are financed by the Ministry of Labour, Family and Social Affairs under 5-year contracts. Subsidies amount to at least 80% of the real costs of running the therapeutic centres. Addicts receiving treatment in the therapeutic communities are expected to participate financially. Both ministries publish tenders for grants every year.

The legal basis for the financing of drug demand reduction activities is the Prevention of the Use of Illicit Drugs and Dealing with Consumers of Illicit Drugs Act. In this respect, the act introduced the obligation to finance drug demand reduction programmes. Activities such as the information, education and promotion of health are financed by the state budget. Local action groups are financed by the budgets of the local communities. Activities in hospitals and clinics are financed by the Health Insurance Institute. Drug demand activities provided by social services, the educational system and NGOs are financed by the state budget. Future umbrella organizations of NGOs will be financed by the Governmental Office for Drugs.

Verified programmes of NGOs are eligible for at least 80% financing by the national or municipal budget.

It should be pointed out that in the 1990s, non-governmental organizations received significant financial resources from foreign institutions, such as for example: the Soros Foundation, Lindesmith Centre, PHARE (European Commission) and Pompidou Group (Council of Europe). PHARE and the Pompidou Group also organized study visits and education for civil servants.

1.5 Co-ordination

In 1992, the National Committee for the Implementation of a National Programme for the Prevention of Drug Abuse was established. The Committee formally stopped working in 1999.

Although a National Programme for the Prevention of Drug Abuse in the Republic of Slovenia was adopted in 1992, the Committee has since its inception always had problems with producing its own strategy and it never became more than a "chat room". It was not clear what its competencies were and the mechanisms for the realization of its decisions were not elaborated and/or taken into account.

Today, there are at least three types of co-ordination at the *government level*:

- The Governmental Office for Drugs has overall responsibility for co-ordinating the work of the ministries and governmental bodies. It is widely acknowledged that this co-ordination is at present weak. In the first year and a half of its existence, the inter-ministerial commission, which should govern its work, has not yet met.
- Co-ordination of Centres for the Prevention and Treatment of Drug Addiction was established at the Ministry of Health and it is the co-ordinating body established to provide a uniform treatment approach in all treatment centres and to foster the exchange of treatment experiences.
- The Ministry of Labour, Family and Social Affairs has established a Commission for Social Rehabilitation whose aim is to co-ordinate the policy in the field of social rehabilitation. Members of the Commission are mainly NGOs dealing with therapeutic communities financed by the Ministry.

At the *non-governmental* and so-called "para (non-)governmental"[15] level there has been:

- Occasional and non-systematic informal co-ordination between local (drug addiction prevention) community groups. They have been organized in approximately 25 Slovene local communities and have been instituted in three forms: (a) as formal governmental bodies of local/municipal authorities (in the Slovene capital Ljubljana as the Office for the Prevention of Addiction), (b) as NGO Associations, (c) as commissions or working groups affiliated or functioning under local municipalities. Their tasks involve mostly the co-ordination of the formal (GO and NGO) and informal subjects functioning in DDR in a specific local community.
- In the capital of Ljubljana there have been two attempts at co-ordinating NGOs. In 1998, CONZIS was formed as a network of different kinds of social welfare-oriented NGOs, fighting mostly for the development of a stable system of funding for NGOs drawing on municipal funds. This network also included a few drug demand reduction NGOs. The second network was the Consortium of Outreach and Harm Reduction-oriented Organizations in Ljubljana. It was founded as an informal co-ordination group in 1999, but has failed to sustain its further development and institutionalization.
- The high-threshold organizations (related to different systems of treatment communities) occasionally meet and consult with each other in smaller informal networks.

The Prevention of the Use of Illicit Drugs and Dealing with Consumers of Illicit Drugs Act introduced the legal basis for the existence of the following co-ordinating bodies: the Governmental Commission for Drugs, the Office for Drugs, the Council for Drugs, the Co-ordination of Centres for the Prevention and Treatment of Dependence and the Association of Non-governmental Organizations (as an umbrella organization)

At the end of 2000, there was no umbrella organization of NGOs. However, such an organization has been founded in 2001.

A central platform for drug demand reduction organizations and drug demand reduction programmes does not exist. Information can be obtained from the Governmental Office for Drugs, the Ministry of Health and the Ministry of Labour, Family and Social Affairs and the Social Chamber. Some information can also be obtained from the Office for the Prevention of Addiction in Ljubljana.

1.6 *Epidemiology*

Historical overview

Until the 1990s, not much concern had been expressed about the illegal use of drugs in Slovenia. In the late 1960s and early 1970s, solvents, cannabis, LSD, tranquillizers and minor pain relievers became relatively popular, especially among students and young people, while opiates were used only to a very limited extent. "Injection use was rare. In the late 1970s, small groups of dropouts started to inject opiates more frequently (opium or opioides stolen from pharmacies). In the late 1980s the incidence and prevalence of injection heroin use has increased."[16]

The "discovery" of the illicit drug problem could be said to be marked by the first Slovenian conference and seminar on drugs, which took place in April 1974.[17] The lectures held at that seminar were published in the first Slovenian report on drugs in 1975.[18] In some of the articles in the report, the authors warned that a higher focus on drug abuse could also have some unplanned adversary consequences (e.g. stigmatization of users). In the following 10 years some of the key organizers of this seminar expressed the fear that this seminar might have been partly responsible for unnecessarily "inventing" the drug problem in Slovenia.[19]

Although in the 1980s some books on drugs were published,[20] as late as in 1983 and 1985 the leading experts on drugs[21] evaluated the actual drug abuse situation as not being critical. In the middle of the 1980s, the first relatively comprehensive cross-sectional study on the prevalence of drug abuse among university students was conducted. One of the main findings was that drug abuse at the time was not as great a problem as in some Western countries during the same period.[22] In comparison with Western European countries, Slovenia seemed to be lagging behind by approximately 10 years as regards the consumption of prohibited drugs among young people.

The turnaround in the perspectives and discourses occurred from 1989 to 1991. Police inspectors discovered at the end of the 1980s and the beginning of the 1990s a visible increase in the illegal production and sale of drugs, which was also seen in the much larger quantities of seized drugs, especially heroin and in the increase of the number of criminal offences (which the penal law defines as the illegal production and sale of drugs and permitting the taking of drugs) as well as other offences, violent acts and secondary crimes linked with drugs.[23] It became obvious that the use of heroin was increasing and that increasingly younger age groups were starting to take heroin and certain other prohibited drugs, and were injecting their drugs.

The new problem was first recognized and made publicly visible by the actions of the users themselves,[24] by young researchers (high school and university students) and by the media more than by professionals and experts. It seems that some professions were reluctant to admit the emergence of the new problem or somehow tended to dismiss its importance.

Situation in the 1990s

Since 1990, a considerable increase in drug abuse has been noticed in Slovenia, among which injection-drug taking, particularly heroin, caused the greatest concern. Together with the development of different drug-oriented services and activities of preventive and treatment nature, epidemiological services were also developed and interest in epidemiological research grew. In this section, the results of the cross-sectional research work will be described rather than the official data of the health and repressive subsystems.

The change in the understanding of the drug problem and of the drug-related discourse at the turn of decade was characterized by the perception that the nature of drug abuse has changed in the period "of some years"[25] or in the period "from five years ago till today".[26] The usual accompanying interpretation of the changed nature of drug abuse was that in previous times drug abuse was connected with typical users' ideological (anti-materialistic) interpretations and interests, while in present times drug abuse has become a "normal" part of the consumerist lifestyle of youngsters.[27]

Cross-sectional research

Only a few of the epidemiological studies of this type were carried out in the 1990s, mostly on populations of school students. In 1991 the first ESPAD-like survey covered a representative sample of 1,029 students of secondary schools in the Slovenian capital of Ljubljana. The students were from 15 to 18 years of age.[28] In 1995 and 1999, two fully internationally comparative ESPAD studies were conducted on representative Slovenian samples. In 1995 and 1998, another two studies using full ESPAD methodology were carried out with representative samples of Ljubljana's students. Table 1 shows extracts of the results of these five studies.

Table 1: Results of five school surveys on drug abuse among 15-year-old school students in Slovenia

Year of survey	1991	1995	1995	1998	1999
Authors	Bulic&Vesel[29]	Jerman[30]	Stergar[31]	Dekleva[32]	Stergar[33]
Sample	1,029	1,531	3,306	1,535	2,375
Age of responding students			15		
Territory	Ljubljana	Ljubljana	Slovenia	Ljubljana	Slovenia
Lifetime prevalence cannabis use in %	13.2*	16.7	13.2	25.8	24.9
Lifetime prevalence heroin use in %	0.0	0.8	0.9	3.6	2.1
Lifetime prevalence ecstasy use in %	N/A	1.8	1.2	7.0	4.1
Lifetime prevalence inhalants use in %	16.3	11.3	12.3	15.6	N/A

Note: * While 13.2% of 15-year-old students have already used cannabis, the corresponding result for the whole sample (15-18 years) was 30.2%.

Only two representative household studies were done in the 1990s covering the Slovenian territory and adult respondents. The first one, done in 1994 (sample size 1,050), showed 3.9% of lifetime use of cannabis, and the other one, done in 1999, 8.1%.

The data on drug abuse among youth can lead us to a tentative conclusion that there were two periods of greater increase of illicit drug use: the first one around the end of the 1980s, and the second one around 1995 and 1998.

Data based on treatment services (mostly health sector)

Data on the treatment of users in medical organizations (psychiatric and non-psychiatric departments, centres for prevention and treatment of drug addiction) and other organizations (NGOs) should be viewed with considerable caution. The planned epidemiological system of data collection (based on the indicator of first treatment demand) has not yet been fully implemented. The majority of the data is either based on partial information (covering only one part of the system of treatment services) or the estimated coverage is low or the criteria for data collection are not standardized across the systems.

Table 2: Data on treatment of Slovenian drug users.

Year	89	90	91	92	93	94	95	96	97	98	99
Indicators											
Average age of visitors to Stigma – a needle exchange service in Ljubljana*				27.5	26.5	27.5	27.0	26.5	24.5		
Aids cases incidence per 1,000,000*	3.5	1	3.5	2.5	3.5	3	7	6	0.5	2	
Aids cases incidence per 1,000,000 of IUD users*	0.5			0.5				1			
HIV prevalence among IDU starting methadone substitution programme in two sites*							0	1	0		
First treatment demand (two treatment centres in Ljubljana and Koper)*			44	207	141	187	125	309			
All treatment demand (two treatment centres in Ljubljana and Koper)*			51	228	175	229	136	434			
Persons in methadone maintenance programme (14 local centres in Slovenia)#							530	530	762	926	1,097
All treated in 14 centres for prevention and treatment of drug addiction#									1,414	2,599	2,342
Hospital admissions for drug dependence and non-dependent drug use*			139	128	126	164	250	300			
Hospitalized drug-related emergencies*			189	185	191	154	162	179			

Notes: * Taken from Petric, 1998.
Taken from Kastelic and Kostnapfel Rihtar, 2000.

Data based on treatment services are more or less inconclusive and do not allow much valid interpretation. The main reason for this lies in the weak and ineffective data collection systems. However, data collected in the recently developed system of the regional drug abuse treatment centres, which more or less cover the territory of the whole of Slovenia, show that the need for treatment has been increasing over the last 3-5 years.

Police and justice data

The seizures of illicit drugs increased in the 1990s. In 1995, the Slovenian police confiscated the first larger quantities of amphetamines (1302 tablets) and ecstasy (7354 tablets), drugs that were previously hardly found on the Slovenian market.

Table 3: Police and court data on drug abuse, addiction and related phenomena

Year	89	90	91	92	93	94	95	96	97	98	99
Indicators											
Illicit drugs related deaths*	9	3	5	9	9	4	12	16	16	18	19
Number of seizures#	32	37	47	116	118	113	170	228	298		
Number of criminal reports*	126	105	202	264	281	407	453	875	964	988	1106
Misdemeanours*		171	135	205	365	418	796	1174	1773	1954	
Quantity of seized heroin in kilograms*		27	9	16	20	14	18	25	30		
Quantity of seized marihuana and hashish in kilograms*		22	28	27	95	61	32	40	49		
Per cent drug addicts among prison population#		1.5	5.3	7.2	9.4	12.1	17.3	22.9			

Note * Ministry of the Interior of Slovenia: Statistical Annuals.
Petric, 1998.

Conclusions

The majority of the statistical indicators show a continuous increase in drug abuse and related indirect phenomena during the 1990s. Among such indicators are: survey data on drug abuse, treatment demand indicators, illicit drug-related deaths, number and quantity of seizures, criminal acts and proportion of drug addicts among prisoners. There are hints indicating that besides the starting wave of illicit drug use at the beginning of the 1990s, a second wave of higher drug consumption has been occurring since the middle of the 1990s in Slovenia.

2 Organizations active in the area of drug demand reduction

2.1 *Slovenian DDR organizations and the selection of their sample*

At the governmental level, there are three ministries that deal primarily with illicit drug use and demand reduction: the Ministry of Health, the Ministry of Labour, Family and Social Affairs and the Ministry of Justice. Their main activities are policy-making and the financing of drug demand reduction programmes. The Ministry of Education and Sports and the Ministry of the Interior play only a secondary role in drug demand reduction.

Since 1999, Slovenia has had a governmental Office for Drugs, whose main aim is the co-ordination of policies at the governmental level. Apart from that, the following governmental bodies are theoretically in operation: the Governmental Commission for Drugs (which has never met – until writing this report), the Council for Drugs (co-ordination of social rehabilitation programmes) and the Co-ordination of centres for prevention and treatment of dependence (co-ordination of methadone centres and other activities at hospitals and clinics) within the Ministry of Health. This co-ordination body has been very active in different roles in the past few years; besides co-ordination it also offers many forms of training and has been leading in developing guidelines.

Among the public institutions dealing with drug demand reduction issues are:

- Inpatient and outpatient public clinics whose main activity is treatment.
- About 60 centres for social work whose main activities are after-care and to a lesser extent prevention.
- The Public Health Institute whose main activity is research.

There are about 80 public institutions dealing with drug demand reduction exclusively and inclusively. They are numerous and geographically equally spread around the country.

Non-governmental organizations also played a pivotal role in the field of drug demand reduction. In the beginning, they were mainly concerned with developing public awareness. Today, their principal activities are treatment (therapeutic communities), harm reduction and prevention. There are, for now, approximately 40 NGOs in Slovenia dealing mostly with drug demand reduction. The development of NGOs and their activities was described in the previous section.

For the purposes of this research project, 37 Slovene organizations in the field of drug demand reduction were selected from two regions in Slovenia: the region of Slovenia's capital Ljubljana and the coastal area, consisting of three communities/towns – Piran, Izola and Koper.[34] These two regions were selected because they are the ones with the highest number of registered drug users/addicts and the highest number of drug demand reduction organizations. The selected 37 organizations are *all of the DDR organizations operating in these two Slovene regions* (the Ljubljana region and the coastal area) and include *all the Slovenian DDR organizations operating at the national level.*

2.2 *Characteristics of the analysed organizations*

Types of organizations and time of their founding

Among the 37 organizations, 21 are governmental, 1 private and 15 non-governmental. A number of 23 organizations operate at the national level and 14 at the local level. Twenty-nine are located in Slovenia's capital Ljubljana (23 of them operate at the national and 6 at the local level), and 8 in the coastal region (Table 4). The reason why the number of local organizations operating in the smaller (coastal) region is higher are twofold: firstly, the coastal region consists of three towns each of which developed some of its own services. Secondly, many of the national level organizations, which are located in Ljubljana, also offer a lot of their services specifically to the inhabitants of Ljubljana's region.

Table 4: 37 organizations surveyed by level of operation and status.

Level of operation	National level		Local level/ Ljubljana		Local level/ coastal region		Local level/ both regions		Total	
Legal status	n	%	n	%	n	%	n	%	n	%
Governmental, public agency	12	52.2	4	66.7	4	50.0	8	57.1	20	56.8
Private firm, enterprise	1	4.4							1	2.7
Non-profit, voluntary	10	43.5	2	33.3	4	50.0	6	42.8	16	40.5
Total	23	100.0	6	100.0	8	100.0	14	100.0	37	100.0

Table 5 shows that among the organizations surveyed, nine deal with DDR exclusively and 28 inclusively. The ones operating at the national level are to a greater degree inclusively-oriented, as many of them are ministries, faculties or research institutes which do not engage solely in the relatively narrow field of drugs.

Table 5: DDR: level of operation by type of organization

Level of operation	**National level**		**Local level**		**Total**	
Type of organization	n	%	n	%	n	%
Exclusive	3	13.0	6	42.9	9	24.3
Inclusive	20	87.0	8	57.1	28	75.7
Total	23	100.0	14	100.0	37	100.0

Time of founding and time of starting DDR activities

The organizations active in DDR in Slovenia are relatively young. All the NGOs (except one, which was founded as a GO, but later changed its status) were founded after 1990 (Table 6) and nearly half of them (45%) were founded in the last time period (1996-1998). Also the majority of GOs have been founded in 1990 or after this year (we included also all the ministries in this group). About one third of the organizations have been founded in the period from 1996 to 1998, which shows that the field of DDR in Slovenia is still in the phase of rather dynamic development.

Table 6: Time of founding of DDR organizations by their legal status

Legal status	**Governmental, public agency**		**Private firm, enterprise**		**Non-profit, voluntary**		**Total**	
Founding date	n	%	n	%	n	%	n	%
Till 1989	5	25.0			1	6.2	6	16.2
1990-1992	7	35.0	1	100.0	3	18.8	11	29.7
1993-1995	6	30.0			5	31.2	11	29.7
1996-1998	2	10.0			7	45.7	9	33.3
Total	20	100.0	1	100.0	16	100.0	37	100.0

Table 7 confirms this conclusion with the data on starting time of DDR activities: 90% of the organizations started them after 1990, and a majority of them after 1993. For the whole sample the modal years of starting DDR activities were 1993-1995, while for the NGOs the modal years are from 1996 onwards. This shows that DDR activities are a rather new enterprise in Slovenia, especially those implemented by the NGOs.

Table 7: Time of organizations' start of DDR activities by their legal status

Legal status	Governmental, public agency		Private firm, enterprise		Non-profit, voluntary		Total	
Starting time of DDR activities	n	%	n	%	n	%	n	%
1992-1989	4	20.0					4	10.8
1990-1992	7	35.0			3	18.7	10	27.0
1993-1995	6	30.0	1	100.0	5	31.3	12	32.4
1996-1998	3	15.0			8	50.0	11	29.7
Total	20	100.0	1	100.0	16	100.0	37	100.0

International comparison (Table 8) shows that Slovenia has a smaller proportion of NGOs than Poland and the Czech Republic (but more than Hungary), and that Slovenian NGOs are on the average the youngest. It means that NGOs in the other three countries have had a longer tradition than Slovenian NGOs.

Table 8: Per cent of NGOs among all analysed organizations and NGOs' founding year, by countries

Characteristic:	Poland	Slovenia	Hungary	Czech R.	All
% of NGOs among all organizations	63.3	43.2	34.8	46.9	47.5
Average year of founding of NGOs	1981,5	1992,3[35]	1990,9	1991,3	1987,9

2.3 *Funding and staffing*

Funding

The organizations participating in this research often treated questions on their financial situation with caution. Some hesitation to answer was noticed. Twenty-six organizations answered the question on overall budget and 30 the question on budget for DDR programmes.

Over one third of all organizations and over one half of NGOs have a budget up to 50,000 EUR (Table 9). There are six organizations with a budget larger than 500,001 EUR. Those are institutes and ministries whose budgets are aimed at supporting DDR programmes of both governmental and non-governmental organizations. While 24% of the national level organizations have a budget less than 50,000 EUR there are 60% of the local level organizations with a budget in this range.

Table 9: Total organizations' budget by their status

Legal status	**Governmental, public agency**		**Private firm, enterprise**		**Non-profit, voluntary**		**Total**	
Budget in EUR	n	%	n	%	n	%	n	%
Up to 5,000	1	7.7					1	3.8
5,001-10,000	1	7.7			1	7.7	2	7.7
10,001-50,000	1	7.7			6	46.1	7	26.9
50,001-100,000	1	7.7			3	23.0	4	15.4
100,001-500,000	5	38.5			2	15.4	7	26.9
Over 500,001	4	30.8	1	100.0	1	7.7	6	23.0
Total	13	100.0	1	100.0	13	100.0	26	100.0
No answer	7				3		10	
Total	20		1	100.0	16		36	

Some respondents declared that 0% of the total budget is directed to DDR programmes although DDR projects are run by their organizations. Their answers were respected. On the other side 41% of all the organizations direct 100% of their budget towards DDR programmes.

Table 10: DDR budget by status of organizations

Legal status	**Governmental, public agency**		**Private firm, enterprise**		**Non-profit, voluntary**		**Total**	
Budget in EUR	n	%	n	%	n	%	n	%
Up to 5,000	4	26.7			2	14.3	6	20.0
5,001-10,000					3	21.4	3	10.0
10,001-50,000	4	26.7	1	100.0	6	42.9	11	36.7
50,001-100,000					1	7.1	1	3.3
100,001-500,000	5	40.0			2	14.3	7	23.3
Over 500,001	2	13.3					2	6.7
Total	15	100.0	1	100.0	14	100.0	30	
No answer	5				2		7	
Total	20		1	100.0		16		36

The biggest proportion of organizations (36,7%) can be found in the category of DDR budgets in the range between 10,001 and 50,000 EUR (Table 10). Almost another third have DDR budgets up to 10,000 EUR. While 53% of the national level organizations have a budget less than 50,000 EUR there are 73% of the local level organizations with a budget in this range.

Many different sources contribute to the funding of the organizations: the state budget, local community budgets, foundations, direct donations from individuals and legal persons, and from members. Financing from public funds (at both national and local levels) is distributed through the organization of public tenders. Table 11 shows that while the proportion of organizations that receive funds from public/governmental agencies stayed the same in the period from 1995 to 1998, the proportions of them receiving funds from foreign sources and also from individual donations have grown slightly.

Table 11: Number and per cent of organizations receiving funds from different sources

Year	1995		1998	
Sources	n	%	n	%
International organizations	2	7.7	5	13.5
Foreign governments/agencies	0	0.0	2	5.4
Other foreign organizations	4	15.4	7	18.9
Public/government agencies	23	88.5	33	89.2
Private sector	3	11.5	3	8.1
Voluntary organizations	2	7.7	1	2.7
Fees/individual donations	5	19.2	11	29.7
Number of organizations operating	26	100.0	37	100.0

Table 12: Organizations receiving funds from public or governmental agencies

Year	1995		1998	
% sources from public/governmental agencies	n	%	n	%
0	3	11.5	9	24.3
1-20	1	3.8	2	5.4
21-40	3	11.5	3	8.1
41-60	1	3.8	1	2.7
61-80	1	3.8	1	2.7
81-100	17	65.3	21	56.7
Number of organizations operating	26	100.0	37	100.0

Table 12 shows that while there is a small proportion of DDR organizations that did not receive any funds from public or governmental agencies in both years analysed, the majority of them did receive funding in both years that made up more than half of their DDR funds from these sources. The structure of funding from these sources has became worse, as in 1998 there were more organizations without funding and less with the highest percentage of funding from public or governmental agencies. On average in 1995, organizations received about 67% of funds from public or governmental agencies, and in 1998 only about 57%.[36]

Table 13: Comparison of four countries regarding their organizations' DDR funds

Total budget in EUR	Poland	Slovenia	Hungary	Czech Republic	Total
Up to 5,000					
Count	6	6	4	6	22
% within Country	15.8	20.0	16.0	14.6	16.4
5,001-10,000					
Count	4	3	5	3	15
% within Country	10.5	10.0	20.0	7.3	11.2
10,001-50,000					
Count	6	11	8	12	37
% within Country	15.8	36.7	32.0	29.3	27.6
50,001-100,000					
Count	9	1	2	7	19
% within Country	23.7	3.3	8.0	17.1	14.2
100,001-500,000					
Count	11	7	4	10	32
% within Country	28.9	23.3	16.0	24.4	23.9
Over 500,001					
Count	2	2	2	3	9
% within Country	5.3	6.7	8.0	7.3	6.7
Total					
Count	38	30	25	41	134
% within Country	100.0	100.0	100.0	100.0	100.0

In Table 13, the structure of DDR funds in four countries is presented. It seems that regarding this structure (proportions of organizations having less or more funds for DDR), Slovenia is not privileged although it has a higher living standard and a greater GDP than the other three countries. Slovenia has the largest proportion of organizations having less than 5,001 EUR for DDR activities. If we divide the data and use as the cutting point 50,000 EUR, then we see that Poland has 42.1% of organizations operating with DDR funds below this limit, Slovenia 66.7%, Hungary 68.0% and the Czech Republic 54.2%. In interpreting this data, one should, of course, take into account the fact that Slovenia has a smaller number of inhabitants in comparison to the other three countries.

Staffing

A share of 45% of the organizations at the national level and 85% of the organizations at the local level have less than ten employees. If we analyse only the staff working on DDR it becomes evident that 70.4% of the organizations working at the local level and 60.9% of the organizations working at national level have up to three staff members. This shows that the development of organizations dealing with drug demand programmes started only recently. In connection with the budget for DDR programmes, it should be noted that a small staff might also be due to a lack of financial resources. By contrast, many of the NGOs, especially those dealing with harm reduction problems, have reported difficulties in contracting qualified staff.

Three organizations answered that no one in their organization deals exclusively with drug demand reduction, although they see themselves as an organization dealing with DDR. This is because in those organizations nobody is assigned specifically to DDR, but rather everybody is working on multiple social assistance programmes (e.g. Karitas).

Table 14: Organizations' professionals by type of training

	All Investigated		National Level		Local Level	
Type of training	n	%	n	%	n	%
Medical training	29	8.1	10	3.2	19	39.5
Psychiatric training	6	1.6	4	1.2	2	4.1
Legal training	13	3.6	13	4.1	0	
Public health training	9	2.5	5	1.6	4	8.3
Social worker training	32	8.9	23	7.4	9	18.7
Psychology training	62	17.3	57	18.3	5	10.4
Educational training	144	40.2	136	43.8	8	16.6
Sociology training	31	8.6	31	10	0	
Management training	5	1.3	5	1.6	0	
Other	27	7.5	26	8.3	1	2.0
	358	100.0	310	100.0	48	100.0

Table 14 gives information on the educational background of the professionals involved in the DDR programmes. Those professionals are not necessarily employed with the organization. At the overall level, educational training seems to be the most frequent background. That is due to the network of prevention activities in primary schools (*Healthy Schools*), which involves more than 100 teachers. At the local level, medical training is the most frequent professional background (39.5%) due to the network of methadone centres run by the local medical centres.

Note that four organizations do not have any professional employees among its paid staff.

2.4 *The organizations' missions and goals*

The organizations' declarations regarding their missions in DDR were classified into five categories. The exclusive organizations' answers were classified into only two types: those which mentioned policy design and co-ordination as their mission were basically co-ordinating bodies, local action teams or organizations founded for the aim of co-ordination. The other exclusive organizations stated as their mission personal care and treatment, and were mostly treatment communities or organizations related to them (Table 15).

Inclusive organizations on their part stated as their aims, apart from these two missions, prevention and intelligence, with the former being the most frequent. General prevention, personal care and policy design accounted for the stated missions of 89% of the researched organizations.

Table 15: Organizations' missions by inclusive/exclusive orientation

Type of organization	**Inclusive**		**Exclusive**		**Total**	
Mission	n	%	n	%	n	%
Prevention	12	42.9			12	32.4
Personal care, treatment and advice	8	28.6	5	55.6	13	35.1
Policy design, co-ordination, implementation	4	14.3	4	44.4	8	21.6
Interest representation						
Intelligence	3	10.7			3	8.1
Other	1	3.6			1	2.7
Total	28	100.0	9	100.0	37	100.0

Organizations were also asked about their first, second and third goals in DDR. The first goal of the organizations at the national level is prevention, whereas the first goal of the organizations at the local level is drug demand reduction (as a general statement). When analysing the goals referred to as the second goals of the organizations, we found that more than 30% of the organizations at both the national and the local level stated treatment and care. Rehabilitation and after-care were listed as the third goal by 30% of the organizations working at the local level, with treatment and care at 20%, while more than one-third of those at the national level indicated treatment and care. Policy development and training of professionals were only exceptionally identified as goals of the organizations at the local level.

In conclusion: Slovenia has a relatively (compared to the other three countries) small proportion of NGOs working in the field of DDR, they are only rarely exclusively-oriented and they are younger than the NGOs in two of the other three analysed countries. Slovenian DDR organizations operate mostly with low DDR budgets (again, compared to the average situation in the other three countries). Slovenian DDR organizations are also relatively poorly staffed. Generally, educational training seems to be the most frequent background of DDR professionals, but at the local level it is medical training that is the most frequent professional background due to the relatively well-developed network of so-called "methadone centres" run by the local medical centres. The most frequent missions of DDR organizations are: (1) personal care, treatment and advice, (2) prevention and (3) policy design, co-ordination and implementation. It is surprising that no organization has drug users' interest representation as its principal mission.

3 Drug demand reduction activities

The activities were studied by questioning the organizations as to their main fields of activity in the area of drug demand reduction. They could mention three specific activities in these fields, their target groups and the year of their inception.

3.1 Main fields of activity in which organizations were engaged

The main fields of activity of the organizations are shown in Table 16. The most frequently mentioned main field of activity of the surveyed organizations is prevention (91.9% of organizations), followed by policy development, training of professionals, research and co-ordination (by order of frequency). Only then follow treatment and care, and rehabilitation and interest representation, which are performed by 38-46% of the organizations.

A comparison of the status of the organizations by field of activity shows some differentiation. NGOs are more often involved in treatment and care, interest representation and policy development, while GOs are more often engaged in fund-raising and co-ordination. In general, we were surprised by how many NGOs declared that they were engaged in policy development and how few were engaged in funding and fund-raising. In these respects they differ from NGOs in the other three countries (see section 5.1).

Table 16: Main activities in DDR by status of organization

Status	Governmental (N=20)		Private (N=1)		NGO (N=16)		Total (N=37)	
Main activities	n	%	n	%	n	%	n	%
Prevention	18	90.0	1	100.0	15	93.8	34	91.9
Treatment/Care	7	35.0	1	100.0	9	56.3	12	45.9
Rehabilitation and after-care	8	40.0	1	100.0	6	37.3	15	40.5
Research, Documentation, Database	12	60.0			9	56.3	21	56.8
Fund-raising	5	25.0			1	6.3	6	16.2
Co-ordination	14	70.0			6	37.5	20	54.1
Interest representation	5	26.3			9	56.3	14	38.9
Policy development	12	60.0	1	100.0	12	75.0	25	67.6
Training	12	60.0	1	100.0	11	68.0	24	64.9
Other	11	55.0	1	100.0	10	62.5	22	59.5

3.2 *Specific fields of activity, their target groups and starting times*

Thirty-four of the investigated organizations gave a positive answer to the question on whether *prevention* is their main activity in the field of drug demand reduction.

Prevention activities *started* to develop sporadically at the local level by the end of the 1980s. The majority of the organizations started their activities in the middle of the 1990s. There are some differences between organizations at the national and the local level. At the local level, the development of prevention activities continuously increased during the 1990s. At the national level, a significant increase in activities was noted after 1995. More than two-thirds of the organizations at the national level stated that they started prevention activities after 1995.

The *target groups* of the prevention programmes are mainly young people, school pupils, the public in general and professionals. None of the organizations operating at the local level indicated a population at risk and university students as targeted groups. University students were indicated only by one organization at the national level. One of the rarely indicated targeted groups was parents, which was mentioned only twice at the national level and once at the local level.

The organizations indicated the various services they provide. At the national level and at the local level, the main activities include the distribution of brochures, leaflets, films, publishing materials, and lectures and seminars. None of the organizations at the local level indicated information campaigning as part of their prevention activities. In fact, public information campaigns are conducted only at the national level and only by inclusive organizations. Street work is provided mainly by the inclusive-type, non-governmental organizations. This is probably due to the "nature" of the street work. It is not a job that can be done from nine to five.

At the national level, a large share of *treatment activities* consists of individual counselling, and at the local level, of methadone treatment. Respondents at the local level often also indicated individual counselling as their activity.

There is indeed a very interesting distribution of treatment activities between the local and national levels. One finding is that organizations at the national level did not indicate medical care, methadone treatment and needle exchange as part of their activities. The reason is that medical centres are organized at the local level. Methadone treatment is linked to local medical centres and therefore organized and provided only at the local level.

Needle exchange programmes are provided only by NGOs and only at the local level. The development of needle exchange programmes has been demand-driven and therefore they only exist in those areas where the prevalence of illegal drug use is high.

The organizations indicated drug users and addicts as the *main target* groups. Besides the target groups mentioned above, the following target groups were indicated at the national level: drug users' families and relatives, abstainers and professionals involved in DDR programmes.

Table 17: **Division of labour in treatment/care activities among organizations by status, level of operation and type of orientation**[37]

Types of organizations	Legal status		Level of operation		Type of organization	
Specific treatment and care activities	Governmental, public agency	NGOs	National	Local	Exclusive	Inclusive
Detoxification	100%		100%			100%
Individual counselling	23%	77%	53%	47%	35%	65%
Treatment	50%	50%	75%	25%	25%	75%
Group psychotherapy		100%	100%			100%
After-care		100%	100%		100%	
Day centres		100%	75%	25%	50%	50%
Outpatient clinics	100%		100%			100%
Methadone treatment	100%			100%	33%	67%
Needle exchange, condom distribution		100%		100%		100%
Medical care	33%	67%		100%		100%
Referral		100%	100%		100%	
Other	100%		75%	25%	50%	50%

At the local level, two respondents mentioned drug users' families. It is noted that abstainers and professionals involved in DDR programmes are not target groups for organizations working at the local level.

A share of 40.5% of the investigated organizations are involved in *rehabilitation and/or after-care* activities.

It is important to highlight the great importance of volunteer work involved in the rehabilitation and after-care activities. This is also the case in prevention activities, treatment and care, and also after-care activities, which are performed with the cooperation of volunteers. Some of the activities are accomplished by volunteers only. In some cases this is due to the lack of financial resources to hire paid staff.

Rehabilitation and after-care programmes started to develop later than treatment and care programmes. They are a logical consequence of treatment and care programmes. As some of the respondents indicated, treatment and care programmes involve rehabilitation and after-care.

The *establishing year* of rehabilitation and after-care programmes was in all cases after 1991. The majority (more than 80%) of the respondents at the local level indicated to have established a programme between 1991 and 1994. At the national level, the majority of rehabilitation and after-care programmes started after 1995.

The *main activities* in the field of rehabilitation and after-care are diverse and dispersed. At the local level, the main activities are counselling and legal advice, assistance in employment and education, and group therapy. None of the organizations at the local level provide assistance with housing, assistance with reintegration into families, nor do they run day after-care centres or engage "clients" in field work.

Table 18: Division of labour in rehabilitation and after-care activities among organizations by status, level of operation and type of orientation

Types of organizations	Legal status		Level of operation		Type of organization	
Specific rehabilitation and after-care activities	Governmental, public agency	NGOs	National	Local	Exclu-sive	Inclu-sive
Day after-care centres	100%		100%			100%
Group therapy, group meetings	33%	67%	50%	50%	50%	50%
Assistance in social re-adaptation		100%	67%	33%	67%	33%
Assistance in education		100%	50%	50%	25%	75%
Assistance in finding employment	40%	60%	60%	40%	40%	60%
Assistance in reinte-gration with families		100%	100%			100%
Assistance in finding housing		100%	100%		100%	
Engaging drug users in field work		100%	100%			100%
Individual counselling, legal advice	83%	17%	20%	80%	17%	83%
Other	67%	33%	100%		33%	67%
Total	63%	37%	58%	42%	35%	65%

It is presumed that these activities will develop later on when the group of "clients" in need of such assistance becomes big enough at the local level. Although some would say that the reason why such activities are not carried out is the lack of financial resources, it is more probable that the reason is the "critical mass" of assistance seekers.

At the national level, the distribution of rehabilitation and after-care activities is even more dispersed than at the local level. Activities provided are assistance to education, assistance to housing, group therapies, assistance to reintegration and assistance to employment, counselling and legal advice. One of the organizations at the national level runs a day after-care centre.

Research, documentation and database activities are conducted by 21 organizations. Taking into account the lack of epidemiological data and other information on illegal drug use in Slovenia, the number of organizations running research activities was surprisingly high. The majority of the respondents *established* research and documentation activities after 1995 (more than 70%). The first organization that started to run a research activity was the Institute of Public Health in 1982.

Activities in the field of research and documentation consist of epidemiological research, running database centres, evaluation, methodology and the development of methods (Table 19).

Table 19: Division of labour in research/documentation/database activities among organizations by status, level of operation and type of orientation

Types of organizations	Legal status		Level of operation		Type of organization	
Specific research and documentation activities	Governmental, public agency	NGOs	National	Local	Exclu-sive	Inclu-sive
Research	74%	26%	63%	37%	5%	95%
Running database, information centres	60%	40%	100%			100%
Conducting evaluation	67%	33%	50%	50%	50%	50%
Development of methods, methodology	25%	75%	100%			100%
Other		100%	100%			100%
Total	63%	37%	71%	29%	11%	89%

The *target groups* are mainly professionals followed by decision-makers and the public in general. A share of 74.1% of all organizations declared professionals to be their target group, 7% mentioned decision-makers and their own organization. It is surprising that 75% of the organizations developing methods and methodology are non-governmental. In contrast, it is assumed that the majority of the organizations engaged in research activities are governmental and conduct their work at the national level.

As previously stated, one would presume that in the light of so many research activities there would be reliable data on drug addicts and drug addiction in general. Since this is not the case, we assume that the research work is for internal purposes. The work is probably aimed at developing better systems of monitoring organizations' activities.

Only six organizations indicated *funding/fund-raising* as part of their activities. The majority were governmental (public) organizations (66.7%). As it is a very small sample, it is therefore difficult to draw conclusions.

The organizations' main *activities* in the field of funding and fund-raising are: fund-raising, organization of sporting events and similar activities (57.1% of all activities) and subsidizing projects (Table 20).

The *starting year* for all of the organizations working in this field was after 1991. The majority started activities in this field after 1995.

The *target groups* are recipients, organizations running DDR and donors and local authorities. The former group was the only one mentioned at the local level. At the national level, both previously mentioned target groups were identified together with donors and international organizations.

Table 20: Division of labour in funding/fund-raising activities among organizations by status, level of operation and type of orientation

Types of organizations	Legal status		Level of operation		Type of organization	
Specific funding and fund-raising activities	Governmental, public agency	NGOs	National	Local	Exclu-sive	Inclu-sive
General support	100%			100%	100%	
Fund-raising, organization of events	75%	25%	75%	25%	75%	25%
Contacts with donors	100%		100%			100%
Other	100%		100%			100%
Total	86%	14%	71%	29%	57%	43%

Co-ordination activities are conducted by 20 organizations.

The organizations' main activity in the field of co-ordination is co-ordination at the regional and national level (64.3% of all activities). This activity was declared as the most important one at the national as well as at the local level. At the local level, only one other activity was indicated: co-ordination of special events and campaigns. This was indicated at the national level as well as the co-ordination of activities within the own organization and the co-ordination of other organizations' activities within specific areas.

The first co-ordination activity commenced in 1990. The majority of the organizations established such activities after 1995.

Table 21: Division of labour in co-ordination activities among organizations by status, level of operation and type of orientation

Types of organizations	Legal status		Level of operation		Type of organization	
Specific co-ordination activities	Governmental, public agency	NGOs	National	Local	Exclu-sive	Inclu-sive
Co-ordination within one's own organization	100%		100%			100%
Co-ordination of other organizations' activities	67%	33%	100%			100%
Co-ordination of special events	50%	50%	75%	25%	25%	75%
Co-ordination at the regional or national level	89%	11%	61%	39%	44%	56%
Total	82%	18%	71%	29%	32%	68%

The respondents most frequently identified the following target groups: governmental, public agencies (32.4% of total), NGOs, governmental organizations and NGOs (28% of total).

Interest representation was identified as an activity by 14 of the organizations. A share of 64% of them were non-governmental.

The *main activities* in this field consist of protecting drug users' rights, lobbying, advocacy and legal advice and representation (Table 22). Lobbying and advocacy is the activity of non-governmental organizations. As shown in the data, the activities are aimed at ensuring the social rights of drug users rather than protecting human rights in general.

Table 22: Division of labour in interest representation activities among organizations by status, level of operation and type of orientation

Types of organizations	Legal status		Level of operation		Type of organization	
Specific interest representation activities	Governmental, public agency	NGOs	National	Local	Exclu-sive	Inclu-sive
Legal advice, representation	33%	67%	100%			100%
Protecting drug users' rights	50%	50%	87%	13%	25%	75%
Lobbying, advocacy		100%	50%	50%	25%	75%
Other		100%	100%			100%
Total	31%	69%	81%	19%	19%	81%

The beginning *year* of the activity was in two cases dated before 1990, although the majority of the organizations established activities after 1995.

The *target groups* are mainly drug users (overall level 32%). Public institutions were stated in 27.7% and public opinion in 16% of the cases.

Policy development and legislation is an activity which 67% of all organizations perform. It is interesting to note that almost half (48%) of the organizations indicating this activity are non-governmental.

The organizations' *main activities* in the field of policy development and legislation are the development of strategies and legislation, and participation in the strategy and policy development process.

Policy development activities were established at the local and at the national level after 1991. The majority of policy development activities at the local level were founded in the period 1991-1994, whereas the majority of those at the national level were established after 1995.

Table 23: Division of labour in policy development/legislation activities among organizations by status, level of operation and type of orientation

Types of organizations	Legal status		Level of operation		Type of organization	
Specific policy development and legislation activ.	Governmental, public agency	NGOs	National	Local	Exclusive	Inclusive
Development of policy	86%	14%	71%	29%	14%	86%
Participation in policy processes	40%	60%	55%	45%	40%	60%
Total	52%	48%	59%	41%	33%	67%

Respondents mentioned parliament, government and policy-makers as *target groups* at the national level. At the local level, only one target group was indicated: policy-makers.

At this point, it should be noted that respondents were asked to answer this question during the time when an overall discussion on the new law on drug demand reduction took place in Slovenia. The preparation of the new legislation, which started in 1996, engaged many of the organizations in the field of drug demand reduction. Some of them were asked by the government to cooperate in drafting the legislation (especially those at the national level). The others became involved at a later stage to secure their interests, especially in the parliamentary discussions.

The first activity on *training of professionals* (Table 24) originated in 1989 and was established at the national level (High School for Social Work). A significant increase in the activities is seen after 1995 – mostly at the national level.

Table 24: Division of labour in training of professionals activities among organizations by status, level of operation and type of orientation

Types of organizations	Legal status		Level of operation		Type of organization	
Specific training of professionals activities	Governmental, public agency	NGOs	National	Local	Exclu-sive	Inclu-sive
Teachers, Trainers	100%		100%			100%
Policemen, Judges	100%		100%			100%
Students	100%		100%			100%
Professionals DDR programmes	43%	57%	82%	18%	21%	79%
Volunteers		100%	67%	33%	33%	67%
Other	50%	50%	50%	50%	50%	50%
Total	46%	54%	81%	19%	22%	78%

The *target groups* of the activities at the local level are only professionals in DDR programmes. The majority of the organizations in the field of drug demand reduction were established at the beginning of the 1990s. Therefore, the training of professionals had to be one of the main activities in the 1990s in order to train those who founded organizations dealing with drug demand reduction and to train the first professionals and volunteers in the field. Respondents from the organizations at the national level indicated professional involved in DDR programmes as their main target group, although teachers, trainers, policemen, judges, custom officers, students and volunteers were also mentioned.

A number of 22 organizations indicated that they conducted *other activities* apart from those stated in the previous questions on specific DDR activities. The respondents generally mentioned all of the activities in the field of DDR that they provide.

3.3 *The most important activities*

Respondents were asked to choose two DDR activities from all of the activities that they perform. The first question asked them to mention the most important of their activities, and the second, to state which activity they would most like to develop further in the near future.

Table 25 shows *the most important activities* as stated by the respondents. It is an interesting distribution because the organizations indicated very different activities as being the most important ones.

The most important activities of the organizations at the national level are: distribution of leaflets and brochures (13.0%), training of professionals (13.0%) and individual counselling (8.7%). At the local level, the most important activity is individual counselling (30.8%) followed by methadone treatment (7.7%). On the whole individual counselling (16.7%) is shown to be the most important activity.

Only one activity is run by a private organization, 18 (50%) by governmental (public) organizations and 13 (36%) by NGOs.

The background of the professionals is as follows: 52% of the activities involve psychologists and social workers, 25% medical doctors and 16% psychiatrists.

Table 25: The most important of the organizations' activities

	Legal status			Level of operation		
Type of organization *Specific activity*	Governmental, public agency	Private firm, enterprise	Non-profit, voluntary	National level	Local level	Total
Distribution of brochures, leaflets						
Count	1		3	3	1	4
% within legal status	5.0		20.0	13.0	7.7	11.1
Street work						
Count			2	1	1	2
% within legal status			13.3	4.3	7.7	5.6
Special events (concerts, ...)						
Count	1			1		1
% within legal status	5.0			4.3		2.8
Public information campaigns						
Count	1			1		1
% within legal status	5.0			4.3		2.8
Individual treatment						
Count	3		3	2	4	6
% within legal status	15.0		20.0	8.7	30.8	16.7
Treatment						
Count	1			1		1
% within legal status	5.0			4.3		2.8

	Legal status			Level of operation		
Type of organization: *Specific activity:*	**Governmental, public agency**	**Private firm, enterprise**	**Non-profit, voluntary**	**National level**	**Local level**	**Total**
Therapeutic communities						
Count			1	1		1
% within legal status			6.7	4.3		2.8
Day centres						
Count			1	1		1
% within legal status			6.7	4.3		2.8
After-care						
Count			1		1	1
% within legal status			6.7		7.7	2.8
Methadone treatment						
Count	2				2	2
% within legal status	10.0				15.4	5.6
Needle exchange, condom distribution						
Count			1		1	1
% within legal status			6.7		7.7	2.8
Assistance in social re-adaptation						
Count		1		1		1
% within legal status		100.0		4.3		2.8
Research						
Count	2		1	2	1	3
% within legal status	10.0		6.7	8.7	7.7	8.3
Support in fund raising						
Count	1		1	1	1	2
% within legal status	5.0		6.7	4.3	7.7	5.6
Co-ordination at the regional and national level						
Count	2			1	1	2
% within legal status	10.0			4.3	7.7	5.6
Development of strategy, policy, legislation						
Count	1			1		1
% within legal status	5.0			4.3		2.8
Participation in strategy, policy, legislation development process						
Count	1			1		1
% within legal status	5.0			4.3		2.8
Training of teachers						
Count	1			1		1
% within legal status	5.0			4.3		2.8
Training of professionals						
Count	2		1	3		3
% within legal status	10.0		6.7	13.0		8.3
Other						
Count	1			1		1
% within legal status	5.0			4.3		2.8
Total						
Count	20	1	15	23	13	36
% within legal status	100.0	100.0	100.0	100.0	100.0	100.0

The organizations were also asked about activities that should be *intensified in the future*. The list is long and many different wishes were mentioned. A share of 16.2% of the respondents wished to develop training programmes on prevention, 10.8% wished to improve co-ordination at the regional and national levels, and to develop the training of professionals involved in DDR programmes.

It is interesting to note that the activities, which we found to be lacking at all, do not have high priority for development in the future (for example assistance with housing).

Two organizations at the local level declared that there was no activity to be intensified in the future. These organizations expressed two wishes: to intensify the development of training programmes concerning prevention and to intensify co-ordination activities at the regional and national levels. For the national level organizations, most emphasized the wish to intensify the training of professionals.

The wishes for the further intensification of activities are very disperse also regarding the two different statuses of organizations. GOs wish to intensify training programmes concerning prevention, while NGOs' answers show no specific or important focuses (more than two NGOs stated "none").

Table 26: Activities to be intensified in the future

	Level of operation		Legal Status			Total
	National level	Local level	Government, public agency	Private firm, enterprise	Non-profit, voluntary	
Distribution of brochures, leaflets						
F	1		1			1
%	4.3		5.0			2.7
Development of training programmes						
F	2	4	5		1	6
%	8.7	28.6	25.0		6.3	16.2
Street work						
F	1	1			2	2
%	4.3	7.1			12.5	5.4
Other (cooperation with media)						
F	1		1			1
%	4.3		5.0			2.7
Treatment (general)						
F	2	1	2		1	3
%	8.7	7.1	10.0		6.3	8.1

	Level of operation		Legal Status			Total
	National level	Local level	Government, public agency	Private firm, enterprise	Non-profit, voluntary	
Therapeutic community						
F	2		1		1	2
%	8.7		5.0		6.3	5.4
Day centres						
F	1	1			2	2
%	4.3	7.1			12.5	5.4
After-care, employment, educational support						
F		1			1	1
%		7.1			6.3	2.7
Day after-care centres						
F	1			1		1
%	4.3			100.0		2.7
Group therapy, group meetings						
F		1	1			1
%		7.1	5.0			2.7
Assistance in social re-adaptation after treatment						
F	2				2	2
%	8.7				12.5	5.4
Research (epidemiological ...)						
F	2		1		1	2
%	8.7		5.0		6.3	5.4
Running database centres						
F	1		1			1
%	4.3		5.0			2.7
Co-ordination of other organizations' activities within specific areas						
F	1				1	1
%	4.3				6.3	2.7
Co-ordination at the regional, national level						
F	1	3	3		1	4
%	4.3	21.4	15.0		6.3	10.8
Participation in strategy, policy, legislation development processes						
F	1		1			1
%	4.3		5.0			2.7
Training of professionals involved in DDR programmes						
F	4		2		2	4
%	17.4		10.0		12.5	10.8
None						
F		2	1		1	2
%		14.3	5.0		6.3	5.4
Total						
23	23	14	20	1	16	37
%	100.0	100.0	100.0	100.0	100.0	100.0

4 Organizations' attitudes towards the drug problem and their perceptions of drug demand reduction policies

4.1 *Perceptions of the extent and structure of the drug problem*

The institutional response to drug use-related problems is assumed to be strongly influenced by the perception of the magnitude of the problems. In this part of the report, we will analyse the set of questions which asked the organizations' representatives to estimate the extent and structure of illegal drug use in Slovenia.

Some of the respondents took these questions as an opportunity to play the challenging intellectual "what-will-be" game, while the majority of the respondents did not like the questions. They referred to the widely divergent estimates of the number of drug users occasionally stated by national experts, and more or less all of them claimed that nobody really knew the exact numbers.

Moreover, we gained the impression that although the questions were clearly stated, the respondents somehow understood the terms used very differently, for example, what exactly are "drugs", "use" and "drug users".[38] Due to the central role and moral satiation of these terms in recent public discourses, some respondents did not feel comfortable in attempting to define these terms more precisely. This might be the reason why 7 out of 37 respondents declined to answer even the first two relatively "easy" questions on the general use of drugs, and even more respondents were not ready to answer the next, more detailed questions on the use of specific drugs.

Table 27 shows that the estimates regarding the use of all illicit drugs in Slovenia in 1998 varied from 3,000 to 300,000, which means an extraordinary difference of 100 times, representing from 0.15% to 15% of the entire Slovenian population. Even if we do not take into account the two extremes of one-sixth of the respondents (we cut off five estimates at each extreme), the difference between the lowest and highest estimate is still fivefold. The mean estimate is almost 80,000 (Table 28) or 4% of the Slovenian population. The dispersion of the estimates is so large that the standard deviation almost equals the mean value.

The distribution of the predictions regarding general drug use in 2003 is quite similar to the estimates regarding drug use in 1998. The dispersion is just as large, but the distribution and the mean value drift a little bit to the side of the growing use of drugs. The lowest prediction is again 3,000 and the highest 400,000. The predicted mean value is somewhat more than 90,000 (Table 28) and on average it indicates that expectations predict the growth rate of drug use at 18% for the next five years (based on the averages of the absolute numbers). This prediction seems rather conservative and is lower than, for instance, the predicted rate of Slovenian economic inflation.

Table 27: Estimated number of drug users in 1998

Estimated drug use	Frequency	Per cent
3,000-10,000	4	13.3
10,001-50,000	8	26.7
50,001-100,000	13	42.9
100,001-300,000	5	16.6
Total	30	100.0
No answer	7	
Grand total	37	

Table 28: Estimates of drug use in 1998 and 2003 and predicted relative change: descriptive statistics

	N	Minimum	Maximum	Mean	Std. Dev.
Estimated drug use 1998	30	3,000	300,000	76,816.6	65,536.8
Predicted drug use 2003	29	3,000	400,000	90,603.4	80,333.1
Relative change in per cent	29	0	33.3	23.7	19.4

The estimates of drug use by NGOs and GOs are almost the same. By contrast, the estimates made by organizations dealing with drug demand reduction inclusively are about twice as high as those made by organizations with an exclusive orientation. Similarly, estimates by national organizations are twice as high as those of organizations working at the local level. However, none of these differences reach the level of statistical significance.

Table 28 shows the extent and direction of the predicted relative change in drug use. Percentages are calculated on the basis of the individual values estimated for drug use in 1998 as a base rate. None of the respondents expected drug use to diminish, while six of them expected the growth rate of drug use to remain unchanged. The most pessimistic respondent predicted an increase of 66%, while 24% growth was expected on average (based on the average of the percentage of predicted growth).

Variance analyses show that the different subgroups of respondents (by level of operation, local or national, and by status, NGO or GO) do not differ significantly in predicting changes in drug use, but the respondents of NGOs and national organizations tend to be more pessimistic in their predictions than those of GOs and local organizations.

The estimates and predictions relating to the structural aspects of the market with respect to the specific groups of drugs are even more heterogeneous. Table 29 shows that in the case of amphetamine use in 1998, the most conservative estimate was a 2% market share, while the most radical assessment set the share at 79%. In general, our respondents believed that the three largest shares in the market of illicit drugs are held by cannabis (58%), amphetamines (21%) and opiates (11%). Other drugs have much smaller shares.

The basic picture does not change much if we compare the estimates of recent use with predictions (for 2003). In absolute numbers, the shares (% of the markets) of specific drugs are not expected to change by more than 2% (Table 29). Our respondents expect the use of opiates and cannabis to decline, and the use of amphetamines, hallucinogens and mostly cocaine to grow over the next five years. But the change is not assumed to be really big

or important; in relative terms the highest growth is expected in cocaine use (the share in 2003 is expected to be 28% higher than in 1998).

Table 29: Estimated (1998) and predicted (2003) market shares of different drugs used (in %)

	Estimation 1998			**Prediction 2003**		**Predicted growth**
	N	*Mean*	*Std. Deviation*	*Mean*	*Std. Deviation*	**03/98**
Opiates	26	11.1	6.3	10.9	7.0	- 2%
Cocaine	26	3.7	3.2	4.7	3.5	+ 28%
Cannabis	26	58.4	22.8	56.0	21.3	- 4%
Hallucinogenic	26	2.9	3.0	3.1	4.2	+ 7%
Amphetamines	26	20.5	18.9	22.5	18.4	+ 9%
Other	26	3.5	6.6	3.0	5.9	-12%
Total		100.0		100.0		

Our subjective assessment as regards our respondents' opinions about the structure of drug use is that much has been written about and is known in Slovenia about opiates, but this is out of proportion with what is known about amphetamines, cocaine and even cannabis. Our final observation is that the perceptions of Slovenian respondents seem to reflect a trend of a relatively stable development over the next five years both as regards the extent of drug use and its structural characteristics.

4.2 *Organizations' attitudes*

Attitudes towards drugs and drug-related (moral) reactions were measured using a scale of eight items. The items were designed to measure the attitudinal dimension ranging from permissiveness to restrictiveness regarding illegal drug use.[39]

The ranges of the responses in seven out of eight cases represented the whole continuum (from 1: agree to 5: disagree), and the standard deviations also seemed to be rather high (Table 30). In fact, all of the distributions were closer to being bimodal than to a normal Gauss distribution. It means that the questions were formulated so as to make it difficult for respondents to adopt a central position in responding, and that the items and the scale could very well differentiate the respondents.

Table 30: Characteristics of organizations' representatives as regards eight attitudinal items

Attitudes:	N	Min	Max	Mean	Std. Dev.
Taking illegal drugs can sometimes be beneficial. (BENEF)	36	1	5	3.3	1.7
Adults should be free to take any drug they wish. (FREED)	36	1	5	3.1	1.8
We need to accept that using illegal drugs is normal for some people's lives. (NORM)	36	1	5	2.4	1.6
Smoking cannabis should be legalized. (LEGAL)	36	1	5	3.5	1.5
The best way to treat people who are addicted to drugs is to stop them from using drugs altogether. (TREAT)	36	1	5	3.0	1.7
The use of illegal drugs always leads to addiction. (DETERM)	36	1	5	3.7	1.5
Taking illegal drugs is always morally wrong. (MORAL)	36	2	5	4.1	1.1
All use of illegal drugs is misuse. (MISUSE)	36	1	5	3.3	1.7

The average responses (means) are located in the more permissive half of the continua (e.g. in the "agree" part of the responding continuum of the items TREAT, DETERM, MORAL and MISUSE, and in the "disagree" part of the item NORM, in five out of eight cases, most explicitly under the item MORAL. All other averages are quite close to the central points (values from 3.08 to 3.53) of the response continua.

Taking into account the highly morally satiated nature of drug-related issues, the averages that are around the central point and the predominantly bimodal distributions of responses, we may conclude that the attitudes of the Slovenian respondents are on average rather permissive, but that a substantial subgroup of restrictively-oriented professionals exists. The attitudes could also be described as being "divided".

The structure of attitudes was further analysed using variance analysis with two independent variables: status (GOs and NGOs) and the level of operation (local and national). Table 31 shows that these two variables are by and large not responsible for the variance seen in these eight attitudinal items, as there were no systematic tendencies in the differences among the means. The only two statistically significant differences (at the 0.05 level) show that local organizations disagree more often with the statement *Taking illegal drugs is always morally wrong* than national organizations, and that exclusive organizations disagree with the statement *Smoking cannabis should be legalized* more often than inclusive ones.

Table 31: Means of eight attitudinal items regarding the level of operation, status of organizations and their inclusive/exclusive orientation in DDR

	Benef	Freed	Norm	Legal	Treat	Determ	Moral	Misuse
By status								
Governmental, public (N=17)	3.7	3.1	2.5	3.7	2.9	3.8	4.3*	3.4*
Non-profit, voluntary (N=14)	3.0	3.0	2.4	3.3	3.1	3.6	3.6*	2.9*
By level of operation:								
National level (N=22)	3.3	2.8	2.6	3.6	3.0	3.4	3.9#	3.2
Local level (N=14)	3.4	3.6	2.1	3.5	3.1	4.1	4.6#	3.6
By inclusive/exclusive orientation:								
Exclusive (N=9)	4.1	4.0*	3.1	4.4#	2.4	3.4	4.3	3.1
Inclusive (N=28)	3.1	2.8*	2.2	3.2#	3.2	3.8	4.1	3.4

Note: * $p<0.10$, # $p< 0.05$.

A factor analysis of the eight items showed that a one-factorial solution is meaningful, furthermore that the resulting factor, which explains 52% of the variance, is rather highly satiated with all the eight items and that the reliability of a scale composed of these eight items would be rather good. Therefore, a new variable (named restrictive/permissive orientation) was formulated as a linear function of the responses to the eight items, with a theoretical minimum of 1 and maximum of 5 points.[40] One of the respondents reached the maximum (5) and two of them nearly the minimal (2) value points. The new variable will be used in further analyses.

4.3 *Perceptions of policies*

The perceptions of current national drug policies were tested using two sets of questions. The first one asked about the orientation of drug policy, more specifically about the five typical possible dimensions of drug policy: health promotion, harm minimization, demand reduction, supply control and the law enforcement approach to users. The five dimensions were evaluated on a 5-point scale (5 = Definitely yes, 4 = Rather yes, 3 = Equal, 2 = Rather no, 1 = Definitely no).

Table 32 shows that on average the answers concerning these five orientations all focused around the central point (in the middle between "yes" and "no"), and the difference between the smallest and the largest average is only 0.82 points. According to these perceptions, the strongest orientation of Slovenian drug policy is towards harm minimization, and the least pronounced towards supply control, while the other three orientations (health promotion, demand reduction and law enforcement) are somewhere in between (actually very close to the middle point). The perception of the primacy of harm minimization can be further illustrated using the result that nearly two-thirds of all respondents felt that Slovenian drug policy is positively focused on harm minimization (65.7% of answers "rather yes" or "definitely yes"), which is nearly two times higher than the proportions of comparable answers concerning other drug policy orientations.

Table 32: Perceptions of the five dimensions of drug policy: descriptive statistics of data on a 5-point scale (1= definitely no, 5 = definitely yes)

	N	Min.	Max	Mean	Std. Dev.
Health promotion	36	1	5	3.1	1.0
Harm reduction	35	2	5	3.7	0.8
Demand reduction	36	1	4	3.1	0.9
Supply control	36	1	4	2.9	0.9
Law enforcement	36	1	4	3.0	0.8

Analyses of variance proved that there are no statistically significant differences in the perception of drug policy orientations between organizations operating at the national or local levels, between GOs and NGOs or between exclusively- and inclusively-oriented organizations.

On the basis of the newly-developed variable (restrictive/permissive orientation), all the organizations were divided in three groups of approximately equal size. These were the groups of the most restrictive, the moderate and the most permissive organizations (Table 33). The comparisons of the three groups produced only one (marginally significant) difference. This difference was found in the perceptions of the law enforcement orientation of Slovenian policy. The most permissive organizations perceived this orientation as much more pronounced than the group of the most restrictive organizations.

Table 33: Perceptions of the salience of the five dimensions of drug policy by the three groups of organizations, differentiated by the level of permissiveness

	Health promotion	Harm minimization	Demand reduction	Supply control	Law enforcement
most restrictive (N=12)	3.1	3.8	2.7	2.7	2.7
moderate (N=10)	3.2	3.6	3.3	3.1	3.0
most permissive (N=14)	3.0	3.8	3.2	3.0	3.4
stat. sig. (ANOVA)	-	-	-	-	0.1

Our conclusion is that the sample of Slovenian organizations has a rather non-differentiated perception of the national drug policy orientation with a relative emphasis on harm minimization. However, it is important to note that all of the subgroups of organizations share this perception that the strongest emphasis of the policies pursued is on harm reduction. This perception is also shared by the authors of this report. We feel that the institutional agents of the harm reduction policy are the most highly organized ones and the closest ones to the sources of our national funds. It is less clear whether this situation developed as a consequence of a broad national professional consensus or as a consequence of other factors.

The answers to the next two questions could be used to (partially) answer the question of the (non)differentiation of the Slovenian national drug policy. The respondents were asked to mention up to three main strengths and weaknesses of the Slovenian national drug policy (Tables 34 and 35).

Table 34: Main strengths of the national drug policy*

Strengths	n	%
Awareness of the drug problem, public discussions, better understanding of the problem	4	6.2
Efficient network of organizations, effective cooperation	6	9.2
Competent, expert-based and professional	1	1.5
Prevention programmes, preventative programmes at schools, new subjects of drug prevention	8	12.3
Therapy programmes (new treatment and care centres), therapeutic communities	4	6.2
Harm reduction programmes	13	20,0
Effective policy, conception, legislation, (variety of programmes, openness for changes)	18	27.7
Supply control, law enforcement (legislation and control), repression, relatively good control of supply (drug market), new legal institutions for police (controlled purchase, secret parcel) for combating drug criminality	1	1.5
Other	7	10.8
No strengths at all	3	4.6
Total responses	65	100.0

Note: * Respondents were allowed to mention three strengths. If they mentioned one strength two or three times, it was categorized as belonging to one of the categories in the table and the multiple answers were taken as only one answer.

The first impression gained from Tables 34 and 35 is that the respondents mentioned more weaknesses (82, or on average 2.2 per respondent) than strengths (65, or 1.8 per person).

The second impression is that the most frequent answers in both tables contradict each other. Among the strengths were the "effectiveness of policy, conception and legislation (variety of programmes, openness for changes)", which was mentioned 18 times, and the "efficient network of organizations and effective cooperation" mentioned 6 times, while at the same time 27 respondents mentioned a "lack of policy, there is no drug policy, lack of a conceptual approach, lack of a national programme of priorities, lack of programmes" and a "lack of co-ordination, there is no co-ordination, there is big chaos, incoherence of ideas, communication on the vertical level" 21 times as the main weaknesses. These outright contradictory perceptions could point to heterogeneity and complexity of perceptions (and reality). Another explanation could be that the applied coding system and the coding process were too crude and produced such results. It is, for instance, possible that a respondent evaluates national policy on the whole as not co-ordinated enough, but at the same time mentions the perfect co-ordination in one of the sectors of this policy as its main strength. It could also be the case in relation to national level drug policy which due to its own lack of efficiency allows professionals to organize their own mechanisms of co-ordination in one specific sector. In any case, the magnitude of the answers mentioning a lack of policy and lack of co-ordination point to the predominant (negative) perception of national policy.

Table 35: Main weaknesses of the national drug policy*

Weaknesses	n	%
Lack of awareness of the drug problem (drug users are not recognized as patients)	4	4.9
Lack of professionals, experts	-	-
Ineffective programmes	3	3.7
Focus on law enforcement, repressive approach, proclamation of war on drugs	3	3.7
Lack of policy, there is no drug policy, lack of a conceptual approach, lack of a national programme of priorities, lack of programmes	27	32.9
Lack of co-ordination, there is no co-ordination, there is big chaos, incoherence of ideas, communication on the vertical level	21	25.6
Lack of research, information, no information/ data on the number of drug users, absence of research institute	5	6.1
Insufficient funding, financial problems	6	7.3
Lack of evaluation, lack of control and monitoring of programmes	5	6.1
Barriers in development of non-governmental institutions	-	-
Other	8	9.8
Total responses	82	

Note: * Respondents were allowed to mention three weaknesses. If they mentioned one weakness two or three times, it was categorized as belonging to one of the categories in the table and the multiple answers were taken as only one answer.

In our opinion the above-mentioned contradictory answers could be another reflection of the rather divided attitudes to drugs (section 4.2) in Slovenia. The representatives of the restrictive and permissive attitudes probably evaluated specific elements of the national drug policy in diametrically opposing ways.

To a certain extent, it is surprising and encouraging to see that respondents did not mention a lack of knowledge, experts, effective programmes, research and monitoring or even funding to be the main weaknesses to any higher degree. These issues were mentioned in about one-sixth of all responses.

As regards the specific orientations of national policy, harm reduction was mentioned thirteen times on the positive side, as well as preventive programmes eight times and therapy and treatment programmes four times, while supply control and law enforcement were very rarely mentioned, neither as a strength nor as a weakness. This result is in accordance with the findings related to the previous set of questions (Table 32) on the orientation of national policy. It seems as if it is the professionals' perception that places the emphasis on harm minimization and views this largely as positive.

5 Differentiation and integration into the system of Slovenian DDR organizations

The question of differentiation and integration into the system of the Slovenian DDR organizations will be dealt with in the next three sections of this part of the report. In the first section, the division of work between GOs and NGOs will be analysed, the next looks at the grouping of organizations by functional type and in the last section, the system of interaction among all the analysed organizations is examined more closely.

5.1 *Division of work between NGOs and GOs*

Table 36 shows that the majority of DDR organizations are inclusive ones. The exclusive ones (regarding their functional type[41]) are: four high-threshold NGOs, three local action groups, one co-ordinating governmental body and one medical centre. Regarding the overall number of these types of organizations, it may be concluded that local action groups and high-threshold NGOs often tend to be exclusively oriented in their activities, while other types of organizations perform their DDR activities mostly only as part of their overall workload.

Table 36: Inclusive/exclusive orientation of DDR organizations by legal status

	Legal status			
Orientation to DDR	Governmental, public	Private firm, enterprise	Non-profit, voluntary	Total
Exclusive	4		5	9
Inclusive	16	1	11	28
Total	20	1	16	37

Table 37 shows that in Slovenia, the proportion of exclusive, more specialized organizations is smaller than on average in the other three countries (and in fact it is lower than in any other of the three countries). We can only speculate about the reasons for this finding. It could be also related to the smallness of Slovenia and its dense social networks. It can be related to a rather decentralized structure of urbanization (a majority of inhabitants live in smaller towns and villages).

Table 37: Inclusive/exclusive orientation of DDR organizations by country

	Country	
Orientation to DDR	Slovenia	Czech Republic, Hungary, Poland
Exclusive	9 (24%)	51 (36%)
Inclusive	28 (76%)	93 (64%)
Total	37 (100%)	141 (100%)

Table 38 shows that among the most important missions of organizations, the most frequent are personal care and treatment, prevention and policy design. NGOs seem to place a little more emphasis on prevention and treatment than GOs do; nonetheless, GOs choose policy design as their mission much more often than NGOs did.

Table 39 shows a similar, albeit more differentiated picture regarding organizations' main goals in the field of DDR. NGOs state as their main goals prevention and treatment, and rehabilitation a little bit more frequently, while GOs clearly prevail regarding the goals of research and funding. The biggest difference between both types of organizations is found in the general statement of "drug demand reduction", which was mentioned by the GOs as a kind of overarching indirect goal, which is an inherent part of their general functions.

Table 38: Mission of DDR organizations by legal status

	Legal status			
Mission of organization	Governmental, public (N=20)	Private firm, enterprise (N=1)	Non-profit, voluntary (N=16)	Total (N=37)
Prevention	5		6	11
Personal care, treatment and advice	6	1	7	14
Policy design and coordination	6		2	8
Research, documentation	2		1	3
Other	1			1
Total	18	1	14	37

Table 39: Three most important goals in the field of DDR (multiple responses are added together)

	Legal status			
Organization's goals in DDR	Governmental, public (N=20)	Private firm, enterprise (N=1)	Non-profit, voluntary (N=16)	Total (N=37)
Drug demand reduction (general statement)	10		3	13
Prevention/information	11		13	24
Treatment and care	10	2	10	22
Rehabilitation (after-care)	3		4	7
Research/documentation	4			4
Funding/fund-raising	2		1	3
Co-ordination	2		2	4
Interest representation				
Policy development/legislation	4		2	6
Training of professionals	3	1	2	6
Other			2	2
Total	49	3	39	91

Table 40 shows the activities performed by the organizations by status. The general impression is that GOs and NGOs do not differ to a large extent regarding their type of activity. For instance, there is no type of activity, which could be performed by GOs or NGOs exclusively. But there are differences in at least four types of activities (regarding the share of each type of organization among all):

- GOs offer a disproportional high share of coordination activities and an even higher proportion of funding/fund-raising activities.

- The NGOs' share of treatment and care activities is greater than the GOs' share. This type of disproportionality is even higher regarding interest representation activities, which are offered much more frequently by NGOs.

Table 40: Type of activities, performed by organizations of different status

Status of organization *Type of activity*	**GO** n=20	**Private** n=1	**NGO** n=16	**All** n=37
Prevention	19	1	14	34
Treatment and care	7	1	9	17
Rehabilitation/after-care	8	1	6	15
Research/documentation	12		9	21
Funding/fund-raising	5		1	6
Co-ordination	15		5	20
Interest representation	5		9	14
Policy development	13	1	11	25
Training of professionals	12	1	11	24
Total	96	5	75	176

Table 41: GO and NGO organizations, which offer specific kinds of activities in international comparison (in per cent)

	Slovenia			**Czech Republic, Hungary, Poland**			**Diff. SLO others:**
Status of organization *Type of activity*	GO n=20	NGO n=16	All n=37	GO n=66	NGO n=70	All n=144	
Prevention	95	88	92	79	96	88	+4
Treatment and care	35	56	46	41	54	47	-1
Rehabilitation/after-care	40	38	41	26	43	35	+6
Research/documentation	60	56	57	58	36	46	+1
Funding/fund-raising	25	6	16	39	26	31	-15
Co-ordination	75	31	54	55	43	49	+5
Interest representation	25	56	38	12	29	21	+17
Policy development	65	69	68	53	33	42	+26
Training of professionals	60	69	65	67	67	67	-2

Table 41 shows an international comparison of the Slovenian situation with (the average) situation in the three other countries. According to the results, a higher proportion of Slovenian organizations (of all types, aggregated) compared to the other three countries offer preventive and educational, rehabilitation, research, co-ordination, interest representation and policy development activities, while a smaller proportion is engaged in funding activities, with about the same share offering treatment and care, and training activities. The two largest differences are in policy development and interest representation, which are offered by 17% and 26%, respectively, of Slovenian organizations.

Let us take a closer look at GOs and NGOs to analyse what the more typical activities of NGOs and the typical activities of GOs in Slovenia and in the other three countries are (on which we base our comparison). We have used the percentage of organizations of each type engaged in specific activities and have defined a 20% difference as the threshold, arriving at the following differences:

- In Slovenia 56% of NGOs are engaged in research, while only 36% of NGOs in the other three countries are; 56% of NGOs in Slovenia engage in interest representation work and only 29% of NGOs do so in the other countries; 69% of NGOs in Slovenia are active in policy development, while only 33% of NGOs in other countries are.
- By contrast, only 6% of NGOs in Slovenia are engaged in funding/fund raising, while 26% of NGOs in the other three countries are.
- In Slovenia 75% of GOs do co-ordinating activities, while only 55% of GOs in the other three countries engage in such activities.

Table 42: What are the typical activities of GOs and NGOs?

Type of activity	Slovenia	Czech Rep., Hungary and Poland (average)
Prevention	-	NGO
Treatment and care	**NGO**	NGO
Rehabilitation/after-care	-	NGO
Research/documentation	-	**GO**
Funding/fund-raising	GO	GO
Co-ordination	**GO**	GO
Interest representation	**NGO**	NGO
Policy development		**GO**
Training of professionals		-
Total number of differentiated fields:	4	9

Table 42 analyses the differences in percentage between the organizations of two types (GOs and NGOs) regarding their involvement in different activities. The criterion used for stating that one specific activity is more typical for an NGO is: the percentage of NGOs offering this activity had to be at least 10 points more than the corresponding percentage of GOs offering this activity. In cases where the differences were at least 20%, the corresponding fields in Table 42 have been highlighted.

Table 42 shows that in Slovenia treatment and care, and interest representation activities are distinctively the more characteristic activities of NGOs, while funding and especially co-ordination are more typical GOs' activities. The third column in Table 41 shows the same analysis for the other three countries. A comparison reveals that Slovenia does not differ from the other three countries qualitatively (regarding the kind and contents of the activities in which either NGOs or GOs are dominant), but it does differ as regards quantity. The differentiation between GOs and NGOs is found more often (i.e. regarding more kinds of activities) in the other three countries.[42]

Table 43: Perception of the strengths of national drug policy by status of organization

Status of organization *Strenghts*	**GO** n=20	**Private** n=1	**NGO** n=16	**All** n=37
1 Awareness of the drug problem, public discussions, better understanding of the problem	1		3	4
2 Efficient network of organizations, effective cooperation	2		4	6
3 Competent, expert-based and professional			1	1
4 Prevention programmes, preventive programmes on schools, new subjects of drug prevention	5	1	2	8
5 Therapy programmes (new treatment and care centres, therapeutic communities)	3			3
6 Harm reduction programmes	6	1	6	13
7 Effective policy, conception, legislation (variety of programmes, openness for changes)	8		7	15
8 Supply control, law enforcement (legislation and control, repression, relatively good control of supply (drug market), new legal institutions for police (controlled purchase, secret parcels) for combating drug criminality	1			1
Total	24	2	22	51

The differences in the perceptions of the organizations of their strengths and weaknesses in national policy were also analysed. Table 43 shows some differences among both types of organizations. NGOs disproportionally perceive the awareness of the drug problem and the efficient network of organizations as one of the national drug policy's strengths, while GOs are proud of the prevention programmes and therapy programmes, which other types of organizations very rarely see as a strength. Both groups agree that effective policy and harm reduction programmes represent the most obvious strength of Slovenian drug policy.

Table 44 shows the differences among NGOs' and GOs' perception of the weaknesses of national drug policy. They both perceive a lack of policy and lack of co-ordination as the two biggest weaknesses (which contradicts the results in Table 43). Another interesting finding is that insufficient funding was not mentioned very often, and when it is, almost exclusively by NGOs. It seems that GOs are not aware of this (NGO) problem.

Table 44: Perception of the weaknesses of national drug policy by status of organization

Status of organization *Strengths*	**GO** n=20	**Private** n=1	**NGO** n=16	**All** n=37
1 Lack of awareness of the drug problem (drug users are not recognized as patients)	2		2	4
2 Lack of professionals, experts				0
3 Ineffective programmes			2	2
4 Focus on law enforcement, repressive approach, proclamation of war on drugs	2		1	3
5 Lack of policy, there is no drug policy, lack of a conceptual approach, lack of a national programme of priorities, lack of programmes	10	1	9	20
6 Lack of co-ordination, there is no co-ordination, there is big chaos, incoherence of ideas, communication on the vertical level	10	1	7	18
7 Lack of research, information, no information/ data on the number of drug users, absence of research institute	2		2	4
8 Insufficient funding, financial problems	1		5	6
9 Lack of evaluation, lack of control and monitoring of programmes	1		1	3
10 Barriers in the development of non-governmental institutions				0
Total	25	2	27	60

Conclusion: In comparing Slovenia with the other three countries analysed, some differences were found regarding the differentiation of work between GOs and NGOs. In Slovenia, the proportion of NGOs among all analysed organizations was smaller than the average of the four countries. Slovenia also has a smaller proportion of exclusively-oriented organizations than any of the other three countries compared. Although there is some differentiation of the work between GOs and NGOs, signs exist that this differentiation is smaller (to be more precise, it is not visible in so many fields of activities) than in the other countries. Regarding the specific kinds of activities, Slovenian NGOs are comparatively "stronger" in the fields of interest representation, research and policy development, but "weaker" in fund raising than the NGOs in the other three countries. Regarding the perception of the national drug policy, Slovenian GOs and NGOs alike evaluate the harm reduction orientation as a strong point, but they also differ in their evaluations of the funding problems. It seems that GOs do not consider this to be such a serious problem as NGOs do.

5.2 *Functional differences among organizations*

In this chapter, we will analyse the characteristics of the different kinds of organizations regarding their functions. For this analysis, we have intuitively formed seven groups of organizations (Table 45). These groups correspond in part to the pattern of interactions and coalitions among the analysed organizations which has been sometimes observed by the authors. The criteria for grouping the organizations were logical: we put organizations that have often been perceived as performing similar tasks or being in similar positions into the same group.

Table 45: Categorization of DDR organizations in seven groups by function

	Name of the group	List and description of the organizations	N
1.	Ministries and governmental	Four ministries and their bodies (offices, institutes, commissions), one para-governmental professional chamber	8
2.	Research and academic	One high-level, professional school, two research institutes	3
3.	Medical, clinical	One clinic, three local community medical drug centres, one medical local preventive centre	5
4.	Local community	Local community action groups	3
5.	High threshold	Treatment communities, users' parents associations, one private treatment and rehabilitation-oriented firm	6
6.	Low threshold	Street work, outreach and peripatetic organizations	4
7.	Preventive, counselling, other	Prevention-oriented networks, counselling (mostly school and community-related) services for youngsters, information centres, one sporting association	8

Although the decisive factor for categorizing the organizations into these seven groups was not the level of operation (local or national) or their status (GO or NGO), there are no NGOs in the first three categories[43] and no GOs in categories 5 and 6 (Table 46). Nonetheless, in category 7 we have an equal number of GOs and NGOs.

Table 46: Seven types of organizations grouped by function and by status

Organizations by their status *Name of the functional group*	**Governmental**	**Non-governmental**	**Private**	**N**
1. Ministries and governmental	7	1		8
2. Research and academic	2	1		3
3. Medical, clinical	5			5
4. Local community	2	1		3
5. High threshold		5	1	6
6. Low threshold		4		4
7. Preventive, counselling, other	4	4		8
Total	20	16	1	37

In the following, these seven groups of organizations are compared regarding the responses of their representatives to three kinds of questions in our survey. Due to the very small number of organizations in the specific groups, our results do not allow us to deduce any general conclusions.

Figure 1 shows the average drug-related attitude (permissive/restrictive) of the seven groups of organizations. As predicted, the most restrictive are the high-threshold organizations, and the second-most restrictive are the medical organizations. Another predictable finding was that the most permissive ones are the low-threshold organizations. By contrast, the less easily predictable finding was the fact that research organizations tend to be very permissive, second to the low-threshold organizations. Quite close to the average position are the ministerial bodies, though these are closer to the permissive end than to the restrictive.

Figure 2 shows the estimates of the extent of drug abuse in 1998. The estimates of the research and academic institutions seem to be more than twice as high as the estimates of other organizations. This means that the large dispersion of the estimates of the extent of drug abuse would be much smaller without the research organizations, and even smaller if we omit the estimates of the low-threshold and preventive organizations. Are these three groups of organizations more pessimistic or more realistic? Our data cannot give an answer to this question. However, we could attempt to make a hypothetical interpretation by saying that the perception of the greater extent of drug abuse goes hand in hand with the more permissive attitude (compare Figure 1) towards drugs (or, alternatively, the more permissive attitude allows one to see more of drug use in society).

Figure 1: Average permissiveness/restrictiveness of the 7 groups of organizations

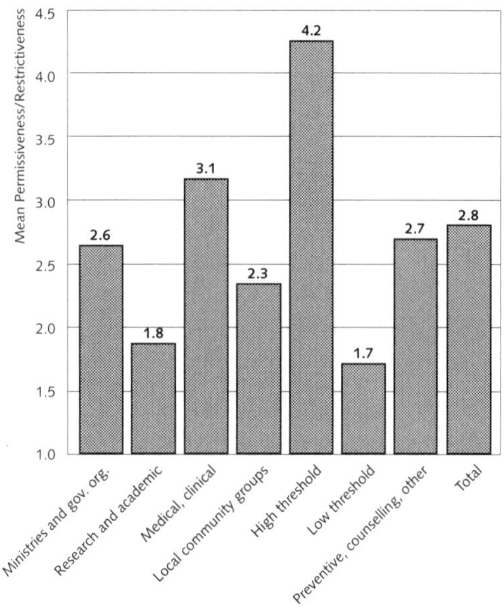

Figure 2: Estimates of the number of drug users by type of organization

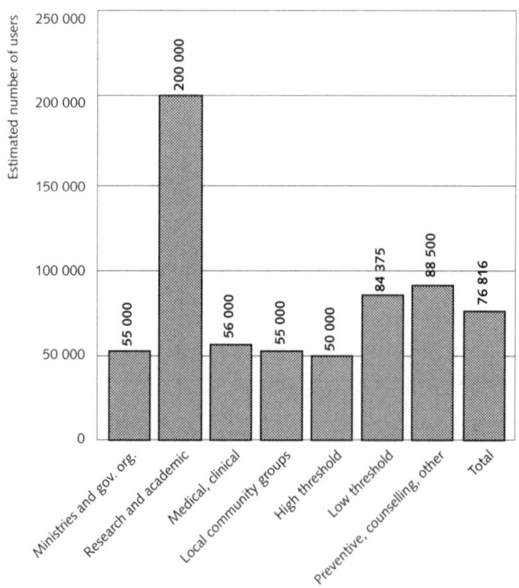

The following figures show the average evaluations of the organizations. Table 47 and Figure 3 show how the organizations evaluate themselves and their own work, and how they believe to be evaluated by their political surroundings. The evaluations were made on the 5-point scales (from 1 – grossly deficient to 5 – excellent, "first rate").

By far the lowest seems to be the self-evaluation of the medical organizations (more than 1 point worse than the average; the differences are statistically significant at the level 0.06). Were they evaluating themselves in a more modest way or were they employing more demanding criteria or was their performance really worse than that of other organizations? There is no way to answer these questions on the basis of our data. By contrast, low-threshold, local community groups and preventive programmes evaluate themselves as – at least – "good, solid, convincing".

Table 47: How the seven functional types of organizations evaluate themselves and how they perceive their evaluation by their political surroundings

Kind of evaluation *Functional type of organization*	Self-image	Image of oneself by politics	Difference between both evaluations
Ministries and governmental org.	3.67	3.50	-0.17
Research and academical	3.33	3.33	0
Medical, clinical	2.60	3.25	+0.62
Local community groups	4.00	4.00	0
High threshold	4.00	4.17	+0.17
Low threshold	4.25	2.67	-1.58
Preventive and counselling	4.25	4.29	+0.04
Total	3.77	3.72	-0.05

In comparing self-evaluation with perceived evaluation by the political environment, two interesting groups of organizations emerge. On the one hand, medical organizations that feel that the outside evaluation of their work overrates them. This may be due to the traditionally higher esteem given to medical organizations (regardless of their real value). On the other hand, low-threshold organizations felt that they were dramatically underrated by their political environment. The difference was more than one and a half points, denoting the difference between the two points: one somewhere between "good, solid, convincing" and "excellent, first rate" and another between "adequate, satisfying" and "problematic, to be improved". This difference probably reflects the (economically and politically) hard times, which some of the low-threshold organizations actually experienced in the period before 1999.

Figure 3: Self-evaluation of the seven types of organizations

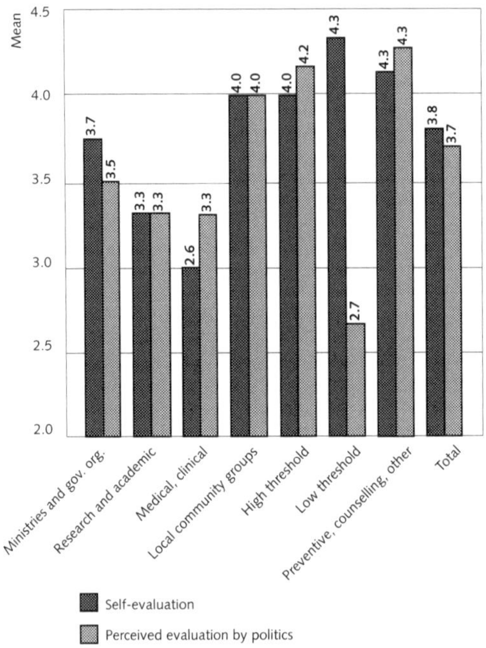

Our analysis showed that organizations grouped intuitively by functional type (sometimes) differ significantly as regards their permissiveness/restrictiveness, their perceptions of the drug problem and their evaluations of their own work. Although these differences are not necessarily very interesting in themselves, we decided to analyse in the next chapter the role of these seven groups of organizations in the whole system of the organizations analysed. Our expectation was that their different characteristics will be related to their different positions within the system of interaction among the organizations.

5.3 *Structure of interaction within the system of DDR organizations*

The relations among 37 organizations were measured by collecting data on 12 dimensions of their interactions. All organizations were asked whether they: received resources, expertise and support from others or provided these goods to others; received clients by others or referred clients to others; communicated informally, engaged in strategic cooperation or common activities with other organizations, and whether they took the interests of other organizations into consideration.

Using the methods of network analysis we calculated (normalized out-degree) indexes of centrality for nine key dimensions of the 12 dimensions of interactions mentioned. For each of these dimensions, we determined the "important" (central) organizations. An organization was considered as "important" if its index of centrality was at the point of 90 or a higher centile.[44] This procedure showed:

- Regarding the provision of funding, there are three by far outstanding organizations: The Ministry of Health, the Ministry of Social Affairs and the local action group in Slovenia's capital Ljubljana.
- Regarding expertise, the four most active organizations are: the Ministry of Health, the co-ordination of centres for the prevention and treatment of drug addiction (which also functions under the Ministry of Health), the Governmental Institute for Health Protection and the (para-governmental) Social Chamber.
- Regarding support, the three organizations providing support are the Ministry of Health, the Ministry of Social Affairs and the Governmental Office for Drugs.
- As regards organizations to which others refer clients, the most important are: the Methadone Co-ordination Project, the high-threshold NGO Project Men, another high-threshold NGO called "Pelikan" (working under Karitas) and the Central Medical Clinic in Ljubljana.
- As regards organizations that refer clients to the responding organizations, the ones that did most referrals were again the Methadone Co-ordination Project, the Central Medical Clinic in Ljubljana and the NGO Project Men.
- As regards informal communication, the most communicative organizations were the Ministry of Social Affairs, the Governmental Office for Drugs, the Governmental Institute for Health Protection and the NGO Project Men.
- Regarding strategic counselling, the strategically most important ones were the Ministry of Health, the Ministry of Social Affairs and the Governmental Office for Drugs.
- Regarding joint activities, the most active were the Ministry of Health, the Ministry of Social Affairs and the Methadone Co-ordination Project.
- Regarding the role of the organization and whose interests should be taken into account, the most important were the Ministry of Health, the Ministry of Social Affairs and the Governmental Office for Drugs.

In a next step, we counted how many times (on how many of the nine dimensions) a certain organization was chosen as the most important one. It turned out that only 10 out of 37 organizations were chosen at least once as the important ones in any of the dimensions. Table 48 shows how often specific organizations were chosen (occupying the upper percentile in the scale of importance regarding specific kinds of interaction).

Table 48: Organizations most frequently chosen as the most important in each interactional dimension, and their basic characteristics

Characteristics *Organization and no. of times chosen*	**GO or NGO**	**National or Local**	**Ljubljana or Coastal region**	**Permissive or restrictive organization[45]**
Ministry of Health (6)	GO	N	L	=
Ministry of Social Affairs (5)	GO	N	L	P
Office for Drugs (4)	GO	N	L	P
Methadone Co-ordination (4)	GO	N	L	P
High-threshold Project Men (2)	NGO	N	L	R
Institute for Health Protection (2)	GO	N	L	P
High-threshold "Pelikan" (2)	NGO	N	L	R
Central Medical Drug Clinic in Ljubljana (2)	GO	L	L	P
Local action group Ljubljana (2)	GO	N	L	R
Social Chamber (1)	NGO	N	L	P
Total (modal form of important organizations chosen	7xGO 3xNGO	9xN 1xL	10xL 0xC	6xP 3xR

The ten most important organizations have many similarities. They are mostly governmental (only two of them are NGOs) and most work at the national level; all of them are located in the Slovenian capital of Ljubljana and seven are among the more liberal half (according to the responses of their representatives).

Table 49 compares seven functional types of organizations[46] with respect to their centrality regarding the different dimensions of interaction between the organizations. The results show that there are significant differences between the seven functional types of organizations as regards the five types of relations: organizations providing resources, providing expertise, referring or accepting clients, and whose interests are viewed as important and taken into account. A closer look at these criteria shows that

- Ministries and governmental offices have been significantly more important with respect to being providers of resources and expertise, and in the sense of their interests being taken into account.

Table 49: Average (normalized out-degree) centrality of seven groups of organizations regarding nine criteria/types of relations between organizations. (Note: those entries that represent the two most central groups of organizations are highlighted)

TYPE OF RELATION: *TYPE OF ORGANIZATION:*	**Provided resources**	**Provided expertise**	**Provided support**	**Referred clients**	**Accepted clients**	**Informal com-munication**	**Strategic counselling**	**Common activities**	**Taken into account**
Ministries and governm. (N=8)	**18.4**	**28.5**	37.5	10.4	10.4	45.5	29.9	32.3	**28.5**
Std. Deviation	22.6	14.4	16.4	5.7	5.7	13.9	14.8	13.8	22.6
Research and academical (N=3)	0.9	**35.2**	29.6	7.4	7.4	49.1	27.8	27.8	**24.1**
Std. Deviation	1.6	8.9	11.6	7.0	7.0	16.3	12.1	16.9	11.2
Medical, clinical (N=5)	1.1	15.6	25.0	**13.3**	**13.3**	35.6	20.6	22.2	10.6
Std. Deviation	1.5	8.0	12.4	7.2	7.2	10.7	12.5	8.1	6.6
Local community groups (N=3)	**13.9**	13.0	23.1	9.3	9.3	34.3	19.4	21.3	10.2
Std. Deviation	19.4	14.0	19.7	8.9	8.9	18.9	21.7	15.8	17.6
High threshold (N=6)	0.9	19.4	24.1	**19.0**	**19.0**	45.4	21.8	21.8	7.9
Std. Deviation	1.4	8.4	5.5	6.2	6.2	11.9	8.1	6.9	6.2
Low threshold (N=4)	0.7	20.1	25.0	8.3	8.3	39.6	15.3	17.4	9.7
Std. Deviation	1.4	7.7	9.9	6.8	6.8	15.9	11.7	10.7	9.2
Preventive, counselling, other (N=8)	1.7	13.2	17.7	6.6	6.6	34.4	12.5	14.9	4.9
Std. Deviation	2.9	8.2	8.1	3.6	3.6	10.1	7.4	9.1	4.4
Total (N=37)	5.9	20.3	26.2	10.8	10.8	40.5	20.9	22.6	13.7
Standard Deviation	13.4	11.9	13.1	7.0	7.0	13.3	12.9	12.1	15.1
ANOVA stat. signif. p <:	0.10	**0.05**	-	**0.05**	**0.05**	-	-	-	**0.05**

- Research and academic organizations have been significantly more important with respect to being providers of expertise and in the sense of their interests being taken into account.
- Medical and clinical organizations have been significantly more important with respect to referring clients to others and accepting clients who have been referred to them.
- High-threshold organizations have been significantly more important with respect to referring clients to others and accepting clients who have been referred to them.
- Local community groups have been significantly more important with respect to being providers of resources.
- Low-threshold, and prevention and counselling were never found among the two most important types of organizations.[47]

In the previous paragraph, the dimensions of interaction mentioned were those in which the density of the relations was thinner, because the groups of organizations mentioned possessed such rare goods, services or possibilities that the relations with all organizations in respect to these goods could not be reciprocal, thus leaving the field of relations not as densely occupied.

Other types of relations by contrast, did not represent or refer to such rare resources so that it was possible to involve a broader circle of organizations in providing or in participating in these activities. Thus, the differences between the groups of organizations were large in respect to providing support, informal communication, strategic counselling and common activities. Also in these fields of relations, the centrality of the ministries, research and high-threshold organizations is more pronounced.

As expertise is supposed to be one of the most important resources in building effective systems, we analysed the dimension of providing and receiving expertise in more detail. Organizations were asked to state to which organizations they offered expertise and from which ones they received it. As all the organizations were asked these questions, it enabled us to compare the subjective, self-attributed importance in providing expertise with the objective importance attributed by others.[48]

Figure 4 illustrates the differences between the seven groups or types of organizations in this regard (providing expertise). Bars signed "estimated by others" show to what degree organizations were central (nominated by others) as providers of expertise, while bars "estimated by selves" show what degree of centrality these organizations claimed for themselves (that they provided expertise to others).

A comparison of both sets of bars shows that ministries were quite realistic in their perception of themselves as (rather important) providers of expertise, while research and academic, low and high threshold organizations underestimated their role as expertise providers. All the others overestimated their role, with the medical organizations overestimating it the most.

Figure 4: Self- and Other evaluations of organizations as being providers of expertise

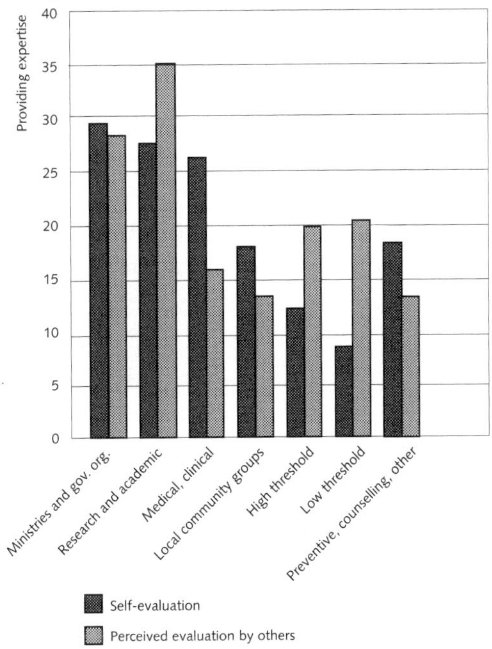

6 Summary of findings, conclusions, implications for policy and research

DDR in Slovenia is a relatively new and underdeveloped field of activities. The majority of the organizations in the field of drug demand reduction in Slovenia were established after 1990 and nearly half of them started their DDR activities as late as in 1995 or even later. An analysis of their budget and staff revealed that the yearly budget allocated to DDR programmes did not exceed EUR 50,000 for more than half of the organizations. The number of paid staff in the majority of the organizations was between 0-10. The impression we gained that the Slovenian organizations were young and inadequately funded, also survived the test of comparison with the other three analysed countries.

Respondents declared the mission of the organizations to be mainly prevention and treatment, and care. Prevention and treatment, and care were indicated as the main goals and the main activities of the organizations. When responding about the activities to be intensified in the future, these two categories were pointed out as well. In comparing the activities of the Slovenian organizations to those of the three other countries (Czech Republic, Hungary and Poland), we discovered that a large proportion of Slovenian organizations are engaged in interest representation, policy development and research.

The estimates of actual drug use diverged widely, while the predictions of future drug use were conservative. However, a more permissive orientation and a "closeness" to research were connected to higher estimates of drug use.

The respondents agreed that the most emphasized dimension of Slovenian drug policy was harm minimization, and quite a number of them saw it as a strength rather than a weakness. However, it was not clear, whether or not Slovenian drug policy is effective and co-ordinated; in fact, whether it existed at all as a product of a deliberate and planned effort. Many respondents viewed it as deficient and non-existent.

Organizations were optimistic regarding their image of overall performance. The lowest perception of the image of overall performance was found in the category of medical organizations. The gap between the images of self, clients and even media on the one hand, and politics on the other hand, was the biggest in the case of low-threshold organizations, which saw themselves as being the least approved by the world of politics, while the respondents from the medical organizations perceived that their political surroundings evaluated them better than they did themselves.

Among the most important and central organizations regarding the nine different dimensions of interactions were mostly governmental and national organizations, which were all located in the Slovenian capital of Ljubljana. The majority were among the more permissive organizations.

The analysis of the situation of NGOs and the division of work between them and GOs showed that the NGO sector in Slovenia is less developed than pointed out by the average of related indicators in the four researched countries. Moreover, the division of work and the differentiation of GOs and NGOs seemed to be less developed than in other countries.

A comparison of the different sub-groups of organizations showed that it is not their status (GO or NGO) or level of operation (national or local), but their function (medical, low-threshold, research, etc.) and even more the level of their permissive/restrictive orientation, which discriminates them the most.

Slovenian organizations seem to have rather permissive attitudes on average, but there are also substantial differences among them. A comparison with the other three countries shows that the attitudes of the Slovenian organizations were the most dispersed (or divided ones).

As regards the division of work among the organizations and their contributions in the network of services, resources and interactions, the superior role of the GO is easily recognized. Among the ten most important organizations, only two are NGOs with respect to the different kinds of interactions, and they deal mostly with implementing high-threshold programmes.

The analysis of the Slovenian findings and their comparison with the answers of the three other countries' organizations point to some unanswered questions and to some possible research and policy implications:

1) The need is quite obvious to strengthen the position of the NGO sector in DDR. Policies should enable a stable environment for the development of NGOs, continuous and predictable funding. The proportion of the NGOs active in the field of DDR and their relative interactional importance should be greater, as this would contribute to a more dynamic and effective development of the field.
2) An even greater differentiation of services and roles should be the aim. To attain this goal conditions should be created for developing more and stronger, exclusively-oriented organizations, and possibly also locally-oriented ones. Although in the relatively small country of Slovenia, the differentiation will always be smaller than, e.g. in a much larger country like Poland, it would help to provide more specific resources and to meet more specific needs.
3) Besides maintaining relatively well-developed harm reduction programmes, greater emphasis should be given to supporting effective health promotion and demand reduction (treatment, after-care, etc.) programmes.
4) Although a great share of all organizations were engaged in policy development and co-ordination, quite a number of them complained that there is "no policy" and not enough co-ordination. The reasons are probably complex and diverse. It is possible that this perception is related to the dynamic nature of developments in the field of DDR, and

it is also possible that the perception of a lack of policy reflects something else: a lack of support for very specific orientations and programmes. We feel that there is not much need for reducing the heterogeneity or unifying the content of the different programmes and their orientations, but rather that the rules that govern this area should be made more transparent and the processes for setting priorities more public.

5) As regards research, the need for building a comprehensive epidemiological system is obvious. What is even more lacking is evaluative research which would provide answers to many of the questions related to the above-mentioned four points. Apart from the need for research, we would like to emphasize the need for developing different forms of accredited training and education, ranging from short courses to post-graduate, masters and doctoral degrees in education in the field of DDR.

Notes

1 Zeleznik-Vouk, 1987.
2 Ibid.
3 Ibid.
4 Nacionalni program ..., 1992.
5 Uradni list SFRJ 2/64, Uradni list SFRJ 3/78.
6 Uradni list SFRJ 40/73.
7 Kazenski zakonik, 1999.
8 Uradni list RS 108/1999, Uradni list RS 44/2000.
9 Uradni list RS, 98/1999.
10 Uradni list RS 33/91.
11 Uradni list RS 60/95.
12 Uradni list RS 60/95.
13 Uradni list RS 12/91.
14 Uradni list RS 54/92.
15 "Para non-governmental organizations" are those having a mixed or unclear status.
16 Petric, 1998.
17 In 1973, the police reported 52 criminal acts related to drugs (Marolt, 1975).
18 Vodopivec, 1973.
19 Vodopivec, Pecar, personal communication with the first author of this report.
20 E.g. Milcinski et al., 1983.
21 Pojavnost ..., 1985; Milcinski, 1983.
22 Unexpectedly this study was done by a group of medical students (Gosar et al., 1984).
23 Petric, 1988.

24 The first association of drug users was founded in 1991.

25 Tomori, 1992a.

26 Tomori, 1992b.

27 Tomori, 1992a.

28 The authors of this study, which has been frequently quoted for about five years as the only representative cross-sectional epidemiological research, were two 17-year-old high school students (Bulic and Vesel, 1992).

29 Bulic and Vesel, 1992.

30 Jerman, 1996.

31 Stergar, 1995.

32 Dekleva, 1998.

33 Stergar, 1999.

34 In 1998 these local communities had the following number of inhabitants: Ljubljana – 270,441; Koper – 47,543; Izola – 14,335; Piran – 17,257. The catchment area of services in these towns could have been 2-3 times greater.

35 The calculation of this relatively early average year of founding was influenced by one NGO, which was founded in 1954, first as a GO, but in the 1990s refounded as an NGO.

36 In this calculation we did not take into account the absolute funds, instead we calculated the averages from the percentages of public funding in all funding.

37 In Tables 17-24 the percentages refer to the part of all organizations performs a certain activity, which belong to one of the groups, e.g. GO or NGO, national or local, exclusive or inclusive.

38 Drug users were defined as users of any illicit drugs in the last 12 months.

39 The scale was originally developed by Gould et. al, 1996. For the details on the development of the scale see the chapter on drug-related attitudes in a comparative perspective in this book.

40 For the details on the development of the scale see the chapter on drug-related attitudes in a comparative perspective in this book.

41 See section 5.2.

42 The scope of this analysis is limited by the fact that we did not take into account the importance (strength, economy, extensiveness of activities, etc.) of analysed organizations but only their number.

43 ... that is, with one exception. It refers to an organization, which formally has the status of an NGO, but is functionally totally dependent on the state and is performing tasks, which should or could (and have been) performed by the corresponding ministry.

44 As there were 37 organizations all together, it means that usually there were three organizations (or occasionally 4 or 5) nominated as the "important" ones.

45 The classification of organizations into permissive or restrictive was made using two methods. By the first method an organizations was denoted permissive if its score on the permissive/restrictive variable (see section 4.3) was below 3,0, and it was denoted restrictive if its score was over 3.0. Using the second method, an organization was denoted permissive if its score on the permissive/restrictive variable was under the median of this variable, and it was denoted restrictive if its score on the permissive/restrictive variable was over the median of this variable. The first method resulted in six permissive, three restrictive and one "neutral" organization, and the second method produced six permissive and four restrictive organizations. In Table 39, the results of the first method are displayed.

46 See the previous section for the definition of the seven functional types of organizations.

47 Although low-threshold organizations were the third-most important group regarding the provision of expertise (after ministries, governmental and research organizations).

48 However, the research did not allow us to measure the quantity and quality of the expertise. We were only able to count the number of organizations which received expertise from a certain organization as a measure of its importance.

References

Bulic, O./Vesel, D. (1992) *Droge, spolnost & AIDS med mladostniki*. Ljubljana: Gimnazija Ledina.

Curk, A. (2001) *Zbirka zakonskih in podzakonskih aktov povezanih s podrocjem drog*. Ljubljana: Urad Vlade RS za droge.

Cvelbar, R. (1996) *Evaluation of the Evolution and Effectivness of Social Policy in the Sphere of Drug Demand Reduction*. Ljubljana: Fakulteta za druzbene vede.

Dekleva, B. (1998) *Droge med srednjesolsko mladino v Ljubljani*. Ljubljana: MOL in Institut za kriminologijo pri Pravni faklulteti v Ljubljani.

Gosar, A. et al. (1984) 'Zloraba drog med studenti v Ljubljani', *Medicinski razgledi*: 175-204.

Jerman, T. et al. (1996) *Razsirjenost uporabe drog med mladimi v mestu Ljubljana*. Ljubljana: Zavod za zdravstveno varstvo Ljubljana.

Kastelic, A./Kostnapfel Rihtar, T. (2000) *Kako preprecujemo in zdravimo odvisnosti od prepovedanih drog v sistemu zdravstvenega varstva*. Ljubljana: Koordinacija centrov za prepecvanje in zdravljenje odvisnosti od prepoveanih drog pri Ministrstvu za zdravstvo RS

Kazenski zakonik (1999) Ljubljana: Uradni list RS.

Marolt, D. (1973) 'Domnevna razsirjenost drog v Sloveniji ter delo organov za notranje zadeve', in: Vodopivec, K. (ed.), *Kaj vemo o drogah*. Ljubljana: Mladinska knjiga.

Milcinski et al. (1983) *Droge v svetu in pri nas*. Ljubljana: Delavska enotnost.

Nacionalni program za preprecevanje zlorabe drog v Republiki Sloveniji (1992) *Casopis za kritiko znanosti* Vol. 20, No. 146-147.

Nolimal, D. (1992) 'Razsirjenost zlorabe alkohola, tobaka in drugih drog v Sloveniji', *Zdravstveni vestnik* 61: 127-131.

Petric, K.V. (1988) *Phare Project on Drug Information Systems, National Report Slovenia*. Ljubljana: Ministry of Health of Slovenia.

Pojavnost alkoholizma in drugih bolezni odvisnosti v SR Sloveniji: zlorabe drog in odvisnosti od njih (1985) *Zdravstveno varstvo*: 1-49.

Stergar, E. (1995) *ESPAD evropska raziskava o alkoholu in drogah med solsko mladino*. Ljubljana: Institut za varovanje zdravja RS.

Stergar, E. (1999) *Raziskava o alkoholu in preostalih drogah med dijaki prvih letnikov ljubljanskih srednjih sol*. Ljubljana: Institut za varovanje zdravja RS.

Tomori, M. (1991) 'Zloraba drog pri mladih – nevarno tveganje', in: Kastelic, A. (ed.), *Zloraba drog*. Ljubljana: Rokus.

Tomori, M. (1992) 'Zloraba psihotropnih snovi – kaksna je slovenska scena danes', *Zdravsteni vestnik* 61: 123-125.

Uradni list Republike Slovenije. Letniki 1991-2000.

Uradni list SFRJ. Letniki 1974-1978.

Vodopivec, K. (ed.) (1973) *Kaj vemo o drogah*. Ljubljana: Mladinska knjiga.

Zeleznik–Vouk, J. (1987) *Osnutek akcijskega programa preprecevanja zlorab drog*. Ljubljana: Republiski sekretariat za zdravstvenoi in socialno varstvo.

Annex: List of researched organizations

Ministry of Labour, Family and Social Affairs of the Republic of Slovenia

Ministry of Health of the Republic of Slovenia

Coordination of Centres for Prevention and Treatment of Drug Addiction (affiliated to the Ministry of Health)

Youth Department at the Ministry of Education, Science and Sports of the Republic of Slovenia

Educational Research Institute

Governmental Office for Drugs of the Republic Slovenia

Institute for Public Health of Republic Slovenia

Association *Project Man*

Hope - Association for Addicts and their Relatives of Slovenia

AIDS Foundation Robert

Association for Preventive and Voluntary Work

Organisation Janez Smrekar – Project "The Rock"

Association *Pelican* (Caritas) - Department for Drug Addicts and Relatives

Sport Union of Republic of Slovenia

B & Z Engineering for Education, Counselling and Research

Foundation *Sounds of Reflection*

Association *DrogArt* – Harm Reduction, Drugs and Electronic Media

Social Chamber of Slovenia

Institute of Criminology at the Faculty of Law in Ljubljana

High School for Social Work

Network of Health Promoting Schools (affiliated to the Institute for Public Health of the Republic of Slovenia)

Ministry of Justice of the Republic of Slovenia

Centre for Treatment of Drug Addiction at the Clinical Department for Mental Health at University Psychiatric Hospital Ljubljana

Stigma – Association for the Reduction of Drug Related Harm

Youth Aid Center (affiliated to Ljubljana's Centres for Social Work)

Centre for Prevention and Treatment of Drug Addiction of the Town of Ljubljana

Office for Prevention of Addiction of the Town of Ljubljana

Prevention Information Counselling Centre for Children, Adolescents and Parents

Institute of Public Health of Ljubljana

Svit – Society for Addicts and Their Relatives

Local Action Group for Prevention of Drug Abuse Piran

Community Incontro

Project *Umbrella*

Centre for Prevention and Treatment of Drug Addiction Piran

Institute of Public Health Koper - Centre for Prevention and Treatment of Drug Abuse

Local Action Group Koper

Centre for Social Work - Counselling Service for Youths and Parents in Izola

Part II

Comparative Analyses

CHAPTER 6

What Are The Interrelationships Between Drug Problems and Drug Policy?

Lessons from the Analyses of the Institutional Context

Ladislav Csémy and Zsuzsanna Elekes

The four national reports published in this volume provide detailed information about development of drug problems and approaches to the solution of the problems in the Czech Republic, Poland, Hungary and Slovenia in the 1990s. The reports differ from traditionally published reports by a unique application of research focused on the institutional context that allows for a completely different approach to the problem and, at the same time, it offers other interpretation possibilities and opens new questions. In this comparative chapter, we would like to deal with the issue of mutual interaction between the changing situation in the drug scene and drug policies, i.e. the manner how society responds to the problems. In our analysis, we will focus on the four above-mentioned countries and we would like to take advantage of the possibilities offered by applied research of organizations.

We start from the assumption that the drug policy of each country consists of a number of elements that limit the rights, possibilities, responsibilities and competencies of the actors, i.e. individuals and social subjects, in particular areas. Drug policy is a response of society to problems induced by drugs; however, it is seldom a direct response to a particular problem, it is rather the result of professional and political attitudes that prevail. Changes in drug policy often take place when the drug scene changes to an extent that existing approaches become ineffective.

The Drug Problem in the Four Countries Under Investigation

Drugs cause problems in many sectors of society; therefore, it is necessary to use various indicators for the evaluation of the relevance and significance of drug-related problems. As a rule, indicators relate to the prevalence of drug use in the population, incidence of undesirable health consequences (drug addiction treatment, cases of intoxication, infectious diseases, drug-related mortality), and drug-related criminal activities. It is more or less possible to compare the seriousness of drug problems in the individual countries. It is a certain limitation that the unified definition of the indicators has only been enforced in Europe after EMCDDA's co-ordination efforts started, i.e. since the 1990s. All four European countries studied have joined the European trend through supporting programmes in the frame of PHARE. Naturally, there were also drug problems before the socio-political changes in 1989; however, the extent and form of the problem cannot be compared to the rapid changes that occurred in the 1990s.

The ESPAD study (Hibell et al., 2000) carried out in 1995 and 1999, was the first methodologically sophisticated international study that allowed for comparison of prevalence of experience with drugs among 16-year-old persons. A summary of experiences of young people from the four countries studied is shown in Figure 1. It is impossible to interpret the results included in the chart as an indicator of drug problems, in contrast to what we have repeatedly seen in the media. However, together with other results, they provide rather convincing evidence on changes that took place in this part of Europe in the 1990s. In particular, they illustrate the unprecedented increase in the availability of drugs in society. At the same time, they demonstrate drug demand, i.e. an interest of young people experiencing drugs and their effects.

The changes between 1995 and 1999 show that the prevalence of experience with drugs among young people has increased in all four countries. Cannabis use was the most frequent in the Czech Republic and Slovenia; the highest increase in use of non-cannabis drugs was in Poland. Lowest values were detected in Hungary; however, the change is also markedly in this country. In comparison with other European countries participating in the study, the Czech Republic and Slovenia are the countries with the highest spread of drug use.

Figure 1: Changes between 1995 and 1999 in lifetime experience of cannabis and any illicit drug other than cannabis

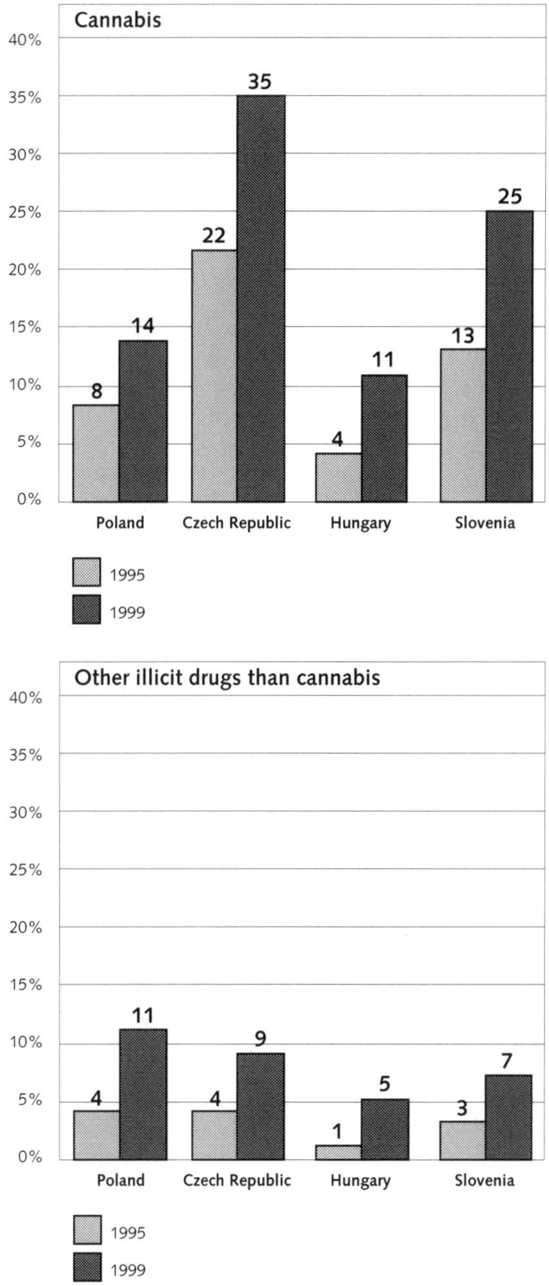

Source: ESPAD, 1995; ESPAD, 1999.

Dramatic increases in drug supply after 1989 and the fast spread of use among adolescents and young adults are clearly revealed in the increase in health consequences. Treatment demand has gone up markedly. Increased need of treatment intervention and social help initiated the conversion and development of an institutional system, formerly organized in all Central European countries in the frame of the centrally controlled state health care system. As far as drug addicts were concerned, psychiatric treatment was the only option for them.

The differentiation of the institutional system for addicted persons took place in the context of a deep reform of the health care systems in Central European countries during the 1990s. A number of new elements were introduced such as privatization of health care facilities, development of private facilities, possibility to choose a physician or service provider freely, etc. In connection with the return of democratic freedoms, there was a fast development of civil society.

Non-governmental organizations (NGOs), previously hardly known, or functioning on a formal basis only, have become an important sector with an impact on the whole society. Analysis of the institutional development in the field of drug demand reduction has shown that the highest number of new organizations was established in 1993-1996. Then, there occurred rather a structural differentiation and improvement of the quality of offered services. Understandably, care for drug-addicted people under new conditions has brought about a number of problems for which the previous system was not ready. This also related to the system of evidence and health statistics. The central data collection systems in the field of drug-related problems was based on obligatory reporting and was unable to cover new facilities such as non-governmental organizations. Therefore, they were not part of the public health network despite the fact that they took care of addicted people and offered various forms of treatment.

As a consequence, existing data on treatment and the number of problem users are not necessarily representative. Despite the mentioned limitations, the existing data are an important source of information. Table 1 offers the number of people who went for treatment in 1995-1999, taking the limitations with regard to the central data collection systems into account. It is important to note, however, that case definition is not always the same due to the differences in statistical reporting in the individual countries. Therefore, the comparability of data is limited.

Table 1: Trends in treatment for disorders caused by misuse of drugs in 1995-1999

Year	Czech Republic[a]	Hungary[b]	Poland[c]	Slovenia[d]
1995	1,763	3,553	4,223	n.a.
1996	2,662	4,718	4,772	n.a.
1997	3,441	8,494	5,336	1,414
1998	4,533	9,458	6,100	2,599
1999	n.a.	n.a.	n.a.	2,342

Notes:
[a] Hospital discharges for drug use related disorders (ICD F11 - F19).
[b] Number of treated persons in the health care system (residential and outpatient facilities).
[c] Patients admitted to residential treatment due to drug addiction.
[d] Aggregate data on the number of treated drug users (methadone substitution centres).

The data show a significant increase in the number of treated people in the second half of the 1990s. As far as the main diagnosis is concerned, the highest proportion of people were treated in connection with the use of opiates (Czech Republic 34% of all cases, Hungary 32%, Poland 42%, Slovenia 93%; most data in Slovenia were, however, obtained from methadone substitution facilities). Clients who abuse more than one drug (poly-drug use) form another large group (Czech Republic 31%, Hungary 19%, Poland 31%). High representation of amphetamines was only reported in the Czech Republic where they represent 25% of people hospitalized for drug-related addictions. The reason being that homemade metamphetamine, known as pervitin, used to be the most popular drug in the Czech Republic for many years.

In what follows, other important indicators from the public health sector (intoxication, HIV infection, hepatitis, drug-related deaths) will be reported. Due to different data collection methods, different levels of incorporation of non-institutionalized population, etc., the data itself are, however, of little validity and incomparable. Therefore, only trends which these data provide will be indicated.

Trends in the criminal justice and law enforcement sector show a rapid increase of the number of drug-related crimes. Differences in legislature and different law enforcement practices restrict data comparability. However, the direction of changes is the same in all countries (Hungary 429 criminal cases in 1995 and 2,860 criminal cases in 1999; 4,282 and 15,628 in the same period in Poland; 407 and 988 in Slovenia; and 1,131 and 7,720 in the Czech Republic).

A part of our research on DDR (drug demand reduction) organizations was dedicated to the issue of dissemination of drugs in the population. It does not concern here an epidemiological survey but rather data based on estimates made by representatives of the organizations studied. The questions were formulated in order to gather information about: (a) the estimation of the total number of users in a particular country, (b) the relative share of various types of drugs on the drug scene and (c) the expected changes until 2003.

Table 2: Estimations of the number of drug users by country for the years 1998 and 2003

	Estimated number of drug users in 1998 (mean of estimates in thousands)	Estimated number of drug users in 2003 (mean of estimates in thousands)	Change between 1998-2003 (in per cent)
Poland	751	1081	+44
Czech Republic	256	303	+18
Hungary	284	482	+70
Slovenia	77	91	+18

The estimation of the number of drug users in the four countries studied in 1998 and 2003, expressed as the average of answers from the inquired organizations, is included in Table 2. It is interesting that the estimation for 1998 is quite close to the number of adolescents who had some experience with any type of a drug when we compare and extrapolate them in relation to the results of the ESPAD study. According to the comparison of averaged estimations between 1998 and 2003, the organizations expect that the number of users in all countries will increase. The last column represents the percentage of the expected size of the change.

According to the organizations' information, the expected slight increase in the Czech Republic and Slovenia would indicate relatively developed and stabilized drug scenes. It is possible to interpret the expected markedly increase in the number of drug users in Poland and Hungary in particular with a claim that the drug scene in these two countries is dynamic and future increasing social impacts of drug abuse are expected.

As far as the estimated relative shares of various types of drugs are concerned, it is not surprising that marijuana represents the highest share (see Table 3). Then, there is a high share of energizing drugs, amphetamines and opioid types of drugs. In all four countries, expectancies of changes in the ratio of specific drugs is practically negligible and varies only between -4% and +4%.

Table 3: Estimated share of cannabis, opiates and amphetamines in the overall use of drugs in 1998 and 2003 (values in percentages)

	Cannabis			Opiates			Amphetamines		
	1998	2003	Change	1998	2003	Change	1998	2003	Change
Poland	29	32	+3	29	28	-1	26	26	0
Czech Republic	48	48	0	18	20	+2	27	24	-3
Hungary	33	31	-2	25	27	+2	31	27	-4
Slovenia	58	56	-2	11	11	0	21	22	+1

We reviewed available data about drug-related issues in the four countries studied and it seems that more things are similar than different. All the indicators show an apparent increase in drug-related problems after 1990 and especially in the second half of the 1990s. It is clear that there are differences between the countries surveyed; this would, however, require more comparable and reliable data.

Can a survey of organizations bring new information regarding drug issues?

In order to formulate substantial characteristics of drug policies in a particular country, existing institutions that deal with drug issues, programme documents and existing legislative arrangements are usually surveyed. If we were to use this approach, it is very likely that we would come to a conclusion that there is an institution in each country which is responsible for governmental drug policy, that there are similar programme objectives for drug control (or so-called national drug strategies), and that legislature usually attempts to come close to legislative standards of the European Union, etc.

Research of organizations allows us, however, to view drug issues from a different angle. Looking at drug issues from the perspective of those who implement them in various fields may help society in general, but particularly those who co-ordinate drug polices, to reflect their viewpoints and principles.

Table 4: Strengths of the national drug policy (in percentages[a,b])

	PL	CZ	H	SLO	Total
Prevention programmes	55	29	15	25	31
Effective policy, conception, legislation	28	33	2	56	29
Awareness of the drug problem, public discussions, better understanding of the problem	45	18	32	13	27
Efficient network of organizations' effective cooperation	23	38	2	19	21
Harm reduction programmes	5	18	0	41	15
Therapy programmes	28	11	10	13	15
Supply control, law enforcement (drug market), new legal institutions for police for combating drug criminality	20	18	12	3	14
Competent, expert-based and professional	10	11	7	3	8
No strengths at all	8	9	39	6	16

Notes [a] Due to multiple choices, the column total may exceed 100%.
[b] Figures are based on the following number of organizations responding to the question: Poland 40, Czech Republic 45, Hungary 41, Slovenia 32.

Table 5: Weaknesses of the national drug policy (values in percentages[a,b])

	PL	CZ	H	SLO	Total all
Lack of policy, there is no drug policy, lack of a conceptual approach, lack of a national programme of priorities	72	72	39	77	65
Lack of co-ordination, incoherence of ideas	30	41	39	60	41
Insufficient funding, financial problems	57	30	20	17	33
Lack of awareness of the drug problem	28	9	10	11	15
Ineffective programmes	26	9	12	9	14
Focus on law enforcement, restrictive approach, proclamation of war on drugs	13	13	10	9	11
Lack of professionals, experts	11	13	5	0	8
Lack of evaluation, lack of control and monitoring programmes	4	2	5	14	6
Lack of research, information	4	0	5	14	5
Barriers in development of non-governmental institutions	15	0	0	0	4

Notes: [a] Due to multiple choices, the column total may exceed 100%.
[b] Figures are based on the following number of organizations responding to the question: Poland 47, Czech Republic 46, Hungary 41, Slovenia 35.

In our research, two groups of questions dealt with drug issues in the strict sense of the word. The first group of questions gather information about strengths and weaknesses of drug policies. In the questionnaire, the questions were formulated as open questions. On the basis of content analysis, categories were established and answers were encoded accordingly. Tables 4 and 5 present a summary of the distribution of answers. The values in the tables represent the percentage of organizations that made up the respective categories.

A total of 158 organizations answered the question related to the strengths of drug policies. Activities in the field of prevention were reported as a strength of drug policies most frequently. Approximately one third (31%) of all organizations mentioned this category. Effective drug policy and awareness of the drug problem in society (29% and 27% of all organizations) occupy the next positions. When we look closely at the individual countries, we get an interesting and differentiated picture. Indeed, prevention and social awareness of the drug problem were regarded as the strongest parts of national drug policy in Poland (55% and 45% of all Polish organizations). Therapeutic programmes and efficient drug policy (28% in both categories) were rated much lower.

In the Czech Republic, the effective cooperation of organizations was considered as the strongest part (38%), efficient and conceptual drug policy (33%) and prevention (29%) followed.

In Hungary, the achieved level of attention to drug problems in society was rated as the strongest element (32%). There were relatively low values in other categories – 15% regarding prevention, and 12% regarding supply control. However, Hungary is the country where most organizations reported no strengths at all (39% of the organizations!).

In Slovenia, the significance of efficient and conceptual drug policy was emphasized the most (56%); and the importance of harm reduction programmes was also very highlighted (41%), and 25% of organizations regard prevention as strength.

The data regarding the weaknesses of drug policies were surprising with regard to the conformity of the answers. There was an unusual agreement that lack of policy, conceptual approach, priorities and programmes are main weaknesses (65% of 169 organizations). It might look contradictory that in some cases (e.g. in Slovenia or the Czech Republic, see Table 4) policy and conceptual approaches are seen both as a strength and a weakness. However, this can be explained by the fact that drug policy in itself is considered of high importance and that the field of drug policy is broad and encompasses many aspects. Insufficient co-ordination or cooperation between the organizations was reported as a drawback. It is a paradox that this aspect was most often expressed in Slovenia, the smallest of the four countries, where it might seem that it is easier to provide for co-ordination and cooperation than in Poland with its 40 million inhabitants.

It is no wonder that insufficient funding belongs to the highlighted weaknesses. It is typical for the public sector of all transforming countries that resources are limited; and drug demand reduction is largely funded from the public sphere. It is also worth mentioning that Poland was the only country where the category "barriers in the development of the non-governmental sector" was mentioned. It is even more interesting given the fact that Poland was the first country where NGOs developed and existed even in times when it was unimaginable in other Central European countries. It is quite possible that the presented barriers relate to difficulties in financing which were also reported most often in Poland (57%).

Table 6: Overview of the results of the ANOVA multiple comparisons[a]

	Slovenia	Hungary	Czech Republic
Poland	Health promotion (n.s.) Harm reduction (Pl<Sl) Demand reduction (n.s.) Control of supply (n.s.) Law enforcement (Pl<Sl)	Health promotion (n.s.) Harm reduction (Pl>Hu) Demand reduction (n.s.) Control of supply (Pl<Hu) Law enforcement (Pl<Hu)	Health promotion (n.s.) Harm reduction (Pl<Cz) Demand reduction (n.s.) Control of supply (n.s.) Law enforcement (Pl<Cz)
Czech Republic	Health promotion (n.s.) Harm reduction (n.s.) Demand reduction (n.s.) Control of supply (n.s.) Law enforcement (n.s.)	Health promotion (n.s.) Harm reduction (Cz>Hu) Demand reduction (n.s.) Control of supply (n.s.) Law enforcement (n.s.)	
Hungary	Health promotion (n.s.) Harm reduction (Hu<Sl) Demand reduction (n.s.) Control of supply(Hu>Sl) Law enforcement (Hu>Sl)		

Note [a] (n.s.) = Difference in the mean values of the given two countries is not statistically significant, (*abrev. name of the country* < or > *abrev. name of the country*) = difference of the mean values of the given two countries is statistically significant at least on P<0,05, the inequality sign indicates which country has a higher or lower mean value.

Comparison of strengths and weaknesses of drug policies seems a very promising approach that brings about plausible information for the development of drug strategies in particular directions. In addition, it is easily possible to modify the method and apply it for the purposes of regional comparisons in the framework of one country (this approach has been applied in 2000 in the Czech Republic).

The question asking the respondents to describe the current orientation of the drug policy in the country they lived in was the second source of information about drug policy orientation. It was actually an application of a Lickert-type scale on five dimensions of drug policy: health promotion, harm reduction, demand reduction, control of supply and law enforcement. It is possible to treat the values of the variables as ordinal values, and it means that it is possible to calculate a group average for each of the five dimensions that describe drug policy. We tested the differences in averages of the four surveyed countries and we discovered that there are "significant differences in national drug policy profiles" on the basis of this approach. Table 6 provides a summary of statistically significant differences detected by ANOVA (multiple comparison test).

Data conversion to a standard score allows for better representation of differences between the individual countries. When the values are expressed by means of a standard score, the average of the values of the whole set (i.e. all countries) equals zero. Group averages, i.e. average values of the countries, represent the position of the particular country in comparison with the average of the whole set as well as other countries. Figure 2 is an attempt to present the differences in the profiles of the individual countries.

The countries studied do not differ with regard to the dimensions of demand reduction and health promotion. In contrast, the highest polarization of the profile exists in the fields of harm reduction and law enforcement, and is slightly less in the field of supply control. The available information allows for the following interpretation of priorities of national drug policies of the individual countries: Poland is a country where law enforcement and control of supply are the least accentuated characteristics of the national drug policy and harm reduction is neither regarded as a priority for drug policy. The highest average value is in the field of demand reduction.

The profile of the Czech Republic is the most balanced, and it means that none of the fields was given a significantly higher priority. The values in the dimension of harm reduction and law enforcement slightly exceeded the average value. On the contrary, in Hungary there are clearly the highest deviations between the individual fields. Law enforcement and control of supply were reported as marked priorities of drug policy; again in contrast, harm reduction was given the lowest average value in comparison with the other countries. In Slovenia, the profile is similarly balanced as in the Czech Republic except for the field of harm reduction.

Figure 2: Priorities of national drug policies

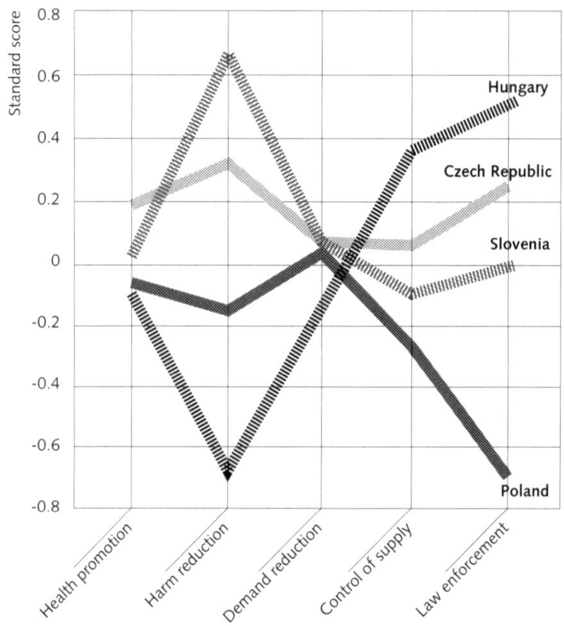

Coming back to the comparison between country pairs included in Table 6, we discovered no statistically significant differences between the Czech Republic and Slovenia in any of the monitored fields. It means that the priorities of drug policies in both countries are perceived identically and it is possible to regard them as balanced policies containing liberal elements.

Poland and Hungary are the most different with respect to their drug policy profile. Low average values in the fields of law enforcement and control of supply measured in Poland indicate that there is distrust in the efficiency of repressive measures. The result is also interesting in the context of recent legislative changes rendering drug laws in Poland more strict. The profile of Hungary gets rather close to a conservative view of priorities of a drug policy; approaches that represent repression (law enforcement) were fancied while liberal approaches represented by harm reduction were refused.

The results of the analysis of the strengths and weaknesses of drug policies and the analysis of profiles of national drug policies provide a differentiated view of drug policies in the four Central European countries. Such a view can only result from research that focuses on DDR organizations.

Links between drug problems and drug policy

Our previous conclusions logically lead to the exploration of the relationships between drug-related problems and drug policy. Is there a relationship between drug-related problems and drug policy? Are we able to find sufficiently convincing arguments for the support of this relationship? Monographs about drug epidemiology and many scientific reports (WHO, 2000; Stimson et al., 1999; Bammer et al., 1999) emphasize the necessity of good and comparable data for a rational intervention of society and they regard standardized monitoring of drug problems as the best verification of efficiency of intervention. However, practical experiences with drug policies often bring cases that relativize the above-mentioned assumption. In this regard, the drug policy of the United States of America, i.e. a drug policy of a country that has the widest knowledge database as far as the extent of drug problems in a country is concerned, is the most discussed drug policy. Many papers mention incorrect priorities of the U.S. drug policy that remain unchanged despite the fact that results of many researches indicate that the drug policy could be more effectively and cheaper, and should be shifted towards a policy with a higher priority for public health issues (*The Lancet*, 2001; Kleiman, 1998).

Even in Western European countries, it is difficult to find a positive relationship between the extent of drug problems and drug policies. Romesjo (2000: 294-295), in his review of the study edited by Waal (1998) also refers to this fact:

> **In comparison of data from countries with either restrictive or harm-reduction policy, Waal finds no consistent correlation between policy, drug use prevalence and HIV incidence or prevalence. He presents several explanations, such as insufficient data and time sequence, the insignificant influence of policy on prevention and cultural and situational factors.**

In our research, we also failed to find a direct correspondence between drug problems and drug policy in the four Central European countries. Considering the difficulties faced by experts in developed Western European countries, it is possible that it was not even realistic to expect to find it. In this context, we must underline the fact that Central European countries unlike Western European countries had to face the rapidly increasing drug problem in a historically short period of the 1990s. It is understandable that the conceptual and institutional framework of drug policy was established in the short time available; however, it will take more time in many fields in order to achieve a more significant progress. This especially relates to research and monitoring of drug problems, standardization of approaches in data collection and standardization of measuring instruments and techniques. After the assumptions will be established, it will be possible to gather quality and comparable data. It will only be then that the obtained knowledge will have efficient impacts on the objectives of drug policy. This is what we learned from the research of the institutions, and we believe that this is not little.

References

Bammer, G./Beers, M./Patel, M. (1999) 'The Role of Field Epidemiology in the Investigation of Drug Problems', *Drug and Alcohol Review* 18 (3): 329-330.

Hibell, B. et al. (2000) *The 1999 ESPAD Report. Alcohol and Other Drug Use Among Students in 30 European Countries.* Stockholm: The Swedish Council for Information on Alcohol and Other Drugs, CAN. Council of Europe (Pompidou Group).

Kleiman, M. (1998) 'Drugs and Drug Policy: The Case for a Slow Fix', *Issues in Science and Technologies* XV (1).

Romesjo, A. (2000) 'Patterns on the European Drug Scene. An Exploration of Differences', *Review Addiction* 95 (2): 294-295.

Stimson, V. G./Fitch, C./Rhodes, T./Ball, A. (1999) 'Rapid Assessment and Response: Methods for Developing Public Health Responses to Drug Problems', *Drug and Alcohol Review* 18 (3): 317-325.

The Lancet (2001) *Rethinking America's "War on Drugs" as a Public-Health Issue*, Editorial, *The Lancet* 357: 9261.

Waal, H. (Ed.) (1998) *Patterns on the European Drug Scene. An Exploration of Differences.* Oslo: National Institute for Alcohol and Drug Research.

World Health Organization (2000) *Guide to Drug Abuse Epidemiology*, WHO/MSD/MSB 00.3.

CHAPTER 7

The Perception of the Drug Problem and Opinions on National Policies

Can We Think Beyond Borders?

Tünde Györy and Robert Sobiech

When analysing social problems, one has to take into account that the specific conditions of a problem may be defined in many different ways by the various organizations and groups involved. Such definitions usually have a significant impact on the beliefs shared by public opinion. Moreover, they contain more or less explicit recommendations for problem-solving and play a significant role in policy design. Opinions on the problem's conditions as well as opinions on the preferred counteractions are crucial in any attempt to understand national responses to drug abuse. Hence, opinions on drug problems shared among the organizations surveyed constitute an important part of our research.

One of the research objectives is to provide evidence on the differences in problem definition in the four countries. We assume that organizational and social settings play a crucial role in shaping dominant beliefs and opinions. Therefore, we are interested in finding out to what extent the definitions are shaped by "national" factors (e.g. specific conditions, natural history of the problem and types of social policies). On the other hand, we assume that due to numerous similarities in the problem's interpretation one could outline "group" or "sector" approaches to the problem in which professional concepts and organizational characteristics have a greater influence. Thus, in addition to analysing the influence of national differences, an attempt is also made to trace the impact of the above factors. We assume the following variables to be particularly influential: type of knowledge utilized by organizations in their activities, the focus on individual or policy approach, the maturity of organization and type of professionals employed.

In order to analyse the relations described above, the following elements of the problem's definitions were selected:

- Scope of the problems (opinions on the number of drug users and the expected change on a 5-year horizon).
- Structure of the problem (opinions on dominant drugs and the expected change on a 5-year horizon).
- Character of national policy (main focuses, strengths and weaknesses).

Scope of the problem

Estimates provided by respondents reflected differences in the population of drug users in the countries studied (Table 1). The average number of Polish drug users was estimated at 750,000, in the Czech Republic and Hungary the number varied between 250,000 and 280,000, in Slovenia it was 75,000. It should be mentioned at this point that the figures provided by respondents show differences in the size of each country rather than that they reflect the perceived scope of the problem. A more accurate picture is revealed when one relates the estimations to the populations of the respective countries (Table 2). It turns out that the highest rate (38 drug users per 1,000 citizens) is estimated in Slovenia, followed by Hungary and the Czech Republic (28 and 25 per 1,000). The lowest rate (19 drug users per 1,000) is found in Poland.

Table 1: Estimated number of drug users, 1998

	Czech Republic	Hungary	Poland	Slovenia
Mean estimated number of drug users, 1998	256,100	284,063	750,833	76,817

Table 2: Estimated number of drug users in 1998 per 1,000 inhabitants

	Czech Republic	Hungary	Poland	Slovenia
Drug users in 1998 per 1,000 inhabitants	24,9	28,1	19,4	38,7

The types of activity conducted by the organizations seem to be one of the most important factors influencing the above-described differences. An analysis of the problem's perception provides contradictory evidence. In all countries except for the Czech Republic, the use of scientific knowledge results in a higher estimation of the number of drug users. In Hungary, the estimates provided by organizations conducting research (400,000) are twice as high as in the remaining organizations. In Poland, the mean value of the number of drug users estimated by such organizations is around 832,000, compared to 685,000 provided by the other organizations. In Slovenia, the respective estimate was around 30% higher (Table 3). The assumption concerning the impact of the scientific activities on the perception of the scope of the problem is only partially supported by data from a dominant source of information. It is worth noting that there was no direct influence of the problem's scope from organizations which relied on official statistics as the main source of data. Only in Poland, organizations which gathered information on the drug problem from professional literature came up with a lower estimate (130,000 compared to the mean value of 750,000 drug users).

Table 3: Estimates of drug users in 1998 and conducting research

Country	**Conducting research**	**Estimated number of drug users, Mean**	**N**
Czech Republic	yes	209,882	17
	no	316,538	13
	Total	256,100	30
Hungary	yes	410,000	13
	no	197,894	19
	Total	284,062	32
Poland	yes	832,500	16
	no	685,500	20
	Total	750,833	36
Slovenia	yes	92,266	15
	no	61,366	15
	Total	76,816	30
Total	yes	386,918	61
	no	335,902	67
	Total	360,214	128

A striking difference appears in the case of "individual perspective", i.e. organizations, i.e. those whose activities are focused on meeting individual needs, particularly treatment and care. In each country (especially in Poland

and Slovenia) it turned out that such organizations came up with much lower estimates of the number of drug users than other organizations did (Table 4). An analysis of the data gathered shows that care and treatment organizations influence the definition of the problem. The opposite relationship did not appear.

The territorial level of action did not differentiate perceptions either. In Slovenia, the problem is perceived as being larger by representatives of national organizations, while in Poland significantly higher estimates of drug users are provided at the local level. No such differences are observed in Hungary and the Czech Republic.

Table 4: Estimated number of drug users in 1998 and provision of treatment and care

Country	Provision of treatment and care	Estimated number of drug users (Mean)	N
Czech Republic	yes	215,000	14
	no	292,062	16
	Total	256,100	30
Hungary	yes	277,187	16
	no	290,937	16
	Total	284,062	32
Poland	yes	515,263	19
	no	1,014,117	17
	Total	750,833	36
Slovenia	yes	51,269	13
	no	96,352	17
	Total	76,816	30

The period of initiation of drug demand activities turns out to be a key factor related to the problem's estimates. In Hungary, organizations which started their activities after 1994 come up with significantly higher numbers of drug users compared to the estimates of the institutions which were founded earlier (Table 5). In Hungary, the mean value provided by the oldest organizations is 175,000 drug users, while the estimate supplied by the newly-established institutions is 462,500. Converse relations are observed in Poland and Slovenia. In Poland, the number of drug users provided by organizations which started drug demand reduction programmes before 1990 is 851,000 while the estimate by new organizations is 620,000. In Slovenia, the respective numbers are 121,000 and 77,000 drug users.

Table 5: Estimated number of drug users and date of initiating drug demand reduction activities

Country	**Initiation of DDR activities**	**Estimated number of drug users (Mean)**	**N**
Czech Republic	1910-1989	255,000	3
	1990-1994	243,571	14
	after 1994	269,846	13
	Total	256,100	30
Hungary	1910-1989	175,500	10
	1990-1994	271,923	13
	after 1994	462,500	8
	Total	290,000	31
Poland	1910-1989	8,515,789	19
	1990-1994	645,833	12
	after 1994	6,200,000	5
	Total	750,833	36
Slovenia	1910-1989	121,666	3
	1990-1994	63,545	11
	after 1994	77,531	16
	Total	76,816	30
Total	1910-1989	544,714	35
	1990-1994	307,880	50
	after 1994	274,964	42
	Total	362,263	127

An analysis of the data on the number of drug users reveals a very limited impact of the type of professionals on the problem's definition. Four dominant groups of professionals were selected to test the possible influence, i.e. medical, social work, psychology and educational professions. It turns out that the existing difference among professional definitions reflects national characteristics rather than a particular professional background. The closest similarity appears in psychologists' descriptions. In Poland, Slovenia and the Czech Republic estimates provided by psychologists are distinctly different from the numbers offered by other organizations. In Poland, the estimates of organizations which employed psychologists are almost three times higher than in other institutions (934,000 compared to 327,000). The differences are smaller in Slovenia (90,000 compared to 58,000) and in Hungary (329,000 compared to 207,000). The figures provided by the remaining professional groups vary in each country. For example, only in Poland organizations with medically trained staff come up with higher estimations; in

Slovenia and in Hungary such organizations give the lowest figures. Higher estimations are provided by organizations with social workers in Poland and Slovenia, while institutions with a staff with an educational background provide the highest figures in the Czech Republic and Slovenia.

Attitudes towards drugs turn out to be linked to the different estimations of the number of drug users. However, in each country one observes a slightly different relationship. In Hungary and Poland respondents with restrictive attitudes provide the lowest assessment of the number of drug users. In Hungary and Slovenia, a permissive approach is linked to the highest estimations.

Perceptions of future threats seem to be another important element of problem definitions. Therefore, an emphasis was placed on discovering the perceptions of future changes, i.e. organizations' forecasts based on their estimations of the number of drug users in 1998 and 2003.

As shown in Tables 6 and 7, forecasts of a substantial increase appear in the case of Poland and Hungary. In Hungary, the expected increase in the number of drug addicts (mean value) is around 160%. In Poland, the anticipated rise exceeds 100%. These countries, especially Hungary, also had a very high rate of internal differentiation. It turns out that five Hungarian and five Polish organizations expect an increase by more than 200%. Moreover, one of the Hungarian organizations foresaw a 2000% growth and one of the Polish organizations a 1000% increase, which had a significant impact on the mean values. Compared with Hungary and Poland, Slovenia and the Czech Republic expected only a minor change (24%-32% increase).

Table 6: Expected rise in number of drug users, 1998-2003 (1998=1)

	Czech Republic	Hungary	Poland	Slovenia
Mean expected rise	1,32	2,63	2,05	1,24

Table 7: Expected rise in number of drug users (1998=1)

Country	Expected rise in number of drug users, Mean	N	Standard deviation
Czech Republic	0,32	30	0,3887
Hungary	1,63	26	3,7354
Poland	1,05	33	1,7665
Slovenia	0,24	29	0,1943
Total	0,79	118	2,0463

Opinions on the current and future situation seem to illustrate the specific situation of each country. In Hungary one refers to the problem with a high number of drug users (per 1,000 inhabitants) and expectations of a considerably rising number of drug users. In Poland, the estimates of the number of drug users and anticipated increases are relatively low. Opposite estimations are given in Slovenia (numerous drug users and expectations of relatively slow growth). The Czech Republic is a country with very moderate estimations both with regard to the current and future situations.

Regardless of national differences some interesting diversities appear when the organizational context is included in the analysis. A significantly lower increase in the number of drug users is reported in cases of "knowledge-consuming organizations", especially by organizations which conduct research. Such organizations expect a 46% growth compared to the 110% increase expected by other organizations ($p<0,036$). Expectations of moderate growth expressed by such organizations appear in all countries except Slovenia and particularly in Poland (63% growth compared with a 136% increase in other organizations) as well as in Hungary (53% versus 213%). The same relationships appear in Hungary and Poland in cases of organizations, which were involved in the policy process and utilized official statistics and professional literature as sources of information.

A significant growth in the number of drug users is reported in the case of "individual perspective" organizations, especially organizations which provide treatment and care. They expect a 104% increase compared to the 55% rise declared by the remaining organizations ($p<0,2$). Again, the strongest growth is foreseen by Polish and Hungarian organizations.

Table 8: Expected rise in the number of drug users and initiated drug demand reduction activities (1998=1)

Initiated drug demand reduction activities	**Expected rise in number of drug users, Mean**	**N**
1910-1989	1,21	31
1990-1994	0,51	47
after 1994	0,33	39
Total	0,63	117

A more pessimistic development is anticipated by organizations, which initiated their activities before 1990 (121%). Organizations which started their programmes in the early 1990s expect a 51% increase, the remaining ones a 33% growth. The above link is observed mostly in the case of Polish and

Hungarian organizations. It is worth noting that the oldest institutions usually come up with moderate estimates of drug users in 1998.

Differences in the anticipation of problem development (however, not statistically significant) are revealed in estimates supplied by organizations in which various professional groups are employed. Similar to the case of drug users' numbers, a sharp increase (95%) is expected by Hungarian and Polish organizations occupying psychologists and social workers (121%). There is no evidence of attitudes having an impact on the development of the drug problem. Increases in the number of drug users are expected by respondents with moderate attitudes.

Opinions on the structure of drug supply

Opinions on dominant drugs are found to be another important characteristic of problem definition. Each organization was asked to come up with a structure of drug supply and its changes over a 5-year period. The data gathered are utilized both to create a country profile and to indicate future trends. The first task was to discover the similarities and differences in the assessment of the problem's conditions in 1998 and expected changes on a 5-year horizon. Secondly, we tried to discover factors influencing the perception of the supply structure.

A comparison of dominant drugs in the four countries reveals two models of supply (Table 9). The first one emerges in the Czech Republic and Slovenia. In both countries cannabis constitutes almost half of total supply. The share of amphetamines is assessed as 20%-25% of the total market. Opiates are less popular and do not exceed 11%-17%. On the other hand, in Hungary and Poland cannabis, amphetamines and opiates make up almost equal parts of the supply structure. Their share is around 25%-30%.

Striking differences are discovered in the forecasts provided by the respondents. The most stable situation occurs in the Czech Republic. The only considerable increase (40%) is expected in the case of hallucinogens. Slovenian organizations anticipate a 40%-50% increase in cocaine and amphetamine supply. Substantial changes in the cocaine share are predicted in Hungary (145% increase) and Poland (205% increase).

Table 9: Opinions on drug supply in 1998 and in 2003

	Czech Republic		Hungary		Poland		Slovenia	
	'98	Forecast (1998=1)	'98	Forecast (1998=1)	'98	Forecast (1998=1)	'98	Forecast (1998=1)
Opiates	17,66	1,17	24,97	1,18	28,62	1,03	11,11	0,97
Cannabis	45,57	0,99	29,83	0,93	27,96	1,25	58,38	0,98
Cocaine	4,58	1,08	4,38	2,45	4,89	3,05	3,69	1,51
Amphetamines	25,77	0,95	30,97	0,87	25,44	1,08	20,53	1,39
Hallucinogens	7,81	1,40	9,56	0,96	8,21	1,17	3,00	0,99

Opiates

The highest share of opiates is stated in Poland (28%) and Hungary (25%). The lowest proportion is given in Slovenia (11%). The data presented in Table 9 suggests that each of the countries surveyed has its own distinct profile. Opinions on the share of opiates in the drug supply structure do not turn out to be directly connected to forecasts on opiates. Both in the Czech Republic (where opiates make up 17% of total supply) as well as in Hungary (which has one of the highest shares of opiates, i.e. 25%) experts await a 17%-18% increase. In Poland, where opiates are found to be the most popular drug, respondents expect only a 3% growth. Slovenian organizations expect even a 3% decrease.

It is worth mentioning that only a significant minority of Polish organizations expects an increase in opiate supply (82% of them forecast a decrease or a stabilization). Opinions vary more widely in Slovenia (35% of the organizations anticipated a slight growth). A profound differentiation occurs among Hungarian and Czech respondents.

Organizations conducting drug demand reduction programmes with a number of staff of more than 20 come up with significantly higher proportions (35%) of opiates than smaller organizations. Organizations founded between 1990-1994 believe that opiate consumption plays a more significant role on the drug scene than organizations established after 1994 and before 1990. Expectations of significant growth are found more frequently among exclusive organizations.

"Individual perspective" organizations, i.e. treatment and care organizations and rehabilitation centres perceive opiates as a very serious problem. They claim that opiate consumption plays a more important role in the drug consumption scene than representatives of organizations working in other fields of drug demand reduction do.

Figure 1: Forecasts on opiates by number of organizations

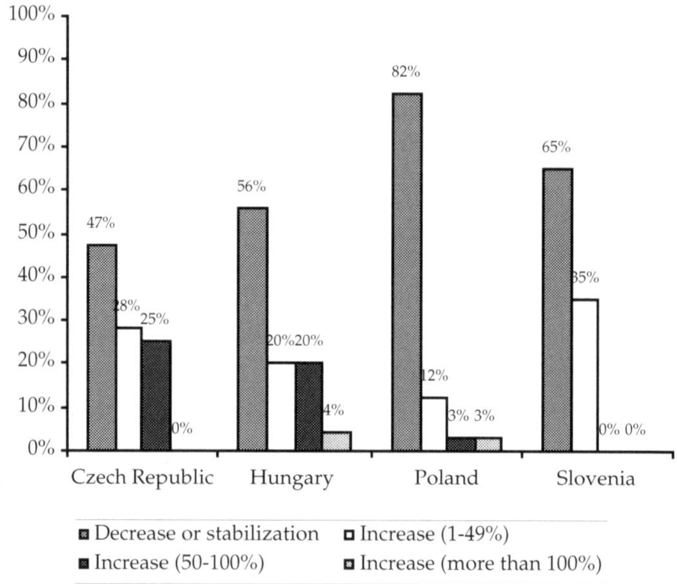

Cannabis

Cannabis occupies a central place among illicit drugs. Its share in total drug supply is estimated as one of the largest in each country. It is especially true for the Czech Republic (46% of total supply) and Slovenia (58%) where cannabis play the most important role in the illicit drug scene. There are only insignificant differences between the share of cannabis and drugs in Hungary and in Poland.

Basic discrepancies appear among forecasts by Polish respondents and representatives of the other three countries' organizations. In the Czech Republic, Hungary and Slovenia a decrease in cannabis supply is foreseen of between 1 and 7%. In the case of Poland, respondents expect a 25% increase.

As shown in Figure 2, a considerable share of the organizations in each country expects a decrease or stabilization in the cannabis supply. Such expectations are expressed particularly by Czech organizations. Polish respondents are more pessimistic in this respect. However, more than 60% of Polish experts state that the cannabis supply on the drug scene would decrease or stabilize, the remaining predict a more significant increase than the other three countries.

Figure 2: Forecasts on cannabis by number of organizations

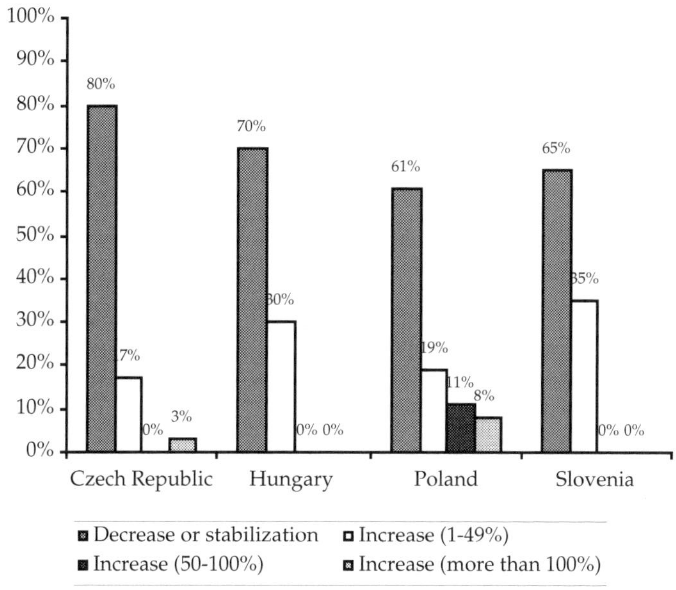

When analysing data on the perception of cannabis some surprising differences among the organizations surveyed are revealed. The smallest organizations (with a staff of less than 10) come up with the highest proportion of cannabis (41% of total drug supply). Organizations founded after 1994 are more pessimistic and assess the proportion of cannabis on the drug scene at about 46%. According to organizations founded at earlier dates, the proportion is about 34%-38%. Inclusive organizations assess that 40% of the illicit drug scene belongs to cannabis.

Respondents in organizations conducting treatment, care and rehabilitation programmes calculate the share of cannabis at 36%-38%, which is a significantly lower proportion than other estimations. It is worth stressing that the highest estimates, i.e. 42%-43% are provided by "policy-oriented" organizations.

A comparison of opinions on the share held by opiates and cannabis leads to some astonishing conclusions. While a higher share of opiates is declared mostly by big, "individual- oriented" and exclusive organizations, the strong position of cannabis is emphasized by small, newly-established and "policy-oriented" organizations. One may claim that a perception of those two drugs is influenced by a separate set of factors. It seems plausible that particular concern for opiates is expressed by the relatively old, well-developed organizations providing direct services to drug users. On the other hand, a focus on cannabis is perceived by organizations which seem to be relatively new actors in the drug demand reduction field.

Cocaine

Cocaine is defined as one of the least popular drugs (3.5-5% of total supply) on the illicit drug scene. There are only slight differences among the countries surveyed (see Table 9).

However, forecasts provided by the respondents show that serious changes are expected in the future. The proportion of cocaine is expected to increase in all four countries. The lowest rise is expected in the Czech Republic (8%), which is significantly low in comparison to other countries. In Slovenia, the cocaine share is expected to rise by 51%, in Hungary by 145%. The highest increase is anticipated in Poland, where the cocaine share is expected to double (208%). Czech respondents are most optimistic. A share of 76% of the organizations expects a decrease or stabilization (Figure 3). A lack of major changes is also anticipated by more than half of the Hungarian organizations. Polish respondents believe that the supply of cocaine will increase dramatically. Only 27% of Polish organizations expect a decrease or a stabilization. Two-thirds of Polish experts forecast a rise of at least 50%. A more moderate forecast is made in Slovenia, where 62% of the organizations expect a rise.

Estimations of cocaine and forecasts of future developments seem to be influenced by similar factors as in the case of cannabis.

The smallest organizations (with a maximum staff of 20) believe that cocaine accounts for 4%-5% of illicit drugs. Organizations which employ more staff come up with lower estimates (1.5-2.7%). Similar differences appear between organizations founded after 1994 (5.6%) and organizations founded before 1989 (3.6%).

Inclusive organizations come up with higher assessments (5%) than exclusive ones (4%). It should be stressed, however, that exclusive organizations expect a 136% rise, while inclusive organizations expect a 98% increase of cocaine over a 5-year period.

Figure 3: Forecasts on cocaine by number of organizations

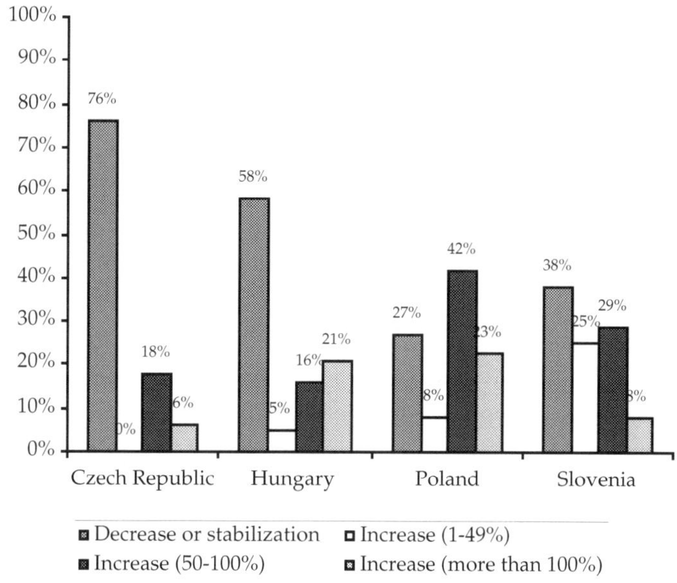

Significant differences appear among organizations with respect to their legal status. Non-governmental organizations state that cocaine represents nearly 6% of the total supply, while governmental organizations assess the share at 3.4%. NGOs believe that the cocaine proportion will increase by 187%, which is a significantly higher expectation than in the case of governmental organizations (33% growth).

Organizations working at the local level come up with estimates that are twice as high (6%) as their counterparts at the national level (3%). The same difference is seen in opinions on future developments. While national organizations think that the cocaine proportion will rise by 154%, organizations at the local level believe that the rise will be around 47%.

Amphetamine

Amphetamine is the second-most popular drug in all countries except Poland. It constitutes the biggest share (31%) of the illicit drug scene in Hungary. In the Czech Republic and Poland, the proportion of amphetamines is almost equal (ca. 25%). The amphetamine share is the lowest in Slovenia (20%). It is worth stressing, however, that Slovenian organizations expect the highest increase in amphetamine supply. While Czech respondents anticipated a 5% decrease and Hungarian respondents a 13% decrease, Slovenian experts expect an increase of almost 40%.

The above-mentioned forecasts are also reflected in Figure 4. The majority of Hungarian, Czech and Polish organizations do not anticipate major changes in amphetamine supply. On the other hand, 58% of Slovenian organizations forecast an increase of the amphetamine share.

Organizations with staff of less than 50 provide a significantly higher estimate of amphetamines (25-30%) compared to those which employ more than 50 persons (18%). Slight differences appear between exclusive organizations (amphetamine share is assessed at 28% of total supply) and inclusive ones (24%). Organizations at the local level (28%) come up with a higher proportion of amphetamines on the illicit drug scene than organizations at the national level (24%).

"Individual oriented" organizations i.e. those working in the field of treatment, care and rehabilitation are more likely to come up with higher proportions of amphetamine usage (26%-28%) than other organizations (23%-24%).

Figure 4: Forecasts on amphetamine by number of organizations

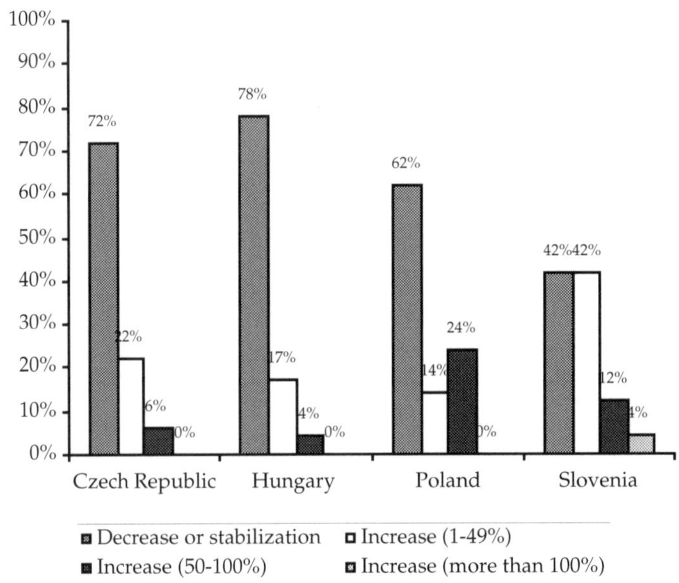

Hallucinogens

Hallucinogens belong to the least widespread drugs in the four countries studied. The average proportion of hallucinogens among illicit drugs is defined by Czech, Hungarian and Polish experts at 8%-10% of total supply. Hallucinogens are very rarely reported in Slovenia (3% of total supply). Czech respondents believe that the share of hallucinogens will rise by 40%. In Poland, 17% growth is expected. Hungary and Slovenia anticipate a slight decrease.

There is very little diversity in the assessment of the share held by hallucinogens in 1998 and its future development. Insignificant differences appear in the case of small (up to 50 persons employed) and older organizations (established before 1990), which come up with slightly higher estimates.

Figure 5: Forecasts on hallucinogens by number of organizations

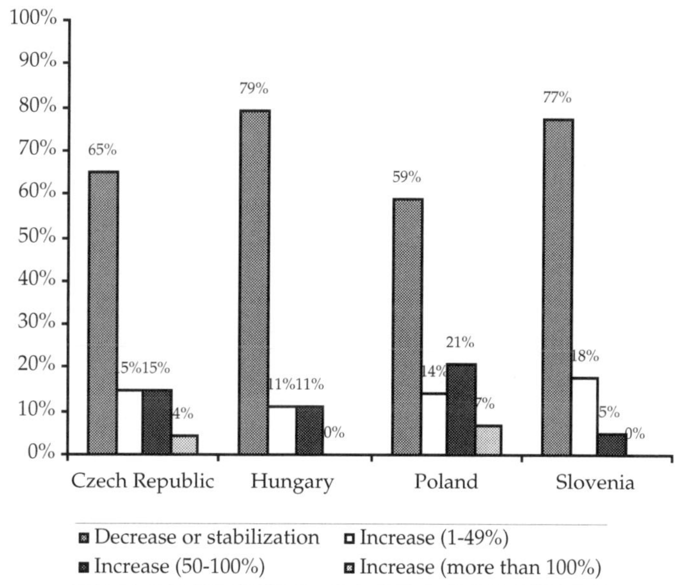

Summary

An analysis of opinions on the drug supply structure and its future changes reveals both national differences as well as diversities influenced by the type of organizational setting. Of particular interest seems to be a tendency to overestimate the share of some major drugs, which is observed among small, relatively newly-established, exclusive, non-governmental organizations. It turns out that access to information on the problem plays a minor role in the perception of the drug scene. The emphasis placed on the importance of drugs like cannabis or cocaine could be interpreted as a way of legitimizing a relatively new threat. It is worth noting that a similar concern for recognized drugs like opiates and amphetamines is expressed by old, well-developed organizations usually providing treatment and care for users of the above-mentioned drugs. Therefore, according to a more plausible explanation, the estimates provided by relatively new actors play an important role in the attempt to secure their positions in national response systems.

Opinions on national policies

One of the objectives of the analysis of national responses is to trace the influence of specific conditions as well as the impact of organizational settings and attitudes. On the one hand, it is assumed that most organizations would regard national policy as a set of countermeasures resulting from specific conditions of the problem. On the other hand, it seems that like the differences in the estimations of the problem's scope and opinions of dominant drugs, the perception of national policy could be influenced by a specific organizational context or existing opinions and beliefs.

Table 10 shows that it is perceived that each country has a different type of national policy. Hungary illustrates a policy based on law enforcement and control of supply, where the other elements, i.e. health promotion, harm reduction and demand reduction, are less visible. The Czech Republic seems to link control measures with health promotion and harm reduction. Slovenia puts the strongest emphasis on eliminating the negative effects of drug dependence. No dominant approach is discovered in Poland. What seems to be a leading feature in Poland is a relatively limited input from the law enforcement side.

Table 10 also reveals some differences as well as similarities in opinions with regard to national policies. One of the main differences appears in the assessment of the law enforcement focus. In Hungary, this feature is described as a dominant element of national policy. A similar emphasis takes place in the Czech Republic, where law enforcement and harm reduction are described as the principal features of the national response system. The law enforcement focus is least present in Poland.

Table 10: Opinions on national policy by country (means on 1-5 scale)

Country		Health promotion	Harm reduction	Demand reduction	Control of supply	Law enforcement
Czech Republic	N	45	46	44	45	42
	Mean	3,29	3,35	3,07	3,11	3,33
	Std. Dev.	1,20	1,20	1,19	1,21	1,10
Hungary	N	44	44	44	43	42
	Mean	2,96	2,21	2,82	3,49	3,67
	Std. Dev.	1,29	1,05	1,23	1,12	1,30
Poland	N	49	49	48	48	48
	Mean	3,00	2,80	3,04	2,73	2,19
	Std. Dev.	1,23	1,00	1,20	1,18	1,12
Slovenia	N	36	35	36	36	36
	Mean	3,08	3,74	3,06	2,92	3,03
	Std. Dev.	1,03	0,78	0,89	0,94	0,81
Total	N	174	174	172	172	168
	Mean	3,08	2,98	2,99	3,06	3,02
	Std. Dev.	1,20	1,17	1,14	1,15	1,24

A similar situation occurs when the control of supply approach is assessed. National policies in Hungary and the Czech Republic are perceived as the ones most closely oriented towards control of supply. Respondents in Poland and Slovenia do not indicate that component as a dominant characteristic.

There are no significant differences concerning demand reduction. Organizations in all countries come up with similar indicators. The only exception is Hungary, where the national policy is perceived as less oriented towards drug demand reduction. An interesting comparison can be made in the case of harm reduction. This feature is strongly emphasized by Slovenian organizations. It also appears in the assessment provided by Czech organizations. Harm reduction turned out to be the weakest element of Hungarian and Polish policy. There are almost no differences in the perception of health promotion.

One can claim that the perception of a national response to the drug problem has been strongly influenced by two policy options: external control of the problem and a reduction of the negative consequences of drug use. The former has confidence in the ability to curb the problem by controlling the supply of drugs or by enforcing existing regulations. The latter implies that radical solutions to the drug problem cannot be found in the foreseeable future and therefore the national response should concentrate on limiting the scope of the negative effects of drug consumption.

It turns out that the perception of policy in each country is strongly influenced by organizational settings and prevailing attitudes to the drug problem. The first diversity of opinions appears in the case of the "supply control" approach. This approach is defined as a key element of national response more often by governmental than by non-governmental organizations ($p<0,1$). This feature is also emphasized by organizations active at the national level ($p<0,2$). It seems that such differences reflect the existing responsibilities as well as the position in the organizational structure. The more central the position, the broader the outlook of an organization and the more distinct the tendency to perceive control of supply as a dominant element of national policy. This relation is also observed among "individual oriented" organizations, i.e. those providing direct services to drug users. For example, organizations active in the field of treatment and care place little emphasis on the control of supply ($p<0.26$). They are also, however, more keen on defining national policy as "harm reduction-oriented" ($p<0.1$).

The most significant influence ($p<0.001$) appears in "knowledge-oriented" organizations, i.e. organizations which use data and information in their everyday activities (research, evaluation). Organizations which conduct research more often define national policy as "supply control"-oriented. They also stress the role of such characteristics as harm reduction ($p<0.045$) and law enforcement ($p<0.06$).

The focus on the "supply control" dimension is closely related to the organization's position and the type of information used. The perception of harm reduction and drug demand reduction turns out to be influenced by participation in a policy-making process. As shown in Table 11, organizations involved in policy development or legislation more frequently characterize national policy as harm reduction-oriented ($p<0.001$) and drug demand reduction-oriented ($p<0.05$).

The above-mentioned results reflect existing differences in the use of information on the problem. It turns out that "knowledge-oriented" organizations, like those conducting evaluations, more frequently describe national policy as harm reduction-oriented.

Involvement in policy development radically affects changes in the perception of reality. One could therefore argue that relatively new concepts like harm reduction tend to exist in organizations linked to policy-makers' circles that are a permanent element of the problem's conditions. The former observation raises the question of the effective transmission of policy priorities to the specifically interested public.

Therefore, the position in the organizational structure, the type of knowledge used and the link to policy-making turns out to be the most significant factors influencing perceptions of national policy. It is worth stressing that the professional background appears to be of lesser importance. Neither a medical background nor a psychological or educational one play a role in defining the features of the national response to the drug problem.

Table 11: Opinions on national policy and involvement in policy development and legislation (means on 1-5 scale)

	Involvement in policy development and legislation	N	Mean	Standard deviation
Health promotion	yes	83	3,13	1,22
	no	91	3,03	1,18
Harm reduction	yes	82	3,36	1,11
	no	92	2,64	1,12
Demand reduction	yes	82	3,17	1,04
	no	90	2,83	1,21
Control of supply	yes	82	3,07	1,14
	no	90	3,04	1,17
Law enforcement	yes	81	3,06	1,17
	no	87	2,99	1,31

Attitudes towards the problem turn out to be another profound source influencing the perception of national policies. An assessment of the national response depends to a startling extent on the normative definitions used by organizations. Permissiveness and a restrictive approach differentiate the organizations' opinions, especially in the areas of control of supply and law enforcement. Respondents with restrictive attitudes perceive the national policy as more law enforcement-oriented ($p<0.001$) as well as more supply control-oriented ($p<0.04$). One may claim that the more restrictive the approach, the higher the expectations of the implementation of tough measures. By contrast, advocates of a permissive approach usually consider national policy as not liberal enough (see Table 12). However, the differences are not statistically significant. They define the national response less oriented towards health promotion than it happens to be the case in the restrictive group ($p<0,18$).

Table 12: Opinions on national policies and attitudes towards the problem (means on 1-5 scale)

	Attitude	N	Mean	Standard deviation
Health promotion	permissive	56	2,73	1,14
	restrictive	53	3,26	1,18
Harm reduction	permissive	56	2,86	1,14
	restrictive	51	2,92	1,04
Demand reduction	permissive	56	2,80	1,03
	restrictive	52	3,10	1,21
Control of supply	permissive	56	3,23	1,21
	restrictive	53	2,75	1,19
Law enforcement	permissive	55	3,53	1,17
	restrictive	52	2,56	1,13

Our research also reveals interesting differences in the perception of national policies among the countries surveyed (Tables 13 and 14). Apart from defining the selected characteristics of national responses to the drug problem, respondents were also asked an open question on the perceived strengths and weaknesses of the national policy.

Awareness of the problem is defined as the main advantage of national policies in Hungary (24% of all responses). Respondents in Hungary stress the importance of public debate, public recognition of the problem by the lay public, and an understanding of causes and effects of drug abuse. It is worth noting that public visibility of the problem is almost the only strong point in Hungary. The second category of strengths in Hungary turns out to be prevention programmes: 11% of responses by Hungarian organizations stress the importance of the different forms of prevention activities. The third noticeable characteristic is supply control activities (9% of organizations put emphasis on this element). According to the dominant opinion (16% of responses), however, national policy has no strengths at all. It is also worth mentioning that Hungarian organizations provide the smallest number of positive (as well as negative) national policy's features.

The strengths of Polish policy turn out to be similar to those indicated by Hungarian organizations. Prevention programmes (24% responses) and awareness of the problem (20% responses) are perceived as the main strong points. Polish organizations also stress the importance of a well-developed system of therapy centres (12% responses). A comparable proportion of respondents point out the effectiveness of the policy, emphasizing the flexibility of legislation, which results in a diversity of programmes and openness to change. Efficient cooperation among drug demand organizations is identified as a main asset of Czech policy (19% responses). Similar approval is expressed in the case of policy and legislation, and prevention programmes.

The most coherent opinions on national policy are observed among Slovenian organizations. Almost half of all responses place an emphasis on efficient policy (28%) and on the strengths of harm reduction programmes.

Table 13: National policy strengths

	Count Column %	Czech Republic	Hungary	Poland	Slovenia	Row Total
STRENGTH		1	2	3	4	
Awareness	1	8	13	18	4	43
		9.0	24.5	20.2	6.3	14.6
Efficient network	2	17	1	9	6	33
		19.1	1.9	10.1	9.4	11.2
Competent experts	3	5	3	4	1	13
		5.6	5.7	4.5	1.6	4.4
Prevention programmes	4	13	6	22	8	49
		14.6	11.3	24.7	12.5	16.6
Therapy programmes	5	5	4	11	4	24
		5.6	7.5	12.4	6.3	8.1
Harm reduction	6	8	0	2	13	23
programmes		9.0	0.0	2.2	20.3	7.8
Effective policy	7	15	1	11	18	45
		16.9	1.9	12.4	28.1	15.3
Supply control	8	8	5	8	1	22
		9.0	9.4	9.0	1.6	7.5
Other	9	6	4	1	7	18
		6.7	7.5	1.1	10.9	6.1
No strengths at all	10	4	16	3	2	25
		4.5	30.2	3.4	3.1	8.5
	Column	89	53	89	64	295
	Total	30.2	18.0	30.2	21.7	100.0

Note: Per cents and totals based on responses.
158 valid cases; 23 missing cases.

Table 14: National policy weaknesses

Count Column %		Czech Republic	Hungary	Poland	Slovenia	Row Total
WEAKNESS		1	2	3	4	
Lack of awareness	1	4	4	13	4	25
		3.7	6.0	10.2	4.9	6.5
Lack of experts	2	6	2	5	0	13
		5.6	3.0	3.9	0.0	3.4
Ineffective programmes	3	4	5	12	3	24
		3.7	7.5	9.4	3.7	6.3
Focus on law	4	6	4	6	3	19
enforcement		5.6	6.0	4.7	3.7	4.9
Lack of policy	5	33	16	34	27	110
		30.8	23.9	26.6	32.9	28.6
Lack of coordination	6	19	16	14	21	70
		17.8	23.9	10.9	25.6	18.2
Lack of research	7	0	2	2	5	9
		0.0	3.0	1.6	6.1	2.3
Insufficient funding	8	14	8	27	6	55
		13.1	11.9	21.1	7.3	14.3
Lack of evaluation	9	1	2	2	5	10
		0.9	3.0	1.6	6.1	2.6
Weak NGOs	10	0	0	7	0	7
		0.0	0.0	5.5	0.0	1.8
Other	11	20	8	6	8	42
		18.7	11.9	4.7	9.8	10.9
Column Total		107	67	128	82	384
		27.9	17.4	33.3	21.4	100.0

Note: Per cents and totals based on responses.
169 valid cases; 12 missing cases.

The diversity of strengths seems to reflect the main differences in national responses to the drug problem. Despite the national differences, there is a meaningful consent on the weak points. Respondents are in agreement that each country lacks a coherent policy. The main criticism concerns a missing overall strategy related to the lack of well-defined national priorities. Such claims constitute around 30% of the responses in Slovenia and in the Czech Republic and around 25% of all negative features expressed by Polish and Hungarian organizations. The second category of policy weaknesses often mentioned turns out to be a lack of co-ordination and poor communication among the organizations. This element very often appears in responses of Slovenian (25%) and Hungarian organizations (24%). Insufficient funding constitutes the third group of policy limitations. Financial problems are encountered mostly by Polish organizations (21% of all mentioned weak points in Poland concern insufficient funding). Financial claims are less visible in the Czech Republic and Hungary (13%-11%). They also constituted one of the less important sources of criticism in Slovenia (6%).

Concluding remarks

The analysis of opinions on the drug problem and related policies reveals the existence of a national as well as an organizational impact on the definition of the problem. It turned out that situation in each country is perceived by organizations in a specific, distinct way. The data presented in Table 15 indicate that national differences still play a crucial role in defining the drug problem. It reveals that we deal with four separate national cases rather than with more or less comparable patterns.

Table 15: Opinions on drug problem in four countries

Country	**Scope of the problem**		**Supply structure**		**National policy**
	*Drug users in 1998**	*Drug users forecast*	*Dominant drug*	*Expected increase*	*Dominant feature*
Czech Republic	Moderate	Low	Cannabis	Hallucinogens	Harm Reduction Law Enforcement
Hungary	Moderate	Low	Amphetamine Cannabis Opiates	Cocaine	Law Enforcement Supply Control
Poland	Low	High	Opiates Cannabis Amphetamine	Cocaine	Demand Reduction Health Promotion
Slovenia	High	High	Cannabis	Amphetamine Hallucinogens	Harm Reduction

Note: * Per 100.000 inhabitants

The closest similarities between the present (perceived) situation and forecast have been observed in Czech Republic and Hungary. In both countries a moderate scope on the drug problem and expectations of a slight increase are discovered. Cannabis is defined as the dominant drug, however Hungarian organizations stress also the importance of amphetamine and opiates. The perceptions of a relatively stable situation contradict opinions on law enforcement as one of dominant features of national policy.

A higher diversity of the definition of the drug problem is identified in Poland. A relatively narrow scope on the number of drug users is correlated with a forecast of a significant increase. Despite expectations of turbulent times and the central position of opiates and amphetamine, national policy is perceived to be focused on demand reduction and health promotion.

Slovenia seems to be the most distinct example of a co-existence of perceived situation of high drug use and a strong emphasis on harm reduction. The described characteristics reflect prevailing opinions in each country, i.e. they do not explain existing models of policy design. Lack of coherent policy is unanimously considered the main weakness of national responses to DDR.

In addition to significant national diversities in the definition of the problem, our research reveals also that organizational settings have considerable influence on this matter. Different opinions are significantly more often mentioned by certain types of organizations. In this context, three relationships seem to be of particular importance (Table 16).

Table 16: Opinions on drug problem and type of organisation

Organisation	**Scope of the problem**		**National policy**
	Drug users in 1998[*]	*Drug users forecast*	*Dominant feature*
Individual oriented	Low	High	Harm Reduction
Policy oriented	-	Low (Hungary, Poland)	Demand reduction Harm Reduction
Knowledge utilised	High	Low	Supply Control
Old	High (Poland, Slovenia)	High	-
New	High (Hungary)	-	
Repressive		-	-
Permissive	High (Hungary, Slovenia)	-	Law enforcement Supply control

Note: * Per 100.000 inhabitants

The position in the organizational system and the type of developed activities play a major role in the perception of the drug problem. The most striking difference has been identified between 'individual-oriented" (i.e. particularly organizations dealing with care and treatment) and "policy-oriented/knowledge consuming" organizations. Care and treatment organizations assess the problem's scope more optimistic and forecast a substantial growth in the near future. On the other side, organizations involved in the policy process and organizations, which use different forms of knowledge in their everyday work, are more likely to overestimate the current number of drug users and expect only a slight increase.

The second set of factors is related to forms to legitimize that the problem really exists. The oldest organizations provide more often a rather pessimistic diagnosis of the current situation and they foresee a significant increase. One can argue that such opinions reflect the need to demonstrate that the problem still exists, and in this way justifying the need for further existence of the occupied position in organizational system.

It is rather strange that only a low correlation was found between attitudes toward drug problem and its definition. It turns out that permissive and restrictive attitudes do not influence the perception of the present situation and forecasts. The only relationship worth mentioning is the one between permissive attitudes on the one hand, and the classification of national policy as law enforcement - and supply control oriented, on the other.

One of the most intrinsic questions is to what extent opinions and perceptions described above will change in the near future. It seems most probable that future developments will modify both the situation in the countries as well as the existing definitions. One can expect that the globalization of the drug scene will eliminate many of existing national differences. On the other hand, the unification of management styles and techniques, similarities in professional education or increased open access to information may not only standardise the activities developed by organizations but will also have an impact on the opinions of their members. In summary, we may state that our research has shown that national responses to the drug problem have to large extent been influenced by specific country conditions. However, it is easy to imagine that this country-focused orientation can not be taken for granted in the long run.

CHAPTER 8

The Division of Labour Between NGOs and Governmental Organizations

Renata Cvelbar and František David Krch

The countries participating in this research, Hungary, the Czech Republic, Poland and Slovenia, have developed institutional frameworks in the field of drug demand reduction (DDR) each in their own specific way. The developmental history of drug demand reduction organizations differs from country to country. The institutional framework depends on the administrative structure of a country and on the various laws tackling drug demand reduction, including legislation on health insurance, social assistance and non-governmental organizations. A whole range of cultural, social, political and other factors have influenced the development of institutions in the field of drug demand reduction.

1 Legislation, governmental concepts and strategies

From a legislative point of view, provisions on illicit drug use were first encompassed in criminal legislation. Drug demand reduction provisions have traditionally been part of various acts in the field of health care and social assistance. These acts encompassed mainly provisions regarding treatment of drug users, financing of treatment, and in some cases provisions regarding social assistance for drug users.

It is only since recently that the countries included in this survey have introduced special legislation dealing with drug demand reduction. These *lex specialis,* where existent, cover prevention, treatment and rehabilitation of drug users. When examining similarities in the legislation of Hungary, the Czech Republic, Slovenia and Poland, it is noted that all of them have signed and ratified the basic international treaties in the field of illicit drug use. These include the United Nations Conventions dealing with illicit drugs, namely the Single Convention on Narcotic Drugs from 1961, the Convention on Psychotropic Substances from 1972, and the United Nations Convention against Illicit Traffic in Drugs and Psychotropic Substances from 1989.

Although the international legal framework has defined the development of national legislation, legislation has developed at different 'speeds' in the four countries. The legislation on drug demand reduction followed the development of criminal legislation. It is not always clear what factors were conducive to the development of drug demand reduction policies and laws. One of the factors could be the extent of the drug problem. Epidemiological data show that during the 1980s incidence and prevalence of illicit drug consumption increased in Slovenia, Hungary, the Czech Republic and Poland. Triggered by public concern legislation on drug demand reduction started to develop. At the same time amendments and changes to the legislation on criminal law were noted. One of the factors contributing to the development of preventive and treatment measures was probably a shift in attitudes towards drug users, who are perceived as persons in need of medical and psychosocial treatment.

Important actors in influencing the policy-making process in the four countries are various international organizations who, at the beginning of the 1990s, systematically involved policy-makers of all four countries in educational programmes on drug demand reduction. In that respect the United Nations International Drug Control Programme (UNDCP), the European Union through the PHARE projects, and the Pompidou Group of the Council of Europe played an important role. An analysis of study visits for policy-makers in the 1990s would probably show that the most influential policy-makers from all four countries attended the same study visits. Thus an informal network of policy-makers was established. Cooperation between the countries is formalized through a Memorandum of Understanding between the Visegrad countries, Slovenia and UNDCP. The document is important as it defines, among other things, cooperation on institutional development, the establishment of a co-ordinating body, and it also deals with drug demand reduction.[1]

Important roles were also played by international non-governmental organizations, such as the Soros foundation and the Lindsmith centre. International organizations influenced the development of a number of drug demand reduction programmes including methadone maintenance and needle exchange programmes. They also influenced the administrative structure in the field of drug demand reduction, for example by establishing co-ordination bodies in Slovenia.

Although external factors have significantly influenced the legislation on drug demand reduction, its development has been different in the four countries due to cultural, social, political and other reasons. Law enforcement and criminal legislation play a major role in developing legislation and programmes in the field of drug demand reduction. It can significantly influence the development of programmes such as methadone maintenance and needle exchange programmes. Suffice to say that in all countries included in the survey these programmes were introduced implying that the criminal legislation allows or tolerates provision of places and equipment for needle exchange and other harm reduction activities.

The following is a short description of the development of drug demand reduction legislation in the four countries:

In *Poland*[2] the first Law on the Prevention of Drug Dependence was adopted as early as 1985. It provided a basis for the activities of various ministries and the adoption of a Governmental Programme on Prevention of Drug Dependence. This programme has been re-adopted each year by the Council of Ministers. The main strategy in Poland is the National Programme Against Drug Abuse for 1991-2001. The law was amended and in 1997 a new law on Strategies to Counteract Drug Dependence was adopted. This law is important, since it was the first in Poland to penalize possession of illicit drugs (small quantities excepted).

In the *Czech Republic*[3] the policy on drug demand reduction was developed by the National Co-ordinating Office for Narcotics, which was established after signing the Agreement on the Establishment of the National Co-ordinating Office for Narcotics in 1991. The anti-drug policy of the Czech Republic focuses on prevention. A special law on drug demand reduction does not exist but the laws on health and welfare deal with issues such as treatment of drug addicts, social rehabilitation and methadone treatment.

In *Hungary*[4] the Criminal Code of 1993 prescribes severe punishment for trafficking and production of illegal drugs, and it declares drug addiction as a health problem by introducing the possibility of a convicted person choosing medical treatment over prison. There is no *lex specialis* on drug demand reduction in Hungary. A strategy on drug demand reduction was adopted in October 2000. This strategy emphasizes the importance of drug demand reduction policies. This is a shift from previous trends, where supply reduction was the main priority in Hungary.

In *Slovenia*,[5] the law specifically focusing on drug demand reduction, the Act on Prevention, Treatment and Rehabilitation of Drug Addicts, was adopted in the beginning of 2000. The law deals with prevention, treatment, social rehabilitation and after-care for illicit drug users. It defines responsible institutions for drug demand reduction and financing of non-governmental organizations. So far, there has not been any comprehensive formal strategy on drug demand reduction. According to the above-mentioned law, a strategy on drug demand reduction should be prepared and adopted by the Parliament in the near future.

Table 1: Institutional response to drug demand reduction

Country	Law on drug demand reduction	Strategy on drug demand reduction
Poland	Yes	Yes
Czech Republic	No	Yes
Hungary	No	Yes
Slovenia	Yes	No

Along with the adoption of drug demand reduction laws and strategies, roles and responsibilities of governmental institutions dealing with illicit drug use were re-defined. Traditionally illicit drugs were the domain of the ministries of interior and police, and the ministry of justice. When surveying the institutions being involved in drug demand reduction, it was noted that the key actors at governmental level are ministries responsible for health, education and social affairs.

In all four countries institutions and organizations dealing with drug demand reduction started activities before 1985. Their activities concentrated on medical treatment of illicit drug users. Only few non-governmental organizations were involved at that time. The development of institutions and organizations in the field of drug demand reduction has intensified in the beginning of the 1990s. The majority of governmental and non-governmental institutions were established between 1991 and 1994. In all countries except Poland more than 80% of non-governmental organizations started drug demand reduction activities after 1992.

One of the reasons Poland has started activities related to drug demand reduction earlier than Slovenia, Hungary and the Czech Republic is that illicit drug use has a longer tradition in Poland. The first systematic capturing of information about the problem of illicit drug use took place in the early 1920s and the first law on drug demand reduction passed the Polish parliament in 1985.[6] All non-governmental organizations, with the exception of organizations in Poland, started to involve in drug demand reduction activities relatively late.

2 Division of labour between non-governmental and governmental organizations

The institutional response in the area of drug demand reduction is a compromise between needs on the one hand and institutional capacities, social possibilities, and resources on the other. Needs are not only determined by the factual scope and the nature of the drug problem, but also by the way the problem is perceived by experts, civil service, general public and risk population. The institutional needs are, on the one hand, clearly defined by the problem (e.g. physical consequences of an addiction define the need for detoxification facilities; high risk of transmission of infectious diseases defines the need for needle replacement programmes etc.). On the other hand different interpretations of the drug issue sometimes obscure the needs, depending which aspect is stressed (medical, social or hygienic aspect, importance of primary prevention or harm reduction etc.).

In the institutional context of drug demand reduction non-governmental organizations (NGOs) today play an important role in all countries reviewed. Depending on the legislation as well as on social and cultural traditions of individual countries (e.g. tradition of certain interest or religious organizations) these organizations include various professional or lay associations, charities, church organizations or foundations. Some NGOs have a similar organizational structure as governmental organizations (GOs), some are voluntary associations such as self-help organizations or non-profit voluntary organizations established on the basis of voluntary work and independence, such as associations in Slovenia. The formal structure of NGOs usually increases with growing demands for funding, because granting of financial resources is always related to certain formal requirements (type of registration and accounting of an organization, method of supervision of its activities etc.).

It is clear from the proportion of NGOs among drug demand reduction institutions in the countries reviewed (Table 2) that NGOs have an important role in the existing drug demand reduction systems. The proportion of NGOs among the institutions reviewed ranged between 34.8% in Hungary to 63.3% in Poland. While in Hungary, Poland and Slovenia approximately one third of NGOs were dealing with drug demand reduction exclusively, in the Czech Republic it was more than 60%. In all four countries reviewed NGOs were active both on the national and local level.

In view of the fact that private organizations do not play a significant role in the drug demand reduction area, this chapter does not analyse these organizations more in depth. There were in total six private organizations in the four countries (2 in the Czech Republic, 3 in Hungary, 2 in Poland and 1 in Slovenia). It seems that in none of the countries reviewed the present legislative and financial conditions are conducive for the involvement of private organizations in the field of anti-drug programmes. It can also be assumed that there is a persistent lack of trust towards the private sector in civil service, health care and social affairs. The possibility cannot be ruled out that in an environment of non-transparent and unclear legislation certain non-profit NGOs may in fact be "hidden" private organizations.

Table 2: Governmental and non-governmental organizations by involvement in drug-related activities

	Czech Republic		Hungary		Poland		Slovenia	
	GO n (%)	NGO n (%)	GO n (%)	NGO n (%)	GO n (%)	NGO n (%)	GO n (%)	NGO n (%)
DDR exclusively	5 (20.8)	14 (60.9)	6 (23.1)	6 (37.5)	4 (25)	12 (38.7)	5 (23.8)	4 (26.7)
DDR part of other activities	19 (79.2)	9 (39.1)	20 (79.9)	10 (62.5)	12 (75)	19 (61.3)	16 (76.2)	11 (73.3)
Total	24 (51.1)	23 (48.9)	26 (61.9)	16 (38.1)	16 (34)	31 (66)	21 (58.3)	15 (41.7)

2.1 *Legislative context*

Legislation determines whether at all and on which conditions certain types of institutions can be established. Legislative changes enabling decentralization of institutional power, related to principal changes in the political system at the end of the 1980s and beginning of the 1990s, had therefore primary importance for the emergence and development of non-state drug demand reduction organizations in post-communist countries. The only exception was the situation of drug demand institutions in Poland, where the legislative system enabled the establishments of NGOs already in the previous period. Tables 2 and 3 show that more than 50% of NGOs in Poland were founded before 1990 (almost 24% of NGOs in Poland were established before 1980) and that the same number of institutions (54.8% of all NGOs) started drug demand reduction programmes before 1990. In Poland, 25% of state organizations and 19.4% of non-profit, voluntary organizations started drug demand reduction programmes even earlier than 1984. While it is sometimes noted that NGOs cannot prove their sustainability, the Polish example shows that this is not always the case. It seems however, that long-standing NGOs sometimes adopt certain negative features of GOs (too formal organizational structure, low flexibility). NGOs founded before 1980 are more likely to be larger organizations with a clear formal structure and based on voluntary work. They are often directed by the notion of public interest, which is not exclusively focused on the drug issue (see Table 2). This might be another reason why 73.2% of NGOs in Poland worked with volunteers while in other countries the figure was not higher than 12.2% (Table 4).

Table 3: GOs and NGOs by date of establishment (results in percentages)

	Czech Republic		Hungary		Poland		Slovenia	
	GO	NGO	GO	NGO	GO	NGO	GO	NGO
before 1990	45.5	8.7	43.5	18.8	66.7	54.8	23.8	6.7
1990-1995	40.9	56.5	39.1	62.5	13.3	41.9	61.9	53.3
after 1995	13.6	34.8	17.4	18.8	20.0	3.2	14.3	40.0

Note: Data are missing from 15 organizations.

Table 4: GOs and NGOs by date of starting DDR programmes (in percentages)

	Czech Republic		Hungary		Poland		Slovenia	
	GO	NGO	GO	NGO	GO	NGO	GO	NGO
before 1990	20.8	0	28.0	12.5	50.0	54.8	19.0	0
1990-1995	62.5	60.9	40.0	62.5	18.8	38.7	61.9	53.3
after 1995	16.7	39.1	32.0	25.0	31.3	6.5	19.0	46.7

Note: Data are missing from 10 organizations.

The data presented in Tables 3 and 4 clearly indicate to which extent the liberalization of society prompts differentiation of institutions. Most drug demand reduction programmes (both in GOs and NGOs) which were initiated before 1990 started in Poland and Hungary. The youngest drug demand reduction programmes implemented by NGOs were reported by organizations in Slovenia and the Czech Republic, which may have both positive consequences (differentiation of the institutional context of drug demand reduction, release of new resources, efforts to initiate missing programmes, transfer of programmes to new regions, growth of the above-standard offer etc.), as well as negative consequences (instability and poor continuity of programmes, attempts to use the significance of the drug issue as a means to obtain funding, instability of resources etc.).

2.2 *Personnel and financial resources*

The growing needs as well as growing possibilities (with emergence of new institutions) in the field of services aimed at drug demand reduction on the one hand, and growing professional and financial resources on the other hand, are two factors mutually influencing each other. During the 1990s the number of organizations with a legal status was growing, which was not possible under the previous legislation. With the changing institutional structure in the drug demand reduction field also the professional demands were changing. Professional resources multiplied and – what is especially important – adjusted themselves according to demand and to the more differentiated institutional context. Thanks to NGOs, the institutional response was expanded and psychosocial and hygienic aspects at the onset (start) of addiction and follow-up care started to receive more attention. The focus shifted from mainly medical treatment for drug addicts to primary prevention and low-threshold contact establishments. The importance of social work was recognized more widely. International experience and changes in the educational system after 1990 led to a broader and more differentiated personnel pool in the countries reviewed.

Mechanical comparison of mean figures of the individual institutions may be misleading (it might reflect the choice of institutions rather than the actual situation). We therefore sought to identify the proportion of employees dealing exclusively with drug issues (DDR staff in Table 5) out of the total average number of paid staff (Staff in Table 5). The result is summarized in Table 5. While in state organizations on average only between 8.4% (Slovenia) and 31.1% (Hungary) of staff were employed in programmes dealing with drug issues, in NGOs between 48.3 (Czech Republic) and 71.2% of paid staff was dealing with drug issues. These figures tell us the same as Table 2 (NGOs more frequently deal with drug issues exclusively), but at the same time they suggest that the intensity is higher than it is shown in Table 2. It may also be that state institutions in the countries reviewed employed more auxiliary staff than NGOs and that some GOs were dealing with drug issues only marginally or because they "had to". High numbers of staff in GOs might be distorted by large central state institutions and hospital wards for addicts. In general, the larger the country (Poland), the more state employees.

Table 5: GOs and NGOs by staff and legal status (results in average n/organization)

	Czech Republic		Hungary		Poland		Slovenia	
	GO	NGO	GO	NGO	GO	NGO	GO	NGO
Staff	82,8	14,3	53,1	9,5	29,4	51,4	41,5	6,4
DDR staff	14,2	6,9	16,5	5,1	42,9	36,6	3,5	4,1
DDR per cent	17,1	48,3	31,1	53,7	14,6	71,2	8,4	64,1
Volunteers	0	10,8	0,1	12,2	0	73,2	20	11,5

Czech, Polish and in general also Hungarian GOs did not employ volunteers. On the contrary, Slovenian state organizations employed more volunteers than NGOs (20). At same time, Slovenian organizations reported on average the lowest numbers of staff.

Table 6 shows mean figures of staff with university-level education employed by governmental and non-governmental institutions in individual countries. Table 6 reflects the situation on the labour market in the given country and also to which extent drugs are perceived as a medical, psychological or social problem. In light of the proportion of prevailing professions in drug demand reduction programmes in individual countries we may for example assume that in Hungary the tendency is to treat drug addiction predominantly as a medical problem (on average the highest number of physicians in both GOs and NGOs). In Poland, drugs are seen more as a psychological problem (on average the highest number of psychologists). In Slovenia, drugs are seen as a psychosocial problem and state institutions put emphasis on educating people. The Czech Republic is economizing on professional staff (on average the lowest numbers of staff with university education per institution). However, it is obvious that some of these differences are a result of the selection of institutions.

Table 6: DDR organizations by training of staff and legal status (results in average n/organization)

	Czech Republic		Hungary		Poland		Slovenia	
	GO	NGO	GO	NGO	GO	NGO	GO	NGO
Physician	0,9	0,2	7,0	2,2	0,3	0,7	1,0	0,4
Psychiatrist	1,1	0,6	1,7	0,5	0,9	0,9	0,2	0
Psychologist	1,1	0,9	0,6	0,4	8,9	7,9	2,1	0,9
Sociologist	0,1	0,1	0,2	0,2	0,6	0,2	1,1	0,5
Social worker	0,5	1,3	1,1	1,0	0,1	0,2	0,7	0,8
Public health officer	0,1	0	0,2	1,2	0	0,1	0,3	0,1
Educationalist	1,4	1,1	0,7	0,8	3,3	9,0	5,9	0,9

By comparing GOs and NGOs, it is clear that in the Czech Republic, Hungary and Slovenia NGOs employ on average less staff with university-level education. These findings correspond to a certain extent to the criticism of some NGOs that they operate on a poor professional level. The situation in Poland however is reversed, with NGOs employing more staff with university-level education (e.g. educationalists) than GOs. We may therefore assume that long-term experiences (compared with other countries, Polish NGOs are on average the longest-standing ones) prove increased demand for professional education. A comparison of GOs and NGOs also shows certain differences in their profiles: GOs employ on average more physicians, psychiatrists and psychologists, whereas NGOs employ more professionals specialized in social work, public health and education. These differences are least distinct in Slovenia. Programme orientation of organizations (their activities) and also their attitudes towards the drug problem and its solution will probably correspond to these differences in profiles of GOs and NGOs.

Table 7 informs about the average budget of GOs and NGOs in 1998. Table 9 shows sources of funding as reported by GOs and NGOs. The figures are only approximate and are of disputable validity. The number of institutions (also given in per cent), which did not provide an answer to this question, is an indication to what extent the financing of GOs and NGOs in individual countries is transparent. The proportion of budget dedicated by GOs and NGOs to DDR programmes (DDR in per cent in Table 7) has a more informative value than the comparison of average budgets in individual countries.

Table 7: Average budget of DDR organizations in 1998 and legal status (results in thousand EUR – average values)

	Czech Republic		Hungary		Poland		Slovenia	
	GO	NGO	GO	NGO	GO	NGO	GO	NGO
Total budget	3875,1	135,6	39013,6	1656,5	18776,3	774,8	69000,8	223,9
DDR budget	421,2	59,7	435,8	31,3	231,2	203,0	153,7	52,0
DDR per cent	10,9	4,4	1,1	1,9	1,2	26,2	0,2	23,2

With the exception of the Czech Republic state organizations were allocating on average less resources for drug programmes (in proportion to the overall budget) than NGOs. Among NGOs, the relatively lowest proportion of budget dedicated to DDR programmes was reported by Hungarian organizations (1.9%), the highest proportion was reported from Poland (26.2%). This disproportion may depend on the exclusivity of interest in drug issues and on the proportion of DDR staff in the total number of staff. It may also reflect the adoption of institutional structures of non-governmental institutions in the country. Polish and Slovenian NGOs reported on average the highest numbers of staff employed exclusively in DDR programmes. Polish NGOs also reported the highest mean DDR budget (4 times higher than in NGOs in other countries). However, we have to be very careful when interpreting data on budgets as it is a very sensitive issue and some institutions did not provide figures.

The number of GOs and NGOs revealing their budgets and the costs of their DDR programmes (Table 8) may be regarded as *per se* valid and relatively important information. NGOs in all four countries were more informed or willing to provide information about their budget (it was a common practice for them), while GOs either did not know their budget situation (large state institutions) or did not disclose it for other reasons. This discrepancy was most marked in the Czech Republic and Poland, where more than 90% of NGOs disclosed their budget, while less than 50% of GOs did not disclose it. Surprisingly the situation was reverse in Hungary, where relatively more GOs provided information about their budget compared to NGOs.

Table 8: **Information about budgets**

	Czech Republic		Hungary		Poland		Slovenia	
	GO	NGO	GO	NGO	GO	NGO	GO	NGO
Disclosed budg.	11	21	18	12	7	30	14	12
(%)	45.8	91.3	69.2	75	43.8	96.8	66.7	80
Disclosed DDR budget	19	21	13	10	7	28	16	13
(%)	79.2	91.3	50	62,5	43.8	90.8	76.2	86.7

Table 9: **DDR organizations by source of funding (in 1998) and legal status (average in percentages)**

	Czech Republic		Hungary		Poland		Slovenia	
	GO	NGO	GO	NGO	GO	NGO	GO	NGO
Foreign sources*	4.3	8.8	2.3	18.5	3.4	6.7	2.8	14.9
Public / Govern. agencies	95.6	71.6	91.3	50.2	90.0	80.2	92.4	54.4
Private sector	0	5.3	2.1	26.7	0	4.5	0	3.1
Voluntary Organ.	0	1.3	0	1.4	0	1.3	0.4	0
Fees / Individual donations	0	12.8	4.3	3.1	0	5.6	4.3	12.0

Note: * Total funding from international organizations, foreign governments' agencies and other foreign organizations

NGOs in all four countries included in the survey reported a larger proportion of foreign resources within the overall budget than GOs. In the Czech Republic and Poland NGOs reported approximately two times higher funding from abroad than GOs. In Hungary the figure was eight times higher in NGOs than in GOs. In Hungary and Slovenia GOs reported that they were receiving funds for DDR programmes also from individual donations. The highest proportion of foreign resources within the overall budget was reported in Hungary and Slovenia. The lowest proportion of foreign resources within the overall budget was reported in Poland, where the budget of NGOs came mainly from state funds. This also supports the hypothesis that the longer NGOs exist the more they resemble to a certain extent GOs. Among other things these NGOs master the ways to obtain state funding and "get accustomed" to it, which may be a stabilizing factor for such an institution and a stimulus for long-term programmes. The lowest proportion of income from state sources was reported by NGOs in Hungary.

2.3 *Goals and activities*

Goals in the drug demand reduction field stated by organizations in individual countries not only tell about the actually implemented activities but also which activities are regarded as important for the particular GOs or NGOs and for tackling the drug problem. A number of factors determine which specific drug-related issues are addressed by the institutions reviewed. Besides specific national DDR features and institutional differences they may also reflect the selection of those institutions, which are the most notable among GOs and NGOs in each country. Each organization reported not more than three goals. The following table shows which share of organizations formulated a goal in a particular area. The proportion is calculated from the total number of GOs or NGOs (N) in a given country.

Table 10: Different DDR goals by status of organization and country (results in percentages)

	Czech Republic		Hungary		Poland		Slovenia	
	GO	NGO	GO	NGO	GO	NGO	GO	NGO
N	24	23	26	16	16	31	21	15
DDR (general statements)	25	47.8	23.1	50	6.3	6.5	47.6	20
Prevention/ Inf.	50	91.3	38.5	68.8	81.3	71	47.6	66.7
Treatment and care	29.2	39.1	42.3	18.8	37.5	38.7	33.3	53.3
Rehabilitation	25	17.4	11.5	6.3	12.5	29	9.5	26.7
Research/ documentation	20.8	-	3.8	-	6.3	3.2	19	-
Funding	25	4.3	11.5	6.3	-	-	14.3	-
Co-ordination	29.2	-	7.7	-	25	-	14.3	6.7
Interest repres.		-	4.3	-	-	-	-	- -
Policy develop./ legislation	16.7	4.3	-	-	12.5	-	19	13.3
Training of profes.	12.5	21.7	26.9	18.8	25	16.1	14.3	13.3

Prevention and distribution of information were the two most frequently stated goals by GOs and NGOs in all four countries. While in the Czech Republic, Hungary and Slovenia prevention activities were carried out mainly by NGOs, in Poland prevention was more frequently cited as a goal by GOs. NGOs in the Czech Republic and Slovenia more frequently than GOs cited treatment and care as a goal. In Hungary the situation was reverse and in Poland the ratio between GOs and NGOs was balanced. GOs in the Czech Republic and Hungary stated more frequently rehabilitation as their goal, while in Poland and Slovenia this goal was more characteristic for NGOs. Research and documentation were in all countries characteristic for GOs rather than NGOs, as well as funding, co-ordination, policy development and legislation. Only one organization, an NGO in the Czech Republic, stated interest representation. This NGO (named ANO) is an umbrella organization for NGOs active in the field of DDR. There was only one NGO (in Slovenia) which stated co-ordination as its goal.

While interpreting results compiled in Table 11 it is important to take into account that the institutions included in the survey were encouraged to cite up to three different prevention, treatment and care activities. Table 11 shows only the per cent of organizations, which stated one, two or three activities in the given area. The results are based on information that a given organization was implementing a particular activity in previous years. The information was not verified as was the level of implementation, which means that different activities could have been implemented in a largely different way.

Table 11: DDR activities reported by legal status and country (results in percentages)

	Czech Republic		Hungary		Poland		Slovenia	
	GO	NGO	GO	NGO	GO	NGO	GO	NGO
Prevention	91.7	100	65.4	87.5	81.3	96.8	90.5	93.3
Treatment	33.3	56.5	53.8	31.3	31.3	64.5	33.3	60
Rehabilitation	25	34.8	26.9	25	25	58.1	38.1	40
Research	66.7	34.8	42.3	37.5	68.8	35.5	57.1	60
Funding	45.8	17.4	34.6	40	25	25.8	23.8	6.7
Co-ordination	58.3	30.4	42.3	26.7	68.8	61.3	71.4	33.3
Interest represent./ protection of civic rights	12.5	26.1	3.8	12.5	25	38.7	25	60
Policy develop.	66.7	34.8	23.1	-	81.3	48.4	61.9	73.3
Training	66.7	65.2	65.4	50	68.8	77.4	57.1	73.3

Among all activities, state and non-state institutions in all four countries were most frequently involved in various prevention activities. More emphasis on prevention can be observed in NGOs, either because they see prevention as a key element within drug demand reduction, or because certain prevention activities are relatively easy to report. NGOs operating in the Czech

Republic, Poland and Slovenia most frequently reported treatment and rehabilitation activities, while in Hungary GOs were more likely to be involved in these activities. However, these activities differ greatly (see details in Table 13). The fact that NGOs active in the DDR area are well integrated in the institutional context and play an important role, was reflected in the finding that NGOs also participate in activities such as co-ordination or policy development. In Slovenia NGOs are even more involved in DDR legislation and policy initiatives than state organizations. It is rather surprising that in Hungary more NGOs than GOs mentioned their involvement in funding activities (granting or mediating of financial resources). Interest representation and especially protection of human and civic rights, i.e. activities which are focused mainly on changing the public opinion and the protection of rights of drug users, are in all four countries dominated by NGOs.

Table 12: Preventive activities reported by legal status and country (in percentages)

	Czech Republic		Hungary		Poland		Slovenia	
	GO	NGO	GO	NGO	GO	NGO	GO	NGO
Lectures/ seminars	58.3	82.6	34.6	43.8	37.5	61.3	33.3	26.7
Distribution of inform. materials	37.5	26.1	15.4	50	18.8	32.3	61.9	60
Training program.	4.2	8.7	7.7	18.8	18.8	29	19	26.7
Counselling	-	4.3	3.8	31.3	12.5	12.9	28.6	33.3
Street work	4.2	8.7	-	-	-	-	-	20
Organization of information points, clubs, camps	4.2	17.4	7.7	18.8	-	12.9	9.5	13.3
Special events	4.2	8.7	3.8	-	6.3	3.2	14.3	13.3
Public information campaigns	-	8.7	11.5	-	25	9.7	14.3	6.7

Table 12 shows that prevention programmes in the DDR area are in the majority of countries focused mainly on mediation of information (lectures and workshops in schools, publishing of information about harm caused by drugs, and drug misuse in general etc.), although it seems that more differentiated and targeted prevention programmes are beginning to appear. In the Czech Republic, Poland but also in Hungary lectures and seminars are among the most popular prevention activities, whereas in Slovenia the distribution of information materials prevails. The majority of prevention activities were targeted at students, young people, and the general population. There were no significant differences between individual countries in this respect. As far as the distribution of labour between state and non-state institutions is concerned, it seems that NGOs are slightly more active in the area of prevention, or that they state prevention activities as often (or as easily?) as GOs.

NGOs were unequivocally more active in training programmes and in organizing information points, clubs or summer camps. In the Czech Republic and Slovenia, NGOs also more frequently organized street work, whereas organizations in Poland and Hungary did not report any involvement in street work. This finding might not reflect the real situation but might be related to the limited selection of organizations. Although some prevention activities suit better the legal status, personnel structure and focus of either governmental or non-governmental organizations, in many respects GOs and NGOs became competitors and may take over each other's activities regardless of their status.

Table 13: Treatment and care activities by legal status and country (in percentages)

	Czech Republic		Hungary		Poland		Slovenia	
	GO	NGO	GO	NGO	GO	NGO	GO	NGO
Individ. counselling	-	17.4	3.8	6.3	6.3	19.4	14.3	53.3
Treatment (general)	16.7	13	26.9	6.3	12.5	16.1	9.5	6.7
Therap. community	4.2	13	-	-	6.3	12.9	-	-
Group psychotherapy	4.2	21.7	-	6.3	-	9.7	-	6.7
Family therapy	-	8.7	-	-	-	16.1	-	-
Day centres	-	8.7	3.8	-	-	9.7	-	20
Outpatient clinic	16.7	8.7	-	-	12.5	6.5	4.8	-
After-care	-	-	7.7	12.5	-	6.5	-	6.7
Methadone treatm.	4.2	-	-	-	-	-	14.3	-
Needle exchange, condom distribution	-	4.3	3.8	6.3	-	-	-	6.7
Medical care	-	-	3.8	-	-	3.2	4.8	6.7
Referral	-	-	-	-	-	3.2	-	6.7

In the field of treatment and care a higher differentiation of activities can be observed than in the area of prevention, as well as bigger differences in representation of certain activities in state and non-state organizations. Czech GOs organized primarily de-toxification programmes, hospital treatment for drug addicts and outpatient clinics. NGOs usually cited individual counselling, therapeutic communities, group and family therapy as main activities in this area. The situation in other countries was similar, with certain variations. In Hungary and Poland de-toxification was organized mainly by non-governmental organizations. In Hungary only one state organization reportedly maintained a day centre. Methadone programmes were reported only by one state institution in the Czech Republic and three GOs in Slovenia. Other harm reduction activities (i.e. needle exchange and condom distribution) were a priority mostly for NGOs, whereas in Poland no organization reported this type of DDR activity. In Poland and Slovenia family therapy was not "popular" among organizations included in the survey. Organizations in the Czech Republic and Hungary did not cite referral as one of their activities. In the Czech Republic after-care was included in rehabilitation.

Table 14: Rehabilitation activities reported by legal status and country (in percentages)

	Czech Republic		Hungary		Poland		Slovenia	
	GO	NGO	GO	NGO	GO	NGO	GO	NGO
Day after-care centres	8.3	13	11.5	-	6.3	6.5	4.8	-
Hostels	-	8.7	-	-	-	12.9	-	-
Group therapy and meetings	12.5	8.7	7.7	-	6.3	22.6	9.5	20
Assistance in social readaptation	-	4.3	7.7	25	6.3	12.9	-	13.3
Assistance in finding housing	-	-	-	-	-	9.7	-	6.7
Reintegration within their families	-	-	-	6.3	-	-	-	6.7
Help and motivation in education	-	-	-	-	-	-	-	20
Assistance with employment	-	4.3	-	-	-	9.7	9.5	13.3
Support of mutual support of drug users and their involvement in street work	-	-	-	6.3	6.3	-	-	6.7
Individual counselling, legal advice	-	4.3	7.7	-	-	3.2	23.8	6.7

In the majority of the countries reviewed, with the exception of Hungary, NGOs are more active than GOs in the area of rehabilitation. However, in general only very few organizations reported any forms of re-socialization included in the survey. Despite the incessantly stressed social aspect of the drug problem and the importance of adequate social and work integration of drug addicts, almost half of the activities included in the survey were not carried out by any organizations in the Czech Republic and Hungary. Slovenian NGOs reported the most differentiated system of social support and after-care, including day after-care centres, hostels, and various other forms of social assistance. Absence of certain forms of rehabilitation seems to confirm not only their high personnel and financial costs, but also the hypothesis that (compared for example with the large number of prevention programmes) the bulk of work in the drug area is carried out by only a few organizations, and that a large number of institutions deal with drug issues only marginally and for different reasons. On the basis of the survey results we may also assume that the majority of governmental organizations active in the drug area does not pay adequate attention to the social aspect of drug use and to family, social and work rehabilitation. There is generally an emphasis on the medical aspect of drug use and the social aspect of the problem does not – despite official statements to the contrary – receive the attention it deserves.

2.4 *Attitudes and perceptions of the drug issue*

The kind of activities an organization carries out and its experience and focus determine the way the organization perceives the institutional context and its weak and strong sides. The following Table 15 informs about attitudes to national policies adopted by state and non-state organizations in individual countries. The table reflects the share of organizations which assess the national policy in a certain way. N is the number of state and non-state organizations, which cited advantages or disadvantages of the national DDR policies (the percentages in the table are calculated out of the total N).

Governmental and non-governmental organizations in individual countries have similar attitudes about the strengths of national anti-drug policies. There are, however, major differences when comparing the countries with each other. In the Czech Republic the governmental and non-governmental institutions differ most in their assessment of the effectiveness of networks and cooperation, level of repression, strengthening of legal control (which is highly appreciated by GOs), and in the assessment of effectiveness of harm reduction programmes (more appreciated by NGOs). In Hungary both GOs and NGOs are quite reserved when assessing positive sides of the national policy. GOs compared to NGOs appreciate more that there is awareness of the drug problem and public discussion on drug issues. In Poland, NGOs appraise the quality of therapeutic programmes more positively than GOs. State organizations on the other hand value the level of repression and strengthening of legal control. In Slovenia, NGOs stress public discussion, awareness of the drug problem, effectiveness of drug networks, and cooperation. Slovenian state organizations perceive the effective DDR policy, legislation, clear concept, and prevention programmes as a strong aspect of the national programme.

Table 15: Main strengths of the national policy on the drug problem by legal status and country (in percentages)

	Czech Republic		Hungary		Poland		Slovenia	
	GO	NGO	GO	NGO	GO	NGO	GO	NGO
N	22	21	25	12	15	23	17	14
Awareness of the drug problem, public discussion, understanding of the problem	18.2	19	40	25	46.7	43.5	5.9	21.4
Efficient network, effective cooperation	50	28.6	4	0	40	8.7	11.8	28.6
Competent, expert-based	13.6	9.5	4	8.3	13.3	8.7	0	7.1
Prevention programmes	27.3	28.6	12	16.7	60	56.5	29.4	14.3
Therapy programmes	13.6	9.5	12	0	6.7	34.8	23.5	0
Harm reduction progr.	13.6	23.8	0	0	6.7	4.3	35.3	42.9
Policy, conception, legislation	36.4	33.3	4	0	26.7	30.4	64.7	50
Supply control, law enforcement	22.7	14.3	8	8.3	33.3	13	5.9	0
Other	9.1	19	12	8.3	6.7	0	17.6	28.6
No strengths at all	4.3	9.5	40	41.7	0	13	11.8	0

In all four countries inefficient and unsuitable anti-drug policies, as well as lack of concept in anti-drug policies and lack of co-ordination were regarded as the weakest points of national policies. This suggests that in any context these are sensitive issues and difficult-to-solve problems. Lack of co-ordination in this context is equivalent to poor co-ordination of anti-drug programmes and institutions involved in the field, insufficient vertical communication, and inconsistent strategies and approaches. In this respect state and non-state institutions did not differ greatly. However, these results are not unequivocal. What one organization perceives as negative can be viewed positively by another organization. While 45.5% of governmental and 36.4% of non-governmental organizations in the Czech Republic criticized co-ordination, almost the same number of organizations regarded it as a main strength of the national policy. As far as the evaluation of co-ordination of DDR programmes is concerned, Polish organizations were equally ambivalent, while a negative assessment prevailed in Hungary and Slovenia.

Table 16: **Main weaknesses of the national policy on the drug problem by legal status and country (in percentages)**

	Czech Republic		Hungary		Poland		Slovenia	
	GO	NGO	GO	NGO	GO	NGO	GO	NGO
N	22	22	25	12	16	29	19	15
Lack of awareness of the drug problem	4.5	9.1	12	0	12.5	37.9	10.5	13.3
Lack of professionals	4.5	22.7	4	8.3	0	13.8	0	0
Ineffective programmes	13.6	4.5	12	8.3	18.8	24.1	0	20
Focus on law enforcement, repressive approach	4.5	22.7	8	8.3	6.3	17.2	10.5	6.7
Lack of policy, lack of conceptual approach and progamme of priorities	68.2	72.7	48	33.3	75	72.4	84.2	60
Lack of co-ordination	45.5	36.4	44	33.3	43.8	24.1	68.4	46.7
Lack of information and research	0	0	8	0	12.5	0	15.8	13.3
Insufficient funding, financial problems	31.8	27.8	20	16.7	43.8	62.1	5.3	33.3
Lack of evaluation, control and monitoring of program.	0	4.5	0	16.7	12.5	0	21.1	6.7
Barriers in development of non-governmental institutions	0	0	0	0	6.3	20.7	0	0

A clearer differentiation in the attitudes of state and non-state institutions can be seen in some other areas. Non-state organizations in the Czech Republic and Poland criticize the existing policy as being too repressive towards drug users. In Hungary and Slovenia the attitudes of both GOs and NGOs were less critical. Non-governmental institutions in the Czech Republic, Poland and Hungary criticized the lack of experts in the anti-drug area. Only non-governmental organizations in Poland claimed that there are problems and barriers, which prevent the development of non-governmental institutions.

2.5 *Conclusions*

Based on the results of this study it can be summarized that in all the countries included in the survey there are rather extensive networks of organizations active in the anti-drug field, which differ with regard to their legal status and implemented activities. Although only few institutions, the majority of them non-governmental organizations, were dealing with drug-related issues exclusively at the time of the survey, their number is nevertheless increasing. These organizations also continue to broaden their range of activities and make them more specific. Non-governmental, non-profit organizations play an important role within the existing institutional context. Gradually a differentiation of labour between governmental organizations and non-governmental organizations is occurring, as well as a differentiation between individual organizations regardless of their legal status.

Non-governmental, non-profit organizations, which emerged especially in the beginning of the 1990s, quickly took over the territory not saturated by governmental organizations, respectively the territory in which the existing legislation and personnel resources did not enable state organizations to operate. With the credo "somebody has to do it" the Slovenian NGOs for example started the first methadone and replacement programmes, which are not run by state organizations. Other activities of NGOs are to a major part determined by human resources (important aspects are the professional composition, experience and interests of a team) as well as financial resources. NGOs often run programmes in areas, which the state with its directly managed agencies addresses only to a limited extent or not at all (e.g. street work programmes, programmes of early intervention, harm reduction, therapeutic communities, after-care programmes). The principal advantage of NGOs lies in their higher flexibility and sensitivity to the needs of the drug scene. We can assume that in the future productivity and the success of a programme will play an increasingly important role regardless of the status of the organization, which means that successful organizations will expand into areas "traditionally" covered by other types of organizations.

By comparing the state and non-governmental organizations reviewed it may be assumed that:

- Non-governmental organizations employ on average less staff than state organizations. However, NGOs have less support staff and more qualified employees and volunteers who are more involved in drug demand reduction programmes.
- The budget of the majority of NGOs is on average more transparent and information about their budget is more easily available than in GOs. The transparency of NGOs' budgets often has a legal background. NGOs more often than GOs use foreign resources. NGOs largely depend on funds from public and governmental sources, which form more than half of their budget.

- It may be assumed that the longer NGOs exist they tend to adopt a more formal structure, increase and differentiate their staff, and become more dependent on state sources. In accordance with the changing financial and personnel resources they differentiate and at the same time stabilize their activities, and are involved in longer-term programmes.
- Non-governmental organizations are active in all types of drug demand reduction programmes. NGOs are also involved in the legislation process in the relevant areas, in policy development, training, and co-ordination.
- More emphasis on prevention observed among non-governmental organizations (as a declared goal and activity) may reflect both the fact that non-governmental organizations (or their staff) are more socially oriented and understand the problem of drugs in a broader context, but also the fact that traditional prevention programmes are in general easier to implement (they require lower costs, lower experience and a lower level of personal involvement). The majority of prevention programmes consisted of lectures and seminars for young people and the general public, as well as the production and distribution of information materials.
- Non-governmental organizations are more often oriented towards harm reduction (e.g. street work, needle exchange and condom distribution). They are also more active in certain socially-oriented programmes (e.g. clubs, summer camps, group therapy). This is reflected in the staffing of non-governmental organizations, which employ more professional social workers, public health workers, educationalists and family therapists.
- Activities of non-governmental organizations in the areas of treatment, care and rehabilitation are more differentiated. This means that non-governmental organizations are more flexible than state organizations in engaging in new programmes and venturing into "niches" within the institutional context. They are clearly more active especially in the sphere of rehabilitation and re-socialisation of drug addicts. However, out of the total number of non-governmental organizations there are only a few organizations that are involved in this respect. The majority of governmental organizations in the countries reviewed do not pay enough attention to social, family and work rehabilitation.

Notes

1 The Memorandum of Understanding was signed in Prague in 1995. The aim of the document is to encourage the cooperation between Visegrad countries, Slovenia and UNDCP. It has three parts: Law enforcement, institutional building and drug demand reduction.

2 References to Polish legislation and policy-making are taken from J. Zamecka and R. Sobiech in this volume.

3 References to Czech legislation and policy-making are taken from L. Csémy and D. Krch in this volume.

4 References to Hungarian legislation and policy-making are taken from Z. Elekes and T. Gyry in this volume.

5 References to Slovenian legislation and policy-making are taken from B. Dekleva and R. Cvelbar Bek in this volume.

6 R. Sobiech and J. Zamecka in this volume.

CHAPTER 9

Are the Differences in Attitudes Towards Drugs Related to Different Demand Reduction Structures and Services?

Bojan Dekleva and Joanna Zamecka

1 Introduction

The emergence of illegal drug use in the last two decades in the four countries studied (Czech, Hungary, Slovenia, Poland) has been related to different policy responses. Mostly in the 1990s, many new activities, professional doctrines and specific policies have been developed. The totality of the emerging institutional response has sometimes been described as not enough planned, non-systematic or even chaotic.

The 1990s brought about also many new responses and strategies which had been unknown in the previous decades (or were at least not made explicit). Among the newest responses and ideas are programmes, which do not necessarily aim at the elimination of illegal drug use but instead shift the main purpose of drug control to harm reduction, risk reduction and regulation of use.[1] Because of the relative newness of these responses and because of the relative newness of the field of illegal drugs control itself in the four countries studied, it seems sometimes that the harm reduction orientation stands in direct opposition to other orientations. This is indicated by the fact that seemingly in the professional and public circles a kind of discourse develops which favours an "either-or" perception of the drug policy question.

Although we feel that this perception unnecessarily simplifies the complex questions of drug use and drug policies, we cannot escape the feeling that it – to some degree – actually informs and influences drug policy development, which on its turn is informed by specific lay and professional attitudes. This has been the reason to include the topic of drug-related attitudes of the researched organizations' representatives in our research.

2 Research background

The research instruments which were central in this analysis were taken from the British Social Attitudes project. The authors of the 13th British Social Attitudes report's chapter on illegal drugs claim that in the situation, where the state is promoting the "war against drugs" policy, while "a policy of 'harm reduction' dominates drug agencies throughout the country" it is important "to be able to gauge accurately the public mood" regarding illegal drugs. On the one hand, "... policy makers at least need to be aware of the extent to which their goals and assumptions have public backing", and on the other "... it can be important that the public be educated in the light of expert opinion".[2]

Starting from the comparative research on Swedish and British drug policies the authors discovered that the "distinction between 'liberal' and 'restrictive' perspectives towards drugs is of considerable use when considering attitudes towards drugs".[3] They describe the "restrictive perspective as one which sees drugs as dangerously addictive and which emphasizes abstinence on the part of the individual, and prohibition on the part of the policy makers. Conversely, a liberal perspective is more likely to accept that individuals can, and do, exert control over their use of drugs, that drug use is not necessarily harmful *per se* and that prohibition creates as many problems as it solves. Often other social problems are seen as greater threats to individuals and society than drug-taking".[4]

The development of the drug scale was guided by Thompson's derivation of an index of prejudice against homosexuals. The scale consists of eight items (statements) that were chosen from sixteen on the basis of a factor analysis and verifications of the scale in two rather big samples. The scale proved to be of high reliability.

Their analysis showed that more restrictive attitudes were characteristic for the older, less educated/qualified, more authoritarian and more xenophobic groups of respondents.[5] They were also found more often in respondents with conservative political party identification than in those with labour and liberal-democrat party identification. Their results also show that attitudes have been changing over time (during the last decade; towards more liberal ones) and that people who have used illegal drugs in their lifetime tend to have more liberal attitudes towards drugs.

For our research the data on the attitudes of drug agencies' professionals of two countries are more relevant because they can serve as a comparison framework for our results. The authors compared British and Swedish professionals and found that they differ very much in their attitudes.

3 The aims, presuppositions and hypotheses of the analysis

The main idea of this part of the research is that drug-related attitudes matter. In other words, that they in a systematic way discriminate between the four countries studied and that they are related to what DDR (drug demand reduction) organizations actually do and the way they are structured.

The main research aims were:

- to test the feasibility of the drug-related attitudes scale in the four countries,
- to compare the four countries regarding their DDR organizations' representatives attitudes, and
- to analyse the relations between these attitudes and the organizations' characteristics.

To reach these aims we have to make some assumptions. The most general one and the most critical one (given the fact that our study is based on comparative research) is that our instrument (the questionnaire) is valid and the responses to its questions are interculturally comparable. Another, more specific, and very crucial presupposition is that the responses/attitudes of the surveyed organizations' representatives are in a significant way related to the organizations' orientations as a whole which inform the organizations' activities, decisions and development. In our research we have unfortunately no possibility of testing this presupposition. But according to the available information, the surveyed organizations' representatives were mostly chosen among organizations' executive managers or professionals responsible for their activities. Because of this observation we assume that an organization representative's attitude actually represents his or her "organization's attitude".

In making hypotheses about the importance of the drug-related attitudes and their relations to the institutional output (organizations' characteristics and activities) we do not say much about the hypothesized causality. On the one hand the attitudes of managerial level staff probably influence the organizations' output; on the other hand they reflect the global conditions in their respective socio-political and cultural environments (countries). The relations between the mentioned (groups of) factors and indicators (attitudes, DDR activities, organizational characteristics, environmental conditions, etc.) are undoubtedly complex and dynamic, with time also being one of the most important factors.

4 The drug scale

The questionnaire used in our research included – besides many questions on organizations, their characteristics and activities – eight statements, which were expressing some typical opinions about the problem of illegal drugs. Four of them express liberal and four of them restrictive opinions (see Table 1). These statements address a number of key issues related to illegal drugs and can be heard in everyday discussions about drugs as well as in expert conferences and discussions about policy developments around the world. The attitudes were measured by 5-points Likert-type scales (1 = agree, 5 = disagree).

Of the 181 respondents in our sample, 170 expressed attributed scores to all eight statements, five gave answers to seven of eigth items only[7] and six did not answer any of the statements.

Table 2 shows the descriptive statistics of the responses to these eight items.[8] What the table does not show is that all the distributions are bi-modal (or in one case even three-modal), which means that our respondents tended to have very divergent opinions. This means that it is less relevant to speak about (statistical) means but let us nevertheless observe that on average our respondents took the most decisive (negative) positions on the following statements: *Taking illegal drugs can sometimes be beneficial* and that *Smoking cannabis should be legalized*. On the other side they were – on average – most close to the neutral point in judging the statement that *We need to accept that using illegal drugs is normal for some people's lives*. This is at the same time the statement where the opinions diverged the most (the largest standard deviation), while the most coherent set of opinions was related to the statement that *Smoking cannabis should be legalized* (the smallest standard deviation).

Table 1: The list of eight attitudes[6]

Liberal 1:	Taking illegal drugs can sometimes be beneficial.
Liberal 2:	Adults should be free to take any drug they wish.
Liberal 3:	We need to accept that using illegal drugs is normal for some people's lives.
Liberal 4:	Smoking cannabis should be legalized.
Restrictive 1:	The best way to treat people who are addicted to drugs is to stop them using drugs altogether.
Restrictive 2:	The use of illegal drugs always leads to addiction.
Restrictive 3:	Taking illegal drug is always morally wrong.
Restrictive 4:	All use of illegal drugs is misuse.

Table 2: Descriptive statistics of the scores on the eight statements (N=175)

Statements:	Minimum	Maximum	Mean	Std. Deviation
Taking drugs can be beneficial (L1)	1	5	4,08	1,43
Adults should be free to take drugs (L2)	1	5	3,21	1,79
Using drugs is sometimes normal (L3)	1	5	2,99	1,75
Cannabis should be legalized (L4)	1	5	4,13	1,33
Best treatment is not to use drugs (R1)	1	5	2,90	1,67
Use of drugs always leads to addiction (R2)	1	5	3,41	1,63
Taking drugs is morally wrong (R3)	1	5	3,44	1,63
All use of illegal drugs is misuse (R4)	1	5	2,57	1,66

Since all items are designated to relate to a single (hypothetical) dimension of attitudes on drugs we analysed the data using factor analysis.[9] The analysis of Pearson's correlation coefficients between pairs of items proves that almost all of them (25 of 28) are statistically significantly and strongly correlated (Table 3) in a meaningful (as hypothesized) way.

The factor analysis (principal component method with the criterion of factor extraction of eigenvalues greater than 1) initially extracted two factors, which together explained 56% of total variance. As the factors were rather highly correlated (in Oblimin solution) a one-factor solution was also tested. In this solution the communalities are between 0,30 and 0,56 and the extracted factor explained 43% of variance. The Cronbach's Alpha coefficient for the scale of eight items was 0,80. Table 4 shows the satiations of the general attitudinal factor with the eight statements.

Table 3: Correlations between eight attitudinal items

Statements:	1.	2.	3.	4.	5.	6.	7.	8.
1. Taking drugs can be beneficial	1,00							
2. Adults should be free to take drugs	0,39	1,00						
3. Using drugs is sometimes normal	0,42	0,52	1,00					
4. Cannabis should be legalized	0,56	0,36	0,36	1,00				
5. Best treatment is not to use drugs	#-,14	-0,31	-0,33	-0,34	1,00			
6. Use drugs always leads to addiction	-0,26	#-,06	-0,34	-0,22	0,30	1,00		
7. Taking drugs is morally wrong	-0,28	-0,25	-0,28	-0,31	0,22	0,45	1,00	
8. All use of illegal drugs is misuse	-0,44	-0,38	-0,42	-0,52	0,40	0,35	0,35	1,00

Note: All the correlations in the table are statistically significant, usually at the level p<0,001, except those, marked with the sign "#", which are not statistically significant.

Table 4: The factor structure matrix for the eight attitudes

Eight statements:	**Correlations with the factor:**
Taking drugs can be beneficial	0,687
Adults should be free to take drugs	0,635
Using drugs is sometimes normal	0,714
Cannabis should be legalized	0,723
Best treatment is not to use drugs	-0,563
Use of drugs always leads to addiction	-0,543
Taking drugs is morally wrong	-0,579
All use of illegal drugs is misuse	-0,753

Although Gould, Shaw and Ahrendt named this dimension "liberal/restrictive" we decided to label it "the permissive/restrictive factor" (or dimension), in order to avoid associations to the names of specific political parties or orientations.

On the basis of this factor analysis we conclude that it is possible to make a combined score/scale of all the eight original items by adding their individual scores.[10] For the aim of making the results more easily interpretable we divide this sum by 8. Consequently, the new composite attitudinal variable ranges theoretically between 1 and 5. The result 1 represents the most permissive attitude and the result 5 the most restrictive one.[11] The scale's mean is 3,26 and its standard deviation 1,06. The distribution of values on the new scale is much closer to the Gaussian normal distribution ideal.

For the following analyses we form – on the basis of this single attitudinal variable – three subgroups of responding organizations (by dividing the sample into three groups of almost equal size):

- the permissive group:
  N=58, score between 1,00 and 2,63, mean = 2,00,
- the moderate group:
  N=61, score between 2,71 and 3,88, mean = 3,37,
- the restrictive group:
  N=56, score between 4,00 and 5,00, mean = 4,44.

5 Comparison of four countries regarding their permissive/restrictive orientation

Table 5 shows general differences between countries regarding the average permissive/restrictive orientation of their organizations. On average the most restrictive attitudes are shown by Polish organizations and the most permissive by Slovenian ones, while the Czech ones are very close to the Slovenian ones, and the Hungarian are between the Polish and the Czech ones (but closer to the Polish ones). The differences are statistically significant (analysis of variance, $p<0{,}001$).

Table 5: Average drug-related attitude of four countries' organizations.

Country:	Mean	St. dev.	N
Czech Republic	2,79	0,83	45
Hungary	3,50	1,03	45
Poland	3,82	0,88	49
Slovenia	2,78	1,13	36
Total	3,26	1,06	175

Using the same instruments and methodology as Gould and others[12] allows us to compare our data with theirs. In comparing Sweden with Great Britain they found an average score of 3,8 for 80 Swedish organizations and a score of 2,0 for 40 British organizations. This means that Poland is in this aspect very close to Sweden (it is in fact even more restrictive than Sweden), while Slovenia and the Czech Republic are closer to Great Britain than to Sweden (but they are not as permissive as Great Britain is).

The four countries do not only differ in their average permissive/restrictive orientation but also in the distribution of organizations of different orientation (Table 6). In Poland and Hungary we can see more organizations with restrictive than with permissive attitudes, and in Slovenia and the Czech Republic the opposite is true. While Poland has a majority of restrictive organizations and Slovenia a majority of permissive ones, Slovenia is the only country with – even in the classification of organizations in three groups – a bi-modal distribution. This means, that – with a majority of permissive organizations – it has more restrictive organizations than moderate ones. In this characteristic it differs from the Czech Republic, which has a very similar (overall permissive) average, but with – nearly – as many moderate organizations as permissive ones (Table 6). In this comparison Slovenia looks as the most heterogeneous or the most polarized country among the four. Hungary seems to be the only one with a majority of organizations with moderate positions. Similar conclusions can be drawn from comparing the standard deviations of permissiveness/restrictiveness, with Slovenia having the largest (of the four) and the Czech Republic the smallest (Table 5).

Table 6: Restrictive, moderate and permissive organizations by country

		Permissiveness/Restrictiveness			**Total**
Country		Permissive group	Moderate group	Restrictive group	
Czech R.	Count	22	18	5	45
	% within Country	48,9	40,0	11,1	100,0
Hungary	Count	10	19	16	45
	% within Country	22,2	42,2	35,6	100,0
Poland	Count	7	16	26	49
	% within Country	14,3	32,7	53,1	100,0
Slovenia	Count	19	8	9	36
	% within Country	52,8	22,2	25,0	100,0
Total	Count	58	61	56	175
	% within Country	33,1	34,9	32,0	100,0

Table 7: The ratio between the number of restrictive and permissive organizations in the four countries

Country	**Ratio between restrictive and permissive organizations**
Czech Republic	0,2
Hungary	1,6
Poland	3,7
Slovenia	0,5

6 Permissive/restrictive orientation and some organizational characteristics

The following organizations' characteristics were analysed regarding their permissive/restrictive orientation:

- Time of founding
- Legal status
- Level of operation
- DDR exclusive/inclusive orientation
- Presence of specific groups of staff (e.g. voluntary workers or medical staff).

6.1 Time of founding

In this chapter we analyse the relation between the founding time of organizations and their attitudes. The hypothesis could be that the newer organizations (those, which have been founded more recently) would show more often a more permissive orientation, while the older, more traditional ones would also have more traditional, in this case, restrictive drug-related attitudes.

Table 8 shows that organizations with a more permissive orientation tend to have been founded later than the moderate and the restrictive ones. The average difference between them is about four years, with the average founding year of the permissive organizations being 1986,8.

Table 8: Average time of founding of organizations of different orientation

Permissiveness/Restrictiveness	**Mean**	**N**	**Std. Deviation**
Permissive group	1986,8	58	18,4
Moderate group	1981,1	55	23,9
Restrictive group	1982,8	56	20,9
Total	1983,6	169	21,2

The global differences in time of founding between permissive and restrictive organizations could be also due to a specific interaction between countries, attitudes and times of founding of organizations. If for instance in a country, where the organizational system was built earlier, the predominant orientation would be restrictive (irrespective of the time of founding of organizations) and vice versa, we could find a strong relation between the permissive/restrictive orientation and time of founding, which would be produced only because of systematic differences among countries regarding the time of the most intensive development (and setting) of their DDR institutional system. To test this possibility we calculated the average time of founding of DDR organizations in the four countries (Table 9).

Table 9: Average time of founding of organizations in the four countries

Country	**Mean**	**N**	**Std. Deviation**
Czech Republic	1984,40	47	21,47
Hungary	1989,56	43	8,94
Poland	1975,81	48	27,51
Slovenia	1987,00	37	17,10
Total	1983,86	175	20,84

The data in Table 9 only partly confirm the hypothesis described before. The differences between founding year of permissive and restrictive organizations could be due to the fact that in Poland, where organizations are "older", they are also on average more restrictive, while in the Czech Republic and Slovenia, where they are "younger", they are predominantly permissive. By using this explanation we would expect that the most permissive organizations were to be found in Hungary which is obviously not the case. Therefore, it can be tentatively concluded that there are at least two factors influencing the organizations' drug-related attitudes: the country of their origin and the time of their founding.

Comparing means in Table 8 could be misleading also because organizations' founding years are not normally distributed. While the majority of organizations have been founded in the last decade there were some organizations founded as early as in 1910. There might be also some inconsistencies in collecting data on founding years because during the time of the change of political systems (around 1990) some of the organizations, which had been in fact founded many years ago, changed their status, their affiliations, and might have been – only formally – re-founded. It is to be doubted that the researchers in the four countries documented these complex and sometimes confusing changes in the same (consistent) way.

Because of this argument we decide to analyse the relation between the founding time and the permissive/restrictive orientation also in a categorical way (instead of by calculating means). Table 10 compares specifically two halves of the 1990s with the previous decades. It shows, that while the minority (17,6%) of organizations founded before 1990 shows permissive attitudes today,[13] such attitudes are shown by a relative majority (about 43%) of all organizations founded after 1990. However there are no differences between organizations founded in the first and in the second half of the 1990s.

Table 10: Time of founding by drug-related attitudes

		Permissiveness/Restrictiveness			Total
Founding year		Permissive group	Moderate group	Restrictive group	
till 1990	Count	12	31	25	68
	% within Founding y.	17,6	45,6	36,8	100,0
1991-95	Count	32	21	22	75
	% within Founding y.	42,7	28,0	29,3	100,0
1996-	Count	14	9	9	32
	% within Founding y.	43,8	28,1	28,1	100,0
Total	Count	58	61	56	175
	% within Founding y.	33,1	34,9	32,0	100,0

This result could be interpreted as showing that the cutting years in terms of the organizations' attitudes were close to the years of the change in the political systems in the four countries. The rather large majority of the organizations founded before 1990 show a moderate or restrictive orientation, while the relative majority of the organizations founded after 1990 show a permissive orientation.

6.2 *Organizational status*

In this part only the GOs and NGOs will be compared, as the other two groups ("private" and "other") are too small. Table 11 shows that GOs' attitudes tend to be mostly (prevalently) moderate, while NGOs are more polarized, tend to be either restrictive or permissive, with the last ones being more prevalent. This means that the NGOs allow for the realization of more specific and also divergent interests while the GOs represent more "average" interests.

Table 11: Legal status of organizations by their drug-related attitudes

		Permissiveness/Restrictiveness			Total
Legal status		Permissive group	Moderate group	Restrictive group	
Governmental, public agency	Count	22	41	20	83
	% within legal status	26,5	49,4	24,1	100,0
Non-profit, voluntary	Count	34	17	33	84
	% within legal status	40,5	20,2	39,3	100,0
Total	Count	58	61	56	175
	% within legal status	33,1	34,9	32,0	100,0

6.3 *Level of operation*

Table 12: Level of operations of organizations by their drug-related attitudes

		Permissiveness/Restrictiveness			Total
Level of operation		Permissive group	Moderate group	Restrictive group	
National level	Count	29	35	31	95
	% within Lev. of operation	30,5	36,8	32,6	100,0
Local level	Count	29	23	23	75
	% within Lev. of operation	38,7	30,7	30,7	100,0
Total	Count	58	61	56	175
	% within Lev. of operation	33,1	34,9	32,0	100,0

The three kinds of attitudes are more or less equally distributed among national and local organizations (differences are not statistically significant). But nevertheless local organizations' attitudes tend to be more permissive and national organizations' more restrictive (although the majority of them are moderate). Among the national organizations there are 7% more restrictive than there are permissive ones, while among the local organizations there are 26% more permissive than there are restrictive ones.

6.4 *DDR exclusive/inclusive orientation*

This characteristic does not discriminate between organizations with different drug-related attitudes.

6.5 *Presence of voluntary workers and medical staff*

Table 13 shows that organizations where no voluntary workers are present are on average more permissive, while the presence of voluntary workers characterizes restrictive organizations. The relation between the variables is statistically significant at the level $p<0{,}05$. The engagement of volunteers in the field of DDR hence seems to be associated with more restrictive motivations.

Table 13: The presence of volunteers in organizations by their drug-related attitudes

		Permissiveness/Restrictiveness			Total
Volunteers active in organization:		Permissive	Moderate group	Restrictive group	group
No	Count	44	42	29	115
	% within VOLUNT1	38,3	36,5	25,2	100,0
Yes	Count	13	15	22	50
	% within VOLUNT1	26,0	30,0	44,0	100,0
Total	Count	57	57	51	165
	% within VOLUNT1	34,5	34,5	30,9	100,0

Table 14 shows that organizations with no medical staff tend to be more permissive, while the presence of medical staff marks more restrictive organizations. The same relation is characteristic for each of the four countries. The relation between the variables is, however, not statistically significant neither in any of the four countries nor in the joint data set.

Table 14: The presence of medical staff in organizations by their drug-related attitudes

		Permissiveness/Restrictiveness			Total
Presence of medical staff in organization:		Permissive group	Moderate group	Restrictive group	
No	Count	45	36	33	114
	% within MEDIC1	39,5	31,6	28,9	100,0
Yes	Count	13	19	21	53
	% within MEDIC1	24,5	35,8	39,6	100,0
Total	Count	58	55	54	167
	% within MEDIC1	34,7	32,9	32,3	100,0

6.6 *Perceptions of the national drug policy*

In this part we analyse the relations between the permissive/restrictive orientation and the perceived strengths and weaknesses of the national drug policies. We are not interested in perceptions of drug policies in specific countries but in the differentiation in perceptions across countries.

Table 15 shows how organizations of the three kinds perceive strengths of the national drug policies. Data in the table show how many organizations of a certain group chose a specific strength as characteristic of their respective national drug policy.[14]

On the left side of each number in Tables 15 and 16 there are signs "-", "+" or "=". These signs denote whether the specific group of organizations selected (chose) a specific strength or weakness less often, more often or equally often than others.[15] In cases where over-choosing or under-choosing is especially pronounced the respective entry is given in bold type.[16]

In Table 15 it can be seen that all three groups of organizations chose more or less comparable number of strengths. The rank order of the frequency of their choices was – broadly speaking – more similar than different. E.g. all three groups chose as their second most frequent answer the "Awareness of the drug problem". But if we look at the first rank order it can be seen that for permissive organizations the most pronounced strength is "Effective policy, conceptions, legislation", which is also not un-important for the other two groups, while for the other two groups the "Prevention programmes" represent the most frequently mentioned strength. For our analysis the entries in bold type are especially important. They show that "Prevention programmes" and "Therapy programmes" are not something, which the permissive group would evaluate as a strength in the same way as the other two groups. On the other side the restrictive group especially less often perceives "Harm reduction programmes" as one of the strengths of their national policy.

Table 15: Perception of the strengths of national drug policies by the three groups of organizations

Organizations: *The perceived strengths of the national drug policy:*	**Permissive** **N=58**	**Moderate** **N=61**	**Restrictive** **N=56**	**Total**
Prevention programmes	**- 10**	+ 19	+ 17	46
Awareness of the drug problem	- 12	= 13	+ 16	41
Effective policy, conceptions, legislation	+ 16	- 11	- 11	38
Efficient network of organizations	+ 11	= 9	- 7	27
Harm reduction programmes	+ 10	+ 9	**- 4**	23
No strengths at all	+ 10	- 7	- 6	23
Supply control, law enforcement	- 5	+ 8	+ 9	22
Therapy programmes	**- 2**	+ 9	+ 8	19
Competent, experts	+ 5	**+ 6**	**- 1**	12
Other	**- 2**	+ 6	**+ 7**	15
Total	120	124	124	368

In Table 16 we can see that the three groups of organizations more or less agree on the high rank orders of the first three perceived weaknesses ("Lack of policy", "Lack of co-ordination" and "Insufficient funding"). The most pronounced over-choosing we can see is in the case of the permissive organizations perceiving "Focus on law enforcement" as a major weakness of the national policy (and vice versa, the most pronounced under-choosing by the restrictive organizations evaluating the same item as strength). They also less often regard "Ineffective programmes" or "Barriers in development of NGOs" as one of the weaknesses.

Generally speaking, the permissive organizations evaluate national policies as much more competent and effective, while restrictive organizations more often emphasize prevention, therapy and law enforcement as strengths.

Table 16: Perception of the weaknesses of national drug policies by the three groups of organizations

Organizations: *The perceived weakness of the national drug policy:*	Permissive N=58	Moderate N=61	Restrictive N=56	Total
Lack of policy	= 31	= 30	= 29	90
Lack of co-ordination	= 22	+ 23	- 17	62
Insufficient funding	- 15	+ 19	+ 18	52
Lack of awareness of the problem	- 5	+ 8	+ 10	23
Ineffective programmes	**- 3**	**- 4**	+ 13	20
Focus on law enforcement	**+ 17**	**- 2**	**- 0**	19
Lack of professionals, experts	= 4	= 5	- 3	12
Lack of research	= 3	= 3	= 3	9
Lack of evaluation	= 3	= 4	**- 2**	9
Barriers in development of NGOs	**- 1**	- 2	**+ 4**	7
Other	+ 17	+ 16	**- 6**	39
Total	135	128	125	388

In both tables we can see quite a substantial number of answers which were categorized as "other". An interesting observation is that the group of restrictive organizations much more often than others gave answers which were later categorized into this category when nominating the strengths and much less often than others, when nominating the weaknesses.

One of the possible (methodological) reasons for the finding that permissive organizations perceive their national policy as more competent and effective could again have to do with the specific interaction between the countries and their organizations' attitudes. It could be, for example, that in some countries, which are characterized by a more permissive orientation the general opinion would be, that their policy is effective, and in other, more restrictive countries the opinion would be just the opposite. In this case we would get the result that the more permissive organizations perceive the policy as more effective, but this relation would be produced only because the organizations in different countries are not equally distributed regarding their orientation. To verify this hypothesis we analyse in Table 17 some differences among the four countries.

First it can be seen in Table 17 that the four countries did not choose the strengths and weaknesses to the same extent. The least "active" in mentioning both strengths and weaknesses were Hungarian organizations; relatively speaking they mentioned 2-3 times less strengths and weaknesses as the other three countries.

Table 17: Positive and negative evaluations of national drug policy by the four countries

	CZ	H	PL	SLO
Number of organizations	49	46	49	37
Number of chosen strengths	89	53	89	74
Number of strengths reduced	83	52	78	55
Number of weaknesses	107	67	128	82
Number of weaknesses reduced	118	36	114	69
Number of chosen strengths per organization	1,82	1,15	1,82	2,00
Number of strengths reduced per organization	1,69	1,13	1,59	1,49
Number of chosen weaknesses per organization	2,18	1,46	2,61	2,22
Number of weaknesses reduced per organization	2,41	0,78	2,33	1,86
No. of org. which chose "Effective policy, conceptions, legislation"	14	1	10	13
No. of org. which chose "Effective policy, conceptions, legislation" per organization	0,29	0,02	0,20	0,35
No. of org. which chose "Ineffective programmes"	6	6	11	2
No. of org. which chose "Ineffective programmes" per organization	0,12	0,13	0,22	0,05

Note: Each organization could mention up to three strengths and three weaknesses. These answers were categorized into two schemes of 10 categories each. If an organization mentioned two or three times the same category of strength or weakness, we merged their answers and assumed that they mentioned that characteristic only once. In the table the term "chosen ..." refers to the original answers while the term "reduced ... " refers to the number of merged answers.

Although the other three countries were relatively equally active in contributing either positive or negative evaluations of their national policies, we find larger differences among them regarding specific strengths or weaknesses. We test these relations in the case of two items: one of the strengths ("Effective policy, conceptions, legislation") and one of the weaknesses ("Ineffective programmes"). In Table 17 it is demonstrated that Slovenian and Czech organizations (taken together as – on average – more permissive oriented) evaluated their national drug policy two to three times more often effective compared to Polish and Hungarian organizations (taken together). In the case of one of the weaknesses ("Ineffective programmes"), Slovenian and Czech organizations chose it two times less often than Polish and Hungarian organizations.

This is one possible explanation of the results in Tables 15 and 16. There are different ways to interpret these results. One possible (but very simple) interpretation would be, that a more permissive national orientation (that is, drug policy) leads to a more efficient policy (or at least to such opinions by the organizations' representatives). Another interpretation could be that the more effective overall system (which is reflected also in the more effective DDR sub-system) leads to a more permissive orientation of drug experts. Another interpretation could be to explain these relations by referring to some other "third factors".[17]

7 Organizations' activities

Involvement in DDR activity is presented and evaluated in the study by comparing the organizations' definitions of their organizational mission, their DDR mission, preferred goals, development of different DDR activities, opinions about the importance of selected DDR actions and preference of a certain DDR activity to be developed in the future. The next step is an analysis of the relations between some characteristics of all organizations studied and their involvement in DDR activities. The characteristics of organizations discussed here are their level of operating, legal status, exclusive/inclusive DDR orientation and, last but not least, permissive/repressive attitude. An aim of the analysis is to show and explain eventual relations between the characteristics of organizations and the nature of their involvement in DDR activities. We are interested to study whether they are more connected with a permissive/repressive attitude of organizations compared to other organizational characteristics.

7.1 *Mission of organizations*

Table 18 shows that in each country organizations chose most frequently two types of missions. The first mission of personal care and advice, refers to those actions focused on people with problems or on people at risk as a consequence of their drug consumption. The second mission, influencing attitudes and knowledge, is connected to the popularization of the idea of a healthy life without drugs. The Czech, Polish and Slovenian organizations mainly conduct activities in the area of personal care and advice while Hungarian organizations more often focus on influencing attitudes. A relatively large number of Slovenian and Czech organizations indicated their domain of activities to be in the area of policy design and policy co-operation.

Table 18: Mission of organizations by country

DDR Mission	Number of organizations									
	Czech Rep. N=49		Hungary N=46		Poland N=49		Slovenia N=37		Total N=161	
	n	%	n	%	n	%	n	%	n	%
Influencing attitude	14	28.6	20	43.5	14	28.6	7	18.9	55	30.4
Personal care and advice	20	40.8	16	34.8	20	40.8	13	35.1	69	38.1
Support for communities	4	8.2	4	8.1	5	10.2	2	5.4	15	8.3
Policy design, co-operation	9	18.4	4	8.7	1	2.0	7	18.9	21	11.6
Intelligence	2	4.1	1	2.2	1	2.0	4	10.8	8	4.4
Other			1	2.2	8	16.3	4	10.8	13	7.2

The most important mission was personal care and advice for governmental organizations (33%) and NGOs (42%). That mission was also identified by most of the organizations at the national level (49%) and by the majority of organizations with an exclusive DDR orientation (52%). At the local level the majority of each country's local organizations conduct activities in the field of influencing attitudes and knowledge. Organizations with inclusive DDR orientation preferred these two missions also. Personal care and advice as well as influencing attitudes were also the major missions for both repressive and permissive organizations. However, permissive organizations more than repressive ones conceive also other missions, e.g. policy design, support to communities, etc. as being part of directing their work.

7.2 *Organizations' DDR missions*

A mission in the area of drug demand reduction was indicated only by inclusive DDR-oriented organizations. Czech and Slovenian organizations indicated a broader spectrum of DDR activities than the organizations in the other two countries (Table 19). The order of the frequency of activities is the same for these two countries. Prevention activities is the main category. Hungarian and Polish organizations preferred mainly two kinds of mission: prevention and personal care, treatment and advice. They chose them, however, in the opposite sequence. The order of missions indicated by the two largest groups of Polish organizations is the same as in the case of the Czech and Slovenian organizations.

Table 19: DDR mission of organizations by country

DDR Mission	Number of organizations									
	Czech Rep. N=29 (49)		Hungary N=32 (46)		Poland N=32 (49)		Slovenia N=28 (37)		Total N=121 (181)	
	n	%	n	%	n	%	n	%	n	%
1. Prevention	10	34.5	11	34.4	18	56.3	12	32.4	67	41.6
2. Personal care	9	31.0	12	37.5	11	34.4	8	28.6	40	33.1
3. Policy design	7	24.1	3	9.4	1	3.1	4	14.3	15	12.4
4. Intelligence	3	10.3	2	6.3	1	3.1	3	10.7	9	7.4
5. Interest repres.	1	3.1	1	3.1					2	1.7
6. Other	3	9.4	1	3.6					4	3.3

Governmental and national organizations mention many different activities as their DDR mission. The preferences of NGOs and local organizations are less different and they mainly focus on two types of DDR activities: prevention and personal care as well as treatment and advice. Permissive/restrictive attitudes of organizations somehow influence their activities. Most permissive organizations (37%) conduct activities in the area of prevention as well as of personal care, treatment and advice. The majority of repressive organizations (63%) define prevention as their primary DDR activity and only 24% of them mention personal care, treatment and advice.

7.3 *Drug demand reduction goals*

In the four countries studied the preferences of DDR organizational goals were ranked in comparable orders (Table 20).[18] The most favoured goals were prevention, treatment and generally-defined drug demand reduction. The largest differentiation in goals occurred in the Czech Republic and Slovenia where a considerable number (10% and more) of organizations are even involved in nine of eleven goals. The preferences for goals in Hungary and Poland are less differentiated; organizations in these countries mainly focused on five alternatives. Nevertheless, in each country a majority of organizations was mainly interested in three goals. From the remaining goals only rehabilitation reached a relatively high position in the Czech Republic and in Poland while policy development and legislation attracted the attention of a relatively large percentage of Slovenian organizations.

Table 20: Organizations' goals in the field of drug demand reduction by country

Type of goals	Number of organizations									
	Czech Rep. N=49		Hungary N=46		Poland N=49		Slovenia N=37		Total N=181	
	n	%	n	%	n	%	n	%	n	%
1. DDR	17	34.7	14	30.4	3	6.1	11	29.7	45	24.9
2. Prevention	35	71.4	19	41.3	37	75.5	20	54.1	111	61.3
3. Treatment	18	36.7	14	30.4	19	38.8	16	43.2	67	37.0
4. Rehabilitation	12	24.5	3	6.5	11	22.4	6	16.2	32	17.7
5. Research	6	12.2	1	2.2	2	4.1	4	10.8	13	7.2
6. Funding	6	12.2	1	2.2			3	8.1	10	5.5
7. Co-ordination	5	10.2	2	4.3	4	8.2	4	10.8	15	8.3
8. Interest Repr.	1	2.0	1	2.2					2	1.1
9. Policy Develop.	4	8.2	1	2.2	2	4.1	7	18.9	14	7.7
10. Training of Professionals	8	16.3	10	21.7	9	18.4	6	16.2	33	18.2
11. Other	5	10.2	15	32.6	9	18.4	2	5.4	31	17.1

It is important to state that other characteristics analysed did not change the dominant position of the three goals mentioned above. Two things should be noticed, however. First, that those characteristics somehow altered the intensity of organizational involvement in the three most preferred goals. And second, that they modify the differentiation of the preferences for all selected goals. All relations between variables presented below are statistically significant at the level $p<0{,}05$.

Local organizations focus on the first four goals selected in the above table. There is a correlation between operating at the local level and the involvement in goals of generally-defined drug demand reduction; 35% of local organizations preferred that goal while only 16% of national organizations do. The preferences of national organizations are more diversified. There is a relationship between the national level of operation and a relatively high involvement in two goals: training of professionals and policy design. The goal of training professionals is conducted by 26% of national organizations but by only 9% of the local organizations. Policy design is conducted by 13% of national and by only one (1%) local organization.

A comparable observation refers to the legal status of organizations. NGOs have fewer goals than governmental institutions and they are more focused on the first four goals in the above table. There is also a correlation between the non-governmental legal status of organizations and their preference for prevention. Prevention is preferred even by 73% of NGOs and by 49% of governmental institutions. Governmental institutions are active throughout the whole spectrum of drug demand reduction goals. There is a correlation between the legal status and an involvement in three types of goals: co-ordination, research and fund-raising, which are preferred by, respectively, 16%, 14% and 10% of governmental organizations. These three goals are preferred by only one NGO each. It means that both national and governmental organizations are more often than both local and non-governmental organizations interested in achieving not only traditional but also more modern kinds of drug demand reduction objectives.

Exclusive/inclusive DDR orientation does not discriminate between goal preferences. But there is a correlation between an exclusive DDR orientation of organizations and their involvement in two goals: prevention and rehabilitation. Prevention was preferred by 73% of organizations with an exclusive DDR orientation and by 55% of the organizations with an inclusive DDR orientation. Rehabilitation was preferred by 28% of the organizations with an exclusive DDR orientation and by only 12% of the organizations with an inclusive DDR orientation.

There is no statistically significant relationship between the permissive/repressive attitudes of organizations and goal preferences. However, the goal preferences of more permissive Czech and Slovenian organizations are somewhat distinguished from the goal preferences of more repressive Polish and Hungarian organizations.

7.4 Drug demand reduction activities

When we consider the drug demand reduction activity preferences of the organizations, prevention ranks first in each country (Table 21). Also the training of professionals is conducted by a relatively high percentage of organizations in each country. Apart from these two prevailing areas of drug demand reduction activities, a considerable number (more than 50%) of Polish and Slovenian organizations has specialized in co-ordination and policy development. More than half of the Slovenian organizations is also involved in research.

Table 21: Drug demand reduction activities of organizations by country

	Number of organizations									
Type of activity (Activity No. 1)	**Czech Rep. N=49**		**Hungary N=46**		**Poland N=49**		**Slovenia N=37**		**Total N=181**	
	n	%	n	%	n	%	n	%	n	%
Prevention	46	93.9	35	76.1	45	91.8	34	91.9	160	88.4
Treatment	22	44.9	20	43.5	26	53.1	17	45.9	85	47.0
Rehabilitation	15	30.6	13	28.2	22	44.9	15	40.5	65	35.9
Research	25	51.0	19	41.3	23	46.9	21	56.8	88	48.6
Funding	15	30.6	16	34.8	12	24.5	6	16.2	49	27.1
Co-ordination	21	42.9	17	37.0	32	65.3	20	54.1	90	49.7
Interest Repres.	9	18.4	5	10.9	16	32.7	14	37.8	44	24.3
Policy Develop.	24	49.0	7	15.2	29	59.2	25	67.6	85	47.0
Training of Profes.	32	65.3	27	58.7	37	75.5	24	64.9	120	66.3

There is some statistical correlation between certain characteristics of organizations and their involvement in types of DDR activity. The national level of operation is correlated with a relatively high involvement in the following drug demand reduction activities: training of professionals (77%), co-ordination (59%), policy development (58%) and fund-raising (35%). The local level of operation is correlated with treatment and care (57%). The governmental status of organizations is correlated with a relatively high involvement in DDR activity in the fields of co-ordination (59%) and research (58%). A non-governmental status of organizations is correlated with prevention (95%), treatment (55%) and interest representation (33%). An exclusive DDR orientation is correlated with a relatively high involvement in DDR activities in the fields of treatment (63%) and rehabilitation (52%).

The permissive/restrictive attitudes of organizations did not significantly influence their involvement in different types of DDR activity. We see, however, that both types of organizations, i.e. permissive and repressive, are active in prevention as well as in training of professionals. Besides, more than half of the organizations with permissive orientations carry out research and policy development while more than half of the restrictive organizations develop co-ordination of an activity. The remaining activities were conducted by less then half of these two types of organizations.

7.5 *The most important DDR activity*

There is no significant difference between the countries studied in their definition of the most important drug demand reduction activity. Most of the organizations mention two types of DDR activity: prevention and treatment. In the case of Slovenia, treatment is more frequently chosen than prevention. In the other countries those two types of activity are preferred in reversed order.

Table 22: The most important DDR activity of organizations by country

Type of activity	Number of organizations									
	Czech Rep. N=49 (49)		Hungary N=33 (46)		Poland N=48 (49)		Slovenia N=36 (37)		Total N=166 (181)	
	n	%	n	%	n	%	n	%	n	%
Prevention	16	32.7	13	39.4	18	37.5	8	22.2	55	33.1
Treatment	17	34.7	5	15.2	14	29.2	13	36.1	49	29.5
Rehabilitation	3	6.1	2	6.1	3	6.3	1	2.8	9	5.4
Research	1	2.0	2	6.1	1	2.1	3	8.3	7	4.2
Funding	3	6.1	2	6.1	1	2.1	2	5.6	8	4.8
Co-ordination	5	10.2	3	9.1	5	10.4	2	5.6	15	9.0
Interest Repres., Policy Develop.	4	8.2	2	6.1			2	5.6	8	4.8
Training of Profes.			4	12.1	6	12.5	4	11.1	14	8.4
Other							1	2.8	1	0.6

The characteristics of organizations somehow influence their choice of the most important activity. They determine whether prevention or treatment are identified as the most important activity for the organization. NGOs (43%), national organizations (37%), inclusively DDR-oriented organizations (34%) as well as restrictive organizations (44%) more frequently conduct prevention. Treatment is the most important activity for governmental institutions (26%), local organizations (51%), exclusively DDR-oriented organizations (45%) as well as permissive organizations (34%). However, while these two dominant types of DDR activity are defined as the more important ones by even three-fourth of the repressive organizations, they are identified as such only by little more than half of the permissive organizations. The activities conducted by permissive organizations are more differentiated and directed towards other types of action.

7.6 *DDR activity preferred to be intensified in the future*

The DDR activities mentioned by organizations as the most important are also more or less the same ones which they wish to increase in the near future (Table 23). Prevention and treatment are forseen to be developed by a majority of organizations in each country. Besides these two, some organizations wish to increase other kinds of DDR activities. Czech organizations are going to increase policy development. Hungarian organizations decide to increase rehabilitation and training of professionals. Polish organizations want to increase training of professionals. Slovenian organizations prefer to increase co-ordination. The need for developing still other types of action in the future is articulated by single organizations.

Table 23: Organization's DDR activities to be increased in the future by country

Type of activity	Number of organizations									
	Czech Rep. N=46 (4)		Hungary N=39 (46)		Poland N=49 (49)		Slovenia N=37 (37)		Total N=171 (181)	
	n	%	n	%	n	%	n	%	n	%
1. Prevention	11	23.9	14	35.9	20	40.8	10	27.0	55	33.1
2. Treatment	11	23.9	7	17.9	8	16.3	8	21.6	34	29.5
3. Rehabilitation	4	8.7	6	15.4	4	8.2	4	10.8	18	5.4
4. Research	3	6.5	1	2.6	3	6.1	3	8.1	10	4.2
5. Funding	3	6.5	1	2.6	1	2.0			5	4.8
6. Co-ordination	3	6.5	2	5.1	2	4.1	5	13.5	12	9.0
7. Interest Repres.	1	2.2							1	0.6
8. Policy Develop.	5	10.9	1	2.6	1	2.0	1	2.7	8	4.7
9. Training of Profes.	1	2.2	6	15.4	7	14.3	4	10.8	18	10.5
10. Other	4	8.7	1	2.6	3	6.1	2	5.4	10	5.8

National organizations (37%) foremost prefer to increase prevention whereas local organizations want to develop treatment (30%). However, the primary position of prevention and treatment is stable independently of the legal status of organizations and their level of operation. With regard to the remaining types of DDR activity about 10% of governmental institutions want to increase research while about 10% of NGOs declare their wish to increase rehabilitation and training of professionals. About 10% of organizations with an inclusive orientation want to develop training of professionals and about 10% of those with an exclusive DDR orientation intend to develop rehabilitation. Restrictive organizations (39%) intend consequently more often than permissive organizations (25%) to increase prevention in the future. The first group of organizations (16%) is a little bit less interested in developing treatment than the latter group (23%).

8 Conclusions

Assuming that the orientation of a nation's drug policy can be judged by the attitudes of its drug demand reduction organizations then it can be stated that Polish drug policy is the most restrictive in comparison to the other three countries), whereas the Slovenian and the Czech ones are the most permissive and the Hungarian lies in between. The Slovenian situation differs from the situation in the other three countries in the sense that the attitudes of the organizations are most polarized. It is not clear whether this is the outcome of a broader range of interests covered by them or of difficulties in communication and cooperation between them.

The more restrictive organizations are founded before the 1990s and more often tend to have also medical staff and voluntary workers. NGOs tend to be either permissive or restrictive, while GOs tend to be moderate in their orientation.

The organizations differ in their perception of the national drug policy in a particular way. The permissive ones seem to evaluate their respective national drug policies generally as more competent, while perceiving the prevention and therapy programmes as less positive, and regarding the focus on law enforcement as the major weakness. The "inverted" picture of the above seems to come close to the perceptions of the restrictive organizations.

Comparative analysis of organizational involvement in DDR activities shows that there are not many differences among the countries. The findings present a certain degree of correspondence with regard to dominant organizational missions, goals and all kinds of activities: those conducted, those defined as the most important or intended to be increased in the near future. Universal and easy recognizable ideas of prevention, treatment, rehabilitation and training of professionals seem to be the main elements of drug demand reduction missions, goals and activities for the organizations studied. These elements are usually preferred exclusively or by a majority of the organizations in each country. And preference for these goals creates a picture of consensus. The differences refer rather to the diversity of involvement in the remaining, not dominanting other activities. The ideas of co-ordination, research, funding and fund-raising, policy development and interest representation are relatively newer and still not easily recognized objects of DDR missions, goals and activities. Those activities are sporadically preferred and, as we assumed, determined by certain factors. We compared several organizational characteristics in order to identify these factors: the country of origin, level of operation, legal status and exclusive/inclusive DDR orientation of organizations. We were, however, most interested in the influence of restrictive/permissive attitudes of organizations. It is demonstrated that its effect is less significant than the other characteristics. In many cases, a higher diversity of preferred activities is more related to the national level of operation or the governmental status of organizations than to their restrictive/permissive attitude. A high concentration on traditional activities is in some cases more related to the local level of operation, to a non-governmental status or to an exclusive DDR orientation of organizations than to their repressive attitude.

Contrary to intuitive predictions it seems that the organizations' permissive/restrictive attitude is not to a large degree related to their DDR activity involvement. The reasons for this finding are unclear. It is possible that our scheme for coding DDR activities was not well adapted to the aim of differentiating the permissive/restrictive content of the activities.[19] Another interpretation could be that the attitudes mostly influence the rhetorical level, while the structuring of the specific activities is influenced by more pragmatic factors.

The findings most probably reflect the fact that drug-related attitudes do not function as an independent factor; they themselves are being influenced and can be understood only in the broader framework of the countries' social climate and material conditions. However, whereas they do not influence policy and activities as an independent factor, they do so to a greater extent in interaction with other factors. With this interpretation we may explain the fact that differences between countries (in many indicators related to drugs and drug demand reduction) were often larger than differences between permissive and restrictive organizations.

The permissive/restrictive orientation is thus something, which is partly related to the fashions of time, partly to longer-term traditions, partly to the general level of societies' development, and maybe even partly to "geography". Although it is one of the most emphasized dimensions in ideological discourses it was not very clear from our data that it would be also very much related to the concrete level of drug demand reduction activities.

Leaving aside the "scientific"[20] relevance of the permissive/restrictive dimension, it is at least important in terms of ideological and political processes. Hence, its understanding as well as the proper use of this (rhetorical) dimension in public and professional discourses seem a necessary condition for the development of co-ordinated policies across borders.

Notes

1 Cohen, 1999.
2 All quotations are from Gould, Shaw and Ahrendt, 1996.
3 Ibid.
4 Ibid.
5 The respondents were a representative sample of the British public.
6 The development of the scale is described in Gould, Shaw and Ahrendt, 1996.
7 For the aim of including also these five respondents in our analysis we "calculated" the missing answer as the mean answer to the other seven items. Doing so we were able to analyse the answers of 175 respondents.
8 In Tables 1 to 4 the eight statements are written in shortened versions.
9 The obvious limitation of this factor analysis was the fact that none of the eight variables was normally distributed.
10 Before adding the answers we inverted the answers to the permissive statements.
11 Actually one of the respondents agreed with all the permissive and disagreed with all the restrictive statements and achieved result 1, while eight of the respondents achieved the maximum score of 5.
12 Ibid.
13 In fact, at the time of surveying, in 1998/1999.
14 Each organization's representative was allowed to choose three strengths and three weaknesses. In case that someone chose, for instance, two strengths which we later on categorized into the same category (e.g. prevention programmes), we took his answer as nominating prevention programmes only once.
15 For example the number "10" in the cell "permissive" (column) x "prevention programmes" (row) in Table 15 means that 10 of the 58 permissive organizations perceive "prevention programmes" as one of the strengths of the national drug policy. The sign "-" on the left side of the number "10" in the same cell means that the permissive organizations relatively less often than others decided to nominate "preventive programmes" as one of the strengths of the national drug policy.

16 The condition of over- or under-choosing was calculated as a ratio between the theoretical and empirical frequencies. The theoretical frequencies for specific cells were calculated as: column total by row total divided by grand total. If this indicator was over 1,4 or under 0,7 we decided that the over- or under-choosing was "especially pronounced".

17 ... Which would presumably influence both, organizations' orientation and the effectiveness of the policy.

18 Each organization was asked to define a maximum number of three goals. An involvement was stated when an organization indicated a certain goal at least once. This is the reason why the percentages do not add up to 100%.

19 E.g. either a permissive or a restrictive organization could be engaged in something called "prevention" or "information" or "counselling" or "interest representation", but the content of these activities could differ much. Our coding system was not made to differentiate the contents of the activities, but much more to differentiate the forms of these activities, as reflected in traditional categories as "prevention" and "rehabilitation".

20 With this we refer to the quest for "objective" knowledge, e.g. what kinds of programmes are "objectively" better, what kind of educational attitudes "cause" what kinds of behaviour, etc.

References

Cohen, P. (1999) 'Shifting the Main Purpose of Drug Control: From Suppression to Regulation of Use – Reduction of Risk as the New Focus for Drug Policy', *Drug Policy* 10: 223-234.

Gould, A. et al. (1996) 'Illegal Drugs: Liberal and Restrictive Attitudes', pp. 93-116 in: Jowell, R. et al. (eds.), *British Social Attitudes – the 13th Report*. Hants: SCPR.

CHAPTER 10

Networks in Drug Demand Reduction Policy and Practice

Patrick Kenis and Stefan Loos

1 Introduction

In the previous chapters the organizational field of drug demand reduction (DDR) policy and practice in the four countries studied has particularly been described and analysed in terms of so called attribute variables. This means that these chapters have presented the DDR field in terms of (aggregates of) characteristics of the organizations involved, such as their size, their legal status, the type of activities they provide, their opinions and attitudes. Such an analysis has produced interesting insights on the degree of differentiation within the national and local DDR field as well as information on how different characteristics are linked to each other. For example, it has become clear which type of organization does what, to what extend opinions and attitudes differ within a country or across different types of organizations and how these characteristics are linked to each other. In this chapter an additional dimension will be added to the description and analysis of the DDR fields. We will analyse the extend and forms of *integration* within the different national DDR fields.

Analysing integration is important as such, but becomes particularly interesting when combined with an analysis of differentiation. Characteristic for a field like DDR is that its effectiveness is not only contingent on its degree of differentiation (e.g. the range of activities provided) but also by the way the relations or the network among the different organizations is structured. Drug demand reduction is typically a field where organizations are dependent on each other (e.g. for resources or expertise) and where the effectiveness of outcomes could consequently be more contingent on the structure of the relationships between the organizations than on the sum of effectiveness of the different organizations. In a field like DDR, outcomes can often not readily be attributed to the activities of individual organizations but are contingent on integrated and co-ordinated actions of many different agencies (see also Provan and Milward, 1995). What is proposed here is thus a structural analysis of the DDR field in the four countries studied (on structural analysis, see Wellman and Berkowitz, 1997 and Emirbayer, 1997).

In what follows we will present such a structural analysis by studying the structure of different types of relationships between the organizations at the national level in the four countries. The principal aim is to present a number of characteristics of these networks, to compare them with each other and across countries as well as to produce some tentative statements on the causes and consequences of these networks.

2 Analysing networks in DDR policy and practice

The unit of analysis to be studied here is what recently has been called organizational field networks or field nets (see Kenis and Knoke, forthcoming). An organizational field net is a configuration of interorganizational relations among all the members of an organizational field. An organizational field being "...those organizations that, in the aggregate, constitute a recognized area of institutional life: key suppliers, producers, regulatory agencies, and other organizations that produce similar services or products" (DiMaggio and Powell, 1983: 148). The aggregate of national organizations active in the field of DDR in a country can clearly be regarded as a recognizable area of institutional life. In the present chapter we will concentrate on this organizational field in the four countries studied.

The next step in our relational analysis is to consider the thus defined institutional fields as field nets. A field net "... consists of a particular pattern of both present and absent links among the entire set of organizational dyads occurring in a specified organizational field" (Kenis and Knoke, forthcoming). Consequently the organizational field net concept explicitly focuses analytic attention on the dyadic relations, or ties, between every pair of organizations in a field. In the present study we have collected data on 8 types of relationships (see Table 1). These are the type of relationships which are commonly considered when studying relational patterns in organizational fields (see e.g. Knoke, 2000 and Provan and Milward, 1995).

Table 1: Types of relationships studied

exchange of clients	This means that an organization is either referring clients to another organization or an organization is receiving clients which have been referred by another organization
exchange of support	This means that an organization either provides support to another organization or that an organization receives support form another organization
exchange of expertise	This means that an organization either provides expertise to another organization about DDR or that an organization receives epertise form another organization about DDR
exchange of resources	This means that an organization either provides resources (i.e. financial, facilities, equipment) to another organization or that an organization receives such resources form another organization
common activities	This means that two organizations are engaged in common activities in the field of DDR
strategic co-operation	This means that two organizations are consulting each other before making important decisions on DDR programmes
informal communication	This means that the organization's employees exchange information on DDR programmes on an informal basis
prominence attributed	This means that an organization is naming another organization as one of which the interests, goals or opinions are taken into account when taking decisions concerning DDR programmes

Information on these types of relationships has been collected through the questionnaire (see the Annex of this publication) and in which an organization was asked to indicate which of these relationships it has had recently with which other organization in the organizational field it is part of. On the basis of this information 8 NxN matrices resulted in which a 0 is marked for an absent relationship and a 1 for a present relationship (where N is the number of organizations in the organizational field).

Combinations of such present and absent relationships in such a matrix aggregate into various network sub-structures, for example, the occurrence of such components as cliques, groups, positions, action sets, structural holes, as well as into structural attributes of the entire field, such as density, connectivity, and centralization (Wassermann and Faust, 1994 and Knoke, 2000). Consequently, on the basis of the data collected at least 32 networks (i.e. 8 types of relationships in 4 countries) could be described in terms of the concepts mentioned before. In the analysis below we have chosen to describe the different networks in terms of two of these concepts: density and centralization. As spelled out in more detail below, these indicators of network structure primarily demonstrate the intensity in which organizations within an organizational field communicate and are indicative for the hierarchical or power structure of the organizational fields. For the time being this seems to be the type of information which in combination with the descriptions on the degrees of differentiation of the organizational fields provides a good picture of the "organization" of the DDR fields in the different countries.

Table 2 presents the four national-level organizational fields, which form the basis for the network analysis to be presented further on. Data on the 8 different types of relationships between all national organizations in these fields have been collected and subsequently been analysed using two computer programmes for analysing networks (i.e. UCINET[1] and Visone[2]).

Table 2: Number of national-level operating organizations in the field net studied and some aggregate characteristics of the organizations involved

	Number of organizations	Legal status (public/non-profit/private)	Orientation (exclusive/ inclusive)	Founding year (median)	Drug related attitude (mean/St.dev.)[1]
Czech Rep.	15	10 / 5 / 0	4 / 11	1993	2,79 (=P) / 0,83
Hungary	24	14 / 9 / 1	6 / 18	1992	3,50 (=R) / 1,03
Poland	37[2]	11 / 25 / 1	10 / 27	1987	3,82 (=R) / 0,88
Slovenia	23	12 / 10 / 1	3 / 20	1993	2,78 (=P) / 1,13

Notes: [1] Source: Dekleva and Zamecka in this volume. P means "permissive" and R means "restrictive". The basis for this calculation is all organizations included in the national surveys.

[2] Originally 38 national organizations had been identified. One organization at the national level refused to participate in the study.

3 Density in the DDR fields

Network density is a macro-level property, defined as the proportion of present dyadic ties to all potential ties. Density is an important network property with respect to how "close" the different actors are to each other. For example, the speed with which information may be transmitted among the organizations of a field varies inversely with the density of communication ties. A very low-density communication network implies that messages are likely to propagate only slowly through the field via lengthy chains of intermediaries, because relatively few alternative routes are available to link particular dyads indirectly. The average path (the minimum number of indirect steps necessary to connect a dyad) is likely to be longer in low-density networks, meaning that both the time required to transmit messages and the potential for distorted communication are greater than in high-density networks whose path-lengths are much shorter. Many members of low-density fields may be only tenuously connected to one another, and thus they will find it difficult to gain access to information or other resources available elsewhere in the field. By contrast, in a high-density network, the average path length between pairs of organizations are likely to be quite short (including numerous direct ties); multiple alternative routes link the relatively fewer dyads that lack direct ties; and few or no organizations likely remain completely out of the field's information or resources loop (see Kenis and Knoke, forthcoming).

Table 3: Density for the different types of relationships

Type of relationship	**Czech Republic**	**Hungary**	**Poland**	**Slovenia**
Client exchange		4,3	7,5	37,2
Support exchange	14,3	4,4	7,7	58,5
Expertise exchange	11,4	24,3	15,2	71,5
Resource exchange	1,9	7,6	6,4	22,5
Common activities	16,2	22,8	24,6	62,1
Strategic co-operation	19,1	23,2	10,4	57,7
Informal communication	17,4	43,8	18,4	100
Average	13,4	18,6	12,9	58,5

The density of a network ranges between a minimum of 0 (when no relation is present) to a maximum of 100 (when all possible relationships actually exist). Network density is presented in Table 3 in percentages. Since the size of the network enters into the denominator of network density, one should always look at the size of a network separately when interpreting density measures.

On the basis of Table 3 a number of observations can be made. The network with the lowest density is the Czech resource exchange network (1,9%) and the network with the highest density is the Slovenian network on informal communication. All types of relationships taken together, Slovenia has the highest density (58,5%), followed by Hungary (18,6%), the Czech Republic (39,3%) and Poland (12,9%). This result might be biased given the different number of organizations in the different organization fields. It is obvious that the larger a network is (in terms of number of organizations) the smaller the chance becomes that more organizations are linked to each other. This might partially explain the relative low density in Poland. It can be stated, however, that Slovenia seems to have an exceptional high density. What is also interesting to see is that there is not one country which scores highest or lowest on all types of relationships compared to any other country. This is an indication for significant variations between relationships within countries.

The density of relationships in the Czech Republic are highest in the networks of strategic co-operation, information communication, and common activities. The exchange network is the least dense while exchange of support and resources lie somewhat in-between the others. In Hungary, informal communication is the most frequent form of relationship, while the density of the client and support networks is very low. Compared to other countries, the Polish networks score lowest in the network of strategic co-operation and second lowest in all other networks but common activities, which seem to be quite frequent. The Slovenian pattern of relationships in the national organizational field can generally be considered as rather dense. What is especially interesting is that all organizations communicate informally amongst each other.

4 Network Centralization and Actor Centrality in the DDR fields

One of the most prominent structural characteristics in the analysis of organizational fields is the notion of centrality since it gives an answer to the question: "Who has the power?". Centrality is considered a fairly good indicator for power in networks. The network literature distinguishes between centralization as a macro-level property (i.e. at the level of the network) and ego-centric concepts of "actor centrality" that characterize a specific ego's power relative to other network alters. Analysts conventionally consider three types of centrality – degree, closeness, and betweenness (Wasserman and Faust, 1994: 169-219). Variations among the basic centrality measures take into account differences in the directionality of ties (sending or receiving), and the "quality" of the other actors (in terms of their own centralities) to which an ego is connected.

Degree centrality is the simplest definition of actor centrality stating that central actors must be the most active in the sense that they have the most direct relations to other actors in the network. In a directed relation, such as clients received respectively send, one can distinguish between the out-degree and in-degree of an actor. The in-degree of an actor is the number of relations that are adjacent to that actor, which means that in-degree can be seen as a measure of receptivity or popularity of an actor. The out-degree of an actor is the number of relations adjacent from that actor, which implies that out-degree can be seen as a measure of expansiveness of an actor. For example, if actor A says he is sending resources to five other actors, the out-degree of that actor is 5. If nine actors say that they receive resources from that same actor, its in-degree is 9. A relationship, such as informal communication, is by its very nature undirected but differentiating between the in- and out-degree of an actor in such a relationship still makes sense. It now tells us whether or not the statement of actor A about his relation to actor B is confirmed by actor B. For example, actor A says that he or she informally communicates with all other actors in a network, but none of these other actors confirm this relationship. The way we treated this situation is by awarding an unconfirmed relationship half of the value of a confirmed relationship and, consequently, calculate the degree of an actor as the average of his in- and out-degree. To make actor degrees comparable among networks of different sizes, the degree of an actor is standardized by dividing it by the total number of relationships in a network. This standardized actor centrality index ranges from 0 (when the actor has no relationships with other actors) to 1 (when the actor has direct relationships with all other actors in the network and all other actors have no direct relationships among each other). Usually it is expressed as a percentage.

The measure of *closeness centrality* is based on the closeness of an actor to all other actors in the network. It is assumed that the closer an actor is to another actor, the quicker he or she can interact with that actor. Closeness centrality is also a measure for the autonomy of an actor. The closer an actor is to another actor, the less he or she has to rely on other actors to interact with that actor. Generally, closeness centrality of an actor is standardized and made comparable across networks of different sizes. A (standardized) closeness centrality of 1 indicates that an actor has direct ties to all other actors in a network.

Interaction or the flow of information between two non-directly linked organizations often depends on the actors that lie between them. For example if an organization i informally communicates with an organization j and j informally communicates with k, but i does not informally communicate with k, then j controls the flow of information between i and k. Thus, the more often actor j lies between actors, the higher his or her *betweenness centrality* and the more influential he or she becomes. In its standardized version, the index ranges from 0 (the actor does not fall on any 'shortest paths' among other actors) to 1 (the actor falls on all shortest paths among all other actors).

For all three centrality measures macro-level centralization measures can be calculated on the basis of the actor centrality measures. Centralization measures tell us, in general, how variable or heterogeneous the actor centralities in a network are.

4.1 *Network Centralization*

To derive corresponding macro-level *centralization* measures, the ego-actor centrality measures can be aggregated, thus revealing the extent to which the information transmission ties in a field-net tend to concentrate around a single organization, with the other members substantially more peripheral. For example, the maximally centralized "star" network concentrates all relations on one central organization that communicates directly with the others. No direct connections link the N-1 non-central actors. In contrast, a "circle" network is completely decentralized: each organization communicates with just two partners, each of which also exchanges information with another unique actor, thus forming a closed chain with no central organization. Freeman (1979) proposed a mathematical definition of a normed group-level centralization index for a network of N actors. It basically ranges between 0 and 1, with the lowest score occurring when all actors have the same centrality value and higher scores reflecting the tendency of one actor to dominate the others. Thus, network centralization reflects the extent of relational inequality in a network (variation or dispersion among the ego-level centralities), and permits comparison of changes over time or differences across networks.

Table 4: Network centralizations for the different types of relationships

Country	Czech Republic			Hungary			Poland			Slovenia		
	DC[1]	CC[2]	BC[3]	DC[1]	CC[2]	BC[3]	DC[1]	CC[2]	BC[3]	DC[1]	CC[2]	BC[3]
Client exchange				20,3	5,5	52,8	8,8	2,7	61,0	9,9	2,5	25,2
Support exchange	5,5	4,6	25,8	18,2	3,5	35,9	4,3	1,7	24,7	13,4	2,3	39,6
Expertise exchange	14,3	6,2	42,9	7,9	2,0	24,4	4,7	1,9	16,9	8,1	1,70	26,9
Resource exchange	25,0	14,3	100	45,0	4,3	100	10,4	2,6	37,5	15,4	1,5	25,7
Common activities	9,4	3,4	21,3	6,1	1,2	22,1	6,4	2,4	30,5	9,40	1,60	31,7
Strategic co-operation	14,8	5,3	50,4	6,7	1,7	24,4	6,2	2,0	24,4	9,2	1,7	19,8
Informal communication	13,2	4,7	54,7	7,3	2,5	39,9	3,1	1,3	14,7	11,4	1,8	48,5
Prominence				15,0			20,6			9,8		
Average centralization	13,7	6,4	49,2	15,8	3,0	42,8	6,1	2,1	30,0	11,0	1,9	31,1

Notes:
1 DC = Degree Centralization
2 CC = Closeness Centralization
3 BC = Betweeness Centralization

Table 4 presents the scores for three different centralization measures: degree centralization, closeness centralization and betweenness centralization. Centralization scores are presented in percentages. A score of 0% means that there is no centralization at all (all actors are equal), whereas a centralization of 100% indicates a maximum centrality (one actor has a direct link to any other actor and those other actors have no link among each other).[3]

In general it can be observed that most networks presented are rather decentralized. The average degree of centralization is 11,3%. This means that in most networks there are no organizations which have much more direct and/or indirect relationships to other organizations. The co-operation in the networks can generally be characterized as horizontal. An exception seems to be especially resource exchange and to a smaller extend exchange of clients. This reflects the fact that there are often only a small number of organizations, which provide financing for DDR activities (e.g. a ministry) for a much larger number of organizations. The same may apply to referral of clients where one organization (e.g. a hospital) refers clients to a larger and broader range of specific services. It is especially interesting to see that the Slovenian system, which could on the basis of density scores be labelled as "full co-operation" is a very decentralized system. This indicates that the dense co-operation in the field is of a rather bottom-up nature and is not particularly "organized" by any central actor. In contrast the Hungarian organizational field turns out to be less "organized" than we would have expected on the basis of the density scores. Here the centralization in the more formal types of relationships is somewhat higher than in the other countries but less so than one would have expected.

4.2 *Actor centrality*

As explained before, actor centrality refers to an ego-actor's visibility or popularity, as indicated by its involvement in many direct and indirect relations. An actor with many ties enjoys greater centrality compared to an actor with relatively fewer ties. In the following we will present for each of the countries the three actors, which enjoy the highest level of actor centrality for the different types of relationships. We will only present the actor centralities based on degree, i.e. degree centrality (direct ties). The reason is that the different centralization measures are in three of the four countries highly and significantly correlated (in the Czech Republic, Hungary and Slovenia). They seem to measure the same phenomena. In Poland the different measures are, however, not correlating. This indicates that the actors in Poland with many direct relationships are not necessarily the same actors which reach a lot of organizations indirectly through these direct relationships and that these organizations also not necessarily have an important broker position in the network. Not taking into consideration the effect of indirect relations limits somewhat the analysis of the Polish case but is certainly representative for the other three countries.

Czech Republic

Table 5 presents the actor centrality of the three most central actors in the different networks and some of their characteristics. The calculation of centralities is based on direct ties only (degree centrality). In the second column of Table 2 the identification numbers of the organizations are mentioned. We decided that for reasons of anonymity, the names of the organi-

Table 5: Actor Centralities and characteristics of the most central organizations in the Czech Republic[1]

	Organisation[2]	Centrality (in %)[3]	Legal status[4]	Orientation[5]	Founding year	Attitude[6]
Support exchange	1	13.3	GOV	EX	1993	3,5
	15	13.3	GOV	IN	1993	3,5
	10	13.3	GOV	IN	1918	2,8
	6	13.3	NGO	EX	1995	4,0
Expertise exchange	1	25.0				
	10	20.8				
	13	12.5	NGO	EX	1995	3,4
	3	12.5	GOV	IN	1925	3,1
Resource exchange	6	50.0				
	2	25.0	NGO	EX	1990	3,9
	15	25.0				
Common activities	1	17.7				
	10	17.7				
	2	11.8				
Strategic co-operation	1	22.5				
	15	12.5				
	10	12.5				
	2	12.5				
Informal	1	20.5				
communication		15	11,4			
	2	11.4				
Number of organizations in top 3	21		GOV: 14 NGO: 7	IN: 9 EX: 12	Founded before '89: 5 Founded after '89: 16	
Number of different organizations in top 3	7		GOV: 4 NGO: 3	IN: 3 EX: 4	Founded before '89: 2 Founded after '89: 5	Mean: 3,46

Notes:

1 For the Czech republic no data are available on the exchange of clients and prominence.

2 Here an anonymous number for the organization appears. Same numbers in this column refer to the same organization.

3 Percentage or organizations in a network to which the organization has a relation.

4 NGO = **N**on **G**overnmental **O**rganization; GOV = **GOV**ernmental Organization.

5 **EX**clusive = Organization is active in the field of ddr only; **IN**clusive = Organization is also active in fields other than ddr.

6 On a scale ranging from 1'very permissive' to 5'very restrictive'.

zations should be omitted and be substituted by numbers. Whenever the same number appears in this column the same organization is referred to. As such it becomes possible to see how often an organization appears in the top 3 across the different types of relationships. When the organizations appears a second time in the table its centrality score is mentioned but all other organizational characteristics have been omitted (since they are always exactly the same).

Table 5 indicates that in 5 out of the 6 types of relationships organization 1 is the most central actor, followed by organizations 2, 10, and 15, each of whom is central in 4 different networks. Organization 1 is a governmental organization and has an exclusive orientation, which means that its specific task is drug demand reduction. The organization is as such, however, not very central since it has in all cases relations with less than one fourth of the other organizations. In the list 21 central positions appear (for some relationships more than three organizations appear because they have equal centrality scores) but only 7 different organizations can be identified in this list. Of these 7 organizations 4 organizations are exclusive and 3 are inclusive. This might be an indication for the fact that drug demand reduction has been developed as a specialized and distinguished field of activity in the Czech Republic. Other indications for this are that among these 7 organizations there are 4 governmental organizations and that 5 of the organizations have been founded after 1989. The organizations in charge appear, however, not be representative compared to all organizations in the Czech Republic in terms of their attitude. They have an average attitude of 3.46 (which has been classified as restrictive) whereas the Czech Republic overall – i.e. including local organizations – scores 2.79 (which has been classified as permissive).

Given the fact that as we have learned from the previous chapters that the availability of resources seems to be a crucial aspect in the field of DDR in all countries involved it is interesting to have a closer look at the overall resource exchange network.

The data available represent a very small resource exchange network consisting of two exclusive NGOs and one inclusive governmental organization.

Figure 1: Structure of resource exchange at the national level in the Czech Republic

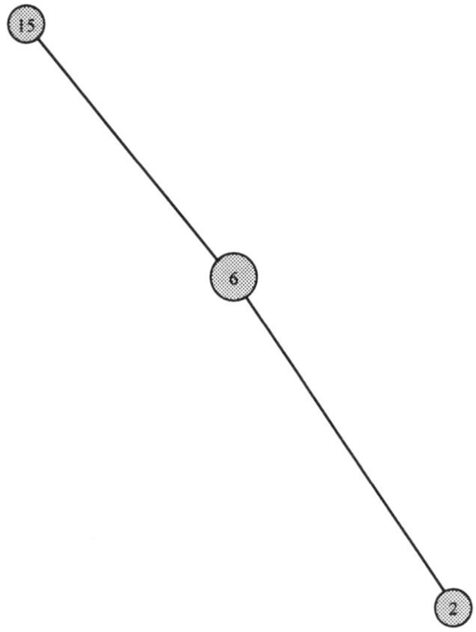

Hungary

Table 6 presents the actor centrality of the three most central actors in the different networks based on the relational data for the Hungarian national organizational field.

The most central actor in the Hungarian national networks seems to be the exclusive NGO 217. This organization is the most central organization in three different networks and the second and third most central organization in two other networks. The reason seems to be that it has a central position in the funding of DDR activities. Centrality scores for the most central actors are in some of the networks rather high (less so, however, for common activities, strategic co-operation and exchange of expertise). This means that generally speaking the Hungarian network seems to be characterized by some "leading" organizations. It is striking, however, that the three organizations, which have the highest scores on "prominence" do not appear as one of the most central organizations in any of the other types of relations. All organizations of the most "prominent" group appear to be governmental organizations. This indicates that organizations strongly feel the influence of public organizations on their functioning.

Table 6: Actor centralities and characteristics of the most central organizations in the Hungary

	Organi-sation[1]	Centrality (in %)[2]	Legal status[3]	Orientation[4]	Founding year	Attitude[5]
Client exchange	244	29.2	GOV	IN	1979	3,6
	209	16.7	GOV	IN	1988	3,9
	214	12.5	NGO	EX	1983	3,6
	226	12.5	Private	IN	1994	3,5
Support exchange	227	25.0	NGO	IN	1984	3,5
	217	20.8	NGO	EX	1992	n.a.
	224	12.5	NGO	EX	1996	3,4
Expertise exchange	217	11.9				
	244	8.2				
	221	8.2	GOV	IN	1992	3,4
Resource exchange	217	47.6				
	224	4.8				
	216	4.8	NGO	IN	1990	3,8
Common activities	214	10.3				
	205	8.7	NGO	IN	1992	3,0
	211	7.9	GOV	IN	1987	4,3
Strategic co-operation	221	10.9				
	224	8.6				
	217	7.8				
Informal communication	217	11.2				
	221	8.7				
	220	8.3	GOV	IN	1992	3,4
Prominence	204	19.5	GOV	IN	1999	3,8
	202	11.9	GOV	IN	n.a.	4,3
	225	11.9	GOV	IN	1994	3,6
Number of organizations in top 3	25		GOV: 11 NGO: 13 Private: 1	IN: 15 EX: 10	Founded before '89: 7 Founded after '89: 17 n.a.: 1	
Number of different organizations in top 3	15		GOV: 8 NGO: 6 Private: 1	IN: 12 EX: 3	Founded before '89: 5 Founded after '89: 9 n.a.: 1	Mean: 3,6

Notes:
1 Here an anonymous number for the organization appears. Same numbers in this column refer to the same organization
2 Percentage or organizations in a network to which the organization has a relation
3 NGO = **N**on **G**overnmental **O**rganization; GOV = **GOV**ernmental Organization
4 **EX**clusive = Organization is active in the field of ddr only; **IN**clusive = Organization is also active in fields other than ddr
5 On a scale ranging from 1'very permissive' to 5'very restrictive'

Overall, there is more variation in the core groups between the different networks than in the Czech networks, indicating a greater degree of functional differentiation (i.e. there are 15 different organizations appearing). As in the Czech Republic, Hungarian networks are also more dominated by governmental organizations than by NGOs. However, in contrast to the situation in the Czech Republic inclusive organizations are here the more dominant ones. Nevertheless, the three exclusive organizations seem to play a crucial role in integrating the different networks, since they occupy 10 out of the 25 top places. It can also be observed that generally speaking, most central organizations are rather young. The majority of the organizations have been founded after 1989.

Given the high score on the exchange of resources (financial, facilities, equipment) it is interesting to have a closer look at the structure of that network (see Figure 2). In this visualization the dominant role of organization 217 becomes clear.

Figure 2: Structure of resource exchange at the national level in Hungary

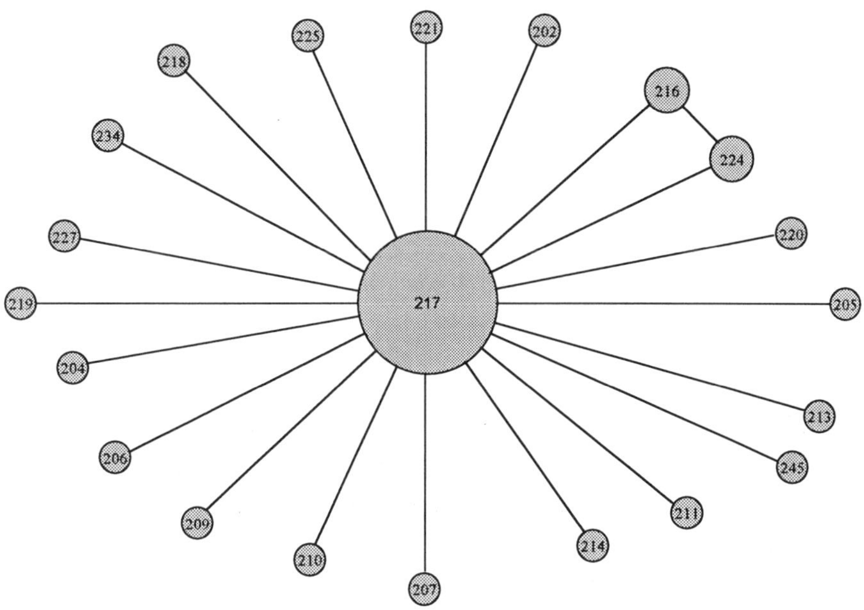

Although this network is rather large compared to the Czech networks, all organizations are reached by this central organization directly. This structure might be effective and especially efficient in cases were the central organization has enough resources to distribute, can handle all the exchanges taking place with other organizations, and will distribute the resources whenever the other organizations need them (see Provan and Milward, 1995). But there is also the danger that the central organization might be a bottleneck, which hinders the necessary, timely and sufficient flow of resources to the other organizations. In such case, a more decentralized network structure or – as a special case – a structure with several intermediate organizations would be preferable.

Poland

Table 7 presents the actor centralities of the most central actors in the different Polish networks.

What is interesting is that in Poland obviously a couple composed of a non-profit and a public organization are rather dominant in most of the networks (organization 9 and – to a lesser extend – organization 15). They have in common that they are both exclusive organizations and have both a rather restrictive attitude with respect to drugs in common. While the client exchange network is dominated by NGOs, governmental organizations are most central in the support exchange and expertise network. In general the variation of organizations between the different networks is smaller than in Hungary which indicates a stronger integration between the different networks. This is also indicated by the fact that the organizations with the highest score in prominence also appear in the other networks.

A closer look at the resource exchange network reveals a picture, which is very different from the ones we have seen before for the Czech Republic and Hungary (see Figure 3).

What we see here is a nearly bi-polar structure with two central organizations: On the one side, we have the exclusive governmental organization (9) and, on the other side, we see an inclusive NGO (29) with a more permissive attitude. While there are several organizations with which they both exchange resources, there are also several organizations exclusively exchanging resources with one of them. This network design not only decreases the burden on each central organization, it also allows for more diversity in the exchange of resources. This figure also illustrates nicely the fact that, as mentioned before, the different centrality measures do not correlate very high in the case of Poland. Organizations in this structure are not only dependent on direct relations but indirect relations play an important role in these kind of structures. For example, it becomes clear that this network is char-

Table 7: Actor Centralities and characteristics of the most central organizations in the Poland

	Organi-sation[1]	Centrality (in %)[2]	Legal status[3]	Orientation[4]	Founding year	Attitude[5]
Client exchange	15	14	NGO	EX	1986	3,8
	21	13	NGO	IN	1978	3,0
	20	9	NGO	IN	1993	4,0
	25	9	NGO	EX	1993	3,1
Support exchange	9	16.7	GOV	EX	1993	4,0
	1	11.8	GOV	IN	1996	2,5
	8	7.9	GOV	IN	1918	3,4
Expertise exchange	9	10.9				
	28	8.3	GOV	IN	1953	3,4
	6	7.4	GOV	IN	n.a.	2,8
Resource exchange	9	18.6				
	29	12.8	NGO	IN	1987	3,0
	28	9.3				
Common activities	9	11.9				
	21	6.7				
	15	6.4				
Strategic co-operation	9	12.3				
	15	12.3				
	30	8.0	NGO	IN	1960	3,1
Informal communication	9	13.8				
	15	6.9				
	21	6.9				
Prominence	9	22.8				
	15	11.4				
	21	9.8				
Number of organizations in top 3	25		GOV: 12 NGO: 13	IN: 12 EX: 13	Founded before '89: 14 Founded after '89: 10 n.a.: 1	
Number of different organizations in top 3	11		GOV: 5 NGO: 6	IN: 8 EX: 3	Founded before '89: 7 Founded after '89: 4 n.a.: 1	Mean: 3,4

Notes:
1 Here an anonymous number for the organization appears. Same numbers in this column refer to the same organization
2 Percentage or organizations in a network to which the organization has a relation
3 NGO = **N**on **G**overnmental **O**rganization; GOV = **GOV**ernmental Organization
4 **EX**clusive = Organization is active in the field of ddr only; **IN**clusive = Organization is also active in fields other than ddr
5 On a scale ranging from 1'very permissive' to 5'very restrictive'

acterized by a number of brokers. It is interesting to note, that organization 29 is not very central in the other networks, while organization 9 is – as has been described above – the most central national organization.

Figure 3: Structure of resource exchange at the national level in Poland

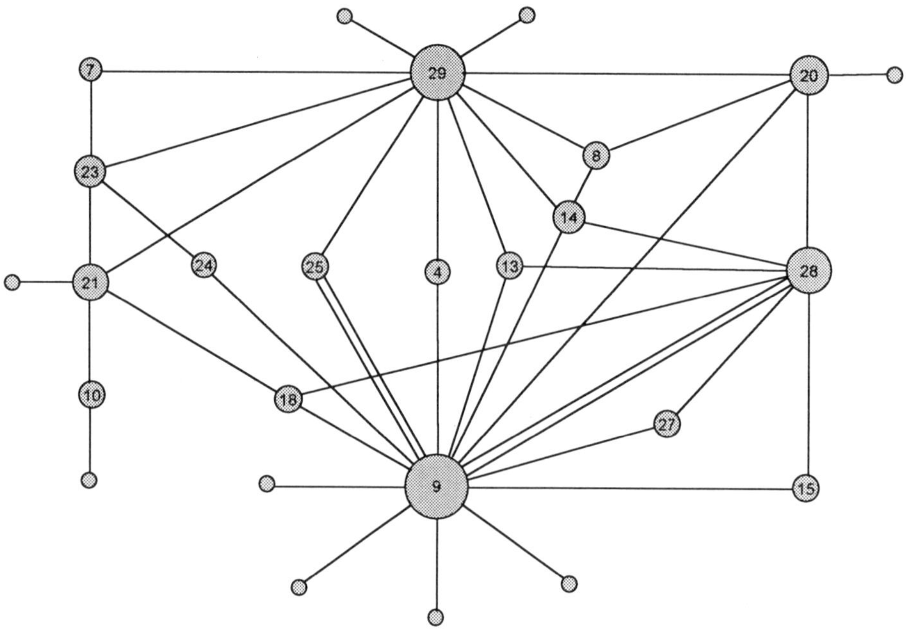

Slovenia

Finally, Table 8 presents the actor centralities of the three most important actors in the different networks in the case of Slovenia.

Given the high density of Slovenian networks it is not surprising that the most central organizations in these networks do not have very high actor centrality scores. The score of the most central organizations is never above 15% and most of them are around 10%. The most central organization in the Slovenian networks are three inclusive governmental organizations: organization 6, founded in 1998, and organizations 1 and 2, both founded in 1991. These three organizations alone occupy 17 out of the 29 top positions in the Slovenian networks, so inter-network core group variability in Slovenia is low. Contrary to the networks in the other three countries, exclusive organizations are not among the most central organizations in the Slovenian national DDR network.

Table 8: Actor centralities and characteristics of the most central organizations in the Slovenia

	Organisation[1]	Centrality (in %)[2]	Legal status[3]	Orientation[4]	Founding year	Attitude[5]
Client exchange	6	12.8	GOV	IN	1998	3,2
	23	8.5	GOV	IN	1995	3,4
	16	8.5	NGO	IN	1998	2,1
Support exchange	1	8.5	GOV	IN	1991	3,9
	6	8.5				
	18	8.1	NGO	IN	1993	3,4
	20	8.1	GOV	IN	1955	2,9
Expertise exchange	3	8.8	GOV	EX	1995	3,4
	16	7.7				
	6	6.9				
	2	6.9	GOV	IN	1991	3,0
	20	6.9				
Resource exchange	2	14.9				
	1	11.4				
	16	8.8				
Common activities	2	10.5				
	6	8.9				
	3	8.0				
	1	8.0				
Strategic co-operation	6	10.3				
	2	8.9				
	16	7.2				
	3	7.2				
Informal communication	6	7.3				
	1	6.9				
	2	6.7				
Prominence	2	13.7				
	1	12.7				
	6	9.7				
Number of organizations in top 3	29		GOV: 24 NGO: 5	IN: 26 EX: 3	Founded before '89: 3 Founded after '89: 26	
Number of different organizations in top 3	8		GOV: 6 NGO: 2	IN: 7 EX: 1	Founded before '89: 1 Founded after '89: 7	Mean: 3,14

Notes: [1] Here an anonymous number for the organization appears. Same numbers in this column refer to the same organization.
[2] Percentage or organizations in a network to which the organization has a relation
[3] NGO = **N**on **G**overnmental **O**rganization; GOV = **GOV**ernmental Organization
[4] **EX**clusive = Organization is active in the field of ddr only; **IN**clusive = Organization is also active in fields other than ddr
[5] On a scale ranging from 1'very permissive' to 5'very restrictive'

Figure 4: Structure of resource exchange at the national level in Slovenia

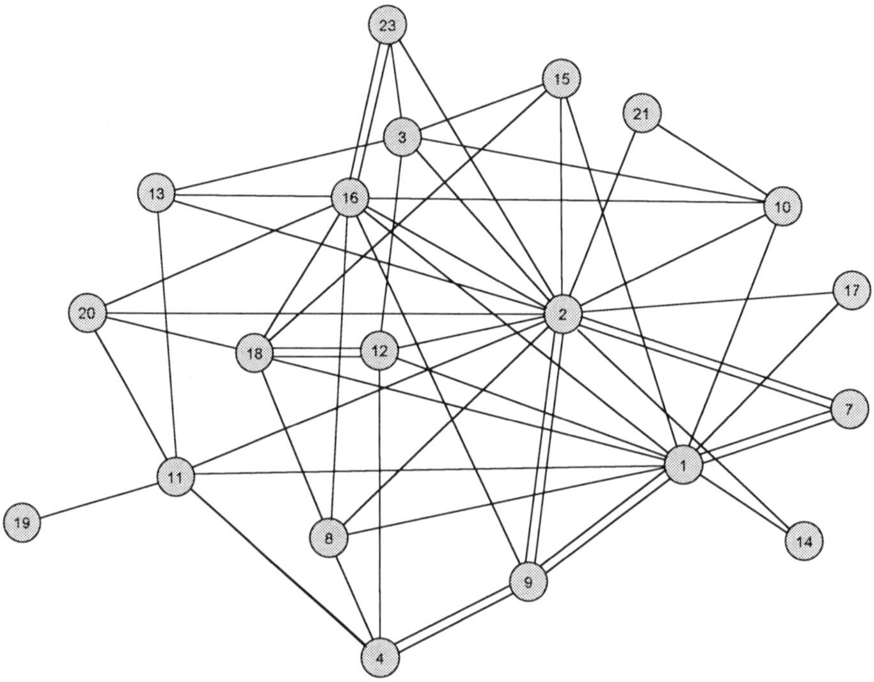

Contrary to the Czech network, the Slovenian exchange network is rather large; unlike the Hungarian network it is not very centralized although central organizations are clearly recognizable. Because of the high density no clear structure can be detected, in contrary to the Polish resource exchange network. What distinguishes it from all other networks visualized so far, are the seven reciprocal relationships.

5 Conclusions

The national organizational field of DDR in the Czech Republic can be characterized as a small, newly developed field with a mixture of non-governmental, inclusive and exclusive organizations in charge. Although there is one clearly dominating organization that is integrating the different networks, overall network density – and therefore integration – is very low.

Hungarian national networks are networks of about the same size – or even smaller – than Slovenian networks. Although the most central organization is an NGO, Hungarian networks are dominated by inclusive governmental organizations. The overall core-group variability is rather high, indicating a lack of central co-ordination and integration, even more so since the most prominent organizations are no central players in the other networks. This might be partly compensated for by the medium density of most Hungarian networks.

Polish networks are certainly the largest and oldest networks analysed here. One central exclusive governmental organization is dominating and bridging the different networks; but its centrality as well as the centrality of other dominating organizations is very low. Since the density of all Polish networks is also low, it seems that integrative forces are weak in the Polish national organizational field.

The low inter-network core group variability, together with the very high density of Slovenian networks indicates that Slovenian networks are highly integrated. The Slovenian national level could, consequently, be characterized as "full cooperation".

Taken together, these networks in the four different countries have shown a wide variety of network structures. Although one might tend to assume that the "content" of a network would have a great influence on its structure (i.e. patient exchange networks are smaller than other networks because only a minority of organizations will be able to deal with patients properly), the results presented so far seem to suggest otherwise. It might be suggested on the basis of these data, that the country is a more important factor than the type of relationship in determining the structure of these networks.

But what has been presented above is rather preliminary and has in the first place an illustrative character. Only basic characteristics of the different networks have been presented. This should be seen as a first step for more detailed and comparative analysis. On the basis of the data presented first vague profiles of the "organization" of the different national organizational fields have become visible. These are very tentative and will have to be sharpened on the basis of subsequent analyses.

Notes

1 See http://eclectic.ss.uci.edu/~lin/ucinet.html.
2 See http://www.visone.de/ and Brandes, Kenis and Wagner (2001).
3 The degree centralities from which the degree centralization measure is derived, were calculated as the average of an actor's in-degree centrality and his or her out-degree centrality.

References

DiMaggio, P./Powell, W. (1983) 'The Iron Cage Revisited: Institutional Isomorphism and Collective Rationality in Organizational Fields', *American Sociological Review* 48: 147-160.

Emirbayer, M. (1997) 'Manifesto for a Relational Sociology', *American Journal of Sociology* 103: 281-317.

Freeman, L. (1979) 'Centrality in Social Networks: I. Conceptual Clarification', *Social Networks* 1: 215-239.

Brandes, U./Kenis, P./Wagner, D. (2001) 'Communicating Centrality in Policy Network Drawings'. *IEEE Transaction on Visualization and Computer Graphics.*

Kenis, P./Knoke, D. (forthcoming) 'How Organizational Field Networks Shape Interorganisational Tie-formation Rates', *Academy of Management Review.*

Knoke, D. (2000) *Changing Organizations.* Boulder, CO: Westview Press.

Provan, K. G./Milward, H. B. (1995) 'A Preliminary Theory of Interorganizational Effectiveness: A Comparative Study of Four Community Mental Health Systems', *Administrative Science Quarterly* 40: 1-33.

Wasserman, S./Faust, K. (1994) *Social Network Analysis: Methods and Applications.* Cambridge: Cambridge University Press.

Wellman, B./Berkowitz, S. D. (Eds.) (1997) *Social Structures: A Network Approach.* Greenwich, CT: JAI Press.

ANNEX

Drug Demand Reduction Institutions Inventory Sheet

INTERVIEWER: The following categories should be used if necessary

00 – no answer
88 – do not know, difficult to say
09 – not applicable
(Do not read them out)

A Organizational characteristics

1 Full name of the organization

....

....

2 English version of the organization's name

....

....

Address

3. Street, number ....
4. Postal code ....
5. City or town ....
6. Country ....
7. Telephone no. ....
8. Fax no. ....
9. Electronic mail ....

10. Legal status of the organization (please cross the appropriate)

1. O Governmental, public agency
2. O Private firm, enterprise, or company
3. O Non-profit, voluntary organization
4. O No legal status

11. Founding date of the organization (year) ....

12. When did your organization initiate drug demand reduction programmes (year)?

    ....

13. This organization (select one only):

    1. O Specializes in drug demand reduction exclusively
    2. O Drug demand reduction programmes are one of a number of other activities

14. Please briefly indicate what your organization's mission is:

    ....

    ....

    ....

    ....

What is:

A) The number of employed staff (staff receiving permanent payment in any form)?
   15. In total .... 16. Drug Demand Reduction Unit.............

B) The number of volunteers in the organization?
   17. In total .... 18. Drug Demand Reduction Unit.............

C) The number of subscribed members (Only if a membership organization)?
   19. In total .... 20. Drug Demand Reduction Unit.............

D) The annual budget of your organization ?
   21. In total .... 22. Drug Demand Reduction Unit.............

INTERVIEWER: Please make the necessary calculations if the respondent answered questions D 21 and D 22

23. The percentage of your annual budget used for Drug Demand Reduction Programme(s)? .... %

What is the proportion of employees involved in the drug demand reduction programme?

24. Full time employees .... %
25. Part-time employees .... %
26. Full time volunteers .... %
27. Part-time volunteers .... %
28. Others .... %

Total number of staff 100%
(involved in drug demand reduction activities)

How many persons are in the following categories in your organization?

	Professionals*	Other persons	Total
Paid staff	29.	30.	31. ....
Volunteers	32.	33.	34. ....
Total	35.	36.	37. ....

* persons with an academic degree or a professional license

INTERVIEWER: Please check total number (see 29)

Please indicate the numbers of professional paid staff in your organization (see 29) with the following backgrounds:

Medical training	38. ....
Psychiatric training	39. ....
Legal training	40. ....
Public health training	41. ....
Social worker training	42. ....
Psychology training	43. ....
Sociology training	44. ....
Management training	45. ....
Other	46. ....

What proportion of your organization's funds devoted to drug demand reduction programmes comes from:

	1998	1995
a. International organizations (e.g. UN, EU, OECD)	47. .... %	48. .... %
b. Foreign governments/agencies	49. .... %	50. .... %
c. Other foreign organisations	51. .... %	52. .... %
d. Public/government agencies	53. .... %	54. .... %
e. Private sector	55. .... %	56. .... %
f. Voluntary organizations	57. .... %	58. .... %
g. Fees and individual donations	59. .... %	60. .... %
	100%	100%

B Activities

61. What are the goals of your organization in the field of drug demand reduction?

a. ....

b. ....

c. ....

INTERVIEWER: Not more than three activities

What are your organization's main activities in the field of drug demand reduction?

62. Prevention / Education / Information

1. O Yes
2. O No

	In which year did activities start?	What is the target group?
Activity A 63.	64.	65. ....
Activity B 66.	67.	68. ....
Activity C 69.	70.	71. ....

72. Treatment and care
    1. O Yes
    2. O No

	In which year did activities start?	What is the target group?
Activity A 73.	74.	75. ....
Activity B 76.	77.	78. ....
Activity C 79.	80.	81. ....

82. Rehabilitation (After-care)
    1. O Yes
    2. O No

	In which year did activities start?	What is the target group?
Activity A 83.	84.	85. ....
Activity B 86.	87.	88. ....
Activity C 89.	90.	91. ....

92. Research/Documentation
    1. O Yes
    2. O No

	In which year did activities start?	What is the target group?
Activity A 93.	94.	95. ....
Activity B 96.	97.	98. ....
Activity C 99.	100.	101. ....

102. Funding/Fund-raising
    1. O Yes
    2. O No

	In which year did activities start?	What is the target group?
Activity A 103.	104.	105. ....
Activity B 106.	107.	108. ....
Activity C 109.	110.	111. ....

112. Co-ordination
    1. O Yes
    2. O No

	In which year did activities start?	What is the target group?
Activity A 113.	114.	115. ....
Activity B 116.	117.	118. ....
Activity C 119.	120.	121. ....

122. Interest Representation/Protection of Civil & Human Rights
    1. O Yes
    2. O No

	In which year did activities start?	What is the target group?
Activity A 123.	124.	125. ....
Activity B 126.	127.	128. ....
Activity C 129.	130.	131. ....

132. Policy Development/Legislation
    1. O Yes
    2. O No

	In which year did activities start?	What is the target group?
Activity A 133.	134.	135. ....
Activity B 136.	137.	138. ....
Activity C 139.	140.	141. ....

142. Training of Professionals (working on drug demand reduction programmes)
    1. O Yes
    2. O No

	In which year did activities start?	What is the target group?
Activity A 143.	144.	145. ....
Activity B 146.	147.	148. ....
Activity C 149.	150.	151. ....

152. Other
   1. O Yes
   2. O No

	In which year did activities start?	What is the target group?
Activity A 153.	154.	155. ....
Activity B 156.	157.	158. ....
Activity C 159.	160.	161. ....

162. Which one of the above mentioned activities best fits what you do in the field of drug demand reduction?

or

Which one of the above mentioned activities is the most important for your organization?

....

....

....

163. Which one of the above mentioned activities would you like to intensify in the near future (i.e. in the next 3 years)? Select one only.

....

164. Which one of the above mentioned activities would you like to stop in the near future (i.e. in the next 3 years)? Select one only.

....

165. Does your organization make use of mechanisms to monitor or evaluate the quality of professional work and services?

   1. O Yes
   2. O No
   3. O Difficult to say

166. If yes in 165, please specify

....

....

167. Does your organization gather any systematic information about its clients (target groups)?

1. O Yes
2. O No

INTERVIEWER: Please circle the appropriate

What is the general opinion on the image of the overall performance of your organization?

	Excellent, "first rate"	Good, solid, convincing	Adequate, satisfying	Problematic, to be improved	Grossly deficient	Difficult to say
168. As seen by yourself	5	4	3	2	1	88
169. By yours clients	5	4	3	2	1	88
170. By the public	5	4	3	2	1	88
171. By the political environment	5	4	3	2	1	88
172. By the media	5	4	3	2	1	88

C Perceptions of the drug problem and policy

173. What is the estimated number of drug users* in your country in 1998 in your opinion?

....

* users of any illicit drugs

174. What is the estimated number of drug users* in your country in 2003 in your opinion?

....

What is your opinion on the prevalence of drug use in your country?
or
Could you describe the current and future structure of drug use in your country in percentage?

INTERVIEWER: This question should reflect the perception of the general drug consumption

		1998		2003
Opiates	(175)	%	(176)	%
Cocaine	(177)	%	(178)	%
Cannabis	(179)	%	(180)	%
Hallucinogens	(181)	%	(182)	%
Amphetamines	(183)	%	(184)	%
Other Drugs	(185)	%	(186)	%
Total		100%		100%

How would you characterize the current national policy on the drug problem in your country? Would you agree that the current policy is focused on

INTERVIEWER: Please circle the appropriate

	Definitely yes	Rather yes	Equal	Rather no	Definitely no	Difficult to say
187. Health promotion	5	4	3	2	1	88
188. Harm minimization	5	4	3	2	1	88
189. Demand reduction	5	4	3	2	1	88
190. Control of supply	5	4	3	2	1	88
191. Law enforcement and control of drug users	5	4	3	2	1	88

192. What are the main strengths of the national policy on the drug problem in your country?

a. ....
b. ....
c. ....

193. What are the main weaknesses of the national policy on the drug problem in your country?

a. ....
b. ....
c. ....

Please indicate whether and to which extent your organization would agree / disagree to the following statements:

194. Taking illegal drugs can sometimes be beneficial

1 2 3 4 5
Agree Disagree

195. Adults should be free to take any drug they wish

1 2 3 4 5
Agree Disagree

196. We need to accept that using illegal drugs is normal for some people's lives

1 2 3 4 5
Agree Disagree

197. Smoking cannabis should be legalised

1 2 3 4 5
Agree Disagree

198. The best way to treat people who are addicted to drugs is to stop them using drugs altogether

1 2 3 4 5
Agree Disagree

199. The use of illegal drugs always leads to addiction

1 2 3 4 5
Agree Disagree

200. Taking illegal drugs is always morally wrong

1 2 3 4 5
Agree Disagree

201. All use of illegal drugs is misuse

1 2 3 4 5
Agree Disagree

D Co-ordination

INTERVIEWER: Name all such organizations in the table below

1. Which organizations has your organization worked together with in the field of drug demand reduction last year and in which way?

Organization	Resources *1	Expertise *2	Support *3	Informal communication *4	Strategic cooperation *5	Common activities *6
1	R P	R P	R P	x	x	x
2	R P	R P	R P	x	x	x
3	R P	R P	R P	x	x	x
4	R P	R P	R P	x	x	x
5	R P	R P	R P	x	x	x
6	R P	R P	R P	x	x	x
7	R P	R P	R P	x	x	x
8	R P	R P	R P	x	x	x
9	R P	R P	R P	x	x	x
10	R P	R P	R P	x	x	x

INTERVIEWER: Mark the answer in the table

Note 1 - 3: Marking both is possible

*1 Resources: Has your organization
[R] received resources (financial, facilities, equipment)
[P] provided resources to these organizations

*2 Expertise: Did your organization
[R] receive expertise concerning drug demand reduction
[P] offer expertise to these organizations

*3 Support: Did your organization
[R] gain support in meeting its objectives
[P] provide support to these organizations

Note 4 - 6: Mark if yes

*4 Informal Communication: Did your organization's employees exchange information on drug demand reduction programmes on an informal basis with the personnel of the following organizations?

*5 Strategic Cooperation: Did your organization consult these organizations before making the important decisions on drug demand reduction programmes?

*6 Common Activities: Has your organization been engaged in common activities in the field of drug demand reduction with the organizations mentioned?

List of Contributors

Ladislav Csémy, Senior Researcher at the Addiction Studies Unit of the Prague Psychiatric Centre

Renata Cvelbar Bek, Advisor to the Government of the Ministry of Labour, Family and Social Affairs of Slovenia

Bojan Dekleva, Professor of Education at the Department of Social Pedagogy of the Faculty of Education, University of Ljubljana

Zsuzsanna Elekes, Senior Researcher at the Department of Sociology and Social Policy of the Budapest University of Economics

Tünde Györy, Research Assistant at the Department of Sociology and Social Policy of the Budapest University of Economics

Patrick Kenis, Professor at the Department of Policy and Organization Studies of the University of Tilburg, the Netherlands; External Research Associate to the European Centre for Social Welfare Policy and Research, Vienna

Franti‰ek David Krch, Psychologist and Senior Research Associate at the Psychiatric Clinic of Charles University, Prague

Stefan Loos, Researcher at the Charité Research Group on Geriatrics at the Evangelisches Geriatrie Zentrum, Berlin

Flip Maas, Programme Coordinator of the Health and Welfare Department at the European Centre for Social Welfare Policy and Research, Vienna

Robert Sobiech, Researcher at the Department of Social Policy of the University of Warsaw and at the National School of Public Administration, Warsaw, Poland

Joanna Zamecka, Associate Professor at the Institute of Social Prevention and Rehabilitation of the University of Warsaw

Wohlfahrtspolitik und Sozialforschung
Herausgegeben vom Europäischen Zentrum Wien
mit dem Campus Verlag, Frankfurt am Main/New York

Wohlfahrtspolitik und Sozialforschung
Herausgegeben vom Europäischen Zentrum Wien
mit dem Campus Verlag, Frankfurt am Main/New York

Public Policy and Social Welfare
A Series Edited by the European Centre Vienna

vols. 1-10 with Campus Verlag/Westview Press, Frankfurt am Main/Boulder, Co.

Vol. 1:	EVERS, A., WINTERSBERGER, H. (Eds.) (1990; 2nd ed.) **Shifts in the Welfare Mix.** Their Impact on Work, Social Services and Welfare Policies pp. 412, DM 68,– (out-of-stock)
Vol. 2:	EVERS, A., FARRANT, W., TROJAN, A. (Eds.) (1990) **Healthy Public Policy at the Local Level** pp. 242, DM 48,–
Vol. 3:	NOWOTNY, H. (1990) **In Search of Usable Knowledge.** Utilization Contexts and the Application of Knowledge pp. 166, DM 38,–
Vol. 4:	MARIN, B. (Ed.) (1990) **Generalized Political Exchange.** Antagonistic Cooperation and Integrated Policy Circuits pp. 284, DM 58,–
Vol. 5:	MARIN, B. (Ed.) (1990) **Governance and Generalized Exchange.** Self-Organizing Policy Networks in Action pp. 386, DM 68,–
Vol. 6:	KRAAN, R. et al. (1991) **Care for the Elderly.** Significant Innovations in Three European Countries pp. 248, DM 48,–
Vol. 7:	PESTOFF, V.A. (1991) **Between Markets and Politics.** Co-operatives in Sweden, pp. 244, DM 48,–
Vol. 8:	KENIS, P. (1992) **The Social Construction of an Industry.** A World of Chemical Fibres, pp. 240, DM 48,–
Vol. 9:	MARIN, B., MAYNTZ, R. (Eds.) (1991) **Policy Networks.** Empirical Evidence and Theoretical Considerations pp. 336, DM 48,–
Vol. 10:	FERGE, Z., KOLBERG, J. (Eds.) (1992) **Social Policy in a Changing Europe** pp. 316, DM 68,–